FREDERICK LEONG
3406 TULANE DRIVE, APT. 14
HYATTSVILLE, MARYLAND 20783

International Perspectives on

——— DSM-III ———

Robert L. Spitzer, M.D.
Professor of Psychiatry
Columbia University
Chief, Biometrics Research Department
New York State Psychiatric Institute

Janet B. W. Williams, D.S.W.
Assistant Professor of Clinical Psychiatric
  Social Work (in Psychiatry)
Columbia University
Research Scientist
New York State Psychiatric Institute

Andrew E. Skodol, M.D.
Assistant Professor of Clinical Psychiatry
Columbia University
Research Psychiatrist
New York State Psychiatric Institute

American Psychiatric Press, Inc.
————————————— Washington, DC

Note: The authors have worked to ensure that all the information in this book concerning drug dosages, schedules, and routes of administration is accurate at the time of publication and consistent with standards set by the U.S. Food and Drug Administration and the general medical community. As medical research and practice advance, however, therapeutic standards may change. For this reason and because human and mechanical errors sometimes occur, we recommend that readers follow the advice of a physician directly involved in their care or the care of a member of the family.

Library of Congress Cataloging in Publication Data
Main entry under title:

International perspectives on DSM-III, Diagnostic and statistical manual of mental disorders, third edition.

Bibliography: p,
Includes index.
1. Psychology, Pathological—Classification. 2. Psychology, Pathological—Diagnosis. 3. Diagnostic and statistical manual of mental disorders, 3rd ed. 4. Psychiatry, Transcultural.
I. Spitzer, Robert L. II. Williams, Janet B.W. III. Skodol, Andrew E.
IV. Diagnostic and statistical manual of mental disorders. V. Title: International perspectives on DSM-III. VI. Title: International perspectives on DSM-III [DNLM: 1. Mental disorders—Diagnosis. WM 141 I1616]
RC455.2.C4I57   1983   616.89′075   83-12226
ISBN 0-88048-017-3

Printed in the U.S.A.

CONTENTS

ACKNOWLEDGMENTS

We should like to thank Dr. Melvin Sabshin for suggesting that this book be written and Mr. Ronald McMillen for supervising its production. We also thank our many contributors for their diligence in preparing these excellent chapters. Finally, we thank Betty Appelbaum for her copy editing and Maggie Bunce for her secretarial assistance.

PREFACE

The Diagnostic and Statistical Manual of Mental Disorders, Third Edition (DSM-III), portrays and symbolizes recent changes in American psychiatry more accurately than any other work. Furthermore, DSM-III, with its translation into many languages besides English, is a most significant facilitator of international scientific dialogue; no other recent psychiatric publication has stirred as much discussion about the dimensions, the definitions, and the boundaries of mental illness. The American Psychiatric Association is proud of this contribution to the science of psychiatry and to its world-wide practice. We are mindful, of course, that we have opened an international dialogue that will produce criticism and questions as well as empirical validation and acclaim. The *International Perspectives on DSM-III* is intended to stimulate such a healthy process of criticism, evaluation, and progress. In addition, this volume will complement the *DSM-III Case Book* in fleshing out DSM-III so that many readers can better understand underlying issues as well as the classificatory details.

American psychiatry has undergone many vicissitudes since World War II. Stimulated in part by the war and its aftermath, psychoanalysis and intensive psychotherapy surged rapidly throughout the United States during the 1940's and 1950's. They remain a potent force, but subsequent developments began to diversify psychiatry in the United States. During the 1950's, a new psychopharmacological approach emerged which had great impact on psychiatric practice generally, including a stunning effect on hospital psychiatry. The 1960's saw the dawning of a community psychiatric approach which attempted to accomplish a massive deinstitutionalization of patients from public psychiatric hospitals in the United States, with treatment to become available in community centers near the patient's residence. During that decade, American psychiatry enlarged its boundaries and its practices so broadly that many critics grew increasingly concerned about the "bottomless pit" of the field. Beginning early in the 1970's, American psychiatry began to narrow its boundaries and to move towards a more rational and an empirical mode. Exciting advances in the neurosciences hastened this development, but socio-economic forces also necessitated a change in direction. The need for much more intensive accountability to many governmental and fiscal intermediaries made it clear that American psychiatry had to become actively responsible to demonstrate the objective data upon which its practices were based.

DSM-III was spawned during this period and it reflects a new era in American psychiatry. Objectification of diagnostic practices serves many simultaneous purposes. It weakens some of the power of psychiatric ideologies, subjective hegemony, and other anti-scientific forces within and outside the profession. It strengthens the movement towards rational empiricism and scientific clinical practice. Psychiatrists all across the world have recognized this trend and most have tended to understand and to support this development.

It is obvious that DSM-III is not a panacea and that it has many imperfections. This volume on International Perspectives is replete with scholarly criticisms, divergent perspectives, and empirical studies supporting different approaches. It is also obvious that each country has its own special problems and needs in regard to psychiatric classification. In developing a new ICD and in future modifications of DSM-III, these national differences must indeed be respected. Nevertheless, this book on International Perspectives demonstrates the presence of many areas of world-wide commonalities as well as differences. The regional perspectives are most illuminating in this regard. Hopefully, the psychiatric classifications for the remainder of this century and beyond will benefit from the dialogues, the insights, and the debates contained in this book. Beyond the broader implications, I believe that *International Perspectives on DSM-III* will have a positive effect on *individual* readers in many countries. The editors and other contributors have both enriched our clinical and theoretical understanding of psychiatry and have contributed significantly to its scientific progress.

Melvin Sabshin, M.D.
Medical Director
American Psychiatric Association

INTRODUCTION

This book reflects the remarkable and unanticipated international interest in the third edition of the American Psychiatric Association's *Diagnostic and Statistical Manual of Mental Disorders* (DSM-III). It presents perspectives on DSM-III from a large number of clinicians and researchers throughout the world, many of whom have made major contributions to psychiatric nosology.

The critical evaluations of DSM-III from an international perspective contained in the chapters of this book are timely for several reasons. First of all, translations of DSM-III into French, German, Italian, and Spanish will soon join the already available translations of the *Quick Reference to Diagnostic Criteria from DSM-III* in Chinese, Dutch, and Japanese. Secondly, work will soon begin on the Mental Disorders section of the tenth revision of the World Health Organization's *International Classification of Diseases* (ICD-10). All of the issues that the contributors to this book discuss in relation to DSM-III will undoubtedly be considered by those responsible for the development of the ICD-10 section. Finally, in March 1983, the Board of Trustees of the American Psychiatric Association approved a recommendation of its Committee to Evaluate DSM-III to constitute a Work Group to Revise DSM-III. This revision will involve changes in the text and criteria to clarify ambiguities, resolve inconsistencies in the criteria, and add new factual information to the text that has become available since 1980 (e.g., the sex ratios for the various disorders). Compatibility with ICD-9-CM (the clinical modification of the ninth revision of the International Classification [ICD-9], used in the United States for recording all medical disorders) will be maintained. The critiques of DSM-III provided by our international colleagues in this book will be studied by the Work Group constituted to revise it.

The book is divided into five sections.

The first section, Background for International Perspectives, describes the significance of DSM-III in American psychiatry and compares its classification with that of ICD-9.

The second section, General Perspectives, contains four critiques of DSM-III by major scholars of international psychiatry. They discuss the strengths and weaknesses of DSM-III from a nosological viewpoint and suggest ways in which future DMSs and ICDs could be improved.

This section is followed by Regional Perspectives, by contributors who have had experience in the use of DSM-III in their respective countries. They were asked to consider DSM-III in relation to their own national diagnostic traditions and to describe its use with their patient populations. In addition, some of these authors report the results of questionnaires they circulated among their colleagues to gather information about reactions to and experience with DSM-III.

The fourth section, Empirical Studies and Future Directions for Research, begins with five articles reporting the results of research on the use of DSM-III with patients. Three of these studies deal with the interjudge reliability of the DSM-III classification; the other two examine the relationship between the DSM-III and ICD-9 classifications as applied to two groups of inpatients. The section ends with a paper describing future directions in research comparing different diagnostic systems.

In the fifth and final section, Conclusion, two of the editors (Drs. Robert L. Spitzer and Janet B. W. Williams) summarize the views of the contributors on the major themes discussed and present their own perspective on these issues.

An extensive bibliography of articles on DSM-III that have appeared in the literature since its publication is presented as an appendix. This bibliography is indexed by subject matter so that the reader can quickly locate articles of particular interest. For the reader's convenience, the DSM-III and ICD-9 classifications and codes are also included as appendices.

We hope the reader will be as excited by the contents of this book as we have been in preparing it. We join with our contributors in believing that it will be an important part of the process of developing future internationally useful classifications of mental disorders.

Robert L. Spitzer, M.D.
Janet B. W. Williams, D.S.W.
Andrew E. Skodol, M.D.
15 April 1983

CONTRIBUTORS

Renato D. Alarcon, M.D., M.P.H.
Formerly:
Associate Professor of Psychiatry
Universidad Peruana
Cayetano Heredia
Lima, Peru

Currently:
Professor of Psychiatry
School of Medicine
University of Alabama in Birmingham
Birmingham, Alabama, U.S.A.

Marc Ansseau
Psychopharmacology Unit, Department of Psychiatry
University of Liège Medical School
Hôpital de Bavière
Liège, Belgium

Peter Berner, M.D.
Professor of Psychiatry
Psychiatric Clinic, University of Vienna
Vienna, Austria

Daniel P. Bobon, M.D., Ph.D.
Department of Psychiatry
University of Liège Medical School
Liège, Belgium

Ian Brockington, M.D., F.R.C.P.
Chairman and Head, Department of Psychiatry
University of Birmingham
Birmingham, England

Professor Giovanni B. Cassano
Director, 2nd Chair of Clinical Psychiatry
Institute of Clinical Psychiatry
University of Pisa
Pisa, Italy

John E. Cooper, B.A., B.M., F.R.C.P., F.R.C. Psych., D.P.M. (London)
Professor of Psychiatry
University of Nottingham
Nottingham, England

Paul Cosyns, M.D.
Professor of Psychopathology
Vrije Universiteit Brussels
Brussels, Belgium

Alv A. Dahl, M.D.
Lecturer in Psychiatry, Institute for Psychiatry
Gaustad Hospital, Oslo University Faculty of Medicine
Oslo, Norway

Hamish Dixon, M.A.
Formerly: Clinical Psychologist, Auckland Hospital
Currently: Senior Psychologist, Child Health Clinic
Wellingon, New Zealand

Maurice Dongier, M.D.
Professor and Chairman
Department of Psychiatry, McGill University
Montreal, Quebec, Canada

Mary-Louise Engels, M.A.
Department of Psychology, McGill University
Montreal, Quebec, Canada

Joanne Fitzpatrick, B.Sc.
Research Assistant, Department of Psychiatry
School of Medicine, University of Auckland
Auckland, New Zealand

A. Missagh Ghadirian, M.D.
Associate Professor of Psychiatry, McGill University
Director of Education, Douglas Hospital
Montreal, Quebec, Canada

Susan Gregory, M.B., Ch.B., M.R.C.Psych., M.Med.Sc.
Research Fellow, University of Nottingham
Nottingham, England

Julien Daniel Guelfi, M.D.
Service de Professeur Pierre Pichot
Clinique des Maladies Mentales et de l'Encéphale
100, rue de la Santé
75674 Paris Cedex 14, France

Koichi Hanada, M.D.
Lecturer of Psychiatry, Department of Psychiatry
Shiga University of Medical Science
Otsu, Japan

John E. Helzer, M.D.
Professor of Psychiatry
Washington University
School of Medicine
St. Louis, Missouri, U.S.A.

Yutaka Honda, M.D.
Senior Lecturer, Department of Neuropsychiatry
Faculty of Medicine, University of Tokyo
Tokyo, Japan

R. Wade Junek, M.D., F.R.C.P.(C)
Clinical Psychiatrist
Atlantic Child Guidance Centre
Halifax, Nova Scotia, Canada

Heinz Katschnig, M.D.
Associate Professor of Psychiatry
Psychiatric Clinic, University of Vienna
Vienna, Austria

Robert E. Kendell, M.D., F.R.C.P., F.R.C.Psych.
Professor of Psychiatry
University of Edinburgh
Edinburgh, Scotland

Gerald L. Klerman, M.D.
George Harrington Professor of Psychiatry
Harvard Medical School
Massachusetts General Hospital
Boston, Massachusetts, U.S.A.

Gerolf A. S. Koster van Groos, M.D.
Hoog Beugt 5
5473 KN Heeswijk-Dinther
The Netherlands

Jerome Kroll, M.D.
Associate Professor of Psychiatry
University of Minnesota
Minneapolis, Minnesota, U.S.A.

Gerhard Lenz, M.D.
Assistant Professor of Psychiatry
Psychiatric Clinic, University of Vienna
Vienna, Austria

José M. López-Ibor, M.D.
Head of the Psychiatric Unit
C. S. Primero de Octubre
Madrid, Spain

Juan López-Ibor, Jr., M.D.
Professor of Medical Psychology and Psychiatry
Head of the Department of Psychiatry
Centro Ramon y Cajal
Madrid, Spain

Professor Carlo Maggini
Associate Professor in Psychopathology
Institute of Clinical Psychiatry
University of Pisa
Pisa, Italy

Professor Graham Mellsop, M.B.Ch.B. (Otago), D.P.M., F.R.A.N.Z.C.P., M.R.C.Psych., M.D. (Melb.)
Head, Department of Psychological Medicine
Wellington Clinical School of Medicine, University of Otago
Wellington, New Zealand

R. James Methven, M.B., Ch.B.
Director, Child Psychiatric Service
Auckland Hospital
Auckland, New Zealand

Professor Pierre Pichot
Clinique desMaladies Mentales et de l'Encéphale
100 rue de la Santé
75674 Paris Cedex 14, France

Nils Retterstøl, Dr. Med.
Professor of Psychiatry, University of Oslo
Medical Director, Gaustad Hospital
Oslo, Norway

Sir Martin Roth, Sc.D. (Hon.), M.A. (Cantab.), M.D., F.R.C.P., F.R.C. Psych.
Professor of Psychiatry, University of Cambridge
Clinical School, New Addenbrooke's Hospital
Cambridge, England

Erik Strömgren, M.D.
Emeritus Professor of Psychiatry, University of Aarhus
Former Medical Superintendent, Aarhus Psychiatric Hospital
Risskov, Denmark

Saburo Takahashi, M.D., Ph.D.
Professor and Chairman, Department of Psychiatry
Shiga University of Medical Science
Otsu, Japan

Tao Kuo-Tai, M.D.
Professor of General and Child Psychiatry
Director of Nanjing Neuropsychiatric Institute
Director of Nanjing Child Mental Health Center
Nanjing, People's Republic of China

Frank T. N. Varghese, M.D., B.S., B.Sc., F.R.A.N.Z.C.P.
Acting Chief Psychiatrist
Research & Training, Mental Health Division
Health Commission of Victoria
Melbourne, Australia

John S. Werry, M.D.
Professor and Head, Department of Psychiatry
School of Medicine, University of Auckland
Auckland, New Zealand

Narendra N. Wig, M.B.B.S, M.D., D.P.M., F.R.C. Psych., F.A.M.S.
Professor and Head, Department of Psychiatry
All India Institute of Medical Sciences
New Delhi, India

Yan Shan-Ming, M.D.
Head, Psychiatrist-in-Chief
Department of Psychiatry
Zhenjiang Psychiatric Hospital
Zhenjiang, Jiangsu, People's Republic of China

SECTION I

Background for International Perspectives

THE SIGNIFICANCE OF DSM-III IN AMERICAN PSYCHIATRY

Gerald L. Klerman, M.D.

DIAGNOSIS AND NOSOLOGY REVISITED

During the past decade, American psychiatry has experienced a major revival of interest in psychopathology and in diagnosis and nosology, culminating in the publication in 1980 of the third edition of the *Diagnostic and Statistical Manual of Mental Disorders* (DSM-III) by the American Psychiatric Association (APA) (1). This revival follows decades of neglect of these topics. From the early 1940s through the mid-1970s, diagnosis and classification were minor concerns of American psychiatry. From World War II on, debates continued over the question "Diagnosis and classification of what?" In the absence of persuasive theoretical and therapeutic answers, the American psychiatric community answered with skepticism, disinterest, and disregard.

One of the main sources of this attitude was the apparent lack of relevance of diagnosis for treatment decisions. This was particularly true when the most valued treatment available was dynamic psychotherapy. If all conditions were indications for psychotherapy, then diagnosis and differential treatment assignments were not necessary. Today, however, treatment decisions cannot be responsibly informed and implemented without a sound nosological base. As effective treat-

Address correspondence to: Gerald L. Klerman, M.D., c/o Psychiatry Service, Massachusetts General Hospital, Fruit Street, Boston, Massachusetts 02114, U.S.A.

ments for mental disorders become diverse, the need for a highly differentiated, diagnostic framework becomes clearer. Spitzer (2), who guided the development of DSM-III, has stated:

> The purpose of a classification of medical disorders is to identify those conditions which, because of their negative consequences, implicitly have a call to action to the profession, the person with the condition, and society. The call to action on the part of the medical profession (and its allied professions) is to offer treatment for the condition or a means to prevent its development, or, if knowledge is lacking, to conduct appropriate research.

DSM-III incorporates a number of developments from recent clinical experience and research advances. It represents or contains five innovations:

1. It represents a reaffirmation of the concept of multiple, separate disorders and places psychiatry once again within the classic medical model that arose in the 18th and 19th centuries.

2. For the first time in an official nomenclature, there are operational criteria, both inclusion and exclusion criteria.

3. These criteria are based, for the most part, on manifest descriptive psychopathology rather than inferences or criteria from presumed causation or etiology, whether this causation be psychodynamic, social, or biological. The exception to this is the category of organic disorders, derived from central nervous system (CNS) pathology. The choice of descriptive criteria rather than etiologic criteria does not in itself represent an abandonment of the ideal of classification and diagnosis based on causation; rather, it represents a heuristic decision to deal with the dilemma that most of the disorders that we currently encounter in psychiatry have no established etiologic or even pathophysiologic basis. There are many competing hypotheses, but none has been clearly established.

4. DSM-III is the first official nomenclature to be tested for reliability in a field test. Never before has a medical specialty involved its practitioners in a field study to test the reliability of a new nomenclature. Never before has statistical evidence been produced concerning the acceptance, reliability, feasibility, and utility of a diagnostic scheme.

5. A multiaxial system has been introduced to accommodate the multiplicity of aspects of patients' lives and experience.

Implicit in the creation of DSM-III and the mode of its formation and promulgation has been a principle of change. Already there is a push for DSM-IV. Thus, we have a diagnostic system that is not static, and one that provides the basis for the generation of evidence to resolve disputes and conflicts.

DSM-III has generated controversy both within the United States and between U.S. psychiatrists and those from other countries, most of whom follow the World Health Organization (WHO) International Classification of Diseases (ICD) (3). As a contribution to understanding the current controversy surrounding these developments, this paper will examine the diversity of the contemporary American psychiatric scene. This diversity will be interpreted in terms of Kuhn's theory of scientific change. Given the existence of multiple competing schools, each with its own paradigm, the emergence of DSM-III represents a partial solution to a set of problems surrounding diagnostic reliability and the selection of patients for differential treatment prescription.

SCHOOLS OF CONTEMPORARY AMERICAN PSYCHIATRY

American psychiatry began in the early 19th century with the creation of mental hospitals. Their medical superintendents—the forerunners of today's psychiatrist—were concerned mainly with the institutional care of people afflicted with "insanity," conditions that today we would classify as "psychotic." The predecessor of today's American Psychiatric Association was the Association of Medical Superintendents of Asylums for the Insane, founded in 1844; its official publication, the *American Journal of Insanity*, later became the current *American Journal of Psychiatry*.

With the beginning of the 20th century, psychiatrists became involved in settings other than asylums: they became active in general hospitals, private practice, and the military services, and were invited as consultants to schools, prisons, and other institutions. With these changes in setting, they saw patients with nonpsychotic conditions, variously called neuroses and personality disorders. Confronted with nonpsychotic patients with diverse symptoms and behaviors, psychiatric opinion began to form various schools that attempted to give meaning to psychopathology and to guide treatments.

Schools of American Psychiatry

It is important to recognize that, at the present time in the United States, no school of psychiatric thought is dominant. American psychiatry has multiple scientific sources. It draws on specialized knowledge within its own broad sphere, ranging from psychoanalysis to psychobiology, and draws from related disciplines—psychology, the neurosciences, and epidemiology—as well. The diversity characterizing the professional scene has resulted in considerable ferment and rivalry among the alternative schools. The extent of this diversity has been described by Armor and Klerman (4) Havens (5), and Lazare (6).

Observers of the American scene have catalogued the diverse schools in various ways. In their influential study of social class and mental illness, Hollingshead and Redlich (7) divided the practitioner community in New Haven into two groups, which they referred to as "Analytic and Psychological" (A-P) and "Directive and Organic" (D-O). Subsequent researchers have described other groupings. In the early 1960s, Strauss and his associates (8), in Chicago, using sociological survey methods, and Armor and Klerman (4), studying a nationwide sample of psychiatrists working in hospitals, identified three psychiatric schools: a biological (or organic) school, a psychological/psychodynamic school, and what was then emerging as a social psychiatric school.

The table identifies the five schools most relevant, in this writer's view, to the current American psychiatric scene with regard to diagnosis and classification and nosology. Observers familiar with the American scene will note that a number of influential groups of practitioners are not represented here. For example, the existential school, identified and described by Havens (5), although it influences many modern thinkers and writers by extending tenets of existential philosophy and literature into therapeutic theory, has had relatively little impact on psychiatric research or practice in terms of diagnosis and classification. Similarly, the many new schools of psychotherapy that have proliferated in recent decades, particularly among nonmedical practitioners (such as Gestalt therapy, humanistic psychology, and transactional analysis), are not discussed; they have been critical of the "medical model" and have little interest in matters of diagnosis and classification. Community mental health also does not appear as a separate school; though it has effected major changes in the delivery of mental health services, its adherents have tended to ignore issues of diagnosis and classification in their writings and clinical practice. The theoreticians and practitioners of community mental health have often been allied in their antidiagnostic stance with the "antipsychiatry movement."

Kuhn's Theory of Scientific Progress

The schools of American psychiatry differ markedly in their concepts of mental illness and in their concern with diagnostic reliability, validity, and appropriateness. The differences in attitude toward diagnosis among the schools encompass moral and ethical judgments; some schools, for example, regard diagnostic efforts as depersonalizing, antitherapeutic, and politically repressive. The force of these ideological elements has often influenced efforts at revision of diagnostic nomenclatures, as manifested in some of the debates and controversies attendant upon the creation and promulgation of DSM-III.

Given this ideological character of the current American psychiatric scene, how can its structure and dynamics be understood? Here the

Contemporary Schools of Psychiatry

School	Major U.S. Proponents	Theoretical Sources	Applications and Emphases
Biological	Kety Winokur E. Robins Snyder	19th-century Continental schools of psychiatry	Pharmacotherapy Genetic studies CNS research
Psychoanalytic	Menninger Erikson Kohut Kernberg	Freudian psychoanalytic concepts and American modifications, particularly ego psychology and self-psychology	Intensive, insight-oriented psychotherapy and psychoanalysis
Interpersonal	Sullivan Fromm-Reichman Fromm Horney Arieti	G.H. Mead, C.H. Cooley, and the Chicago school of symbolic interactionists	Broadened psychotherapeutic framework to include family and group therapies Psychotherapy with ambulatory patients and those with schizophrenia, depression, and other severe conditions
Social	Meyer Leighton Lindemann Caplan	Conceptual and empirical frameworks derived from sociology, anthropology, and other social sciences	Epidemiologic studies Community mental health
Behavioral-cognitive	Wolpe Stunkard Beck	Pavlovian and Skinnerian theory Cognitive psychology	Behavior therapies Cognitive therapy

views of Thomas Kuhn (9) on the nature of change and progress in science appear especially relevant and applicable.

Kuhn has suggested that the history of a science is punctuated by revolutions, the essence of a scientific revolution being the emergence of a new paradigm that provides a significant restructuring of the ways in which the particular science defines its problems and orders its ways of looking at them. In the revised edition of *The Structure of Scientific Revolutions*, Kuhn describes the two components of a "paradigm"—the cognitive and the communal. The cognitive component refers to the theories, concepts, and ideas by which a science is delineated and the rules it employs in conducting research and evaluating evidence. The communal component refers to the collectivity of scientists (or practitioners) who share the ideas and values and who affirm the particular form of scientific "truth."

Kuhn's theory has been the subject of much discussion and controversy. It has been criticized for using the physical sciences as the basis for assessing other sciences, for identifying substantive issues too closely with vicissitudes of composition of scientific communities, and for overstating the allegiance of scientists to a specific paradigm. Nonetheless, Kuhn presents a broad framework for understanding historical change within a science, particularly one as diverse as psychiatry, for which no one school has yet provided a dominant and unifying paradigm.

Kuhn suggests that when a single paradigm emerges as dominant within a science, the status of the science becomes defined, and disputes are resolved. Within this framework two assessments of the scientific status of the current American psychiatric scene are possible. First, each separate school could be regarded as paradigmatic. According to this assessment, the current American psychiatric scene would be regarded as an arena for multiple, competing, scientific paradigms, each with its own cognitive structure (theories and research methodologies) and its own community of investigators and practitioners. The various paradigms compete with each other for scientific dominance, for intellectual status and prestige, and for the allegiance of mental health practitioners, including psychiatrists, psychologists, social workers, and nurses. Second, an alternative view would be that since no school has yet emerged as paramount, psychiatry should be described as a "preparadigmatic" science. Seen from this perspective, psychiatry is still prescientific since a single, dominant paradigm does not exist.

Contemporary psychiatry in the United States, then, involves multiple, competing paradigms. It may be that one paradigm will emerge as dominant in the future, as the scientific discipline may fragment into separate subspecialties. In the current situation, however, the various schools of psychiatry are competing with each other for the support of scientists, practitioners, public policy makers, and the lay public and general intellectual and academic circles.

The attitudes of the various schools toward diagnosis and classification vary; but among the different schools, the biological school, with its historical roots in classic medical thinking, has been the consistent advocate of the existence of multiple diagnostic classes and the importance of diagnosis and classification for biological research and for selection of appropriate therapies. In the 1970s, as DSM-III was being formulated, a number of new ideas emerged, some of which have the characteristics of a new paradigm that has revitalized interest in diagnosis and classification and provided the scientific basis for many of the innovations in the system.

THE DEVELOPMENT OF DSM-III

Anthropologists, historians, and students of cross-cultural psychiatry have observed that every society has its own view of health and illness and its own classification of diseases. Some of these views are consistent with those that have emerged in Western European scientific medicine; others are culturally unique.

Although descriptions of various syndromes and illnesses appear in ancient Egyptian, Greek, and Roman texts, particularly those codified by Hippocrates, the modern concepts of disease and nosology did not emerge in Western Europe until the late 18th century. The general development of scientific thinking and experimental investigation contributed to the concept of multiple discrete illnesses, each with its own signs, symptoms and natural course, outcome and prognosis. This concept was most clearly enunciated by Thomas Sydenham in England, who has been called the father of modern medical nosology.

In the 19th century these views of illness were afforded scientific support and intellectual acceptance by discoveries from the biological sciences. Two discoveries were particularly noteworthy:

1. The correlation of clinical syndromes with structural changes noted at autopsy, by either gross morbid anatomy or histopathology. Pathology emerged as a basic medical science in France, Germany, and Austria in the mid-19th century, and its rationale was codified in the writings of Virchow.

2. The discovery of microorganisms by Pasteur, Koch, and others resulted in delineation of many clinical disorders associated with specific bacteria or other microorganisms. The spectacular success in control of many infectious diseases by treatment with antibiotics or their prevention by sanitary measures or immunization offered the most powerful validation of the concept of discrete disorder.

Advances in diagnostic radiology following the discovery of X-rays and in biochemical tests such as determination of serum glucose provided independent biological confirmation in the living organism of pathological processess correlated with clinical signs and symptoms.

These advances in biology gave medicine a scientific basis, and were rapidly applied to psychiatry, particularly in France, Germany, and Austria. In the latter half of the 19th century, attempts were made to correlate various mental syndromes with autopsy and bacteriological findings. There were notable successes in these searches for biological causes of mental conditions. By 1895, clinical and epidemiological studies had shown that central nervous system syphilis was associated with the syndrome of general paresis, and this association was confirmed by the development of the Wasserman Test, in 1905, and the isolation of the spirochete in the brain, by Noguchi, in 1911. After World War I, Goldberger and his associates in the U.S. Public Health Service discovered the relationship between pellagra and vitamin B deficiency; in addition to elucidating the biological basis of the disorder, this discovery paved the way for effective treatment and, ultimately, prevention.

From the 1920s through the 1950s, there were few new discoveries of biological correlates of the functional psychoses and other clinical disorders in psychiatry. This situation was not true of mental retardation, however: the discovery of the various forms of chromosomal anomalies led to an understanding of Down's syndrome and other retarded states, and the discovery of multiple aminoacidurias further eluciated the pathogenesis of multiple forms of mental retardation.

Nevertheless, the concept of discrete disorders and the medical model applied to psychiatry came under considerable criticism within the profession and from without. Five lines of criticism were debated during the 1960s and 1970s:

1. The most fundamental criticism was the challenge to the legitimacy of psychiatry as part of medicine. Led by Szasz (10), the antipsychiatrists and the labeling theorists in sociology and psychology derided the basic premise of psychiatry that mental disorders, such as psychoses, neuroses, and personality disorders, are true illnesses. They argued that in the absence of anatomic or physiologic evidence of some biological abnormality, the application of the concept of illness to behavioral, emotional, and cognitive states served the need for social control of deviance rather than medical practice.

2. A second line of criticism focused on the low reliability of psychiatric diagnosis made by clinicians and researchers. The absence of agreement on diagnoses among clinicians, especially in dramatic court cases, undermined the credibility of the mental health profession.

3. A third line of criticism pointed to the adverse social and psy-

chological consequences of psychiatric diagnosis. This view was expressed forcefully by Karl Menninger (11) in his influential book *The Vital Balance*, in which he drew attention to the dehumanizing and depersonalizing manner in which psychiatric diagnoses were often employed. This unfortunate consequence of diagnostic practices was expanded upon by the labeling theorists, particularly Scheff and Lemere, who saw diagnosis as central to the social control function of psychiatry. Many labeling theorists went even further, denying the existence of any intrinsic differences between those people who later came to the "labeled" mentally ill and people with other forms of deviance. The most dramatic effort to document this view was reported by Rosenhan (12) in his widely quoted paper "On Being Sane in Insane Places."

4. The fourth line of criticism derived from within the research community, mainly from psychologists and statisticians experienced in multivariate statistical techniques. These critics did not challenge the existence of mental illness or the legitimacy of research in psychopathology, but they did question the categorical or typological nature of the diagnostic systems. They advocated using dimensional approaches, pointing out that there are no sharp boundaries between the normal and the abnormal and that many of the phenomena involved in diagnosis are extensions of normal phenomena, such as anxiety and depression. Lorr, Overall, and Eysenck in psychology and Strauss and others in psychiatry are among the researchers who have expounded this view.

5. Psychiatrists from developing countries and cultural anthropologists criticized the conventional diagnostic system as being rooted in Western European culture and not relevant or valid in other cultures. Anthropologic investigations indicated that various cultures had different concepts of mental illness and that the criteria for abnormality varied from culture to culture and with historical change. This form of historical and cultural relativism seemed to undermine the universality of any diagnostic system.

Revival of Interest in Diagnosis and Classification

Confronted by these challenges, the psychiatric research community responded vigorously. By the early 1960s there was a growing awareness among clinicians and researchers that the absence of an objective and reliable system for description of psychopathology and for psychiatric diagnosis was limiting progress. In 1965 the Psychopharmacology Research Branch of the National Institute of Mental Health sponsored a conference on classification in psychiatry, noting the problems created by inadequate knowledge of diagnosis and classification.

In early 1970, Lehmann (13), commenting on the long period of neglect of diagnosis, nosology, and classification in North American psychiatry, predicted a renaissance of interest. His words were prophetic: within a few years the Washington University criteria for operational diagnosis were published, and soon afterward the Schedule for Affective Disorders (SADS) and Research Diagnostic Criteria (RDC) were developed by the NIMH Psychobiology Collaborative Study (14, 15).

A number of factors contributed to these developments. Three factors are of special note: 1) the advance of new therapeutic modalities, especially the new psychopharmacologic agents, but also new behavioral and psychotherapeutic methods; 2) the availability of high-speed electronic computers allowing management of large-scale data sets and the application of multivariate statistics; and 3) the use of rating scales and other psychometric techniques for quantitative assessment of symptoms, behavior, and personality. By themselves, however, these factors could not have created the changes incorporated into DSM-III—they created the climate for change, but did not define the nature of the changes.

At this point it is useful to return to Kuhn's theory of scientific progress. To recapitulate, Kuhn suggests that scientific progress occurs when a new paradigm emerges to resolve an impasse or, in his terms, to solve a crisis. (9).

The New Paradigm

The new paradigm that emerged in the early 1970s revolved around the use of operational criteria for making diagnostic judgments of a categorical, typological, or nosological nature.

Many rating scales and checklists had been developed in response to the need for a descriptive system. Self-report instruments, checklists, and even specific scales for depression and for anxiety were developed. The new advances in clinical psychopathology drew upon existing psychometric methodologies, particularly those for educational testing, and the growing body of new statistical techniques, specifically those involving multivariate methods.

Within psychiatry, the initial developments involved the quantification of symptoms and behaviors as a means of assessing change during treatment. A large number of reliable and valid scales were developed in the late 1950s and the 1960s, first for psychotic patients, and then for depressed and anxious patients. Lorr, Hamilton, Burdock and Hardest, Zung, Beck, and Overall were major leaders in these developments. In this effort there was active interchange among clinical psychiatrists, clinical psychologists, psychopathologists, and psychopharmacologists. In a large measure they were able to draw upon the extensive knowledge in psychometrics initially developed in the assessment of intelligence and other forms of cognitive and social performance, but gradually applied to psychopathology and abnormal behavior in the late 1930s, and slowly during the 1940s and 1950s.

By the late 1960s, however, considerable difficulty was encountered because of the lack of standardized techniques for the assessment of diagnosis. Psychiatrists and other clinicians had been relying heavily on categorical (typological) nosological approaches, in contrast to the dimensional methods employed in rating scales and personality inventories. There was considerable dissatisfaction, both within clinical practice and among researchers, because of the mounting evidence of the unreliability of psychiatric diagnosis. In addition to the scientific issues, considerable social and political criticism was expressed in the many law suits brought by civil rights advocates, not to mention the continuing criticisms of psychiatric diagnosis and practice by Szasz and the other antipsychiatrists and by the labeling theorists in sociology and social psychology.

The development of operational criteria served to resolve the "crisis." The operational criteria formulated by the Washington University-St. Louis group led by Robins and Guze and codified in the 1972 paper by Feighner (16) opened the way for improved reliability and empirical tests of validity. Fleiss (17) developed the kappa technique for quantifying diagnostic reliability and categorical judgments, and this technique was applied by Spitzer and associates to a wide range of data.

In rapid succession numerous studies demonstrated the ability of the standardized interview technique to provide reliable estimates not only in clinical settings but also in epidemiologic community surveys. These operational criteria and associated measures of reliability were incorporated in the third edition of the *Diagnostic and Statistical Manual*.

The Neo-Kraepelinians

The development of operational criteria constituted the main innovation of the new paradigm that served to resolve the crisis of reliability and relevance that seemed to paralyze research on psychopathology and diagnosis and classification through the 1960s and 1970s. Since the leaders of the Washington University-St. Louis group often adopted a point of view at variance with the main currents of American psychiatry, they aroused considerable discussion and controversy. In an attempt to understand this development, I offered the concept of the neo-Kraepelinians (18). This concept has been discussed in debates about an "invisible college" of investigators (19).

During the past decade, therefore, a small group of neo-Kraepelinians has emerged in American psychiatry and has had major impact on research activity. The neo-Kraepelinian point of view includes a number of propositions:

1. Psychiatry is a branch of medicine.

2. Psychiatric practice should be based on the results of scientific knowledge derived from rigorous empirical study (as contrasted with discursive and impressionistic interpretation).

3. A boundary exists between the normal and the sick, and this boundary can be delineated reliably.

4. Within the domain of sickness, mental illnesses exist; they are not myths. Rather than a unitary phenomenon, mental illness consists of many disorders; and it is the task of scientific psychiatry, and of other medical specialties, to investigate their etiology, diagnosis, and treatment.

5. Psychiatry should treat people requiring medical care for mental illnesses and give lower priority to those in need of assistance for problems of living and unhappiness.

6. Research and teaching should explicitly and intentionally emphasize diagnosis and classification.

7. Diagnostic criteria should be classified and research should validate the criteria for this classification.

8. Departments of psychiatry in medical schools should teach these criteria, not depreciate them, as has been the case for many years.

9. Research efforts directed at improving the reliablity and validity of diagnosis and classification should use advanced quantitative research techniques.

10. Research in psychiatry should use modern scientific methodologies, especially from biology.

These are highly prescriptive and judgmental propositions. The neo-Kraepelinians are not interested in describing current psychiatric practice; they want to change it.

Although the neo-Kraepelinians tend to be most interested in biological, especially genetic, explanations for mental illnesses, a focus on a categorical, nosological approach is not, in my opinion, unique to the biological school of psychiatry. For example, Freud and many of his early followers, such as Abraham and Glover, proposed a classification of mental illness based on psychosexual stages of development. In current research and clinical practice, however, most neo-Kraepelinians emphasize the biological bases of mental disorders and, as a group, are neutral, ambivalent, or at times even hostile toward psychodynamic, interpersonal, and social psychiatric approaches.

The neo-Kraepelinian point of view was first articulated in the textbook by Meyer-Gross, Slater, and Roth published in Britain in 1951 (20). Strongly critical of psychoanalysis, psychotherapy, and social psychiatry, this book was an aggressive reaffirmation of the Kraepelinian approach. In the United States, neo-Kraepelinian activity originated at Washington University, in St. Louis. Its early spokespersons were Eli

Robins, George Winokur, and Sam Guze. Lee Robins has been instrumental in developing new psychiatric epidemiologic methods; Winokur has been most active in familial-genetic studies of affective disorder; and Guze is best known for his research on Briquet's syndrome and reformulation of the category "hysteria." Their junior associates have included Paula Clayton, Donald Goodwin, and Robert Woodruff. The dispersal of several members of Washington University group—Winokur's move from St. Louis to Iowa City, where he is Chair of the Psychiatry Department at the University of Iowa; Goodwin's move to Kansas City, where he is Chair of the Department of Psychiatry at the University of Missouri (Kansas City); and the move of Paula Clayton to Minneapolis as Chair of the Department of Psychiatry at the University of Minnesota—demonstrates the spreading influence of this germinal Washington University psychiatric community.

There is now also a strong locus of neo-Kraepelinian activity in New York, centered particularly around the work of Donald Klein. Klein's view is that psychiatrists cannot prescribe treatment effectively without a careful description of patients' symptoms and syndromes. He maintains that the diagnostic approach based on categorical nosology is the most appropriate approach to research and practice in psychopharmacology, and his volume (written in collaboration with colleagues) on diagnosis and drug treatment (21) has become the most influential textbook of clinical psychopharmacology in the United States. In addition, Klein has been active in the description of new syndromes, such as panic states and "hysteroid dysphoria," and in documenting the distinction between panic states and agoraphobia and other forms of phobia.

Other emerging neo-Kraepelinians include Akiskal in Tennessee, Taylor and Abrams in Chicago, and Wender in Utah.

The Neo-Kraepelinians and DSM-III

It is not clear whether the neo-Kraepelinians represent a distinct school. To the extent that they believe in discrete mental disorders and the primacy of psychiatry as a specialty within medicine, they follow the tradition of Kraepelin and 19th-century classic psychiatric thinking. But to the extent that they are tentative about the etiology of individual disorders and emphasize an empirical, perhaps at times an agnostic, point of view, contributing to the *neo*-aspect of their thinking, they are at variance with the central European Kraepelinian tradition, which has remained more theoretical than empirical.

At this point it is useful to quote from Kraepelin himself, who toward the end of his career wrote (22):

On the other hand, we must seriously consider how far the phenomena on which we normally base our diagnosis really do afford insight into the basic pathological process. While it may be admitted that this procedure is generally valuable there is a fairly extensive area in which such distinguishing criteria are lacking: either they are insufficiently well marked or they are unreliable. This is understandable if we assume that the affective and schizophrenic forms of mental disorder do not represent the expression of particular pathological processes, but rather indicate the areas of our personality in which these processes unfold.

Although DSM-III embodies many, but not all, of these ideas, and although the neo-Kraepelinians played a significant role in providing the research and conceptual background for many of its innovations, it would be a mistake to identify DSM-III entirely with the neo-Kraepelinian point of view. In this respect, Spitzer, the formulator of DSM-III, has explicitly stated his desire not to be considered a member of that invisible college of neo-Kraepelinians, but rather identifies himself with a larger concern with data and empiricism (23).

Returning again the Kuhn's concepts, DSM-III potentially does embody a new paradigm for American psychiatry, blending basic medical concepts of separate disorders, an empirical attitude toward available evidence concerning the etiology or pathogenesis of individual disorders, heavy reliance on psychometric and quantitative approaches to psychopathology, and, most significantly, incorporation of operational criteria as means of increasing reliability and facilitating validity.

IMPACT OF DSM-III ON AMERICAN SCHOOLS OF PSYCHIATRY

With regard to biological psychiatry, there continues to be tension concerning the use of diagnostic categories. Many biological psychiatrists, while accepting the concept of mental disorders, are nevertheless dissatisfied with the current reliance on psychopathological criteria. A number of efforts are under way to supplement, or even supplant, symptomatic criteria with laboratory tests. The hope is that these tests will provide more "objective" means of defining patient groups and thus not only facilitate decisions in clinical practice but promote understanding of pathophysiology and, perhaps, etiology. Currently, the most widely used test is the dexamethasone suppression test (DST). Many biological investigators feel that such biological markers will prove to have greater validity than the symptom diagnostic sets now available.

Within psychoanalytic psychiatry, there has been considerable controversy about the formulation of DSM-III. Much of this controversy has recently subsided. As discussed earlier, there is relatively little within the formal concepts of psychoanalysis that precludes an interest in separate diagnostic categories. In fact, Freud and many of his early associates accepted the distinctions between psychoses and neuroses. Freud himself was instrumental in describing what later came to be the standard categories of neuroses—conversion hysteria, anxiety neurosis, phobia, and obsessive-compulsive states.

During the 1930s and 1940s many attempts were made to relate a predisposition to adult forms of mental illness to particular experiences during childhood stages of psychosexual development. When these failed to be verified by clinical and research experience, diagnostic concern seemed to decline markedly in American psychoanalysis, and diagnosis and classification came under criticism, particularly in the writings of Karl Menninger (11). Psychoanalysts have been disappointed because DSM-III does not have an axis devoted to psychoanalytic mechanisms of defense and ego functions. An attempt was made during the development of DSM-III to develop such an axis, but it received no support from the American Psychoanalytical Association, and was abandoned. Currently there is considerable interest among psychoanalysts and dynamic psychotherapists in developing such an additional axis for future editions of the manual.

Within social psychiatry there has been noteworthy research in psychiatric epidemiology. The new studies, particularly the NIMH Epidemiologic Catchment Area Project (ECA), promise to provide important knowledge about the incidence and prevalence of individual mental disorders and relevant risk factors.

The first use of a structured interview to make RDC diagnoses in a community study in the United States was reported by Weissman and Myers (24). Having demonstrated the feasibility of diagnosis in communities, the NIMH undertook to develop a new structured interview, the Diagnostic Interview Schedule (DIS), which yields diagnoses according to the Feighner system, DSM-III, and the RDC. Five large community studies are under way, each with samples of a minimum of 3,000 people, in New Haven, Baltimore, St. Louis, Raleigh, and Los Angeles. The first results indicate the feasibility of using a structured interview in large-scale community samples and the meaningfulness of the diagnostic prevalence rates that are revealed.

It is hard to discern any specific trend of change with respect to DSM-III within interpersonal psychiatry. Interpersonal psychiatry in the United States has pioneered in the development of new forms of therapeutic intervention whose focus is the individual in relationship to his/her primary groups. Notable have been the advances in family therapy, often using a systems approach, and in group therapy. For the most part, the developers of these techniques have not moved to specify these therapies for particular disorders with anything like the degree of specification that has emerged in behavioral techniques.

Nevertheless, after an early flurry of claims for the efficacy of family interventions in schizophrenia, a more modest approach is now apparent, and it is likely that as systematic trials of family therapy get underway, the investigators will use, as their selection criteria, operational criteria such as those specified in DSM-III.

One exception to this general trend within interpersonal psychiatry is the development of interpersonal therapy for depression by the Boston-New Haven Collaborative Group (25). This form of psychotherapy relies heavily on the ideas of Sullivan and Bowlby, and in the trials of its efficacy, RDC criteria have been used.

Within behavioral psychiatry, the impact of DSM-III can be best seen in stages. While DSM-III was being developed, many psychologists, including those with a behavioral orientation, expressed concern lest DSM-III be considered a "medical" document that precluded the role of nonmedical practitioners in the treatment of patients with mental disorders. This concern seems to have subsided considerably. Behavioral treatments have always claimed specificity, particular interventions being designed for phobias, obsessions, and various forms of sexual dysfunction. In the selection of patients for intervention trials, however, the emphasis has usually been on the presenting symptoms, often assessed by psychiatric techniques. Relatively less attention has been given to differential diagnosis.

This survey of the impact of DSM-III on various schools of psychiatry indicates that, intellectually, the concept of separate syndromes, diagnosed by operational criteria and the multiaxial system, is in principle compatible with the various schools—behavioral, interpersonal, social, and psychoanalytic.

THE IMPACT OF DSM-III ON PROFESSIONAL ACTIVITIES

Clinical Practice

Two features of DSM-III have had the most impact on clinical practice: the use of operational criteria, and the multiaxial classification system.

The use of operational criteria has rapidly been incorporated into clinical practice, with a noticeable increase in the reliability of diagnostic judgments and facilitation of communication among clinicians. DSM-III has been effective in responding to the challenge of diagnostic unreliability. One of the main arguments of the antipsychiatry movement was the apparently low reliability of psychiatric diagnosis and the lack of validity for the categories. In response to this criticism, successful efforts have been undertaken to better understand the sources of unreliability; as they have been located and analyzed, attempts have been made, and are continuing, to overcome obstacles to reliability.

For example, Fleiss and associates (17) applied the statistic kappa (developed by Fleiss) to measure more accurately the degree of concordance among diagnosticians. In addition, training techniques using videotapes and case vignettes have been developed. The utilization of these techniques has resulted in improved reliability not only in research settings but also in clinical practice, as demonstrated by the reasonably high reliability coefficients found in the field trials for DSM-III conducted among a large sample of practitioners.

The other area in which DSM-III has facilitated clinical practice lies in the prescriptions of forms of treatment. As the numbers of psychopharmacologic agents grew in the late 1960s and the 1970s, efforts were undertaken to provide reliable and valid predictors of which types of patients were likely to respond to the various classes of drugs. There seems to be a strong correlation between patterns of response to classes of psychotherapeutic drugs and classic grouping of different categories of psychopathology as embodied in DSM-III. Although responses overlap among classes of drugs, the pattern of response seems to follow the general separation of the major disorders as delineated by the generation of Kraepelin and Bleuler.

This therapeutic utility of diagnostic classification extends also to the selection of patients for psychotherapeutic techniques. The efficacy of differentiated behavioral techniques is closely correlated with distinction among simple phobias, agoraphobia, and obsessive-compulsive states (26). The development of various forms of brief interpersonal, psychodynamic, and cognitive techniques for ambulatory patients with depression, most often nonbipolar, nonmelancholic, and nonpsychotic, also indicates the value of careful diagnosis in the selection of appropriate psychotherapeutic techniques.

During the period when individual psychotherapy was the preferred form of treatment and was considered applicable to all forms of mental illness, differential diagnosis was not a major research or clinical task. This unitary view of treatment was dominant in American psychiatry in the late 1940s and early 1950s, but is no longer tenable. Confronted with multiple forms of drug therapy and a variety of psychotherapies, clinicians need guidance in their selection of the appropriate treatment for individual patients. The revival of psychiatric diagnosis and classification embodied in DSM-III has provided clinicians with reliable and valid criteria for helping them decide which patients would benefit from which kinds of therapy.

The other feature of DSM-III that has gained the most acceptance among clinicians is use of the multiaxial system. This has gone a long way toward alleviating the major discomforts that practitioners have felt with diagnostic systems. It is an attempt to resolve a long-standing dilemma that exists for all medicine: whereas the unit of scientific interest is pathology (the disorder or disease), the unit of clinical practice is the individual patient. Put another way, "Medicine studies diseases but treats patients" (27).

This dilemma has contributed to continuing controversy about the relevance of diagnostic systems for humane practice. Practitioners have long complained that existing classifications hinder patient care in at least two ways. First, they claim that diagnostic categories are inadequate for understanding the complexity of individual patients and for clinical decision-making. For example, it is argued that in evaluating the need to hospitalize suicidal patients, in addition to knowing whether or not the patient is depressed or psychotic, it is also necessary to assess personality dynamics such as the patient's impulsivity or degree of self-control, and to have an adequate understanding of that patient's life circumstances, particularly current stresses, family and income, and other social supports. Second, some clinicians have asserted that assigning patients to categories contributes to a depersonalization and deindividualization of the doctor–patient relationship.

To deal with these objections and to refine diagnostic assignment, DSM-III has incorporated a multiaxial framework. This five-axis system consists of: clinical psychiatric syndromes, entailing chronicity and periodicity aspects as well as symptoms (axis I); personality disorders of adults and development disorders of children and adolescents (axis II); physical illness (axis III); psychosocial stressors (axis IV); and level of adaptive functioning (axis V). The first three axes are typological, involving categories; the last two are dimensional (28).

With these changes DSM-III has gone a long way toward meeting some of the hesitations and criticisms of clinicians with regard to diagnostic systems. As experience evolves, it is likely that further axes will be proposed, particularly one dealing with psychoanalytic defenses and ego functions. At some point, however, there will need to be some limitations on the number of axes, because of practical considerations.

In the long run, the acceptance of DSM-III by clinical practitioners will be the main determinant of its impact, independently of scholarly and research activities.

Research

The impact of DSM-III on research is relatively easier to assess. Inasmuch as the use of operational criteria and emphasis on diagnostic groups arose primarily from within the research community, DSM-III has served mainly to codify existng practices among research groups. It has, however, contributed to an apparent increase in activity in psychopathology and nosology. Numerous efforts are under way to compare the relative reliability and validity of various diagnostic sets for schizophrenia, bipolar illness, and other axis I diagnoses. Within child psychiatry, there is a noticeable increase in concern for descriptive psychopathology, attention now being given to the syndromes of childhood depression (previously its existence was questioned) and to the reliability and validity of other techniques (29). Within therapeutics, DSM-III has served to further codify the importance of careful selection of homogeneous patient groups for therapeutic trials.

It is almost universally accepted that the most powerful evidence for the efficacy of various treatments derives from controlled studies, particularly randomized clinical trials. Prominent medical journals such as the *Journal of the American Medical Associaton*, the *New England Journal of Medicine*, and *Lancet* regularly report results of randomized trials of new drugs, surgical procedures, radiation, and even psychotherapy. Thus, the regulations and guidelines of the U.S. Food and Drug Administration (FDA) not only have contributed greatly to the acceptance of the randomized trial as the standard method for the evaluation of treatment but also have been an important stimulus to the development of diagnostic assessment methods.

Randomized controlled trials in psychiatry have rapidly generated information of high scientific quality and clinical relevance. They have made it possible to specify clinical conditions for which a particular therapy is effective and to identify those for which we do not have adequate evidence, either positive or negative, concerning efficacy, as is the case with many forms of personality disorder represented in DSM-III on axis II.

The FDA has recently indicated that it will require that all future new drug applications (NDAs) define patient groups on the basis of DSM-III criteria, and will also likely require that the patient packet inserts and related material for currently approved drugs be rewritten to conform to DSM-III categories.

Teaching

Although there are few systematic studies available, the evidence suggests increasing acceptance of DSM-III in the teaching of medical students and psychiatric residents. More significantly, DSM-III seems to be increasingly accepted in the teaching of other mental health professionals, particularly clinical and consulting psychologists, social workers, and psychiatric nurses. A number of projects are under way to test the issues in learning and the acceptability of DSM-III in clinical teaching.

Interprofessional Relations

While DSM-III was in its final stages of development, lively discussions developed in various professional groups, particularly the associations of psychologists and psychoanalysts, with a number of relevant articles appearing in *The American Psychologist*.

With the publication of DSM-III, however, the controversy seems to have rapidly subsided. Almost all new textbooks of psychology incorporate DSM-III, and in clinical practice, DSM-III seems to be increasingly accepted as the basis for teaching diagnoses to mental health professionals.

International Relations

The decision of the American Psychiatric Association to develop DSM-III, apart from the ICD, created considerable tension. In an effort to minimize some of this tension, the Alcohol, Drug Abuse, and Mental Health Administration (ADAMHA) and the World Health Organization sponsored a number of projects to improve communication in this area. Commenting on this development, John Cooper (30) noted in a recent issue of the *British Journal of Psychiatry*:

> The mere fact that such a conference and program were conceived and worked through, however, suggests that there is now a widespread and international realization that close collaboration and communication between psychiatrists is of fundamental importance, if psychiatry is to continue its progress towards being recognized as a scientifically based discipline. The twin subjects of diagnosis and classification are an essential part of the foundations that are needed for this progress.

As the time approaches for the development of ICD-10 and/or DSM-IV, it is expected that there will be increasing pressure to bridge the gap between the current World Health Organization and United States efforts. It is likely that all future official nomenclatures—national or international—will include a multiaxial system and operational criteria. Also, formal field trials for feasibility and reliability will doubtless be undertaken. This may be one of the major impacts of DSM-III, namely, the influence it has not only on U.S. psychiatry but on psychiatry in other nations and at the international level.

CONCLUSION

Contemporary U.S. psychiatry is characterized by competing schools—biological, social, interpersonal, psychodynamic, and behavioral, each of which has proposed different theories concerning the nature and origin of mental illnesses and emphasized various modes of treatment. Numerous observers have commented that this division into schools is particularly marked in American psychiatry. So intense are the loyalties and emotions manifested by the adherents of these various schools that psychiatry appears from the outside to be more like an arena of conflicting ideologic sets than a scientific discipline based on commonly shared methodological approaches and incremental advances based on empirical knowledge.

Applying Kuhn's theory of the history of science, one may say that psychiatry seems to be characterized by multiple competing paradigms each of which offers a different conception of the nature of psychiatry and invokes different rules of methods and evidence.

For many years there appeared to be no way out of this unsatisfactory situation. There was no independent means by which the claims of various schools concerning the causation of mental illness and the efficacy of their treatment could be established as valid or dismissed as unproven and unsubstantiated by empirical evidence.

In the past two decades, however, this situation has changed dramatically, particularly in the United States, in other parts of North America, and in England. It may well be that a new paradigm, in Kuhn's sense, has emerged, emphasizing a broader concept of the nature of separate mental illnesses than was the case in 19th-century thinking, but rejecting the unidimensional view that emerged after World War II. Methodologically, the emphasis on quantitative methods from psychometrics and the application of operational criteria have contributed greatly to resolving the crisis surrounding reliability that seemed to paralyze progress through the 1960s. New methods and systematic empirical investigations to test hypotheses have been developed in psychiatric research. In the case of therapeutics, the controlled clinical trial, using standardized diagnostic and assessment methods, with some form of randomization or matching of patients to treatment groups and use of appropriate controls, such as placebos, has emerged as the standard means by which the efficacy and safety of treatments can be evaluated.

The empirical approaches within psychiatric research in the United States have been related mainly to the emergence of a new paradigm. Its methods have been applied primarily to biological research and to the evaluation of drug and behavioral therapy. The association between individual schools and quantitative methodologies is, however, in my view, not intrinsic to the theoretical principles of the schools or their specialized research techniques. For example, in a recent discussion of social psychiatry in the United Kingdom, reference was made to the powerful influence of the British empirical tradition in philosophy and in science—the tradition of Locke, Hume, and Russell, of Newton and Darwin—and in social action—the traditon of Mills, Bentham, and the Webbs—in the theory and practice of social psychiatry. To quote Wing (31): "Empiricism is not, of course, an atheoretical philosophy but it does entail a critical stance toward theories which are seen solely as a source of ideas to be tested, in the hope (though not, it must be admitted, in the expectation) that they might turn out to be useful."

An empirical paradigm in psychiatry emphasizes two aspects of the modern philosophy of science: 1) that the essence of modern science is testing hypotheses through experimental and quasi-experimental methods in the laboratory and in the clinic; and 2) that quantification of phenomena—whether directly observable, as in behavior, or inferred, as with mental processes, conscious or unconscious—is necessary.

REFERENCES

1. American Psychiatric Association: Diagnostic and Statistical Manual of Mental Disorders, 3rd ed (DSM-III). Washington, DC, American Psychiatric Association, 1980
2. Spitzer RL, Endicott J: Medical and mental disorders: proposed definitions and criteria, in Critical Issues in Psychiatric Diagnosis. Edited by Spitzer RL, Klein DF. New York, Raven Press, 1978
3. World Health Organization: International Classification of Diseases, 9th Revision. Geneva, World Health Organization, 1977
4. Armor D, Klerman G: Psychiatric treatment orientations and professional ideology. J Health Soc Behav 9:243–255, 1968
5. Havens L: Approaches to the Mind. Boston, Little, Brown, 1973
6. Lazare A (ed): Outpatient Psychiatry. London, Williams & Wilkins, 1979
7. Hollingshead A, Redlich F: Social Class and Mental Illness. New York, Wiley, 1958
8. Strauss A, Schatzman L, Bucher R, et al (eds): Psychiatric Ideologies and Institutes. New York, The Free Press, 1964
9. Kuhn T: The Structure of Scientific Revolutions, 2nd ed. International Encyclopedia of Unified Science, vol 2, no 2. Chicago, University of Chicago Press, 1970
10. Szasz T: The Myth of Mental Illness. New York, Harper–Hoeber, 1961; Harper & Row, 1974
11. Menninger K, Mayman M, Pruyser P: The Vital Balance: The Life Process in Mental Health and Illness. New York, Viking Press, 1963
12. Rosenhan DA: On being sane in insane places. Science 179:250–258, 1973
13. Lehmann H: Epidemiology of depressive disorders, in Depression in the 1970's. Edited by Fieve RR. New York, Excerpta Medica, 1970
14. Katz M, Klerman G: Introduction: overview of the clinical studies program. Am J Psychiatry 136:49–51, 1979
15. Spitzer RL, Endicott J, Robins E: Research Diagnostic Criteria (RDC) for a Selected Group of Functional Disorders. New York, New York State Department of Mental Hygiene, Biometrics Branch, 1975
16. Feighner J, Robins E, Guze S, et al: Diagnostic criteria for use in psychiatric research. Arch Gen Psychiatry 26:57–63, 1972
17. Fleiss JL, Spitzer RL, Endicott J, et al: Quantification of agreement in multiple psychiatric diagnosis. Arch Gen Psychiatry 26:168–171, 1972
19. Klerman GL: The evolution of a scientific nosology, in Schizophrenia: Science and Practice. Edited by Shershow JC. Cambridge, Mass, Harvard University Press, 1978

19. Blashfield R: Feighner et al, invisible colleges and the Matthew effect. Schizophr Bull 8:1–6, 1982
20. Meyer-Gross W, Slater E, Roth M: Clinical Psychiatry. Baltimore, Williams & Wilkins, 1954
21. Klein DF, Davis JM: Diagnosis and Drug Treatment of Psychiatric Disorders: Adults and Children, 2nd ed. Baltimore, Williams & Wilkins, 1980
22. Kraepelin E: Comparative psychiatry, in Themes and Variations in European Psychiatry. Edited by Hirsch SR, Shepherd M. Charlottesville, Va, University Press of Virginia, 1974
23. Spitzer RL: Letter to the editor. Schizophr Bull 8:592, 1982
24. Weissman MM, Myers JK: Affective disorders in a U.S. urban community. Arch Gen Psychiatry 35:1304–1311, 1978
25. Klerman GL, Weissman MM: Interpersonal psychotherapy: theory & research, in Short-term Psychotherapies for Depression. Edited by Rush J. New York, Guilford Press, 1982
26. Marks I: Review of behavioral psychotherapy, I: obsessive-compulsive disorders. Am J Psychiatry 138:584–592, 1981
27. Klerman GL: Mental Illness, the medical model, and psychiatry. J Med Philos 2:220–243, 1977
28. Mezzich J: Multiaxial systems in psychiatry, in Comprehensive Textbook of Psychiatry, 3rd ed, vol 1. Edited by Kaplan HI, Freeman AM, Sadock BJ. Baltimore, Williams & Wilkins, 1980
29. Cantwell DP: Rediagnostic process and diagnostic classification in child psychiatry (DSM-III). J Am Acad Child Psychiatry 19:345–355, 1980
30. Cooper JE: The last big one? (Comments) Br J Psychiatry 141:531, 1982
31. Wing J: Social psychiatry in the United Kingdom: the approach to schizophrenia. Schizophr Bull 6:556–565, 1980

2

ICD-9 AND DSM-III:
A COMPARISON

Andrew E. Skodol, M.D., and Robert L. Spitzer, M.D.

In 1980 the American Psychiatric Association published its *Diagnostic and Statistical Manual of Mental Disorders*, Third Edition (DSM-III) (1), for use in the United States. Since then, considerable interest in DSM-III has been evident around the world. Most nations officially use the diagnostic terminology and statistical codes of the Mental Disorders section of the *International Classification of Diseases*, Ninth Revision (ICD-9) (2) for psychiatric disorders. The purpose of this chapter is to describe the similarities and differences between ICD-9 and DSM-III.

Since classifications of mental disorders are used for various purposes (e.g., clinical, research, and statistical), a discussion of the degree of correspondence between the two systems can be at several levels. We shall here compare ICD-9 and DSM-III on three levels: 1) the diagnostic process incorporated into or implied by each classification, 2) the diagnostic concepts underlying the diagnostic terms, and 3) the coding systems corresponding to the diagnostic terms.

One of the most obvious differences between the ICD-9 Mental Disorders section and DSM-III is the latter's sheer bulk. Although DSM-III contains only approximately 25% more categories with codes than ICD-9 (including administrative and nondiagnostic codes, DSM-III has 229 codes; ICD-9 has 185), the DSM-III manual, including its various

Address correspondence to: Andrew E. Skodol, M.D., Biometrics Research Department, New York State Psychiatric Institute, 722 West 168th Street, New York, New York 10032, U.S.A.

appendices, is a full-size book of 494 pages, compared with the Mental Disorders section of ICD-9, which occupies 36 pages of that manual. Initially, mental health professionals in the United States were intimidated by this seemingly unwieldy tool, but as familiarity with the system has increased, this complaint has become less frequent.

There are several reasons for the greater size of DSM-III. The major reason is that the American Psychiatric Association's Task Force on Nomenclature and Statistics, which developed DSM-III, attempted to describe every diagnostic category in a systematic and comprehensive fashion, relying on the opinions of advisory committees of experts on the various diagnostic classes and on available research data. Thus, each disorder in DSM-III is described in terms of its essential features, associated features commonly but not invariably present, usual age at onset, typical course, associated levels of functional impairment, common complications, predisposing factors, prevalence, sex ratio, and familial pattern. When information was inadequate to make a statement in any of these areas, such as a familial pattern for conversion disorder, or the sex ratio of social phobia, this was indicated by the statement "No information." Following these descriptions is a discussion of the differential diagnosis for each disorder.

The Mental Disorders section of the ICD-9 is the only section that incorporates definitions of the diagnostic categories. This glossary is justified "because of the special problems posed for psychiatrists by the relative lack of independent laboratory information upon which to base their diagnoses" (P. 177). In contrast to DSM-III, this glossary consists of relatively brief descriptions of the "abnormal experience and behavior" subsumed by a particular category.

TWO CLASSIFICATIONS AND THE DIAGNOSTIC PROCESS

There are two major differences in the diagnostic processes represented by the two classifications. The justification for the glossary in ICD-9 is actually a recognition of the poor reliability with which psychiatrists outside research settings have made diagnoses. Elucidating the problem of diagnostic unreliability (3–9) and developing methods for reducing it (10–18) have been increasing concerns of academic psychiatry throughout the world in the past two decades. DSM-III introduces one solution to the problem of reliability, the use of diagnostic criteria (19–21), into a classification of mental disorders that can serve both clinical and research purposes.

Diagnostic criteria are explicit rules intended to guide clinicians in making a diagnosis. They have been shown in many studies (22, 23) to decrease diagnostic unreliability due to criterion variance—that is, due to idiosyncratic views on diagnosis that may lead clinicians given identical clinical data to reach different diagnoses (24). Typically such criteria embrace both inclusion criteria, the clinical features of a disorder needed to describe a particular clinical syndrome, and exclusion criteria, guidelines for distinguishing among disorders that may have similar clinical features.

The diagnostic criteria in DSM-III cover mainly essential symptoms and indexes of associated symptoms, but for some diagnoses specify a minimal duration (as in schizophrenia), a characteristic course (as in dysthymic disorder), or an age of onset (as in somatization disorder). DSM-III includes diagnostic criteria for all classified disorders except schizoaffective disorder. The manual states that the diagnostic criteria are to be used as guides according to the purpose and setting of an evaluation, but their presence in DSM-III suggests more rigorous guidelines for establishing a particular diagnosis than is usually the case. ICD-9 addresses the problem of closely related diagnoses by listing under each category certain inclusion terms; alternate, commonly used terms referring to identical, or nearly identical, diagnostic concepts; and exclusion terms for disorders that might be confused with the diagnosis in question, but that should be diagnosed under a different rubric in the classification.

A second approach to diagnosis incorporated in DSM-III that makes it differ in format from the ICD is its use of a multiaxial diagnostic system. Multiaxial diagnosis has a long tradition in European psychiatry (25–30), but before the early drafts of DSM-III was virtually unknown to most American mental health professionals. The rationale for a multiaxial system in psychiatry is twofold: 1) it does greater justice to the clinical complexity of mental disorders than does a simple categorical label, and 2) it promotes greater reliability in the assessment of different important features of a mental disorder.

Traditionally, multiaxial systems have included axes for phenomenological syndromes, etiology, duration, course, and severity (31). Use of a multiaxial system is expected to help ensure that accurate syndromal diagnosis will not be confounded by considerations of, for example, etiology. Thus, a major depressive episode with vegetative features may be recognized whether it has been precipitated by a recent stressful life event (reactive) or appears to have "arisen from within," i.e., to be "endogenous."

DSM-III diverges somewhat from European traditions of multiaxial diagnosis in the axes the task force selected. It includes five axes. Axis I is for the majority of clinical syndromes and for conditions not due to a mental disorder that are a focus of attention or treatment. Axis II is for somewhat longer-standing problems, personality disorders in adults, and specific developmental disorders in children. Axis III is for physical conditions important to the understanding or management of an axis I or II disorder. Axis IV is for psychosocial stressors that led to the development or exacerbation of a mental disorder. Axis V is for the highest level of adaptive functioning experienced by the individual in the past year. Though the first three axes are considered the official diagnosis and axes IV and V are reserved for special clinical and research purposes, the use of a multiaxial diagnostic system makes for a diagnostic assessment quite different from that of the traditional single-axis system. Both DSM-III and ICD-9 recognize that the complexity of many mental disorders may require the use of several diagnoses (on each of the first three axes in DSM-III) in order to describe the condition adequately.

A third difference between the approach of the classifications is the inclusion in DSM-III of a definition of the term *mental disorder*. DSM-III conceptualizes a mental disorder as a "clinically significant behavioral or psychological syndrome or pattern that occurs in an individual and that is typically associated with either a painful symptom (distress) or impairment in one or more important areas of functioning (disability)" (P. 6). This definition becomes important in the DSM-III criteria—for example, for personality disorders—and in assessing the clinical significance of certain symptoms such as phobias, obsessions, or compulsions. There is no explicit definition in ICD-9 of the mental disorders classified; the classification is of disorders that psychiatrists have traditionally diagnosed and treated.

Finally, DSM-III attempts to take an atheoretical approach to its classification with regard to etiology. This does not mean that DSM-III claims to be totally atheoretical; in selecting the important features of disorders upon which to base the classification, the developers of DSM-III were guided by theories that have arisen from empirical studies.

What is different about DSM-III, compared with ICD-9, is that explicit statements about the pathogenetic mechanisms that may produce particular disorders have generally not been included in their definitions. Thus, in ICD-9 the definition of hysteria refers to the unconscious nature of symptoms that serve a symbolic purpose, thereby accepting a more or less psychodynamic view of the etiology of the syndrome. By contrast, in DSM-III's conversion disorder the hallmark symptom of a loss or alteration in physical functioning, suggesting a physical disorder, occurs in the context of some psychological factors judged to be etiologically involved (to distinguish this disorder from simply undiagnosed physical symptoms); no mention is made of a specific psychodynamic mechanism. In DSM-III etiology becomes a basis of a diagnostic class only for the organic mental disorders, which by definition present evidence of a "specific organic factor that is judged to be etiologically related to the disturbance" (P. 101); the somatoform disorders, for which no specific psychological factors are required; the psychosexual disorders, in which the disturbance is presumed due to psychological, not organic, factors; and the adjustment disorders, for which stress as an etiological factor is required for the diagnosis.

DIFFERENCES IN DIAGNOSTIC CONCEPTS

There are many differences in the diagnostic concepts underlying the terms classified by DSM-III and ICD-9. This section outlines these conceptual differences. We are reasonably certain that we accurately present the thinking of the APA Task Force and its advisers, but we admit that in many cases we can only approximate the concepts underlying ICD-9, as reflected in its terms, its groupings, and its glossary descriptions. Since ICD-9 is probably more familiar to international readers, we shall begin each comparison with the ICD-9 class or term.

Psychoses and Neuroses: DSM-III
Abandons a Basic Principle

It is immediately evident that the ICD-9 classification divides disorders according to the time-honored distinction between the psychoses and the neuroses. ICD-9 describes psychoses as "mental disorders in which impairment of mental function has developed to a degree that interferes grossly with insight, ability to meet some ordinary demands of life or to maintain adequate contact with reality." It goes on to say that "it is not an exact or well defined term" (P. 177). Although DSM-III includes evidence of "psychosis" in the diagnosis of several disorders (e.g., schizophrenia or paranoid disorders), classifies some disorders as psychotic (e.g., psychotic disorders not elsewhere classified), and notes psychotic features as a subclassification (e.g., of major affective disorders), it does not use the psychotic–neurotic distinction as a principal basis for classification.

The reasons for this change were:

1. The term *psychosis* had (as ICD-9 states) in practice come to be used loosely and to be confounded with the notion of severity (i.e., the DSM-II concept of inability to meet the ordinary demands of life).

2. The term *neurosis* had assumed strongly psychodynamic overtones of etiology that were in conflict with the atheoretical approach desired by DSM-III, as described above.

DSM-III defines *psychotic* more narrowly in its Glossary of Technical Terms as "A term indicating gross impairment in reality testing. . . . When there is gross impairment in reality testing, the individual incorrectly evaluates the accuracy of his or her perceptions and thoughts and makes incorrect inferences about external reality, even in the face of contrary evidence" (P. 367). It goes on to state that evidence of psychotic behavior is the presence of delusions or hallucinations without insight into their pathological nature. This definition was thought to be sufficiently precise to allow for its reliable assessment, whereas the more traditional notion of "psychotic" had been shown to be relatively unreliable (32).

The DSM-III approach to the term and concept of neurosis will be discussed below.

Organic Psychotic Conditions: DSM-III Emphasizes Heterogeneity

DSM-III does not classify the major organic mental disorders as psychoses, since not all meet the above definition with regard to the presence of delusions or hallucinations. When psychotic features are present, they are sometimes noted as a subclassification (e.g., primary degenerative dementia, senile onset, with delusions). DSM-III adopts a broader approach to the diagnosis of organic mental disorders, accepting that a variety of syndromes with circumscribed areas of impairment may be caused by the effects of a physical process on the central nervous system (33,34). Therefore, in addition to delirium and dementia, DSM-III describes seven other organic brain syndromes: amnestic syndrome, organic delusional syndrome, organic hallucinosis, organic affective syndrome, organic personality syndrome, and intoxication and withdrawal (the latter two are for substance-induced syndromes). ICD-9 also recognizes the clinical heterogeneity of organic brain syndromes, but it requires the global cognitive features that may be accompanied by changes in affect, mood, or personality. DSM-III takes this one step further and requires global cognitive changes only in delirium and dementia and provides specific diagnoses for syndromes in which other features may be the sole symptoms. In every case evidence of the organic etiology, from the history, physical examination, or laboratory tests, is required by the criteria.

DSM-III also changes the definitions of delirium and dementia. ICD-9 continues the notion of delirium as an acute and reversible ("with a short course" [P. 177]) brain syndrome, in contrast to dementia, which is chronic, progressive, and usually irreversible. In DSM-III the distinction is between delirium, in which there is cognitive impairment in a clouded state of consciousness and disorientation, and dementia, in which cognitive impairment occurs in a clear state of consciousness. The course and ultimate reversibility or irreversibility are totally dependent on the underlying etiological process.

DSM-III includes a section on organic mental disorders that corresponds to the senile and presenile organic psychotic conditions, but labels the subdivision "Dementias Arising in the Senium and Presenium." The age at onset of the disorder is further deemphasized in that senile and presenile are subclasses, not primary divisions. This decision was based on lack of evidence that the senile and presenile dementias are actually neuropathologically distinct (35, 36). Instead of the ICD-9 depressed or paranoid types and the senile dementia with acute confusional state, both primary degenerative dementias, those with senile and those with presenile onset, can be subclassified according to whether they are accompanied by delirium, delusions, or depression or are uncomplicated.

DSM-III uses the newer term *multi-infarct dementia* rather than *arteriosclerotic dementia*. The clinical features are very similar, but the emphasis is on the actual occurrence of multiple small infarcts (37, 38).

Alcoholic Psychoses and Drug Psychoses: DSM-III Adds Specificity

ICD-9 includes a number of specific diagnoses for alcohol and drug-induced organic mental disorders. DSM-III has a subsection of the organic mental disorders for substance-induced syndromes. The majority of the subcategories of alcohol psychoses have a counterpart in DSM-III (not referred to as "psychoses," however), with some changes in the names and some changes in underlying concepts. ICD-9 states that these conditions are due to excessive consumption of alcohol and that withdrawal can be etiologically significant in some cases. DSM-III is more explicit. For example, alcohol withdrawal delirium (in ICD-9, delirium tremens) is by definition a delirium that develops following cessation of or reduction in heavy alcohol ingestion. ICD-9 does not stipulate that this is a withdrawal state.

Korsakov's psychosis, alcoholic, is renamed "alcohol amnestic disorder," but refers to the same concept. DSM-III has no concept for alcoholic jealousy per se: a person exhibiting persecutory delusions or delusions of jealousy would be diagnosed as having a paranoid disorder and a substance use disorder (see below for discussion of these DSM-III classes). Simple drunkenness is classified in ICD-9 as a nondependent abuse of drugs, whereas in DSM-III it is also an alcohol-induced organic mental disorder, alcohol intoxication, since the signs and symptoms are central nervous system effects of the alcohol, as are all the disturbances in the substance-induced organic mental disorders.

ICD-9 has three specific diagnoses for organic disorders associated with all drugs other than alcohol: drug withdrawal syndrome, paranoid and/or hallucinatory states induced by drugs, and pathological drug intoxication. DSM-III lists nine classes of drugs that have direct effects on the central nervous system: barbiturates and similarly acting sedatives and hypnotics, opioids, cocaine, amphetamines and similarly acting sympathomimetics, phencyclidine or similarly acting arylcyclohexylamines, hallucinogens, cannabis, tobacco, and caffeine, with subcategories in each to describe various clinical pictures. Some of these are associated with intoxication, others, with withdrawal. Some are accompanied by symptoms of psychosis, but others are not. Thus, clinicians can specify both the drug etiologically responsible and the particular syndrome observed. For example, for amphetamines there are categories for intoxication, delirium, delusional disorder, and withdrawal; for cannabis there are categories for intoxication and delusional disorder.

Finally, among the organic psychoses ICD-9 has groupings of transient organic psychotic conditions and other organic psychotic conditions. The former are subdivided into acute confusional state, subacute confusional state, and "other"; the latter, into Korsakov's psychosis or syndrome (nonalcoholic), dementia in conditions classified elsewhere, and "other."

DSM-III includes a subsection of organic mental disorders whose etiology is a physical disorder from outside the Mental Disorders section of the International Classification of Diseases, Ninth Revision, Clinical Modification (ICD-9 CM) (39). (This version of the ICD-9 is used in the United States. See also below.) Here, seven of the original organic brain syndromes described above are listed (minus intoxication and withdrawal), plus an atypical or mixed syndrome.

Both ICD-9 and DSM-III share the convention that the so-called "combination diagnoses" of the ICD-8 should no longer be used. Clinicians are instructed to note the causative physical disorder, such as Huntington's chorea or multiple sclerosis, using an additional code from the appropriate section of the ICD-9.

Schizophrenic Psychoses: DSM-III
Narrows the Definition

There is a major conceptual divergence between the DSM-III and the ICD-9 concepts of schizophrenia. DSM-III narrows the definition of schizophrenia by requiring for its diagnosis an active psychotic period and a continuous duration of disturbance, which may include prodromal and residual phases, of at least six months. The DSM-III definition excludes the ambiguous ICD-9 diagnoses of simple and latent types of schizophrenia, in which the patient had no clear-cut psychotic symptoms, but was classified as having schizophrenia because of behavior peculiarities, anomalies of affect, and functional impairment. ICD-9 recognized the lack of clear conceptualization and definition in these areas and recommended that these diagnoses be rarely used. In DSM-III, such a patient would be likely to receive a diagnosis such as schizotypal personality disorder. The bulk of the research evidence available on these so-called nonpsychotic types of schizophrenia argues for their separate classification, since their relationship to chronic schizophrenia is unclear (40–44).

Acute schizophrenic episode is excluded from the DSM-III concept because of the requirement of a minimum six-month duration. Patients who receive an ICD-9 diagnosis of acute schizophrenic episode would be diagnosed, according to DSM-III, as having schizophreniform disorder (a psychotic disorder not elsewhere classified) if the duration of the disturbance was between two weeks and six months, or atypical psychosis (also a psychotic disorder not elsewhere classified) if the patient was being seen within the first two weeks of a psychotic episode.

At the time of DSM-III's publication there was evidence that schizophrenia with a good prognosis could not be distinguished from schizophrenia with a poor prognosis on the basis of cross-sectional symptoms alone, but required some minimum duration of symptoms (45–47). Since DSM-III's publication, evidence continues to accumulate that the six-month duration requirement for a DSM-III diagnosis of schizophrenia is a more powerful predictor of poor prognosis, defined in terms of diagnostic and symptomatic stability, time in hospital, and impaired social functioning, than are a number of theoretically relevant clinical variables (48, 49).

The DSM-III concept of schizophrenia is further narrowed by the provision that mood-incongruent psychotic symptoms, including certain typically schizophrenic symptoms such as Schneiderian first-rank symptoms, are compatible with the diagnosis of a major affective disorder provided they occur within the context of a full manic or depressive syndrome. Thus, the ICD-9 diagnosis of the schizoaffective type of schizophrenia is likely, in many cases, to correspond to a DSM-III diagnosis of a major affective disorder with mood-incongruent psychotic features. This decision was based on the extensive review of the research literature by Pope and Lipinski (50); it continues to be supported by validity studies, especially in the case of manic episodes with mood-incongruent psychotic features (51, 52).

In DSM-III schizoaffective disorder is grouped with the psychotic disorders not elsewhere classified. It serves as a residual category without diagnostic criteria when the clinician is unable to make a differential diagnosis between schizophrenia and a major affective disorder with psychotic features according to the DSM-III criteria that describe the temporal relationship of the syndromes in cases with mixed features. This decision reflects both a lack of consensus about an adequate definition of schizoaffective disorder (53) and an unresolved controversy as to whether it is a subtype of schizophrenia, a subtype of affective disorder, or an independent diagnostic entity (54).

For the other specific ICD-9 subtypes of schizophrenia, there are counterparts in DSM-III. The term for the hebephrenic subtype has been changed to "disorganized," and there is no mention of somatic delusions in the DSM-III criteria for the paranoid type.

*Affective Psychoses: DSM-III Makes
the Unipolar–Bipolar Distinction*

Affective disorders are not, by definition, considered psychoses in DSM-III, as they are in ICD-9. In some cases the major affective disorders may be accompanied by psychotic symptoms, and in other cases they are not. DSM-III does not limit the psychotic features to those that are mood congruent, as does the ICD-9.

The most striking difference between the DSM-III and ICD-9 classifications of affective disorders is that DSM-III makes the unipolar–bipolar distinction among the major affective disorders whereas ICD-9 does not. The American Psychiatric Association's Task Force evaluation of the available research literature indicated that important differences in external clinical correlates, including family history, clinical course, and response to treatment, existed between patients who had one or more manic episodes or both manic and major depressive episodes (DSM-III bipolar disorder) and those who had only one or more major depressive episodes (DSM-III major depression) (55, 56). ICD-9 diagnoses of manic-depressive psychosis, manic type; manic-depressive psychosis, circular type but currently manic; manic-depressive psychosis, circular type but currently depressed; and manic-depressive psychosis, circular type, mixed, would all be subtypes of bipolar disorder (mixed, manic, or depressed in current episode) according to DSM-III. Recent research evidence does not support the concept of "unipolar mania" without eventual major depressive episodes (57). Manic-depressive psychosis, depressed type, would be either a single or recurrent episode of DSM-III's major depression.

Not all of these ICD-9 affective psychoses would necessarily receive the DSM-III five-digit subclassification of "with psychotic features," since ICD-9 states that "mild disorders of mood may be included here if the symptoms match closely the descriptions given" (P. 186).

Paranoid States: DSM-III Limits the Nature of the Delusions

In ICD-9 the diagnosis "paranoid state, simple," includes delusions of "being influenced, persecuted or treated in some special way" (P. 187). Paranoia in ICD-9 includes systematized grandiose, persecutory, or somatic delusions. DSM-III limits the nature of the delusions in its paranoid disorders to those of persecution or jealousy; it separates acute paranoid disorder from paranoia on the basis of the former's lasting less than six months and the latter's having a duration of more than six months. Research evidence since DSM-III's publication suggests that the limited nature of the delusions may not distinguish a distinct diagnostic entity (58, 59) (see also Chapter 25, Spitzer and Williams: "International Perspectives: Summary And Commentary").

Paraphrenia, classified as a paranoid state in ICD-9, has conspicuous hallucinations without affective symptoms, thought disorder, or deterioration in functioning. Patients with such symptoms could not be classified in the paranoid disorders section of DSM-III, because the DSM-III concept excludes patients with predominant hallucinations. Atypical psychosis might be the corresponding diagnosis, since preservation of the personality is inconsistent with the deterioration in functioning required by the DSM-III criteria for schizophrenia.

Induced psychosis in ICD-9 corresponds to the DSM-III concept of shared paranoid disorder.

Other Nonorganic Psychoses: DSM-III Indicates Reaction to Stress on Axis IV

An ICD-9 depressive psychosis is a reactive psychosis characterized by severe depression, delusions, and often a major suicide attempt. The excitative type of psychosis is a reactive manic psychosis. DSM-III does not use the endogenous–reactive distinction as a basis of classification of affective disorders, since the phenomenology of the episodes does not appear to vary according to whether or not a precipitating event played a pathogenetic role. In DSM-III's multiaxial system, the role of stressful life events in the development or exacerbation of affective disorders (as of other disorders) is noted on axis IV, and may have some prognostic significance.

ICD-9's acute paranoid reaction and psychogenic paranoid reaction are paranoid disorders according to DSM-III, with subtyping made on the basis of duration of symptoms and the role of stress again noted on axis IV. There is no clear corresponding DSM-III category for reactive confusion.

Psychoses with Origin Specific to Childhood: DSM-III Pervasive Developmental Disorders

DSM-III includes categories of infantile autism for severe disturbances in language, social skills, and motor behavior with onset before 30 months of age, and of childhood onset pervasive developmental disorder with severe abnormalities with a later onset. The latter category is very similar to ICD-9's disintegrative psychosis. Both systems recommend that if the disturbance in a child would qualify for a diagnosis of adult-type schizophrenia or major affective disorder, then these diagnoses should be given.

Neurotic Disorders: DSM-III Abandons a Term with Etiological Connotations

The American Psychiatric Association's Task Force on Nomenclature and Statistics found that use of the term *neurosis*, with its strongly psychodynamic connotations regarding etiology, was inconsistent with their attempt to take an atheoretical approach to the classification. Thus, in a controversial move, the task force abandoned *neurosis* as a preferred term for use in diagnostic categories and divided the neurotic disorders, according to their predominant symptoms, into affective, anxiety, somatoform, dissociative, and psychosexual disorders.

In general, ICD-9 "neuroses" are diagnosed with greater specificity in DSM-III, and there is no mixing of phenomenological observations and inferential pathogenic explanations in the definitions. ICD-9 anxiety states are divided into panic disorder and generalized anxiety disorder in DSM-III. Hysteria has been "split asunder" (60) into somatoform disorders (somatization disorder and conversion disorder), dissociative disorders, factitious disorders, psychosexual disorders, psychological factors affecting physical condition, histrionic personality disorder, and malingering. What would be phobic states according to ICD-9 may now be classified as agoraphobia (with or without panic attacks), social phobia, or simple phobia. Depersonalization syndrome corresponds to the dissociative disorder called "depersonalization disorder"; hypochondriasis appears as a somatoform disorder; and obsessive compulsive disorder is an anxiety disorder in DSM-III.

There is no DSM-III category corresponding to neurasthenia. Neurotic depression was judged to be a clinically very heterogeneous category (61,62), and was thus treated in DSM-III in one of several ways: When a full affective syndrome is present for two weeks or more, the patient receives a diagnosis of major depression; if there is chronic mild depression persisting most of the time for over two years, then the diagnosis is dysthymic disorder. Some patients who would receive the ICD-9 diagnosis "neurotic depression" may, according to DSM-III, be diagnosed as having an atypical depression or an adjustment disorder with depressed mood (see below).

Personality Disorders: DSM-III Diagnoses on a Separate Axis

ICD-9 and DSM-III define personality disorders quite similarly: both require long-standing patterns of maladaptive behavior that cause subjective distress or functional impairment. Both systems also allow for the simultaneous diagnosis of a personality disorder and another, more acute disorder, but DSM-III formalizes this approach by placing the assessment of personality functioning on a separate axis, axis II. This ensures that all patients will be evaluated for a personality disorder even in the presence of a more florid (usually) axis I disorder.

The subtypes of personality disorders differ, however, between the two systems. Personality disorder subtypes that appear in both systems include paranoid, schizoid, hysterical (renamed histrionic), anankastic (renamed "compulsive"), and personality disorder with predominantly sociopathic or asocial manifestations (renamed "antisocial" in DSM-III).

Affective personality disorder in ICD-9 becomes either dysthymic disorder (for chronic, long-standing, mild depression) or cyclothymic disorder (for a long-standing pattern of alternating hypomanic and mild depressive periods) in DSM-III. These were classified in DSM-III with the affective disorders because of evidence that suggested a continuity between these patterns and episodes of the major affective disorders (63, 64).

In DSM-III explosive personality disorder becomes intermittent explosive disorder, and is grouped with disorders of impulse control not elsewhere classified. This change was based primarily on the opinion that since the explosive outbursts of affected individuals are not characteristic of their usual baseline behavior (i.e., they are not antisocial), this pattern does not correspond to a *pervasive* pattern of maladaptive behavior, which is the foundation of the DSM-III concept of personality disorders.

Many features of the ICD-9 asthenic personality disorder may be found in the DSM-III dependent type. DSM-III also has a subtype called "avoidant" for socially isolated individuals with an intense fear of rejection.

The major additions in the DSM-III Personality Disorder section are the schizotypal, the borderline, and the narcissistic personality disorders. The schizotypal and borderline types were added, as discussed in the section on schizophrenia, in an attempt to clarify the murky area of borderline schizophrenia and other borderline states. Narcissistic was added because of the high frequency with which people fitting this description seem to be observed in clinical practice and described in the literature.

Sexual Deviations and Disorders:
New Names and Added Specificity

Homosexuality appears in DSM-III only as ego-dystonic homosexuality. The history of the diagnosis of homosexuality in American psychiatry has been widely recounted (65–67). The DSM-III concept requires that the affected individual complain that the weak or absent heterosexual arousal interferes with desired heterosexual relationships and that the persistent homosexual arousal pattern is unwanted and a source of distress. ICD-9, interestingly, deals with this controversial issue by stating, "Code homosexuality here whether or not it is considered as a mental disorder" (P. 196).

Bestiality (renamed zoophilia), pedophilia, transvestism, and exhibitionism are all classified as paraphilias in DSM-III. Other paraphilias include fetishism, voyeurism, sexual masochism, and sexual sadism. ICD-9 lists fetishism, sadism, and masochism under "other sexual deviations and disorders." Transsexualism and disorders of sexual identity, which refer to gender role disorders in preadolescents, are included in the DSM-III gender identity disorders subgroup. The term for the latter diagnosis has been changed to "gender identity disorder of childhood."

In ICD-9 there is one category for psychogenic sexual dysfunctions, frigidity, and impotence. In DSM-III, in keeping with the increased interest in the recognition and treatment of various types of psychosexual dysfunctions (68,69), there are seven specific dysfunctions, plus the ubiquitous "atypical" category: inhibited sexual desire, inhibited sexual excitement, inhibited female orgasm, inhibited male orgasm, premature ejaculation, functional dyspareunia, and functional vaginismus.

Drug Abuse and Dependence: DSM-III Combines Substance Use Disorders

ICD-9 divides its drug abuse categories into alcohol dependence, other drug dependence, and nondependent abuse of drugs; DSM-III groups all syndromes in the diagnostic class "substance use disorders." The concepts underlying the individual diagnoses display some differences, although the names suggest similarity. In ICD-9 dependence is described as "a psychic and usually also physical" state, whereas in DSM-III the dependence category by definition requires evidence of physiological addiction to a substance. ICD-9 says the individual dependent on alcohol or another drug may take it to experience its psychic effects or "sometimes" to avoid withdrawal symptoms, and may or may not exhibit tolerance. DSM-III's definition of dependence requires some evidence of either tolerance or withdrawal. Nondependent abuse of drugs in ICD-9 is for some maladaptive effects of drug use that do not constitute dependence, but are somehow detrimental to the health or social functioning of the individual.

DSM-III's general criteria of abuse are: 1) a pathological pattern of use, 2) impairment in social and occupational functioning, and 3) at least one month's duration. The DSM-III concept of abuse corresponds to the notion of psychological drug dependence in that the individual persists in using a drug to his or her detriment even though he or she is not physically addicted to it. For most DSM-III substance use disorders the diagnosis of dependence assumes that abuse has been present; the reverse, of course, is not true.

Both ICD-9 and DSM-III have categories for alcohol, morphine-type (renamed opioid), barbiturate-type, cannabis, and amphetamine-type dependence, and alcohol, tobacco, cannabis, hallucinogen, barbiturate and tranquilizer (renamed barbiturate and similarly acting sedative or hypnotic), morphine-type (renamed opioid), cocaine-type, and amphetamine-type abuse. DSM-III does not include a category for cocaine or hallucinogen dependence, as ICD-9 does, interpreting the currently available evidence as indicating that physiological dependence as manifested by the development of tolerance or withdrawal does not exist. DSM-III does include tobacco dependence, however, instead of tobacco abuse, although the rationale for the diagnosis in DSM-III is similar to that in ICD-9. DSM-III also adds a category for phencyclidine (PCP) abuse, because of the increasingly widespread use of this drug and the differential treatment implications of syndromes associated with PCP.

Both ICD-9 and DSM-III recognize that multiple drugs may be abused or result in dependence, encourage multiple diagnoses, and provide for various combination diagnoses. ICD-9 includes the direct effects of drugs on the central nervous system as part of several of its abuse syndromes, for example, acute intoxication by alcohol or hallucinogens. DSM-III considers these separate, substance-induced, organic mental disorders that may be superimposed on a pattern of drug abuse, but should be diagnosed *in addition* to the substance use disorder because, under certain circumstances, the acute syndromes require additional treatment.

Physiological Malfunction Arising from Mental Factors:
DSM-III Does Not Make the "Tissue Damage" Distinction

ICD-9 includes a number of categories, named and grouped according to the various organ systems of the body, for psychologically induced physical symptoms or physiological malfunctions that do not involve tissue damage and are usually mediated through the autonomic nervous system. In DSM-III the tissue damage distinction is not made; all patients with a physical disorder in which the symptoms are the expression of a known pathophysiological process (and therefore not a somatoform disorder), are not under voluntary control (and therefore not a factitious disorder or malingering), and are influenced by psychological factors are given the diagnosis "psychological factors affecting physical condition." This category encompasses both malfunctions without known tissue damage and the more traditional psychosomatic illnesses such as asthma, gastric ulcer, and ulcerative colitis, in which tissue damage is evident. Determination of whether there is or is not tissue damage was felt to be unreliable.

The DSM-III concept of "psychological factors affecting physical condition" also includes other, nonpsychosomatic illnesses such as a myocardial infarction, in which psychological disturbance would be expected to affect course or prognosis adversely.

Special Symptoms or Syndromes Not Elsewhere Classified:
DSM-III Groups Majority as Disorders Usually
First Evident in Infancy, Childhood, or Adolescence

ICD-9 includes a group of nonorganic conditions that are judged "not manifestly part of a more fundamental classifiable condition." These are the special symptoms or syndromes not elsewhere classified; they include stammering and stuttering, anorexia nervosa, tics, stereotyped repetitive movements, specific disorders of sleep, other and unspecified disorders of eating, enuresis, encopresis, and psychalgia.

Since the onset of most of these disorders is in childhood or adolescence, most have been classified in DSM-III in subgroups of the major class "disorders usually first evident in infancy, childhood, or adolescence." This large class is subdivided into ten smaller categories (see also below). Most of the ICD-9 special symptoms fall into three groups in DSM-III: eating disorders, stereotyped movement disorders, and other disorders with physical manifestations. Some of the inclusion categories for specific disorders of sleep also are classified as other disorders with physical manifestations; others are unclassified in DSM-III. Psychalgia corresponds in concept to the DSM-III psychogenic pain disorder, which is classified as a somatoform disorder since it fits the general definition for disorders of this class.

Acute Reaction to Stress and Adjustment Disorder:
DSM-III's Multiaxial System
Reconceptualizes Mental Disorders Arising from Stress

ICD-9 has several diagnoses for very transient disturbances of any severity that occur in essentially normal individuals following exceptional physical or mental stress (the acute reactions to stress). These are subclassified according to the predominant symptomatic manifestations: disturbance of emotions, disturbance of consciousness, psychomotor disturbances. The acute reactions to stress are distinguished from longer-lasting disturbances, which are called, in ICD-9, adjustment reactions. Acute reactions are noted to subside within hours or days; adjustment reactions usually last only a few months. The etiologic role of a stressor is evident in the close relationship in time and content to the occurrence of a stressful event. Adjustment reactions may occur following major or minor stressors. The subtyping of adjustment reactions in ICD-9 is made essentially on the basis of symptoms, i.e., disturbance of [other] emotions, conduct, or mixed emotions and conduct; but in the case of depression there is the added feature of distinguishing a brief from a prolonged depressive reaction.

As mentioned previously, DSM-III takes a radically different approach to the classification of stress-related or stress-induced disorders.

With axis IV indicating the role and severity of stressors in the development or exacerbation of a mental disorder for all patients, any mental disorder may be conceived of as a "reactive" disorder. Thus, DSM-III major depressive episode (which might correspond to ICD-9's acute reaction to stress with predominant disturbance of emotions) may or may not be precipitated by a stressor that would be indicated, along with its severity, on axis IV.

In addition, however, there are several DSM-III diagnostic categories in which the etiologic role of a stressor is explicitly included in the diagnostic criteria. One, brief reactive psychosis, refers to a psychotic disorder of less than two weeks' duration that develops immediately after a severe psychosocial stressor, i.e., one that would cause some distress in virtually anyone. Another disorder in DSM-III that includes stress as a necessary feature is post-traumatic stress disorder. This disorder is classified as an anxiety disorder because of the characteristic anxietylike symptoms that develop following severe stressors such as combat experiences, disasters, or victimization in violent crime. Post-traumatic stress disorder overlaps with the ICD-9 acute reactions to stress in terms of the severity of the stressors involved, but the DSM-III concept requires a distinctive symptom picture; various waking and sleeping reexperiences of the traumatic event and numbing of responsiveness to the external world are especially characteristic. DSM-III also recognizes that in addition to an acute onset, such disturbances may have an onset delayed for months following the event, or a chronic course—as opposed to the transient nature of the ICD-9 acute reactions.

Adjustment disorders in DSM-III refer to maladaptive reactions to stress that are not of sufficient severity or duration to meet the criteria for *any* more pervasive disorder. As such, the adjustment disorder categories are residual ones. In DSM-III the assumption is that adjustment disorders will be short-lived and will remit if the stressor ceases or the individual adapts to the stressful situation. DSM-III, like ICD-9, subclassifies these disturbances according to symptom types (DSM-III has more specific types) rather than the age at which the disorder occurs. DSM-III adjustment disorder does not require that the individual be free of all other mental disorders; in fact, preexisting personality disorders or organic mental disorders are noted as possible predisposing factors.

One other category reflects a difference in concept regarding the occurrence of stress and the development of mental disorders between the two classifications. Bereavement is mentioned in ICD-9 as an example of a stressful situation that may lead to an adjustment reaction. Uncomplicated bereavement is listed in DSM-III as a V code condition not attributable to a mental disorder that is a focus of attention or treatment. This reflects a belief that under normal circumstances, a grief reaction at the loss of a loved one is not pathological and may, in fact, be adaptive (70).

Since the DSM-III concept of an adjustment disorder specifies that the reaction in question must be maladaptive, normal grief reactions are excluded. DSM-III gives several general guidelines (based on severity, duration, and type of symptoms) to help the clinician decide whether or not a particular grief reaction is indeed "uncomplicated."

Specific Nonpsychotic Mental Disorders Following Organic Brain Damage: DSM-III Organic Mental Disorders, Section 2

ICD-9 includes categories for several nonpsychotic organic mental disorders that may follow brain damage. Since DSM-III does not make use of the psychotic–nonpsychotic distinction in classifying organic mental disorders (see above), these categories would correspond, on the basis of symptoms, to one of seven organic brain syndromes listed in Section 2 of the Organic Mental Disorders. For these disorders, the etiology is a physical disorder from another part of the ICD-9-CM that is to be coded as a separate diagnosis on axis III of the multiaxial system. Frontal lobe syndrome and some instances of cognitive or personality change of other type correspond to the DSM-III concept of organic personality syndrome. Organic amnestic syndrome may cover most cases of the mild cognitive disturbances also diagnosed under the ICD-9 310.1 rubric.

Depressive Disorder Not Elsewhere Classified: DSM-III Unifies Depressive Diagnoses

In the DSM-III classification of depressive conditions there is no need for the residual category "depressive disorder not elsewhere classified." Major depressive episodes in DSM-III need not either be accompanied by psychotic features or be part of a bipolar disorder, and may or may not be considered a "neurosis." "Atypical" depression, in DSM-III, would apply to cases not meeting criteria for another affective disorder.

Disturbance of Conduct Not Elsewhere Classified: DSM-III Conduct Disorders

Conduct Disorders are another subclass of the large DSM-III diagnostic class "disorders usually first evident in infancy, childhood, or adolescence," since these disturbances have a usual age at onset in the pre-adult years. Both ICD-9 and DSM-III include unsocialized and socialized subtypes of conduct disorder, but DSM-III also subclassifies them according to whether the antisocial behavior is aggressive, i.e., involving personal violence or destruction of property, or nonaggressive. Compulsive conduct disorder (kleptomania) and certain other conduct disturbances fit better in the DSM-III class of "disorders of impulse control not elsewhere classified."

Disorders of Emotions Specific to Childhood
and Adolescence: DSM-III Adopts a Broad Approach
to Classification of Disorders of Children

The DSM-III class "disorders usually first evident in infancy, child-hood, or adolescence" is not limited to emotional disorders but also includes diagnoses for intellectual, conduct (see above), physical (see above), and developmental problems. This expansion of categories reflects a general dissatisfaction with the traditionally limited number of ways of characterizing children's emotional problems and the great increase in research and treatment of child mental disorders. For the emotional disorders themselves DSM-III has categories of oppositional and identity disorders for which there are no specific ICD-9 corre-sponding diagnoses; avoidant and schizoid disorders of childhood and adolescence and elective mutism correspond to the ICD-9 subtype "with sensitivity, shyness and social withdrawal"; and overanxious disorder corresponds to "with anxiety and fearfulness". For the ICD-9 subtype "with misery and unhappiness," DSM-III would consider either major depression or, if it were a question of a milder disturbance reactive to stress, an adjustment disorder with depressed mood. ICD-9 considers DSM-III's separation anxiety disorder an example of an adjustment reaction with predominant disturbance of other emotions.

DSM-III suggests that when children reach the age of 18 they be considered for a corresponding diagnosis of an emotional disorder from the adult sections of the classification. For example, an adolescent with overanxious disorder may, at age 18, meet the full criteria for generalized anxiety disorder. In both the DSM-III and ICD-9 classifications, children and adolescents may receive diagnoses from any section.

Hyperkinetic Syndrome of Childhood:
DSM-III Focuses on Attentional Difficulties

The hyperkinetic syndrome diagnoses of ICD-9 correspond to DSM-III's attention deficit disorder, another subdivision of the "disorders usually first evident in infancy, childhood, or adolescence." The DSM-III focus is, as the name implies, on the attentional difficulties and, to a lesser extent, on impulsivity. Hyperactivity may or may not be present.

Specific Delays in Development: DSM-III Codes on Axis II

Both classifications have a series of diagnoses for specific develop-mental delays, often termed "learning disabilities." DSM-III places these on axis II, requiring their separate and independent evaluation. This is parallel to the thinking with respect to the personality disorders of adults in that these long-standing developmental problems in children might, in the presence of more florid axis I psychopathology, be overlooked.

*Psychic Factors Associated with Diseases Classified Elsewhere:
DSM-III's Psychological Factors Affecting Physical Condition*

DSM-III's single broad diagnosis encompasses both the 316 category of ICD-9 and the 306 category, since no distinction is made on the basis of the existence of tissue damage (see above). The physical disorder or condition is coded on axis III in DSM-III.

Mental Retardation: DSM-III Has Equivalent Categories

ICD-9 uses separate, three-digit rubrics to indicate different degrees of mental retardation. DSM-III lists mild, moderate, severe, and profound retardation as subcategories in the class "mental retardation" of its section on childhood disorders. The I.Q. ranges corresponding to the levels of retardation are identical in the two systems.

CORRESPONDENCE OF CODING FOR STATISTICAL PURPOSES

As can be seen from the above discussion, there are quite numerous conceptual differences between many ICD-9 and DSM-III classes. These differences, in most cases, involve certain basic principles on which the classifications are based, the boundaries between disorders, and the relevant subtypes included in the broader diagnostic classes; they are justified in DSM-III by its proposed clinical use.

How much such differences actually impede the collection of international statistics on morbidity of mental disorders is a matter of debate. Since classifications prior to DSM-III relied solely on brief, general descriptions of the disorders to guide the clinician, it is unlikely that those using such classifications were referring to exactly the same kind of patients when coding a particular diagnostic category. Therefore, the question now, in terms of statistical purposes, seems to be whether diagnoses coded according to DSM-III or ICD-9 are relatively well translated from one system to the other through use of the corresponding codes.

A major goal of the American Psychiatric Association's Task Force was to ensure compatibility between the DSM-III system and the *International Classification of Diseases*, Ninth Revision, Clinical Modification (ICD-9-CM) (39), which is the official system for reporting disease statistics in the United States. Since the appearance of ICD-8, adaptations of the international classifications have been prepared for use in the United States. These adaptations were motivated by a need for classifications that better described the range of conditions encountered in clinical practice. The ICD-9-CM is designed to be compatible with its parent system, the ICD-9, and most of its modifications are accomplished by simply adding new category subtypes in order to describe more conditions. Numerical compatibility in these cases is preserved by adding a fifth-digit subtype to an existing four-digit ICD-9 code or by assigning for a few of the new categories four-digit codes that are not used in the ICD-9. The contents and sequence of the three-digit codes of ICD-9 are unchanged, with a few exceptions, and no new three-digit rubrics are added.

Thus, ICD-9-CM provides fifth-digit codes for four subtypes of presenile dementia, for two subtypes of paranoid and/or hallucinatory states induced by drugs, eight subtypes of hysteria, five subtypes of phobic disorders, etc. The only categories in which numerical compatibility could not be preserved were those for the affective psychoses and the "disturbance of conduct not elsewhere classified." Here the content of the four-digit rubrics in ICD-9-CM are not identical with those in ICD-9. The table (next page) shows the difference between the diagnostic categories corresponding to the numbers in the two systems for the affective psychoses. The relationship between the numerical systems is evident upon inspection of the classifications included as Appendix D in DSM-III, "Historical Review, and Mental Disorders Sections of ICD-9 and ICD-9-CM."

DSM-III departs numerically from ICD-9-CM mainly in its elimination of a number of ICD-9-CM categories believed to be rarely diagnosed in clinical practice in the United States, or to be covered by new DSM-III category subtypes, and in its changing a number of names attached to the codes to reflect revised diagnostic concepts. Examples of categories deleted are: pathological drug intoxication; subacute delirium; simple and latent types of schizophrenia; manic disorder, single and recurrent episodes; paranoid state, simple; paraphrenia; excitative type psychosis; and reactive confusion. Examples of categories or classes renamed include: presenile dementia, changed to primary degenerative dementia, senile onset; alcohol and drug psychoses, changed to substance-induced organic mental disorders; and psychalgia, changed to psychogenic pain disorder.

These changes, coupled with a conceptual rearrangement of the categories and codes in DSM-III, have fostered the belief that DSM-III is not compatible with ICD-9-CM, and therefore not with ICD-9. Close inspection reveals, however, that, for the most part, the DSM-III categories and codes consist of a subset of the larger ICD-9-CM classification. Recently, Thompson and co-workers (71) have created a "crosswalk" from DSM-III to ICD-9-CM: that is, a translation from a diagnostic code listed in one system to the closest approximation of this code in the other system. They found that for approximately 60% of the codes

Diagnoses Corresponding to Four-digit Codes for Affective Psychoses in ICD-9 and ICD-9-CM

Code #	ICD-9	ICD-9-CM
296.0	Manic-depressive psychosis, manic type	Manic disorder, single episode
296.1	Manic-depressive psychosis, depressed type	Manic disorder, recurrent episode
296.2	Manic-depressive psychosis, circular type, but currently manic	Major depressive disorder, single episode
296.3	Manic-depressive psychosis, circular type, but currently depressed	Major depressive disorder, recurrent episode
296.4	Manic-depressive psychosis, circular type, mixed	Bipolar affective disorder, manic
296.5	Manic-depressive psychosis, circular type, current condition not specified	Bipolar affective disorder, depressed
296.6	Manic-depressive psychosis, other and unspecified	Bipolar affective disorder, mixed
296.7	No category	Bipolar affective disorder, unspecified
296.8	Other	Manic-depressive psychosis, other and unspecified
296.9	Unspecified	Other and unspecified affective psychosis

there was an identical code number and terminology that either was identical or contained only minor differences. In about 18% of cases the code numbers were identical and the terminology analogous; in 15% there were different code numbers, but identical or analogous terminology; in only about 7% did the identical codes reflect possible conceptual differences. In all cases, however, a crosswalk was possible. The authors concluded that there were many more conceptual differences between ICDA-8 (an adaptation of ICD-8) and ICD-9-CM than between DSM-III and ICD-9-CM. Therefore, the introduction of DSM-III into the United States should pose no greater problem, perhaps even less of a problem, for international conformity in reporting psychiatric diagnostic statistics than the change that periodically occurs from one revision of the International Classification to another.

CONCLUSION

In summary, there are differences between the DSM-III and ICD-9 classifications of mental disorders. These differences occur at the levels of the diagnostic process represented by each system, the concepts underlying the classifications, and, to some degree, the coding systems used. The changes in diagnostic process incorporated into DSM-III, specifically the use of diagnostic criteria and the multiaxial system for patient evaluation, are innovations expected to improve the diagnostic process and lead to better patient care. The revised diagnostic concepts are a reflection of the continuing search for clinically meaningful categories for describing mental disorders. These will undoubtedly undergo rigorous scrutiny in research studies testing their validity.

The discrepancies between the numerical systems needed for the collection of international statistics on mental morbidity may not be as great as they appear to be at first examination, and therefore may not constitute an obstacle to these important endeavors. In balance, it is hoped that the changes in DSM-III will significantly advance psychiatric nosology.

REFERENCES

1. American Psychiatric Association: Diagnostic and Statistical Manual of Mental Disorders, 3rd ed. Washington, DC, American Psychiatric Association, 1980
2. World Health Organization: International Classification of Diseases, 9th Revision. Geneva, World Health Organization, 1977
3. Schmidt HO, Fonda CP: The reliability of psychiatric diagnosis: a new look. J Abnorm Soc Psychol 52:262–267, 1956
4. Kreitman N, Sainsbury P, Morrissey J: The reliability of psychiatric assessment: an analysis. J Ment Sci 107:887–908, 1961
5. Beck AT, Ward CH, Mendelson M, et al: Reliability of psychiatric diagnosis. II. A study of consistency of clinical judgments and ratings. Am J Psychiatry 119:351–357, 1962
6. Ward CH, Beck AT, Mendelson M, et al: The psychiatric nomenclature. Arch Gen Psychiatry 7:198–205, 1962
7. Sandifer MG, Pettus G, Quade D: A study of psychiatric diagnosis. J Nerv Ment Dis 139:350–356, 1964
8. Sandifer MG, Hordern A, Timbury GC, et al: Psychiatric diagnosis: a comparative study in North Carolina, London & Glasgow. Br J Psychiatry 114:1–9, 1968

9. Kendell RE, Cooper JE, Gourlay AJ, et al: Diagnostic criteria of American and British psychiatrists. Arch Gen Psychiatry 25:123–130, 1971
10. Spitzer RL, Fleiss JL, Endicott J, et al: Mental Status Schedule: properties of factor analytically derived scales. Arch Gen Psychiatry 16:479–493, 1967
11. Spitzer RL, Fleiss JL, Cohen J: Psychiatric Status Schedule: a technique for evaluating psychopathology and impairment in role functioning. Arch Gen Psychiatry 23:41–55, 1970
12. Endicott J, Spitzer RL: Current and Past Psychopathology Scales (CAPPS). Arch Gen Psychiatry 27:678–687, 1972
13. Wing JK, Birley JLT, Cooper JE, et al: Reliability of a procedure for measuring and classifying "Present Psychiatric State." Br J Psychiatry 113:499–515, 1967
14. Endicott J, Spitzer RL: Psychiatric rating scales, in Comprehensive Textbook of Psychiatry/III, vol 3, 3rd ed. Edited by Kaplan HI, Freedman AM, Sadock BJ. Baltimore, Williams & Wilkins, 1980, pp 2391–2409
15. Spitzer RL, Endicott J: DIAGNO II: further developments in a computer program for psychiatric diagnosis. Am J Psychiatry 125:12–21, 1969
16. Wing JK, Cooper JE, Sartorius N: Description and Classification of Psychiatric Symptoms. Cambridge, England, Cambridge University Press, 1974
17. Endicott J, Spitzer RL: A diagnostic interview: the Schedule for Affective Disorders and Schizophrenia. Arch Gen Psychiatry 35:837–844, 1978
18. Robins LN, Helzer JE, Croughan J, et al: National Institute of Mental Health Diagnostic Interview Schedule. Arch Gen Psychiatry 38:381–389, 1981
19. Feighner JP, Robins E, Guze SB, et al: Diagnostic criteria for use in psychiatric research. Arch Gen Psychiatry 26:57–63, 1972
20. Spitzer RL, Endicott J, Robins E: Research Diagnostic Criteria: rationale and reliability. Arch Gen Psychiatry 35:773–782, 1978
21. Spitzer RL, Endicott J, Robins E: Clinical criteria for psychiatric diagnosis and DSM-III. Am J Psychiatry 132:1187–1192, 1975
22. Helzer JE, Clayton PJ, Pambakian R, et al: Reliability of psychiatric diagnosis. II. The test-retest reliability of diagnostic classification. Arch Gen Psychiatry 34:136–141, 1977
23. Grove MA, Andreasen NC, McDonald-Scott P, et al: Reliability studies of psychiatric diagnosis: theory and practice. Arch Gen Psychiatry 38:408–413, 1981
24. Spitzer RL, Williams JBW: Classification of mental disorders and DSM-III, in Comprehensive Textbook of Psychiatry/III, vol 1, 3rd ed. Edited by Kaplan HI, Freedman AM, Sadock BJ. Baltimore, Williams & Wilkins, 1980, pp 1035–1072
25. Essen-Möller E, Wohlfahrt S: Suggestions for the amendment of the official Swedish classification of mental disorders. Acta Psychiatr Scand, Supplement 47, 1947, pp 551–555
26. Stengel E: Classification of mental disorders. Bull WHO 21:601–663, 1959
27. Rutter M, Lebovici S, Eisenberg L, et al: A triaxial classification of mental disorders in childhood. J Child Psychol Psychiatry 10:41–61, 1969
28. Essen-Möller E: Suggestions for further improvement of the international classification of mental disorders. Psychol Med 1:308–311, 1971
29. Rutter M, Shaffer D, Shepherd M: An evaluation of the proposal for a multiaxial classification of child psychiatric disorders. Psychol Med 3:244–250, 1973
30. Ottosson JO, Perris C: Multidimensional classification of mental disorders. Psychol Med 3:238–243, 1973

31. Mezzich JE: Patterns and issues in multiaxial psychiatric diagnosis. Psychol Med 9:125–137, 1979
32. Spitzer RL, Fleiss JL: A reanalysis of the reliability of psychiatric diagnosis. Br J Psychiatry 125:341–347, 1974
33. Lipowski ZJ: A new look at organic brain syndromes. Am J Psychiatry 137:674–678, 1980
34. Lipowski ZJ: Delirium updated. Compr Psychiatry 21:190–196, 1980
35. Seltzer B, Sherwin I: "Organic brain syndromes": an empirical study and critical review. Am J Psychiatry 135:345–349, 1978
36. Wells CE: Chronic brain disease: an overview. Am J Psychiatry 135:22–28, 1978
37. Fisher CM: Dementia and cerebral vascular disease, in Cerebral Vascular Diseases: Sixth Conference. Edited by Toole JF, Siekert RG, Uhisnant JP. New York, Grune & Stratton, 1969, pp 232–236
38. Hackinski VC, Lassen NA, Marshall J: Multi-infarct dementia: a cause of mental deterioration in the elderly. Lancet 2:207–210, 1974
39. National Center for Health Statistics: International Classification of Diseases, 9th Revision, Clinical Modification. Washington DC, US Department of Health and Human Services Publication No (PHS) 80-1260, 1980
40. Stone AA, Hopkins R, Mahnke MW, et al: Simple schizophrenia—syndrome or shibboleth? Am J Psychiatry 125:305–311, 1968
41. Rieder RO: Borderline schizophrenia: evidence of its validity. Schizophr Bull 5:39–46, 1979
42. Spitzer RL, Endicott J, Gibbon M: Crossing the border into borderline personality and borderline schizophrenia: the development of criteria. Arch Gen Psychiatry 36:17–24, 1979
43. Baron M, Asnis L, Gruen R: The Schedule for Schizotypal Personalities (SSP): a diagnostic interview for schizotypal features. Psychiatr Res 4:213–228, 1981
44. Gunderson JG, Siever LJ, Spaulding E: The search for a schizotype. Arch Gen Psychiatry 40:15–22, 1983
45. Astrup C, Noreik K: Functional Psychoses: Diagnostic and Prognostic Models. Springfield, Ill, Charles C Thomas, 1966
46. Tsuang MT, Dempsey GM, Rauscher F: A study of "atypical schizophrenia." Arch Gen Psychiatry 33:1157–1160, 1976
47. Sartorius N, Jablensky A, Shapiro R: Cross cultural differences in the short term prognosis of schizophrenic psychoses. Schizophr Bull 4:102–113 1978
48. Helzer JE, Brockington IF, Kendell RE: Predictive validity of DSM-III and Feighner definitions of schizophrenia: a comparison with Research Diagnostic Criteria and CATEGO. Arch Gen Psychiatry 38:791–797, 1981
49. Helzer JE, Kendell RE, Brockington IF: The contribution of the six month criterion to the predictive validity of the DSM-III definition of schizophrenia. Arch Gen Psychiatry (in press)
50. Pope HG, Lipinski JF: Diagnosis in schizophrenia and manic-depressive illness: a reassessment of the specificity of "schizophrenic" symptoms in the light of current research. Arch Gen Psychiatry 35:811–828, 1978
51. Pope HG, Lipinski JF, Cohen BM, et al: "Schizoaffective disorder": an invalid diagnosis? A comparison of schizoaffective disorder, schizophrenia, and affective disorder. Am J Psychiatry 137:921–927, 1980
52. Abrams R, Taylor MA: Importance of schizophrenic symptoms in the diagnosis of mania. Am J Psychiatry 138:658–661, 1981

53. Brockington IF, Leff JP: Schizo-affective psychosis: definitions and incidence. Psychol Med 9:91–99, 1979
54. Procci WR: Schizo-affective psychosis: fact or fiction? A survey of the literature. Arch Gen Psychiatry 33:1167–1178, 1976
55. Perris C: A study of bipolar (manic-depressive) and unipolar recurrent depressive psychosis. Acta Psychiatr Scand, Supplement 42, 1966, pp 9–188
56. Winokur G, Clayton P, Reich T: Manic Depressive Illness. St. Louis, Ill, CV Mosby Co, 1969
57. Nurnberger J, Roose S, Dunner D, et al: Unipolar mania: a distinct clinical entity? Am J Psychiatry 136:1420–1423, 1979
58. Kendler KS: Are there delusions specific for paranoid disorders versus schizophrenia? Schizophr Bull 6:1–3, 1980
59. Kendler KS: The nosologic validity of paranoia (simple delusional disorder). A review. Arch Gen Psychiatry 37:699–706, 1980
60. Hyler SE, Spitzer RL: Hysteria split asunder. Am J Psychiatry 135:1500–1504, 1978
61. Akiskal HS, Bitar AH, Puzantian VR, et al: The nosological status of neurotic depression. Arch Gen Psychiatry 35:756–766, 1978
62. Klerman GL, Endicott J, Spitzer RL, et al: Neurotic depressions: a systematic analysis of multiple criteria and multiple meanings. Am J Psychiatry 136:57–62, 1979
63. Akiskal HS, Djenderedjian AH, Rosenthal RH, et al: Cyclothymic disorder: validating criteria for inclusion in the bipolar affective group. Am J Psychiatry 134:1227–1233, 1977
64. Akiskal HS, Yerevanian BI: Neurotic, characteriological and dysthymic depressions, in Affective Disorders: Special Clinical Forms. Edited by Akiskal HS. Psychiatr Clin North Am 2:595–617, 1979
65. Spitzer RL: A proposal about homosexuality and the APA nomenclature: homosexuality as an irregular form of sexual behavior and sexual orientation disturbance as a psychiatric disorder. A symposium: Should homosexuality be in the APA nomenclature? Am J Psychiatry 130:1207–1216, 1973
66. Spitzer RL: The diagnostic status of homosexuality in DSM-III: a reformulation of the issues. Am J Psychiatry 138:210–215, 1981
67. Bayer R, Spitzer RL: Edited correspondence on the status of homosexuality in DSM-III. J Hist Behav Sci 18:32–52, 1982
68. Masters WH, Johnson VE: Human Sexual Inadequacy. Boston, Little, Brown & Co, 1970
69. Kaplan HS: The New Sex Therapy. New York, Brunner/Mazel, 1974
70. Clayton PJ, Herjanic M, Murphy GE, et al: Mourning and depression: their similarities and differences. Can Psychiatr Assoc J 19:309–312, 1974
71. Thompson JW, Green D, Savitt HL: Preliminary report on a crosswalk from DSM-III to ICD-9-CM. Am J Psychiatry 140:176–180, 1983

SECTION II

General Perspectives

3

DSM-III: A MAJOR ADVANCE IN PSYCHIATRIC NOSOLOGY

Robert E. Kendell, M.D., F.R.C.P., F.R.C.Psych.

Although nosology is widely regarded as a dull and rather unimportant pursuit, psychiatric classifications involve so many assumptions about the nature of mental disorders that their birth and demise nearly always arouse strong feelings. DSM-III was, and is, a radically new classification, differing in several important ways from all previous national and international classifications, so the controversy it generated before and after its publication was almost inevitable.

In fact, however, none of the major innovations of DSM-III was really novel. The introduction of "operational definitions" for all mental syndromes had been urged by Stengel (1) and Hempel (2) 20 years before, and a fairly comprehensive set of 15 operational definitions had been published by the Washington University school in St. Louis 8 years before (3). A multiaxial format had been advocated for 20 years, by Essen-Möller (4); and several multiaxial systems had been successfully introduced in the 1970s (5,6). Hallowed terms such as *hysteria* had been under attack since the beginning of the century (7), and the misleading implications and inherent woolliness of terms such as *neurosis* and *psychosis* had been exposed a generation before (8). What was new was that all these suggestions were acted upon simultaneously and were incorporated in the official classification of so large and influential a body as the American Psychiatric Association (APA).

Address correspondence to: Professor Robert E. Kendell, University Department of Psychiatry, (Royal Edinburgh Hospital), Morningside Park, Edinburgh EH10 5HF, Scotland

THE MAJOR INNOVATIONS

Operational Definitions

The radical innovations of DSM-III were not merely improvements: they were vital changes that were already overdue. The low reliability of psychiatric diagnoses had been exposed by a dozen studies in the 1950s and '60s, and serious international differences in diagnostic usage had become apparent soon afterward. Although many factors contributed to this low reliability, the most important, and the most easily remedied, was the ambiguity of traditional textbook and glossary descriptions, which presented the typical symptoms of each syndrome without specifying which, or which combinations, of them were adequate to establish the particular diagnosis. Operational definitions are simply a means of specifying precisely which combinations of symptoms and other clinical features are sufficient to substantiate the diagnosis in question, and by eliminating a major source of disagreement they produce an immediate increase in reliability. They also help to emphasize that diagnostic terms are no more than convenient labels for arbitrary groupings of clinical phenomena, concepts justified only by their usefulness and liable at any time to be modified or superseded.

The great achievement of the developers of DSM-III was not just that they appreciated the advantages of operational definitions, but that they mustered the energy and the determination to produce suitable definitions for nearly all the 200 diagnostic categories in the glossary and to obtain the American Psychiatric Association's approval of them. Even with 14 subcommittees and 6 years of effort, this was a formidable task and an impressive accomplishment. As anyone who has ever been involved in such an exercise will know, as soon as a provisional definition is framed, what were previously half-concealed differences among different clinicians and schools are exposed, and arguments ensue; and even when a definition appears satisfactory to everyone concerned, it still has to be applied to substantial numbers of patients before anyone can be sure that it does, in fact, fit the patients it is meant to fit.

Multiple Axes

The second major innovation of DSM-III was its multiaxial format. Multiple axes make it possible to generate a range of clinically relevant information in a standardized format and to prevent different kinds of information, particularly about symptomatology and etiology, from contaminating one another. Menninger (9) and others emphasized long ago how little useful information was often provided by a diagnostic label, yet the unstructured formulation they advocated in its place was useless for all statistical purposes. The introduction of several different axes, each concerned with a distinct type of information, makes it

possible to convey some measure of the wealth of information contained in a formulation without losing the capacity to combine information derived from several different patients for comparative purposes. It also helps to remind clinicians to record important information
they might otherwise overlook.

New Nomenclature and Format

The third major change was a radical revision of both the nomenclature and the grouping of syndromes. All affective disorders were
brought together, instead of some being classified as psychoses and
others, quite separately, as neuroses. Indeed, the old groupings of
psychotic and neurotic illnesses have been abandoned, and the terms
psychosis and *neurosis* all but discarded. Gone, too, are many of the
hallowed terms of psychiatry, such as *manic-depressive illness* and *hysteria*; in their place is a host of unfamiliar neologisms, e.g., paraphilia,
somatoform disorder, and substance use disorder. It is sad to lose old
friends and worse still to discard them deliberately, but words such as
neurosis and *hysteria* had become so encrusted with multiple layers of
meaning and trailed so many false assumptions in their wake that we
are better off without them. *Somatoform disorder* and *paraphilia* may be
unlovely terms, but they are unambiguous and unsullied.

DSM-III and ICD-9

The radical changes in DSM-III have involved breaking ranks with
the World Health Organization (WHO), for they commit American
psychiatry, for at least the rest of this decade, to using a very different
classification from the ninth revision of the International Classification
of Diseases (ICD-9) (10), which nearly all other countries have undertaken to use. This is obviously a matter for regret, and has generated
a certain amount of ill feeling. It is, of course, true that one of the
cardinal functions of classification is to facilitate communication, and
that WHO has to this end devoted much time and energy to persuading
individual governments and national associations to use the ICD instead of their own nomenclatures. But it is unfair to criticize DSM-III
on these grounds, or to represent it as a step back to the bad old days
of the 1950s.

In my view, the American Psychiatric Association was quite justified,
in these particular circumstances, in reintroducing a classification of
its own, because I do not believe that WHO could ever have succeeded
in making such radical changes itself. As Stengel (1) pointed out 20
years ago, international classifications are bound to be "conservative
and theoretically unenterprising," because they are produced by large
multinational committees that have to secure general agreement to all

innovations. Like a convoy, the committee's speed is dictated by that of its slowest members. If major changes were ever to come, an influential national association had to show the way first; and the architects of DSM-III have done all they could to minimize the difference—by providing a rough translation into ICD-9 categories that will serve basic statistical purposes, and by reprinting the whole of the mental disorders section of ICD-9, including its built-in glossary, as an appendix to the manual.

Taken as a whole, DSM-III is a very impressive document. A vast amount of hard work, discussion, argument, and persuasion—in what proportions one can only guess—must have gone into its preparation. The reliability studies and field trials alone involved over 500 clinicians, drawn "from Maine to Hawaii," and nearly 13,000 patients; and the levels of reliability reported were higher than had ever previously been reached outside the ranks of small research teams. Most sections of the classification are considerably better than the corresponding sections of ICD-9 or other rival classifications and are obviously the product of thoughtful and well-informed consideration of the issues involved. The manual is well produced and skillfully laid out, and it was an excellent idea to produce the essential elements—the framework of the classification and the operational criteria and main differential diagnoses for each disorder—separately in the mini-D pocket-size book.

WEAKNESSES OF DSM-III

DSM-III is, of course, a very inadequate classification in the sense that most of its categories, both the new and the long established, are inadequately validated. One can be fairly certain that 50 years hence, when our understanding of etiology is less rudimentary than it is now, classifications of mental disorder—if thus they are still called—will be very different and much better. What matters to us, though, is whether DSM-III is as good as it could have been under present circumstances. In most aspects I think it is. But to my eye it does have several minor shortcomings and a few surprising weaknesses.

The Choice of Axes

The most important of these deficiencies is the choice of axes. Once a decision is made to replace the traditional single diagnostic category with a series of axes, the floodgates open, for the types of information it would be useful or interesting to have recorded are almost limitless. Every new axis, however, increases the complexity of the system, and with it the risk that ordinary clinicians will fail, or refuse, to use the classification in the way its authors intended. New axes should therefore be added only if the case for doing so is very strong.

The use of multiple axes was first suggested as a means of solving the problems raised by a heterogeneous set of diagnostic concepts, some based on symptomatology and others on etiology, overlapping and competing with one another (4). Consider, for example, a woman who becomes manic a week after childbirth. Is this mania or a puerperal psychosis? Glossaries commonly provide rules for dealing with such situations (in the ICD, the instruction is to record the illness as mania); but in practice some clinicians record the illness as mania and some as a puerperal psychosis, with the result that both conditions are underrecorded. A recording system with separate axes for symptomatology and etiology, which would make it possible to study all manic illnesses regardless of their etiology and all puerperal illnesses regardless of their symptomatology, would obviously be preferable. Similar problems are posed by schizophreniform illnesses precipitated by amphetamines, and by deliria and confusional states.

The architects of DSM-III decided they could afford the luxury of five axes, but none of these is wholeheartedly devoted to etiology. As a result, despite the authors' avowed commitment to an atheoretical approach, several of the clinical syndromes on axis I are contaminated with etiological assumptions—adjustment disorders, brief reactive psychoses, and conversion disorders, for example. Nor, in spite of the daunting complexity of the system, is there any means of recording, and hence of identifying, puerperal psychoses. Clinical syndromes are spread across two axes—I and II. Strangely, neither axis has a title; and the only reason given for assigning personality disorders and specific developmental disorders an axis all to themselves is that they are "frequently overlooked when attention is directed to the usually more florid Axis I disorder." This strikes me as a very inadequate reason, particularly as it is quite permissible for patients to be assigned to more than one category on either axis. Surely it would have been better either to have had a single axis only, and hence a simpler classification, or, better still, to have transferred mental retardation to axis II. That axis would then have incorporated all lifelong but stable handicaps, leaving only disorders that are either progressive or potentially reversible on axis I. Admittedly, the distinction between the two is not clear-cut, and a case could be made for including phenomena such as childhood head injuries and schizophrenic defect states on either, axis; but whatever the decision in such cases, both axes would still retain some kind of unifying theme.

Axes IV and V are both optional, which perhaps is just as well, for neither is satisfactory in its present form. It is difficult to believe that either will survive into DSM-IV without radical alteration.

Axis IV (Severity of Psychological Stressors) involves rating all psychosocial stressors, regardless of their nature, on a single seven-point scale. This implicitly assumes that the difference between one stressful situation and another is primarily quantitative, and that it is meaningful to equate "chronic parental fighting" (which may continue from infancy to adolescence) with a single event such as "death of a close friend." As others have pointed out (11), the evidence suggests just the opposite. The effects of chronic parental discord are quite different from those of bereavement, and the effects of repeated sexual abuse quite different from those of the death of a sibling. Indeed, it is very doubtful whether the significance of any of these events is adequately portrayed by a number on a global stress scale.

Axis V (Highest Level of Adaptive Functioning Past Year) is a simple five-point scale that takes no account of the duration of the present episode of illness. Doubtless it does have some limited prognostic use; but the significance of a rating of, say, 4 will be quite different in a man who has had a schizophrenic defect state for 15 years and a woman who has been depressed for 15 months, and different again in someone with Alzheimer's disease.

If these two axes were included simply to get the membership of the APA used to taking an interest in these areas, and as a prelude to something more substantial in DSM-IV, their inclusion is understandable and fairly harmless. But if they were seriously intended to provide useful information either about individual patients or about patient populations, they are a failure. One must suspect that they were the result of a compromise between a group of task force members pressing for detailed and comprehensive ratings in these areas and another group with little interest in social influences. Half a cake is better than no cake; but, as Solomon had the wit to realize, the same does not apply to babies.

New Disorders

There are some 200 categories of mental disorder in DSM-III, many of them the personal creation of Dr. Spitzer's task force. For most of these new disorders I can understand the reasoning involved and can agree that they help to provide a better solution than we had before, even if the formal evidence validating their creation is sometimes very flimsy. It is also true that in some places, such as the subdivision of schizophrenia, the number of categories has been very wisely reduced. In other places, however, one has the feeling that an overly enthusiastic advisory committee was inventing new disorders and noting them on the backs of envelopes.

I am not surprised that Garmezy (12) and Rutter and Schaffer (11) were taken aback by "oppositional disorder" and "avoidant disorder." I had similar feelings when confronted for the first time with eight different types of adjustment disorder, intermittent explosive disorder, isolated explosive disorder, and two kinds of inhibited orgasm. Surely, "isolated explosive disorder" is nothing more than a pretentious term for "he lost his temper," and oppositional disorder, a similarly pretentious label for any mildly troublesome teen-ager. We laugh now at Dr. Cartwright's conviction that Negro slaves who ran away from their plantations did so because they were suffering from "drapetomania" (13), but it seems to me that history is in danger of repeating itself.

Failure to Define Mental Disorder and Its Consequences

Part of the problem is the failure of the task force to define what is meant by mental disorder. In the introduction to the manual a mental disorder is described as a "clinically significant behavioral or psychological syndrome," typically associated either with distress or disability, and as a term that implies the presence of some "behavioral, psychological, or biological dysfunction." The problem with this, as Dr. Spitzer and his colleagues clearly realize, is that it does not make a very useful contribution to deciding where the boundaries of mental disorder should be drawn. The authors have failed, in other words, to provide an operational definition of their most fundamental term. It would be unreasonable to blame them for this, though, for no one else has ever succeeded either. Indeed, most glossaries, including the International Classification, simply ignore the problem: they neither define mental disorder nor comment on their failure to do so.

This failure, or inability, to define mental disorder does, however, have some very awkward consequences; and in these circumstances it might have been wiser to admit that DSM-III, like most other psychiatric classifications, is not really a classification of mental disorders at all. It is a classification of the problems psychiatrists are consulted about; and if in practice shy adolescents and surly teen-agers come, or are brought, to see psychiatrists, then an appropriate pigeonhole must be found for them. But it should not be assumed that just because a consultation has taken place, a mental disorder is necessarily present. It is psychiatrists' collective failure to face this simple fact that understandably raises the hackles of other professions that have their own legitimate interests in abnormal and antisocial behavior.

Dr. Spitzer and his colleagues have followed ICD-9 in providing a series of "V codes" for "conditions not attributable to a mental disorder that are a focus of attention or treatment"; a dozen phenomena, including malingering and borderline intellectual functioning, are listed under this heading. (So, too, is "child or adolescent antisocial behavior," which makes "oppositional disorder" even harder to justify.) Although listing some phenomena under these V codes does establish that everyone who consults, or is taken to, a psychiatrist is *not* necessarily suffering from a mental disorder, the existence of such a list within the glossary assumes that psychiatrists do have a criterion for distinguishing between disorders and problems of other kinds. Unfortunately, the evidence does not support this happy assumption.

Consider bereavement, for example. In DSM-III uncomplicated bereavement is listed under the V codes, although it is made clear that this term can legitimately be applied to someone with a full depressive syndrome. Anyone who develops the identical symptoms after the loss of his job rather than the loss of his brother, however, is deemed to be suffering from a mental disorder—an adjustment disorder (309.00). The task force does not say how it justifies this distinction, though it is fairly easy to see how it arose. Grief after bereavement is not only common and normal in a statistical sense: it is expected and even admired as evidence of genuine fondness for the deceased. But because saying that someone has a mental disorder still carries pejorative overtones, we do not want to regard bereavement reactions as disorders. It is, of course, equally common and statistically normal to break limbs on falling out of windows, yet we have no hesitation about calling a broken femur a disorder. The difference in our attitudes toward the two phenomena is illogical; but until we are able to define what we mean by *mental disorder*, the term is bound to remain a term of convenience, at the mercy of social forces and political pressures of very varied kinds.

The difference in status of pedophilia and homosexuality in DSM-III is an even more vivid example of the problem. Until the 1960s both were universally regarded as mental disorders. However, the extremely effective political pressure exerted on the APA by the Gay Liberation movement from 1970 on eventually compelled the Board of Trustees, in 1973, to issue a formal statement to the effect that homosexuality was not a disease, and to remove it from their classification (DSM-II). Pedophiles, being less numerous and less able to win public sympathy, kept quiet, and pedophilia remained a disease. Dr. Spitzer and his colleagues have done the best they can in the aftermath of that unhappy saga and included "ego-dystonic homosexuality" among the psychosexual disorders, though not in the main group of paraphilias, where pedophilia remains, whether or not it is "ego-dystonic." Eventually the whole gamut of abnormal sexual behaviors will have to be considered anew and an attempt made to adopt a consistent approach to them all, rather than introduce *ad hoc* changes here and there in response to political pressure.

Inappropriate Diagnostic Criteria

For the most part, the operational criteria that are the core of the manual consist of lists of symptoms (observable abnormalities of behavior or reports of abnormal or distressing subjective experiences) that must or must not have been present during a particular time period. In some cases there is a requirement that specific past events should also have occurred: a history of heavy alcohol consumption is essential for the diagnosis of alcoholic hallucinosis, and a history of some recent stressful experience, for a diagnosis of adjustment disorder. There are some situations, though, in which it has been made mandatory for the patient to be above or below a particular age. The diagnosis of schizophrenia, for example, requires "onset of prodromal or active phase of the illness before age 45"; and the diagnosis of somatization disorder requires "a history of physical symptoms of several years' duration before the age of 30."

I am convinced that such stipulations are not merely unwise but fundamentally wrong. It is, of course, true that patients fulfilling the other criteria for schizophrenia rarely present for the first time after the age of 44, and that patients fulfilling the other criteria for somatization disorder rarely present after the age of 29. If they never did so, there would be no need for these age criteria; they would simply be redundant. But if they ever do so—and they certainly do at times in the case of schizophrenia—such patients would have to be coded in some ragbag category (in this case, atypical psychosis, 298.90), despite the lack of evidence that there is any fundamental difference between them and patients presenting at an earlier age. In illnesses with an identifiable pathology it is never stipulated that the patient should be within a particular age range, except for purely administrative purposes (i.e., to ensure that only children are treated by pediatric services or only the elderly by geriatric services). Chicken pox is very rare after childhood, but if a man of 50 presents with a generalized vesicular eruption and a rising titer to the varicella virus, he has chicken pox, not "atypical virus infection." Similarly, myocardial infarction is rare before the age of 30; but if a man of 24 presents with severe chest pain accompanied by ST segment depression and increased transaminases, he has had a myocardial infarct, not an "atypical thoracic incident."

The reason why it is wrong to restrict illnesses to particular age ranges is that what ought to be an empirical observation is thereby converted to an axiom. It is certainly true that schizophrenia does not often develop after the age of 44, and any psychiatrist encountering a patient above that age would well be advised to check his facts very carefully before making the diagnosis; but he should not be debarred from doing so by arbitrary fiat unless there is convincing evidence that such cases are fundamentally different. The same argument would apply to criteria restricting a diagnosis to a single sex, though in fact the authors of DSM-III were careful to define somatization disorder, histrionic personality disorder, and anorexia nervosa in such a way that both men and women could qualify.

In the case of schizophrenia (and also of paranoia) "continuous signs of the illness for at least six months" is also a mandatory requirement. This, I think, is unwise rather than fundamentally wrong. It is unwise for several reasons. In the first place, listing chronicity as a defining characteristic of the disorder makes it impossible to use poor long-term outcome as a validating criterion. A more fundamental objection is that one of the cardinal purposes of making a diagnosis is to determine treatment and predict outcome, and this can hardly be done effectively if the diagnosis has to be delayed for several months and until the outcome is largely determined. Finally, if we were ever to obtain a treatment that effectively controlled the symptoms of schizophrenia within a few weeks, we would find ourselves in a situation in which the illness had ceased to exist, except for a few patients in whom the diagnosis was delayed. I realize, of course, that as schizophreniform disorder is defined identically with schizophrenia, except that the symptoms of the disorder need only have been present for two weeks, the six-month criterion can in effect be ignored by combining schizophreniform disorder with schizophrenia. There is a similar possibility in the case of paranoia. This certainly alleviates the problem, but it would have been better not to have created it in the first place.

In the 1950s and 1960s the diagnosis of schizophrenia was applied by American psychiatrists to a far wider range of patients than it was in other parts of the world (14,15). Indeed, in some centers it had almost become a synonym for mental illness. Part of the motive for introducing operational definitions was to prevent this sort of situation from recurring; and I suspect that the above-noted unusual criteria for the diagnosis of schizophrenia—the age barrier and the chronicity criterion—were included partly as a way of ensuring that the condition would not be "overdiagnosed" as it had been in the past. The motive was admirable, but the means unwise.

Patients who would have been regarded as schizophrenic in DMS-II but do not meet the DMS-III criteria are placed elsewhere, mainly in the group of "psychotic disorders not elsewhere classified," consisting of schizophreniform disorders, brief reactive psychoses, schizoaffective disorders, and atypical psychoses. Atypical psychosis is simply a ragbag, and schizoaffective disorder is almost the only category in the glossary for which no operational criteria are provided. I appreciate that this failure to provide criteria for either schizomanic or schizodepressive disorders can be defended on the grounds that their independent status is by no means established and that it would be difficult to devise any criteria that did not overlap with those for mood-incongruent affective disorders. Nevertheless, the combination of a narrow concept of schizophrenia and no criteria at all for schizoaffective disorders means that a disturbingly high proportion of patients with what used to be called functional psychoses are now left in an un-satisfactory limbo.

Many other criticisms could be made of the detailed criteria for the 200 disorders in the glossary, but it would hardly be appropriate to include here a catalogue of criticisms and suggestions concerned merely with points of detail. I shall limit myself, therefore, to one comment, on the definition of paranoia and other paranoid disorders. These have been defined to include delusions of persecution or jealousy only, and to exclude delusional systems based on ideas of grandeur, hypochondriasis, or bodily defect. We owe the concept of paranoia, and most of the classical studies of paranoid disorders, to the German school of psychiatry, for which the terms *paranoia* and *paranoid* embraced all delusions of self-reference, regardless of whether they were concerned with persecution, grandeur, litigation, jealousy, love, envy, hate, or the supernatural. Because the adjective *paranoid* is commonly used by English-speaking psychiatrists in a restricted, persecutory sense, it seems to have been assumed that the diagnostic concepts of paranoia and paranoid psychosis should be similarly restricted. Like Kendler (16), I think this is unwise and unjustified. There is little evidence that delusional disorders based on persecutory ideation are fundamentally different from those based on delusional ideation of other kinds, and clinical studies of grandiose and hypochondriacal disorders are actively discouraged by relegating them to the ragbag of atypical psychosis.

CONCLUDING COMMENTS

I am uncomfortably aware that so far I have devoted considerably more space to a series of criticisms of DSM-III than I have to praising its strengths and achievements. This is not because I see it as shot through with defects. It is simply because criticism, if it is to be constructive and properly understood, has to be presented in some detail, even if it concerns only a relatively minor issue. Admiration and praise, on the other hand, can be expressed quite adequately in a few sentences. What is more, my own and other people's criticisms must be seen in perspective. Anything so complex and so laden with overtones as a classification of mental disorders is bound to be criticized in one way or another by almost all its users. Indeed, I imagine that most of the members of the task force and its numerous advisory committees would like to see changes themselves, perhaps quite radical ones. Real classifications are always imperfect, and the authors have taken pains to emphasize that they anticipate the need for extensive and more or less continuous revision in the future. In their own words, ". . . this final version of DSM-III is only one still frame in the ongoing process . . ."

Despite its shortcomings, DSM-III is a very impressive document, amply justifying the time and effort that went into its gestation. It is far superior to any previous psychiatric classification. Robert Spitzer and his colleagues, and the American Psychiatric Association itself, have every reason to be proud of their achievement, and the rest of us good reason to be grateful to them.

In the two years since it was published, DSM-III has sold more copies and evoked more interest than its authors and sponsors can ever have dared to expect when they first took up their task. I am in no position to judge how much the manual has influenced the day-to-day diagnostic practice of the majority of American psychiatrists, but its influence on clinical research has been profound and far reaching. No research worker in the English-speaking world can afford to be unfamiliar with its content and its philosophy, even if he does not use its categories and operational criteria himself.

THE FUTURE

What should the next step be in this situation? Although DSM-IV and the tenth revision of the International Classification will not come into use until some time between 1988 and 1990, their planning will take several years, and so will need to start quite soon. ICD-10, in particular, is bound to have a long, slow gestation because so many people and organizations need to be consulted.

For American psychiatry to have a different classification of mental disorders from the rest of the world is, in the long run, highly undesirable, because it hinders international communication. The most important decision to be made, therefore, is whether the American Psychiatric Association and the World Health Organization can get back into step by the end of this decade—and if so, to what extent each classification can change to meet the format of the other—or whether the rapprochement will have to be postponed until the end of the century. Personally, I hope very much that DSM-IV and ICD-10 will at least have the same basic format, and that both will incorporate the operational definitions and other major innovations pioneered by the American Psychiatric Association.

If this proves to be too ambitious a target, then the APA itself will soon have to start planning DSM-IV. Dr. Spitzer and his task force colleagues have said quite explicitly that they regard DSM-III, its categories and definitions, as a provisional document. They appreciate very well that many of the categories they created and others they inherited are inadequately validated and that many of their definitions may prove in practice to have serious shortcomings. So it is no criticism of DSM-III and its architects to say confidently that DSM-IV may need to be very different. It seems likely that the five axes will need to be reconsidered and some of them either dropped or radically revised.

The major issue, though, is likely to be the one that faces all revision committees: How strong does the evidence, or contemporary opinion, have to be that a different way of classifying a particular group of disorders would probably be more satisfactory before a change is made? There are dangers both ways. Widespread changes are always disruptive—to established clinicians, to training programs, and to research workers—and no association can cope with change on the scale of the transition from DSM-II to DSM-III every decade. Careful distinctions will therefore have to be drawn between what is progress and what is merely contemporary fashion. On the other hand, categories and definitions that are clearly inappropriate are best dropped as quickly as possible, even though they may once have been the treasured creation of a distinguished advisory committee.

Whatever form DSM-IV eventually takes, however, it can safely be predicted that it will be firmly based on the sure foundations so carefully laid by Robert Spitzer's task force.

REFERENCES

1. Stengel E. Classification of mental disorders. Bull WHO 21: 602–663, 1959
2. Hempel CG: Introduction to problems of taxonomy, in Field Studies in the Mental Disorders. Edited by Zubin J. New York, Grune & Stratton, 1961, pp 3–22
3. Feighner JP, Robins E, Guze SB, et al: Diagnostic criteria for use in psychiatric research. Arch Gen Psychiatry 26: 57–63, 1972
4. Essen-Möller E: On classification of mental disorders. Acta Psychiatr Scand 37: 119–126, 1961
5. Rutter M, Lebovici S, Eisenberg L, et al: A triaxial classification of mental disorders in childhood. J Child Psychol Psychiatry 10: 41–61, 1969
6. Ottosson JO, Perris C: Multidimensional classification of mental disorders. Psychol Med 3: 238–243, 1973
7. Lewis A: The survival of hysteria. Psychol Med 5: 9-12, 1975
8. Bowman KM, Rose M: A criticism of the terms "psychosis," "psychoneurosis" and "neurosis." Am J Psychiatry 108: 161–166, 1951
9. Menninger K, Mayman M, Pruyser P: The Vital Balance: The Life Process in Mental Health and Illness. New York, Viking Press, 1963
10. World Health Organization: Mental Disorders: Glossary and Guide to Their Classification in Accordance with the Ninth Revision of the International Classification of Diseases. Geneva, World Health Organization, 1978
11. Rutter M, Shaffer D: DSM-III: A step forward or back in terms of the classification of child psychiatric disorders? J Am Acad Child Psychiatry 19: 371–394, 1980
12. Garmezy N: DSM-III. Never mind the psychologists: Is it good for the children? Clin Psychologist 31(3–4): 1, 4–6, 1978

13. Cartwright S: The diseases and physical peculiarities of the Negro race. Charleston Med J 6: 643–652, 1851
14. Cooper JE, Kendall RE, Gurland BJ, et al: Psychiatric Diagnosis in New York and London. Maudsley Monograph No. 20. London, Oxford University Press, 1972
15. World Health Organization: Report of the International Pilot Study of Schizophrenia, vol 1. Geneva, World Health Organization, 1973
16. Kendler KS: Are there delusions specific for paranoid disorders vs schizophrenia? Schizophr Bull 6: 1–3, 1980

4

THE STRENGTHS AND WEAKNESSES OF DSM-III

Erik Strömgren, M.D.

In his introduction to DSM-III, Robert Spitzer states that the preparatory work aroused much "interest (alarm, despair, excitement, joy)." Reading the manual, I, too, passed through all these emotional stages, and a number of others. There is nothing peculiar in that: it seems to be in the nature of psychiatric classifications that they have an enormous emotional impact, a tradition left over from a time when the scientific ambitions of psychiatrists had few targets available except classification.

Since I have been asked to express my personal views on DSM-III, I shall give a short account of my background by way of explaining those views. I took part in the World Health Organization (WHO)-administered preparation of the eighth revision of the International Classification of Diseases (ICD-8) and, to a lesser extent, of the ninth revision (ICD-9). From 1938 until recently, I was a member of the committee on classification of the Danish Psychiatric Association.

DENMARK'S USE OF THE ICD

In 1938 all Danish psychiatrists agreed to use the same system of classification, a system that was based mainly on the *Statistical Guide* of the New York State Department of Mental Hygiene (1). When, in 1948, the sixth edition of the International Classification of Diseases

Address correspondence to: Professor Erik Strömgren, Institute of Psychiatric Demography, Aarhus Psychiatric Hospital, 8240 Risskov, Denmark appeared (2), the Danish Psychiatric Association considered adoption of this revision. But in spite of a serious wish to join in international cooperation in this matter, Danish psychiatrists' reactions were negative—ICD-6 was found inapplicable for Danish purposes. In fact, only five of the member states of the United Nations accepted this revision.

Instead, in 1952 the Danish Association created a new classification (3), which contained a radically new element: it was biaxial. So it is, by the way, not correct, as has been claimed (4), that DSM-III is the first official multiaxial classification. The two axes in the Danish classification were etiology and symptomatological form, respectively. This classification seemed to work quite well, and the main reason for giving it up, in 1965, was the appearance of the eighth edition of the ICD (5), which contained remarkable improvements compared with ICD-6 and ICD-7. It was obvious that the time had come for Denmark, as for most other member states of the United Nations, to adopt the International Classification.

In Denmark ICD-8 worked quite well. The glossary that came out a few years later was a great help, even if it was in no way complete. Unfortunately, however, ICD-8 was not allowed to become the important tool for international cooperation it had been intended to be. It turned out, for instance, that the group of "reactive psychoses," which had been introduced following urgent requests from Japan, the Scandinavian countries, the USSR, and a number of other countries, was practically not used in the Anglo-Saxon countries. As a matter of fact, even the glossary claimed that these psychoses were very rare, in hopeless contrast to the frequency with which this diagnosis was used in many countries.

From the very beginning of the period during which the ICD-8 was in operation, WHO directed a very intensive research program, the results of which influenced ICD-9. When, after ten years of work, ICD-9 (6) was ready, some serious difficulties arose. It was natural for new member states of the UN to adopt ICD-9, and some of those who had already accepted ICD-8 did the same. But for many other countries, among them those in Scandinavia, it seemed impossible, for technical and financial reasons, to change so rapidly after the final acceptance and incorporation of ICD-8. So at present the countries of the world are divided almost equally between those using ICD-8 and those using ICD-9, which is a serious complication since on many points they are incompatible, and the data machines are not able to translate one into the other.

DSM-III

It was quite natural that a special adaptation of the ICD-9, the ICD-9-CM, should be developed for use in the United States. Such adaptations have always been regarded as acceptable so long as they are in accord with the main principles of ICD-9. What at first sight seemed less acceptable was the fact that the American Psychiatric Association (APA) nearly simultaneously introduced a classification, DSM-III, that was clearly incompatible with ICD-9. There were, however, understandable reasons for this step. It was felt that there was a need for a classification containing more exact, operational diagnostic criteria than those contained in the ICD. In addition, the time seemed to have come for experiments with multiaxial classifications. It is well known that ICD-10 may include a multiaxial system, and experiences with DSM-III will be useful in the preparatory work for ICD-10.

Moreover, it is obvious that the preparatory work for DSM-III was extremely intensive and extensive. Many clinical trials were made, more are under way, and others are planned. Of special value also are the various monographs that have accompanied the manual, the *DSM-III Case Book*, etc. If some of the trials mentioned are repeated in countries other than the United States, they will no doubt serve as excellent components of the preparatory work for ICD-10.

One innovation in DSM-III has probably caused more consternation than all the others: elimination of the term *neurosis*. How can this term, which is probably used millions of times every day throughout the psychiatric world, be omitted from an official classification? Personally, I cannot regret this step. I find it refreshing. Few terms are used in so many different ways, or with so many unclear and vague definitions, as *neurosis*. It seems perfectly reasonable to try to substitute operationally defined categories for the many different types of "neuroses" that are included in all previous classifications.

There are, of course, numerous other points in DSM-III that might be subject to discussion; but it is impossible in a brief article to comment on all of them. I shall start my evaluation of DSM-III by mentioning a few main points of a more general nature, after which I shall discuss some of the sections that seem to me to contain controversial issues.

General Evaluation

DSM-III is characterized by the use of five "axes." *Axis* is a popular term, but is usually not defined very precisely. What is meant is obviously that classifications should not be unidimensional, but instead have several dimensions, which can give information besides just the diagnostic classification. The five axes of DSM-III do not constitute a logical system; they were obviously chosen solely for practical purposes. Many other criteria could as well have been selected as "axes"—for instance, age, course, duration, etc.—some of which are taken into account in the definition of some of the diagnostic groups whereas others are taken for granted as obligatory parts of any statistical categorization of the cases classified. Some of these criteria (e.g., course, duration) occasionally play important roles among DSM-III's diagnostic criteria. They are, however, used only in certain chapters, which is probably why they were not promoted to the rank of axes.

The "diagnostic criteria," which are the backbone of DSM-III, are formulated—conceptually and typographically—with admirable clarity. It must have been difficult and laborious to select these operational criteria. It is natural that the degree to which they can obtain acceptance by the majority of psychiatrists will vary from case to case.

Personally, I feel particularly uneasy about the frequently used type of criterion that consists of ascertainment of a certain number of symptoms (or other subcriteria) among a larger number of possible symptoms. For instance, one of the main criteria for "major depressive episode" is "at least four of the following symptoms," following which eight different symptoms are mentioned. What to me seems quite unsatisfactory in this procedure is that the eight symptoms mentioned are obviously regarded as equivalent, in spite of the fact that some of them are far more specific for major depressive episodes than the rest. For example, "poor appetite or significant weight loss . . . or increased appetite or significant weight gain, insomnia or hypersomnia, and loss of energy; fatigue" are not nearly as specific for the diagnosis of a major depressive episode as "feelings of worthlessness, self-reproach, or excessive or inappropriate guilt." It is thus possible to select four of the eight symptoms mentioned also in cases that definitely do not belong to the group "major depressive episode," whereas just one or two of the more specific symptoms should be sufficient to make the diagnosis of this particular disorder certain. It seems most unsatisfactory that no quantification of the very different degrees of importance of the symptoms is attempted. It is to be hoped that further practical trials will provide materials that will allow calculation of coefficients ("weights") for each of these symptoms.

The criticism expressed here can, of course, be applied with equal right to most existing rating scales, including some of the most popular and widely used "research diagnostic criteria," some of which have attained an importance that, in my opinion, they certainly do not deserve. They are tools, just tools, and often very crude tools, the pseudo-exactness of which has obviously given them much more influence than there is any scientific foundation for.

The most controversial of all the criteria specified in DSM-III is probably that of *duration* of episodes, which plays a crucial role in several sections of the classification, especially in the section on "Psychotic Disorders Not Elsewhere Classified," in which the decisive criterion for distinction between "schizophreniform disorder," "brief reactive psychosis," and "atypical psychosis" is just the duration of the episode. Here the subclassification depends primarily on whether the duration is less than two weeks, between two weeks and six months, or more than six months. Until now, I have not met any psychiatrist who could accept such time limits. First, it is, of course, quite arbitrary whether one uses these time limits or others that deviate more or less from them; it is just a question of convention. Second, and more important, even if such conventions were permissible and in some cases might be necessary, their application would be dubious, in the sense that determination of duration can be difficult or impossible. In so many cases it is retrospectively impossible to say exactly when an episode began. (More problems connected with this issue will be discussed later.)

Specific Criticisms

The sections "Disorders Usually First Evident in Infancy, Childhood, or Adolescence" and "Organic Mental Disorders" do not elicit many comments on my part. They seem both very carefully elaborated and based on solid clinical experience. The distinctions among different classes seem logical and practical and reasonably easy to apply.

The structure of the section on organic mental disorders will no doubt prove to be adequate: first, a general description of organic disorders as a broad category; next, descriptions of a number of specific organic syndromes; and, finally, descriptions of the various disorders. There are, of course, some definitions that are not in accord with certain common viewpoints. For instance, there will be objections to the claim that the essential feature of the "amnestic syndrome" is impairment in short- and long-term memory: many psychiatrists will be of the opinion that an amnestic syndrome in its mildest forms may affect only short-term memory.

The diagnostic criteria for the organic affective syndrome seem inadequate in that DSM-III states that to make this diagnosis, it is sufficient if, in addition to the abnormal mood, just two of the symptoms listed as criteria for manic or major depressive episodes are present. This would, for instance, mean that the disturbance of mood would be sufficiently characterized by the presence of insomnia (or hypersomnia) and loss of energy.

Organic mental disorders are divided, in terms of etiology, into two main groups, one in which the underlying physical disorder appears in the ICD-9 section on mental disorders, the other in which the physical disorder is either unknown or classified outside the mental disorder section of the ICD. This procedure looks like a regression to ICD-7—a most embarrassing regression, since one of the most frequently expressed objections to ICD-7 was that it was not comprehensive, in the sense that important mental disorders with an organic etiology could not be found in the mental health chapter, but had to be sought in other chapters.

There is much disagreement with regard to classification of mental disorders of old age. The DSM-III classification will probably not satisfy the majority of psychiatrists. It seems, for instance, too pessimistic to give up the distinction between Alzheimer's and Pick's diseases. With regard to the vascular brain disorders, it is understandable, although regrettable, that DSM-III has succumbed to the fashionable "multi-infarct dementia" terminology. First, cases may present after only one infarct; and, second, etiological differentiation within the group (arteriosclerotic brain disorder, hypertensive encephalopathy, diabetic encephalopathy, thromboangiitis obliterans [Buerger's disease], etc.) is essential for therapy and prophylaxis.

Within the section "Alcohol Organic Mental Disorders," the ICD-9-CM category for alcoholic jealousy is discarded because "the literature does not provide sufficient evidence to support the existence of this syndrome as an independent entity." This viewpoint may depend on the amount of literature consulted.

The syndrome of delirium tremens can be found only under "alcohol withdrawal delirium." Where can typical cases of delirium tremens occurring during heavy consumption of alcohol be classified? The diagnostic criteria for alcohol withdrawal delirium do not give a clear picture of the extremely characteristic syndrome seen in delirium tremens—the visual hallucinations, the suggestibility, and the very special type of disorientation to surroundings, but not to person.

Alcohol hallucinosis is obviously regarded as a withdrawal phenomenon. There would be little agreement on that in international psychiatry. In many cases it is characteristic that when these patients have recovered after alcoholic hallucinosis and have been abstinent for some time, they experience a relapse as soon as they start drinking again. In addition, a certain fraction of these cases become chronic even if the patients stop drinking completely, and their emotions are so well preserved that diagnosing them as schizophrenic does not seem adequate.

Among the cannabis mental disorders there seems to be no place for the long-lasting and chronic cases of psychosis, nor for the acute psychoses arising after a considerable period of abstinence.

In the section "Schizophrenic Disorders" the problem concerning the criterion of duration reaches one of its peaks. To demand a duration of at least six months seems especially dubitable in schizophrenia, in which so often it seems quite impossible to decide when the psychosis really started. If one actually wanted to differentiate between such disorders of more than, and less than, six months, respectively, and if one believed that ascertainment of the duration were possible, then one should be humble and just say "schizophrenic disorder of a duration of more (or less) than six months," and not invent special psychopathological terms for each of the two groups. The term *schizophreniform* in this connection seems especially unfortunate. Professor Gabriel Langfeldt, who originally coined the term, has already stated why (7). Moreover, although it is true that not everybody who has used the term has used it in the same sense as Langfeldt, that does not make it more reasonable to use the term for still one more syndrome.

To most European psychiatrists it will be incomprehensible that in a detailed description of schizophrenic symptoms the term *autism* does not occur at all. Eugen Bleuler (8, 9) regarded autism as one of the central symptoms of schizophrenia, and Manfred Bleuler (10, 11), the psychiatrist who probably has the most intimate knowledge of a great number of schizophrenics, tends to stress autism as perhaps the only really pathognomonic symptom in schizophrenia.

I also think it a serious gap that the presence of schizophrenic psychotic symptoms in clear consciousness is not mentioned as an important diagnostic criterion.

The term *paranoid* is used in DSM-III in a sense that deviates fundamentally from its usage in most European countries, where the term implies that delusions are present. Here, however, as in many other cases, the clear (though disputable) definition given in the glossary does help considerably.

The section "Psychotic Disorders Not Elsewhere Classified" has already been mentioned, especially with regard to the controversial attempt at distinguishing schizophreniform disorder from brief reactive psychosis and atypical psychosis. If only the criterion of duration had been used, one would have to live with it. But when, in addition, a condition for the diagnosis of brief reactive psychosis is that there should be a psychosocial stressor preceding the psychosis, the situation really becomes difficult. In many ways brief reactive psychosis seems to correspond to a subgroup of what is called, in many other countries, "reactive" or "psychogenic" psychoses, in which cases a mental stressor is regarded as decisive for the occurrence of the psychosis; in addition, it is regarded as not uncommon that such psychoses last more than two weeks.

With regard to the type of psychosocial stressor, DSM-III mentions that it should be a stressor "that would evoke significant symptoms of distress in almost anyone." What about stressors of a definitely idiosyncratic ("catathymic") nature that cause psychotic reactions only in people who are specifically vulnerable to certain types of stressors? Where can such psychoses be found in DSM-III?

With regard to schizophreniform disorder, DSM-III states in the beginning that the essential features are *identical* with those of schizophrenia. Later on, however, it is claimed that, compared with schizophrenia, schizophreniform disorder "is more often characterized by emotional turmoil, fear, confusion, and particularly vivid hallucinations." Here some clarification seems necessary.

In the introduction to the section "Affective Disorders," it is stated that the classification differs from classifications "based on such dichotomous distinctions as neurotic vs. psychotic or endogenous vs. reactive." Instead, distinctions are made among three groups: 1) major affective disorders with a full affective syndrome, 2) other specific affective disorders with only a partial affective syndrome (of at least two years' duration), and 3) atypical affective disorders, covering the rest. Furthermore, it is mentioned that within major depression there is a subgroup called melancholia: "A term . . . used to indicate a typically severe form of depression that is particularly responsive to somatic therapy." This is certainly a bold *ex juvantibus* definition, i.e., making therapeutic effect a criterion for diagnosis. Looking at the specific diagnostic criteria for melancholia in this sense, one clearly sees that the great majority of these cases must belong to what is usually called endogenous depression, in which there is indeed a special indication for somatic therapy.

The broader criteria for major depressive episode will, no doubt, embrace a great many cases that belong clinically and therapeutically to the same group, but, in addition, a number of other types of major depression. It may seem questionable whether it is practical to have this very heterogeneous group. As mentioned earlier, if among the criteria for this group the presence of "at least four" of eight different symptoms is valid, the group must contain a great variety of clinical states that have very little in common. Hence, these diagnostic criteria will be of little value if, for instance, the aim is to use them for creating clinically comparable groups for research purposes.

My comments on the remaining groups will be brief. The descriptions of anxiety disorders and somatoform disorders, psychosexual disorders, factitious disorders, disorders of impulse control, adjustment disorders, and personality disorders seem clinically adequate and, on the whole, certainly not inferior to what is known from other classifications. Here again, however, the use of pseudoquantitative criteria will no doubt cause much consternation among clinicians—for instance, when, among the diagnostic criteria for somatization disorder, they find: "Complaints of at least 14 symptoms for women and 12 for men, from the 37 symptoms listed below." It is, of course, very convenient when a restaurant has an à la carte menu. But clinical experience shows, beyond any doubt, that the "culinary" effects depend very much on the kind of selection one makes from the menu more than on the number of items one orders.

CONCLUSION

DSM-III is intended for use in the United States. Would it be applicable in other parts of the world? In some countries, yes; but not in the majority, especially not within the Third World. Psychiatrists in developing countries think that many syndromes that are frequently observed in their countries are not to be found in ICD-9; neither do they find a natural place within DSM-III. This applies especially to the acute reactive psychoses of partly somatic, partly psychosocial, origin. WHO has started an international research project on these so-called "acute psychoses." This group of disorders will no doubt constitute an important subject in the joint World Health Organization/U.S. Alcohol, Drug Abuse, and Mental Health Administration project on the Diagnosis and Classification of Mental Disorders and Alcohol- and Drug-related Problems (12,13).

REFERENCES

1. State of New York, Department of Mental Hygiene: Statistical Guide, 11th ed. New York, Utica, 1934 (72 pp)
2. World Health Organization: Manual of the International Statistical Classification of Diseases, Injuries, and Causes of Death, 6th Revision. Geneva, World Health Organization, vol 1, 1948; vol 2, 1949
3. Dickmeiss P, Lunn V, Strömgren E, Svendsen B Borup: Diagnoseliste med kommentarer. Udarbejdet af Dansk Psykiatrisk Selskabs Diagnoseudvalg 1952. Nordisk psykiatrisk Medlemsblad 6:277–295, 1952
4. Skodol AE, Spitzer RL: DSM-III: Rationale, basic concepts, and some differences from ICD-9. Acta Psychiatr Scand 66:271–281, 1982
5. World Health Organization: Manual of the International Statistical Classification of Diseases, Injuries, and Causes of Death, 8th Revision. Geneva, World Health Organization, vol 1, 1967; vol 2, 1969
6. World Health Organization: Manual of the International Statistical Classification of Diseases, Injuries, and Causes of Death, 9th Revision. Geneva, World Health Organization, vol 1, 1977; vol 2, 1978
7. Langfeldt G: Definition of "schizophreniform psychoses." Am J Psychiatry 139:703, 1982
8. Bleuler E: Dementia praecox oder Gruppe der Schizophrenien, in Handbuch der Psychiatrie. Edited by Aschaffenburg G. Leipzig and Vienna, Deuticke, 1911
9. Bleuler E: Dementia Praecox or the Group of Schizophrenias. New York, International Universities Press, 1950
10. Bleuler M: Die schizophrenen Geistesstörungen im Lichte langjähriger Kranken- und Familiengeschichten. Stuttgart, Georg Thieme Verlag, 1972
11. Bleuler M: The Schizophrenic Disorders. Long-term Patient and Family Studies. New Haven and London, Yale University Press, 1978
12. Strömgren E: The question of the so-called "acute psychoses." Bulletin of Neuroinformation Laboratory, Nagasaki University 8: 61–69, 1981
13. World Health Organization: Current State of Diagnosis and Classification in the Mental Health Field. A Report from the WHO/ADAMHA Joint Project on Diagnosis and Classification of Mental Disorders and Alcohol- and Drug-related Problems. Geneva, World Health Organization, Division of Mental Health, 1981

5

DSM-III: A PERSPECTIVE FROM THE THIRD WORLD

Narendra N. Wig, M.B.B.S., M.D.,
D.P.M., F.R.C. Psych., F.A.M.S.

No psychiatric classification system of the last few decades has generated as much interest and enthusiasm as DSM-III. Though primarily
the national classification of the United States, it has stimulated interest
among psychiatrists all over the world. What began as another revision
of the American Psychiatric Association's classification has developed
intc a major international psychiatric achievement.

Third World countries have not remained indifferent to this development. Psychiatrists in these countries have not only followed the
preparation of DSM-III with keen interest but have also started using
it in research, teaching, and clinical work. The interest in DSM-III is
being further strengthened by anticipation that some of its major advances may be reflected in the forthcoming edition of the International
Classification of Diseases (ICD-10) and hence become part of the official
psychiatric classification of many nations.

Address correspondence to: Narendra N. Wig, M.B.B.S., M.D., Professor and Head,
Department of Psychiatry, All India Institute of Medical Sciences, Ansari Nagar, New
Delhi 110029, India

The author is most grateful to Dr. Shekhar Saxena, Senior Resident, Department of
Psychiatry, All-India Institute of Medical Sciences, New Delhi, for his help at various
stages in the preparation of this paper.

SOME CONCEPTUAL SHORTCOMINGS AND BIASES OF EXISTING PSYCHIATRIC CLASSIFICATIONS

Psychiatric classification is not simply a convenient list of disease categories: it is, indirectly, a way of looking at the whole concept of mental ill-health. Current psychiatric classifications have many conceptual biases that had their origin in 19th-century European philosophical and psychiatric thinking (1). A tendency to emphasize the intrapsychic basis of psychiatric phenomena and search for "underlying" causes even in the absence of overt manifestations is one such example. In Third World countries even psychiatrists find it difficult to apply such concepts as "subconscious" mind to all mental illnesses, and it becomes very difficult to explain such concepts to health workers or laymen. Similarly, the European mind somehow always likes to think in terms of duality—e.g., good or bad, body or mind, organic or functional, genetic or environmental—whereas in many other cultures, such as the Indian or the Chinese, it is much more natural to think in terms of a continuum without clearly defined boundaries. For this reason it is perhaps easier for such cultures to accept apparent contradictions than it is for the European mind.

The European habit of dividing mind into thinking and feeling has led us into the classification of the insanity of thinking (schizophrenia) and the insanity of feeling (affective psychosis) that has dominated psychiatry for almost 100 years. Another example of the arbitrary way in which European psychiatry has influenced psychiatric terminology is in the description of neurotic disorders. Two emotions, anxiety and depression, have been raised to the status of discrete disorders, to the exclusion of numerous other emotions in human experience—e.g., anger, greed, rage, jealousy, hate, or eroticism. In other cultures excess of all emotions is considered bad, and one often wonders why an excess of other emotions is not considered "mental abnormality" in modern psychiatry.

SPECIAL PROBLEMS AND NEEDS OF THE THIRD WORLD COUNTRIES

The so-called Third World contains more than two-thirds of the people living on the earth. Though geographically wide apart, most countries of Asia, Africa, and Latin America have much in common. They are relatively less industrialized; often their populations are large, predominantly rural, and spread over vast distances. Economic resources are limited. Expenditure on health is very small; and in the midst of many pressing health problems, mental health is likely to be relegated to a position of low priority, or no priority.

The number of qualified psychiatrists in most Third World countries is small—on average, about one psychiatrist for a million people. Many countries in these regions will therefore be forced to use nonpsychiatric general practitioners and even less qualified health workers in the delivery of their mental health services for a long time to come (2).

Most Third World countries have shared a common heritage of colonial-era European exploitation in the 18th and 19th centuries. In many of these countries there were well-developed ancient systems of medicine. Though modern science and modern medicine have gradually acquired a position of esteem, the traditional systems of medical care have not totally disappeared. In fact, in many countries of Asia, these systems are still very popular and are even given state support. Traditional resources are being used by a large number of people for mental health care in these countries.

Though modern psychiatry is a relatively new subject in the medical schools, many good departments have been established in recent years. The quantity and quality of clinical research in these centers are rapidly improving. One of the important points made clear by many research publications from developing countries is that symptoms of mental illness in the Third World differ considerably from those described in American and European textbooks. Current systems of psychiatric diagnosis and classification do not seem to take note of or do justice to the psychiatric reality of the Third World.

The developing countries need a classification that is simple, bias free, and, above all, clinically useful and relevant to their psychiatric experiences. Such a classification would be a significant help in providing much-needed mental health care to large numbers of patients under conditions of constraints on resources and manpower. On the other hand, Third World countries cannot isolate themselves from the rapid advances in psychiatric knowledge in the industrialized world. A balance has to be struck between these two partly contradictory needs.

SOME GENERAL COMMENTS ABOUT DSM-III

DSM-III derives its major strength from a number of global advances and relatively drastic changes in its basic approach. Many of the preconceived assumptions of previous classifications that had attained the status of unquestionable truths have been questioned, and some of them have been discarded. DSM-III strives to be "atheoretical," and has succeeded, at least to some extent. For example, the firmly entrenched "theory" of neuroses has been discarded and replaced by more pragmatic and useful classification of these disorders. But some of the other traditional biases of European psychiatry have remained. Though the basic division of psychoses into the two major categories of schizophrenia and affective disorders has been retained, the creation of another category of "psychotic disorders not elsewhere classified" is a significant advance.

Another major strength of DSM-III is reflected in the use that was made of ongoing research and field trials with a direct bearing on the classification. Such work resulted in major changes in the diagnostic categories and criteria during the preparation of DSM-III; and with continuing research, many more drastic changes are likely in the future. This approach will be of considerable help to Third World countries as, with scientifically refined work, these countries will be able to demonstrate conclusively the need for various changes in the current systems of classification to make them truly universal.

Use of a multiaxial system and diagnostic criteria are undoubtedly major advances in clinical psychiatry, and the Third World welcomes these changes. The use of diagnostic criteria should increase the reliability of clinical diagnosis and, along with the multiaxial system, should go a long way toward making therapeutic decisions less arbitrary.

In a way, it is paradoxical that some of these strengths of DSM-III are indirectly its weakness in the Third World setting. At first glance, DSM-III appears unusually complicated and intimidating because of its sheer size; but with familiarity, one probably gets used to its intricacies. Though the diagnostic criteria are its strength, from a Third World point of view, rigidity of criteria creates many difficulties. Complicated definitions and long lists of criteria may be all right for a highly trained worker in a research project, but are very difficult to remember and apply in the average busy outpatient psychiatric clinic of a developing country, with all its constraints of time, privacy, and frequent language problems. Imagine in such a situation considering 14 symptoms for women and 12 for men from the list of 37 symptoms spread over 7 body systems before diagnosing somatization disorder!

Apart from its complicated structure, the insistence on use of the criteria tends to create a false sense of assurance in the diagnosis. One feels that whatever has been neatly put down in the form of crisp criteria is absolute truth. The criteria, however, are seldom more than a crystallization of clinical knowledge accumulated to date.

Strict use of the criteria can also reduce the importance of subtle clinical observation. Students are likely to get into the habit of looking only at the set of criteria and neglecting other observations. For example, it has been a common textbook teaching that anxiety or other affective symptoms in an adolescent may be the beginning of schizophrenic illness, but now such clinical assumptions would be difficult to sustain in the face of rigid diagnostic criteria. It is true that DSM-III repeatedly asserts that it is not a textbook; but, unfortunately, it is becoming one, and is forcing other textbooks to follow its pattern.

For psychiatrists in Third World countries another problem is that many of the current criteria of DSM-III, as would be expected, are based heavily on American experience, which in many cases is not universal. Examples given in the clinical descriptions and criteria are often so culture bound that they provide only poor guidelines for use in developing countries. This is perhaps an inherent problem in modern psychiatry—wherever knowledge of a biological base for a disorder is weak, the diagnostic descriptions or criteria become highly culture-specific.

SPECIFIC COMMENTS ON INDIVIDUAL SECTIONS

The comments that follow relate to the suitability of some of the specific categories of DSM-III for the developing world.

Child Mental Disorders

Grouping in a separate chapter all disorders first evident in infancy, childhood, and adolescence is a long overdue change. Child psychiatry will also benefit from the use of the diagnostic criteria; these, however, are modeled so much after American culture that their use in developing countries is severely limited. Moreover, the concepts behind some of the new categories, such as "separation anxiety disorders" or "reactive attachment disorder of infancy," may require modification for use in developing countries because of differences in family structure and dynamics.

Organic Mental Disorders

The description of discrete syndromes based on clinical features and the inclusion of organic delusional, affective, and personality syndromes are among the strengths of DSM-III. However, Third World psychiatrists also see a number of patients with fever, malnutrition, or drug ingestion presenting with psychotic features without clear disorientation or confusion. A definite diagnosis of an organic mental disorder cannot be made in such cases because organic factors are only strongly suspected to play a role in these psychoses.

Schizophrenia and Other Psychotic Disorders

The section on the major psychoses constitutes one of the most important among DSM-III's changes. The controversy about the proper grouping of the so-called functional psychoses has been raging for nearly 100 years. Kraepelin and Bleuler's dichotomy between schizophrenia and manic-depressive illness has served us well, but probably not well enough. It has interfered with an open approach to the whole issue.

The boundaries of schizophrenia had never been clearly defined. DSM-III has taken the bold step of classifying a shorter-duration, schizophreniform disorder separately from long-duration schizophrenia. The concept of reactive psychosis, which has been pleaded for by Scandinavian psychiatry for a long time, but stoutly resisted by some other European schools, has not been accepted. For the countries of the Third World, both these developments are very important. Many psychiatrists from these countries have been raising their feeble voices for many years about the occurrence of a large number of cases of acute psychosis that is rapid in onset, short in duration, and has a better outcome than classic schizophrenia (3–6). Some have also pointed out the importance of psychosocial stress in these cases and the need to recognize the group of reactive psychoses as different from schizophrenia (7–9). The well-known World Health Organization (WHO) International Pilot Study of Schizophrenia showed that the centers in Third World countries (Colombia, India, and Nigeria) had more acute-type cases than the centers in developed countries (10). More recently, in a WHO study on "The outcome of severe mental disorders," which considers only the first contact of recent-onset cases, similar findings are emerging. At present it seems that both types of cases, i.e., rapid-onset, short-duration and gradual-onset, long-duration, are encountered in all countries; but for some reason, the acute disorders are more frequent in developing countries, which makes the need for better classification of them in these countries more urgent.

The new classification arrangement of the psychotic disorders in DSM-III goes part of the way in meeting the needs of the Third World. The reality of acute and reactive psychoses has been recognized, but the descriptions and criteria are still unsatisfactory. According to DSM-III, for a diagnosis of schizophreniform disorder, the duration must be more than two weeks, and the symptoms must conform to the criteria given for schizophrenic disorder. Many cases of acute psychosis seen in Third World countries do not meet these conditions, and hence are forced into the category of atypical psychosis. As the preliminary findings of an ongoing WHO collaborative study on "Acute psychosis" and an Indian Council of Medical Research's multicenter study on that subject have amply demonstrated, many cases of acute psychosis are observed that last less than two weeks and do not occur in reaction to a major psychosocial stressor.

It is also not logical to expect that symptoms of a short-duration acute psychosis will be identical with those of the relatively long-lasting disorder schizophrenia. In both of the above-mentioned studies it has been found that there are cases of acute psychosis that are difficult to fit into the classic criteria of schizophrenia as described in DSM-III. For example, one of the most common presentations in Third World countries is that of acute psychosis with generalized excitement, overactivity, and disorganized social behavior without either manic mood disturbance or schizophrenic features. Many of the patients with this disorder are observed, on follow-up, to have recovered fully in a short time.

As has been noted earlier, the inclusion of brief reactive psychosis in DSM-III is an important development. This category would be much more useful for Third World countries, however, if it included conditions such as "hysterical psychosis" (see Annex 1), "possession syndromes," and other culture-bound psychotic disorders.

Affective Disorders

The DSM-III grouping of affective disorders seems better than the current International Classification of Diseases (ICD-9) method of classifying depression according to 19 different 4-digit categories. From the Third World point of view, the DSM-III approach of dividing affective disorders into bipolar disorders, major depression, and dysthymic disorders appears quite promising; but more experience with this classification is necessary before a final opinion can be given.

Somatoform Disorders

Provision of a separate classification for somatic disorders is definitely a desirable advance. In light of the reports that as many as 15% to 25% of all patients presenting to any general medical service have no demonstrable physical disorder to explain their physical complaints, the importance of the somatoform classification is considerable. Developing countries need to give added attention to this area so that wasteful use of specialists' time and costly investigations of these physical symptoms can be avoided.

The subclassification of these disorders in DSM-III is not fully satisfactory, however. For example, the concept behind the "somatization disorder" is the result of research by only a few groups of workers, and the criteria given are narrow and culture specific. Often Third World patients have different types of symptoms, and the large number of symptoms required for a diagnosis of somatization disorder forces many patients into the "atypical somatoform" category.

Though in Third World countries one does see definite cases of somatization disorder, conversion disorder, and psychogenic pain disorder that meet DSM-III criteria, there is a still larger number of cases that present a mixture of many of these symptoms and do not fit neatly into any one of the categories. It is obvious that there is need for much more work in this area before a satisfactory system of classification emerges, which is so essential for the development of general hospital psychiatry in developing countries.

Dissociative Disorders

Separation of dissociative disorders from the conversion disorders is, again, an important change. A major difficulty experienced by psychiatrists in Third World countries, however, is the problem of classifying so-called "hysterical fits," one of the most common presentations of patients in these countries (11). Many of the patients with this disorder show classic features of dissociation, and logically should be included in the dissociative disorders category. But there are other cases in which the predominant underlying phenomenon seems to be acute anxiety, and one wonders whether it is correct to put such cases in the category of dissociation. Moreover, there are many patients who have "hysterical fits" along with other symptoms of somatization disorder.

Once again, there is a need for more and better clinical studies in Third World countries to clarify these issues.

Personality Disorders

The increased attention accorded personality traits and disorders by placing them on axis-II is a desirable change. Because of inadequate clinical experience with and research on them in the Third World, no definite opinions can be given on this group of disorders. The basic definition and the specific criteria of these disorders, however, are dependent on cultural norms: what is "maladaptive" in one society may not be so in another, which is likely to limit the clinical utility of fixed criteria in diverse cultures.

Psychosexual Disorders

Like ICD-9, DSM-III has grouped all psychosexual disorders together—a convenient and useful arrangement. Most of the sexual problems commonly seen in Third World countries, e.g., premature ejaculation and impotence, are well covered in the criteria.

There are, however, some specific psychosexual syndromes, frequently observed in many developing countries, that are very difficult to fit into current classification systems. For example, in Indian subcontinent countries such as India, Nepal, and Pakistan, a very common complaint encountered in sexual clinics is what has been tentatively called the "*dhat* syndrome" (12,13). In this syndrome the patient complains of multiple physical and mental symptoms and attributes his ill health to involuntary passage of semen in his urine (see Annex 2). In women there are comparable symptoms, attributed to a "whitish discharge per vaginum"; but not much has been written about this condition.

CULTURE-BOUND SYNDROMES

Though DSM-III does not have a separte section on culture-bound syndromes, it may be appropriate to discuss this subject briefly in the context of Third World countries. The current list of such syndromes is fairly extensive. It includes many reactive psychotic conditions, such as amok and latah, and many varieties of spirit possession syndromes in Africa, Asia, and Latin America. Among neurotic conditions one may note the acute panic reaction associated with a fear of shrinking of the genitals (the koro syndrome of Malaysia), anxiety and exhaustion related to studies (the brain-fag syndrome of Africa), multiple physical and mental symptoms attributed to loss of semen (the dhat syndrome of India), and many other conditions that are as yet poorly described and understood. These syndromes are obviously difficult to fit into the DSM-III classification.

Although it is well recognized that presentations of mental symptoms are markedly influenced by cultural background, it is unfortunate that some of the phenomena observed in the developing countries have been labeled "culture bound." It is not very logical to term "spirit possession" or "fear about shrinking of the genitals" culture bound when "fear of being alone or in public places" or "intense fear of becoming obese" retain the dignified names "agoraphobia" and "anorexia nervosa" and find suitable niches in psychiatric classifications. Creating separate groups of culture-bound syndromes in the classification would be unlikely to serve anyone's interests, least of all those of Third World psychiatrists. What is required at present is more systematic scientific data on these entities, so that more information may be integrated into the mainstream of clinical psychiatry, and the development of a better classification system.

CONCLUSION

There is no doubt that DSM-III is a major advance in psychiatric classification. Its use of diagnostic criteria and multiple axes is likely to have a far-reaching influence on all of clinical psychiatry. The impact may, in some ways, be similar to what happened when statistical measurement and tests of significance were introduced into medical research. The dangers of both these advances are, however, equally obvious. They can only sharpen, but cannot improve, the quality of the original observations. In our current state of limited knowledge, use of specific criteria can encourage a false sense of assurance, and improper use may even impede progress in the long run.

For Third World countries DSM-III brings both hope and frustration. It demonstrates how scientific evidence rather than preconceived theories can form the basis of psychiatric classification. The methods employed in developing DSM-III, e.g., collecting empirical data and conducting field trials, can be replicated in Third World countries in the development of classification systems better suited to their mental health needs.

In terms of actual content, however, DSM-III offers some disappointments for the Third World. The first difficulty is that its American data base limits its usefulness in other parts of the world. Secondly, its complicated structure, which may pose no problem in an academic center, can create serious difficulties when attempts are made to use it in the general mental health services of the developing world, which often work under tremendous constraints in both personnel and resources.

Thus, for the countries of the Third World, the major contribution of DSM-III is the freshness of its approach, which points the way toward developing a truly international classification, based on rigorous scientific data from all parts of the world, without subscribing to any preconceived theory.

REFERENCES

1. Wig NN, Kusumanto SR, Shen Yucun, Sell H: Major schools and traditions in psychiatry: The Third World. Paper presented at the International Conference on Diagnosis and Classification of Mental Disorders and Alcohol and Drug-related Problems. World Health Organization, Copenhagen, 1982 (to be published by WHO)
2. World Health Organization: Organization of Mental Health Services in Developing Countries (WHO Techn Rep Ser No. 564). Geneva, World Health Organization, 1975
3. Wig NN, Singh G: A proposed classification of psychiatric disorders for use in India. Indian J Psychiatry 9: 158–171, 1967
4. Jilek WG, Jilec-Aall L: Transient psychoses in Africans. Psychiatr Clin (Basel): 337–364, 1970
5. German GA: Aspects of clinical psychiatry in Sub-Saharan Africa. Br J Psychiatry 121: 461–479, 1972
6. Kapur RL, Pandurangi AK: A comparative study of reactive psychosis and acute psychosis without precipitating stress. Br J Psychiatry 135: 544, 1979
7. Wig NN, Narang RL: Hysterical psychosis. Indian J Psychiatry 11: 93–100, 1969
8. Pandurangi AK, Kapur RK: Reactive psychosis—A prospective study. Acta Psychiatr Scand 61: 89–95, 1980
9. Singh G, Sachdev JS: A clinical and follow-up study of atypical psychoses. Indian J Psychiatry 22: 167–172, 1980
10. World Health Organization: Report of the International Pilot Study of Schizophrenia, vol 1. Geneva, World Health Organization, 1973
11. Wig NN, Mangalwedhe K, Bedi H, Murthy RS: A follow-up study of hysteria. Indian J Psychiatry 24(2): 120–125, 1982

12. Nakra BRS, Wig NN, Varma VK: A study of male potency disorders. Indian
    J Psychiatry 19(3): 13–18, 1977
13. Neki JS: Psychiatry in South-East Asia. Br J Psychiatry 123: 257, 1973

Annex 1

CLINICAL DESCRIPTION OF HYSTERICAL PSYCHOSIS

An acute psychotic condition following an overwhelming psycho-social stress, often particularly traumatic to the person's self-esteem (e.g., failure in an examination, rejection in a love affair, or an event causing major social disgrace). The onset is usually sudden and dramatic, symptoms developing rapidly in hours or days. The course is usually brief, rarely lasting more than a few weeks. Psychotic behavior appears deliberately exaggerated and attention-seeking, often conforming to the popular concept of "insanity." Symptoms, which are varied and change rapidly, may include excitement, stupor, confusion, and grossly disorganized behavior. Vivid imagery resembling hallucinations may be present. The person's cultural background may often color and modify the manifest psychotic behavior. Hysterical traits in the personality and a history of previous hysterical symptoms are often present.

Annex 2

CLINICAL DESCRIPTION OF THE *DHAT* SYNDROME

A common condition in young males, mostly from the countries of the Indian subcontinent, where there is a strong cultural belief in the harmful effects of loss of semen from the body. Characteristic features are feelings of extreme physical and mental exhaustion, with complaints of poor concentration and memory. Multiple somatic complaints are also present, and the patient attributes all of these to the involuntary loss of semen (*dhat* in the local language) in the urine. There may be a background of guilt about nocturnal emissions or masturbation. The condition is more common in young men of rural background with little education and low socioeconomic status.

6

THE ACHIEVEMENTS AND LIMITATIONS OF DSM-III

Sir Martin Roth, Sc.D. (Hon.), M.A. (Cantab.),
M.D., F.R.C.P., F.R.C. Psych.

ORIGINS AND MAIN FEATURES

Operational criteria for the diagnosis of each category of mental disorder, in the formulation of which strenuous efforts were made to avoid ambiguity, are a central feature of DSM-III. The ancestry of such criteria can be traced to some guidelines provided by the groups under the leadership of Eli Robins of St. Louis, which laid down "inclusion" and "exclusion" criteria for the diagnosis of 15 conditions about which sufficient evidence regarding clinical features, course, and outcome was available in the literature (1). This set of criteria was modified and extended to cover 23 disorders in the Research Diagnostic Criteria of Spitzer, Endicott, and Robins (2). The original purpose was to enhance the possibility of achieving comparable and replicable results in the course of scientific inquiries into the problems of mental disorder. That the aim was worthy and important is evident from examination of the contents of any journal devoted to publication of the results of clinical research in psychiatry. It is commonplace to discover reports by able investigators whose results fail to replicate or may contradict observations previously reported by scientists of comparable stature. It is

Address correspondence to: Professor Sir Martin Roth, Department of Psychiatry, University of Cambridge Clinical School, Level Four, Addenbrooke's Hospital, Hills Road, Cambridge CB2 2QQ, England rarely possible to eliminate the first explanation for such disparities that leaps to mind: that the investigators have not studied comparable patient samples. The diagnostic criteria employed in the selection of patients often prove to have been quite different or only broadly similar.

It was an obvious step to extend the benefits to be derived in research from clearly defined and well thought out operational criteria to everyday clinical practice. DSM-III accordingly seeks to enhance the degree of consistency and reliability of the diagnoses made by psychiatrists in their daily work. The approach is descriptive and empirical. The descriptive accounts of each disorder and the criteria given at the end of each text are confined to statements about the relevant symptoms, signs, patterns of behavior, and test results accessible to objective evaluation. No theories regarding organic, psychodynamic, or any other etiology or interpretations or conjectures that stem from them have been allowed to qualify as criteria. A common ground regarding diagnosis is thus created for psychiatrists who may hold widely diverging views regarding the etiological origins of mental disorders. Despite the subsidiary axes available for the delineation of the patient's status in respect of features other than the main diagnosis, DSM-III is a categorical system of classification and diagnosis. In this it resembles all other sytems that have won a wide measure of acceptance.

A series of field trials undertaken by 800 clinicians who began their work in 1976 preceded the compilation of DSM-III in its final form. The feedback provided regarding clarity, applicability, and reliability of the criteria led to many revisions in the classification, the clinical descriptions, and the diagnostic criteria.

DSM-III is described as a multiaxial scheme of classification. It is the first official scheme of classification to attempt to implement the recommendations originally made by Essen-Möller (3,4) that observations under a number of different headings other than those relevant to the main clinical syndrome should be included in the final diagnostic statement that follows psychiatric evaluation of the patient. This gives expression to the growing consensus among psychiatrists in the last few decades that in many forms of mental illness a traditional categorical diagnosis provides a meager account of the patient who has been submitted to a thorough, systematic, psychiatric examination. It is also accepted that such statements constitute an insufficient foundation for decisions about management.

The term *multiaxial classification* has gained increasing acceptance, as if it were an unambiguous concept already available for application in everyday clinical practice. However, though the principle of descriptive statements along more than one axis is generally accepted, there are conceptual, methodological, and other problems in relation to multiaxial classifications and their application in daily clinical work, which will be examined at a later stage. The introduction of DSM-III has opened up the possibility of initiating cooperative inquiries into a whole range of diagnostic and psychopathological problems using clinical criteria of proven reliability. As it will be extensively employed in the United States for at least a decade ahead, the opportunity provided by this consistency in diagnostic practice should be utilized for promoting knowledge of psychopathology. The information that accrues in relation to diagnosis and classification will be particularly valuable if attempts are made at those centers where research can be conducted to compare DSM-III with other methods of classification in terms of reliability, predictive value, and validity. Interest will attach not only to the proportion of cases that can be assigned by the different systems to the various categories of disorder but also to the proportion of cases that proves unclassifiable.

REFERENCE DIAGNOSES

The main contribution of reference diagnoses has been to the standardization of the Mental State Examination and the consistency in procedure and rigor this entails in examination of the presenting mental picture. The syndromes of DSM-III, like those of other reference diagnoses, comprise phenomena that can be observed or elicited in the course of examination and evaluation of the presenting mental state. But it is open to question whether any of the reference diagnostic schemas, with their sets of clinical syndromes and operational criteria for identifying them, have rendered the process of arriving at the diagnosis in everyday clinical practice obsolete.

In the indubitably organic disorders, the process of arriving at a diagnosis is simple and easily accomplished in its entirety. This is not the case in other forms of mental disorder, including the commonest conditions in psychiatric practice. The findings recorded during the examination of the mental state have to be related to the individual's developmental history, familial and social setting, and personality, his or her previous episodes of illness, the adverse circumstances of the immediate and more remote past, and their meaning for the patient. The contribution made by some of these components to the content and form of the presenting mental state has to be weighed. Evaluation of most of these facets of the total picture has not been standardized. The possibility that consistent and reliable procedures may be extended to components of the diagnostic process other than the mental state examination is not excluded. But it has not, for the present, been achieved, and the task is beset with pitfalls.

THE MULTIPLE AXES OF DSM-III

The information elicited during a psychiatric examination can be recorded on five axes in DSM-III. All forms of mental disorder, with the exception of specific developmental disorders in children and personality disorders in adults, are included under axis I. The developmental disorders of childhood and personality disorders are recorded on axis II; the recording of personality disorder and features on a separate axis constitutes an important refinement, to which further reference is made at a later stage. Axis III provides for noting associated physical disorders, whether these are judged to contribute to causation or judged relevant for other reasons. This axis takes account of new observations placed on record in the last two decades in relation to the association between physical illness and affective neurotic and other syndromes believed to be totally independent of organic causes in the past (5–7). Under axis IV psychosocial stress factors that are judged to have contributed to the genesis of the current illness can be recorded according to a seven-point scale. Axis V is used to describe the highest level of adaptive functioning achieved during a period of a few months at least. Although axes IV and V are intended for research and special purposes, they will doubtless come to be used for comprehensive clinical assessments of many kinds.

A number of conceptual and methodological problems arise in connection with the recording of findings on each of these five "axes." These will be individually considered at a later stage; the comments in this section will be confined to general points about the multiaxial system. The term *multiaxial classification* has been used in a number of contexts to describe schemes of this nature (8), but the validity of this term itself is open to question.

The additional information to be recorded along the multiple axes developed in recent years can enrich clinical description provided it is made clear that the relevance and specificity of the items in question for etiology are uncertain at present. Several problems arise in this connection that ought to be made explicit in DSM-III and similar schemes incorporating a number of axes.

The first point to be noted is that the axes vary in their relevance for the main groups of mental disorder. For example, personality disorder (DSM-III, axis II) has obvious relevance for neurotic disorders, but can be of relatively little interest in cases of senile or multi-infarct dementia. Physical illness (DSM-III, axis III) will be of etiological importance in every case of delirium and clouding of consciousness; it appears to play a more limited role (*vide supra*) in the etiology of some of the affective disorders. The precise strength of such associations is unknown, however. And the contribution to etiology is complicated, involving physiological or psychodynamic mechanisms or a combination of the two.

Similar points with regard to specificity and relevance apply to axes IV and V. But it is apparent that the differential weights that would have to be attached to the four subsidiary axes in DSM-III in any kind of multiaxial scheme ripe for application in clinical practice, cannot be applied at the present time. To determine them an ambitious program of scientific inquiry would have to be mounted to gather factual data with a reasonable measure of precision and an acceptable degree of reliability.

When we turn to the concept of multiaxial classification, the problem presented by the axes comprised within DSM-III is that although they will add information that has some measure of relevance for many forms of disorder, applied uncritically they risk creating greater confluence rather than sharper discrimination among mental syndromes. In the present state of knowledge they cannot bring psychiatric classification closer to the ideal of categories that are jointly exhaustive and mutually exclusive (9).

It is in its promotion of a more structured and systematic multidimensional clinical formulation rather than in its multiaxial *classification* that the special contribution of DSM-III resides. To derive optimal benefit in the immediate future from the multidimensional formulations made possible by the use of DSM-III, the observations listed on the subsidiary axes II–V would need to be augmented by statements regarding their likely relevance and importance, as inferred for the present by relatively crude and subjective means from clinical evaluation.

This refers to the application of DSM-III in ordinary clinical practice, in which its use in the flexible manner described could make it a valuable tool for comprehensive clinical description and analysis. Insofar as research is concerned, the information that will be gathered with the aid of DSM-III has considerable potential for advancing knowledge about the nature and strength of the relationship between the principal diagnoses to be coded on axis I, on the one hand, and possible etiological factors, such as physical illness, personality setting, and life events, in the different varieties of mental disorder, on the other.

Such inquiries will be an essential precondition for a more stringent and logical approach to diagnostic formulation than is possible with the aid of DSM-III at the present time. But to make a reality of such ambitious scientific undertakings the axes would require unambiguous and detailed operational definitions, of proven reliability.

DSM-III AND THE CONCEPT OF HIERARCHICAL ORDER

One of the most valuable contributions made by DSM-III has been the interest it has generated in clinical phenomenology and the fostering of more objective and stringent approaches toward it. However, in trying to avoid all theoretical prejudgments regarding the genesis of mental disorder and seeking to build a diagnosis and classification on empirically observable clinical phenomena, it has perhaps leaned too far backward. In particular, it has ignored certain concepts inherent in traditional descriptive psychiatry that have served to order and organize clinical phenomena in broad categories, on the basis of clinical features held in common, and have expressed, in an open and tentative manner, the relationships among them. This refers to the hierarchical sequence of categories inherent in the Kraepelinian system (10) and the criteria employed for identifying and describing and differentiating among disorders at different levels. In some of the decision trees and in a number of the exclusion criteria, DSM-III has employed principles similar to those in the hierarchial system, but nowhere are these made explicit. Reading the main text one can gain the impression that DSM-III is composed of a large number of well-defined and clearly circumscribed pigeonholes unconnected with each other by psychopathological concepts or clearly defined diagnostic rules of procedure.

It is worthwhile at this stage to take a closer look at the hierarchial scheme that underlies the Kraepelianian system of classification (10). It is inherent in that system that disorders with organic features, i.e., defects in cognition, memory, and/or consciousness, and focal mental disturbances should be given precedence in diagnosis over disorders in which all such features are lacking. In other words, when specific organic features suggesting dementia or delirium are present, any concomitant schizophrenic, depressive, or neurotic symptoms are not allowed to override diagnosis of the appropriate organic syndrome; "functional" features are accorded secondary place in the diagnostic formulation and judged as pathoplastic or related phenomena.

Schizophrenia comes next in hierarchical order. It is given precedence over depressive, manic, and other affective disorders. And manic-depressive disorders take precedence over neuroses. Accordingly, in the presence of indubitable "psychotic," "endogenous," "vital," or "melancholic" depressive features, concomitant neurotic symptoms are not judged to raise alternative diagnostic possibilities. Of course, if "endogenous" features are less than clear-cut, difficulties in diagnosis arise.

Lower down in the hierarchy, the rules become unclear, if only because in the thinking of workers such as Kraepelin (10), Schneider (11), and Jaspers (12), neuroses are not clearly differentiated from "personality disorders" or "psychopathic disorders." Few psychiatrists today, however, would be prepared to accept neuroses as merely disturbances of development identical with personality disorder. Within the presence of a well-defined depressive syndrome with a wide range of symptoms, precedence would be given to the depression over other neurotic symptoms, which would be judged secondary. And neuroses—anxious, phobic, and obsessional—would be given priority over personality disorder, if only because any neurosis that has begun at a definite point in past time has a prior claim on the psychiatrist's concern as far as therapy is concerned.

It is therefore logical for personality disorder to be placed last in the hierarchical order. But as personality variables or a definable disorder of personality is often germane for a total psychiatric formulation, it was wise to place this group of variables, as the creators of DSM-III have done, on a separate axis. This has the further advantage that it prevents "personality disorder" from preempting other psychiatric diagnoses, a practice that often causes opportunities for treatment to be missed, particularly when superimposed mental illness exaggerates or parodies maladaptation of long standing.

It will be apparent that the principle of hierarchical order is not sacrosanct; it is no more than a set of hypotheses, open to challenge and refutation. In relation to certain diagnostic problems, it provides little guidance. There are also issues in relation to which the rules have already been called into question or contradicted (13). But this is one way in which refinements in diagnosis and classification are achieved.

CLINICAL FEATURES IN DSM-III AND THEIR REFINEMENT

Textbook descriptions have often been criticized for the looseness with which they have described the clinical syndromes of psychiatry, thus presenting the possibility of uncontrolled and idiosyncratic variation in the manner in which symptoms and signs were used as criteria. There is substance in this criticism, but it overlooks the possible advantages of flexibility in the application of criteria in the individual cases offered by the textbook accounts. Cross-sectional clinical features do not have precisely the same significance and diagnostic value in every kind of context. The openness of the descriptions of syndromes to be found in the writings of Kraepelin (10) reflected the hypothetical nature of the clinical disorders he delineated. The accounts left a great deal to be discovered, including the precise diagnostic and discriminating value of the different features.

DSM-III eliminates this uncertainty by specifying the manner in which the observations recorded are to be processed in arriving at a diagnosis. But as the sets of features to be found under each rubric represent no more than the choice of one group of experienced investigators, they are in many places arbitrary. This was perhaps inevitable in the present stage of development. It would be unfortunate, however, if the clear operational definitions provided were allowed to create the impression that the problems of diagnosis and differential diagnosis had been resolved.

Ideally, the diagnostic criteria listed under the different rubrics should have quantitative weights or scores proportionate to their value in description and discrimination. An approach toward a more quantitative and less arbitrary set of features could be made with the aid of multivariate statistical methods such as principal components, discriminant function, and cluster analytic techniques. As has been often pointed out, these have not succeeded in defining previously unknown syndromes (14), but they have refined those brought to light by original clinical observation. It would be a pity if the vast body of information that will be set down in the course of arriving at diagnoses with the aid of DSM-III were to be lost and not submitted to statistical analysis. And it would be surprising if well-planned investigations aimed at making optimal use of the information recorded failed to sharpen the available criteria for descriptive and differential diagnosis.

SOME UNSOLVED PROBLEMS

Schizophrenia

It is a good principle in classification that unresolved problems in diagnosis should be made explicit rather than dealt with by means of arbitrary dividing lines. The criteria for the diagnosis of schizophrenia in DSM-III provide an example of this. Continuous signs of illness have to be present for at least six months at some time during the individual's life to qualify the disorder as schizophrenic. This appears to provide a clean separation between the cases that are set on a refractory or chronic course and those of relatively benign prognosis in which the symptoms and signs persist for shorter periods. The latter have to be classified as "schizophreniform disorders" if the symptoms have been present for less than six months but more than two weeks.

This assumes in advance what is in need of proof. If it were possible to divide schizophrenic syndromes into those of good and those of bad prognosis, schizophrenia could no longer be regarded as a unitary disorder. Its indeterminate outcome has been among the features that make retention of its unitary character essential. The advantage from a heuristic point of view is that further comparisons within schizophrenia, as defined by phenomenology alone, may ultimately make it possible to define the reasons for the wide disparities in observed course and outcome. Such findings would be valuable not just for future prediction: they might shed fresh light on the nature of schizophrenic illness.

No such new information can flow from the partitioning of schizophrenic illness in DSM-III. Patients in whom symptoms have persisted for less than six months will be classified under "schizophreniform disorder" or "atypical psychosis" (duration less than two weeks). However, the criteria for the diagnosis of these syndromes differ in respects other than duration from those for "schizophrenic disorders." Comparisons with schizophrenia are therefore invalidated.

Investigations in recent years have shown certain "negative" features of schizophrenic illness to be of high diagnostic specificity—e.g., impoverishment of affect, decline in motivation, with apathy and indifference, marked autism, persistent incoherence, and inconsequentiality or impoverishment of thought. When they can be detected during the early stages of illness, their predictive value may also be considerable. Some studies have claimed correlations between such negative features and abnormal C.A.T. scans (15). There would therefore be merit in giving special weight to such symptoms, or at least in devoting a larger number of criteria to them than DSM-III allows in section A of the diagnostic criteria and in the section on "prodromal or residual symptoms."

The validity of the upper age limit of 45 years, which operates as an exclusion criterion in the diagnosis of schizophrenia, is open to question. The paranoid hallucinatory psychoses of middle and late life have been shown in the last few decades to meet the criteria for the diagnosis of schizophrenia in DSM-III and other diagnostic systems. Moreover, the conditions are genetically homologous with schizophrenia, though the morbid risk for schizophrenia in first-degree relatives is somewhat lower. "Late paraphrenia" responds in a particularly favorable manner to the neuroleptic drugs that are effective in schizophrenic illness of earlier life. In excluding these disorders, DSM-III fails to complete the clinical picture of schizophrenic illness.

The Organic Group of Disorders

The accounts of the main syndromes and the operational criteria for diagnosis of the organic disorders are clear and authoritative. Comments on this section will be confined to the rubrics "organic delusional syndrome" and "organic affective syndrome."

It is well known that an affective or delusional syndrome may evolve in association with somatic or cerebral disease without the characteristic features of the latter such as cognitive impairment or disturbance of consciousness. These disorders, however, differ from the other organic syndromes described in this section. In each of these syndromes somatic or cerebral disease is invariably present. Such disease is also a sufficient cause insofar as the form (as distinct from the content) of most cases of these syndromes is concerned.

This is not true of the organic "affective" and "delusional" organic syndromes described in DSM-III. As the great majority of such conditions develop in the absence of any organic lesions, the latter cannot be necessary. Nor can such organic lesions be sufficient causes in that most patients with cerebral or somatic disease do not develop a typical organic syndrome rather than such purely affective or paranoid concomitants. In other cases, mental disturbances sufficiently consistent, clear-cut, and structured to qualify for a diagnosis of a psychiatric syndrome are absent. The organic lesions doubtless make some contribution to the etiology of a proportion of cases with purely depressive, manic, or paranoid features, but for the reasons indicated, this contribution can be only a limited one. Moreover, these disorders respond to treatment in a manner similar to nonorganic affective and paranoid disorders. The problem could perhaps have been most clearly resolved by assigning these cases to an appropriate category on the *strength of their mental phenomenology* and making an appropriate entry on axis III with respect to associated physical illness.

"Affective Disorders" and "Anxiety Disorder"

The depressive and anxiety states account for a high proportion of the illnesses treated by the modern psychiatrist, particularly in outpatient practice. The territory presents special difficulties in diagnosis, and it is particularly important to provide landmarks as clear and unequivocal as the situation will permit. DSM-III deals with the problem of differentiation between depressive and anxiety disorders by classifying them under entirely separate rubrics. Such a sharp cleavage between affective and anxiety disorders cannot be logically defended; the latter are disturbances of affect in the usual sense of the term. Assigning them to different categories fails to resolve the problems posed by the substantial overlap between anxious and depressive symptoms. More specific criteria and rules of procedure are required for dealing with the difficult issues in relation to depression and anxiety disorders.

When depressive and anxious symptoms coexist, as they often do in endogenous and psychotic states, the depressive symptoms have to be given priority (in accord with the hierarchical principle) over associated anxiety symptoms. The anxiety in endogenous states is also experienced at a deeper level and is qualitatively different from that found in neurotic states, although judgment of this difference depends in part upon empathy. This order of precedence applies to both unipolar states (a concept confined to endogenous disorders in European psychiatry) and bipolar ones. And it is validated by the disappearance of anxiety along with depression when antidepressive treatment is administered.

When, as in DSM-III, the "psychotic" and "endogenous" lines of demarcation are erased, "unipolar" depression is liable to become a capacious category in which endogenous and neurotic depression and simple anxiety states are included. And as agoraphobia often has a coloring of depression, this disorder, along with other phobic states, may be judged "depressive," as recent controversies regarding the pharmacological treatment of these disorders have shown.

Systematic investigations of the relationship between anxiety and depressive states with respect to presenting clinical picture, course, measures of personality, and mood have shown the two groups of syndromes to be distinct, with some measure of overlap (16–21).* We have not resolved the problems of diagnosis and classification in this area. But the findings have provided a data base from which improved operational criteria for differentiation of depressive and anxiety syndromes may be developed.

Schizoaffective Disorder

DSM-III advises that the diagnosis of schizoaffective disorder be considered only when a range of other possibilities, including hybrid conditions such as "schizophrenia with a superimposed atypical affective disorder," have been excluded. The expectation seems to be that the diagnosis of schizoaffective disorder will be rare. Recent reports suggest, however, that an increasing proportion of psychotic disorders are so classified.

It is important that a greater measure of consistency be achieved in arriving at this diagnosis. But this is not likely to materialize until more clear and factually well founded criteria can be advanced. In the presence of a range of psychotic symptoms adequate to justify a diagnosis of schizophrenia, the presence of concomitant depressive symptoms does not call for a revision of this diagnosis. DSM-III lays emphasis on "mood-incongruent psychotic features" that are "prominent" or that persist when affective symptoms are no longer present. Few experienced psychiatrists would allow a single incongruent feature to override a diagnosis of affective psychosis.

Systematic investigations will be needed to provide more clear criteria of demarcation beyond which a hybrid diagnosis should be considered. In the case of schizomanic disorders, the findings of Brockington (22) suggest that mood-incongruent delusions are not associated with a significant deviation from the expected course of manic disorder, whereas cases with passivity feelings and hallucinations pursue a course intermediate between that of manic and of schizophrenic illness.

THE MULTIAXIAL SYSTEM AS A STARTING POINT FOR SCIENTIFIC INVESTIGATIONS

If the strength of the association between the diagnoses recorded on axis I and the other axes could be investigated in a rigorous manner, new

---

*D. Caetano: Enquiries into the classification of affective disorders. Dissertation submitted for the degree of Doctor of Philosophy to the University of Cambridge. Cambridge, Trinity College, 1980

light might be shed on a number of contemporary issues relating to the classification and etiology of mental disorders. There are a number of inquiries on record suggesting significant associations between psychiatric diagnosis and basic personality. For instance, von Zerssen (23) has confirmed that patients with psychotic depression have a distinctively melancholic type of premorbid personality profile. And Caetano* was able, with the aid of the Multiphasic Personality Inventory and the 16 Personality Factors administered after recovery from illness in 89 subjects, to assign 84% to the anxiety or depressive group into which they had originally been allocated on the basis of presenting symptoms.

The current literature on depression is replete with expressions such as "depression with personality disorder," "hysterical dysphoria," "the self-pitying constellation," and "characterologic depression." The difficulty is that the available measures of personality have low levels of reliability and validity, and this can also be said of the categorical forms of personality diagnosis. There are, however, approaches to the problem, particularly to the possibility of comparative studies of patients with different diagnoses whose performance on psychological tests could be investigated after recovery from their current illness.

There is hardly need to emphasize the value of studies that shed light on the strength of the association between diagnoses made on axis I and physical disorders reported on axis III. A number of inquiries in relation to affective disorder and neurosis have reported increased morbidity with respect to physical disease and, in some cases, increased mortality as well (5–7). The difficulty is in deciding what it is relevant to record under this heading. Infectious hepatitis nine months previously or a severe influenza attack six months ago may have been followed by a mild depression, and now the patient is presenting with severe depressive symptoms. A first attack of angina pectoris or a mere suspicion of this disorder 18 months earlier may be of no consequence in relation to the anxiety and depressive symptoms in a 50-year-old male with a normal personality, but in a hypochondrically anxious, body-proud man, it may be the clue, although a well-hidden clue, to a depressive illness of crippling severity. The instructions in DSM-III in relation to the recording of physical illness need to be set down in more detail and inquiries in relation to this feature more carefully standardized if this axis is to be utilized for scientific purposes.

The points made with regard to axis III lead naturally to those that arise in connection with axis IV, for it is the manner in which the individual construes physical illness or any other life-threatening experience that matters. It is for this reason that some people break down

---

*Caetano, op. cit.

after what may appear a trivial illness or accident. According to the instructions in DSM-III in relation to axis IV, an entry should be made only in terms of the stress the *average* person would experience. But the patients who develop the commonest forms of mental disorder do not have a predispositon of "average" character: they are people upon whom psychosocial stressors are liable to impinge with a selective severity. The problem is not insoluble. It calls for the application to the psychosocial stressors of techniques of assessment such as the contextual measure of threat developed by Brown (24), which has been found to have a satisfactory measure of reliability.

The precise intention behind axis V, which is supposed to be employed for recording the level of adaptive functioning achieved during the previous year, requires fuller explanation if this axis is to be put to optimal use. It cannot delineate the highest level of adaptation which the patient has been capable of achieving in the past and to which he may succeed in returning in the future. Many common forms of illness, particularly the neurotic, emotional, and related disorders, often present with a long history of symptoms, although they have usually begun at a definable point in time two or more years previously.

CONCLUDING REMARKS

The contributions of DSM-III may be examined under two main headings.

The first relates to its applications to diagnosis in ordinary clinical practice. The stimulus it has given and the vigorous effort it has elicited in the whole area of clinical diagnosis have already been mentioned. The question arises whether DSM-III should be employed as a comprehensive blueprint for diagnostic practice. A number of problems arise in relation to such an ambitious role for it. Only a limited part of the clinical examination that precedes a final psychiatric diagnosis has been standardized. The findings elicited during examination of the presenting mental state have to be interpreted, and often reinterpreted, in light of a wide range of observations relating to family and developmental history, adaptation in social and familial settings, and any personal vicissitudes that have been suffered (or been conspicuous by their absence) in the weeks or months before the onset of symptoms. DMS-III can provide a valuable guide during the process of reasoning and inferences that leads to the diagnosis, but it is doubtful whether it should be allowed to supplant it. It must not be regarded as a final, closed system, but kept open so that it can not only stimulate fresh research but be modified in accordance with the findings that emerge.

The term *multiaxial classification* applied in some quarters to schemes such as DSM-III's that incorporate a number of axes and dimensions is misconceived. DSM-III provides a sound basis for arriving at a multiaxial clinical formulation, although the weighing of the different axes will have to be undertaken, for the present, with the aid of relatively imprecise clinical means.

The second heading relates to the value of DSM-III as a starting point for scientific investigation of the classification and etiology of mental disorders. The progenitors of DSM-III were instruments intended to enhance the consistency and comparability of the findings reported by different scientific investigators, and it retains a good deal of this original stamp.

Some of the questions that could be addressed with the aid of DSM-III have already been touched upon in the foregoing sections of this paper. The information that is to be collected through the use of DSM-III could probably make a significant contribution to advancing knowledge. But the data that will be gathered under the conditions that prevail in ordinary clinical practice are likely to prove too crude for special scientific exercises.

The data that will prove of real value should perhaps be developed in selected centers in which teams of workers would focus on specific questions. They would need, as a first step, to revise and sharpen the definitions of a number of categories and many features, drawing on recent evidence available in phenomenological studies for this purpose. Some of the most important hypotheses posed are those that link the first axis with the remaining four. In this context, standardization of the clinical procedures and the measures to be applied to obtain relevant and reliable information will demand special attention.

REFERENCES

1. Feighner JP, Robins E, Guze SB, Woodruff RA, Winokur G, Munoz R: Diagnostic criteria for use in psychiatric research. Arch Gen Psychiatry 26: 57–63, 1972
2. Spitzer RL, Endicott J, Robins E: Research Diagnostic Criteria (RDC) for a Selected Group of Functional Disorders, 3rd ed. New York, New York State Psychiatric Institute, 1977
3. Essen-Möller E: On classification of mental disorders. Acta Psychiatr Scand 37: 119–126, 1961
4. Essen-Möller E: Suggestions for further improvement of the international classification of mental disorders. Psychol Med 1:308–311, 1971
5. Whitlock FA: Symptomatic Affective Disorders. A Study of Depression and Mania Associated with Physical Disease and Medication. London, Academic Press, 1982
6. Kerr TA, Schapira K, Roth M: The relationship between premature death and affective disorders. Br J Psychiatry 115:1277–1282, 1969

7. Roth M: The Association of Depressive Illness and Emotional Disorder with Somatic Disease. Montreal, Karger (in press)
8. Rutter M, Shaffer D, Shepherd M: An evaluation of the proposal for a multi-axial classification of child psychiatric disorders. Psychol Med 3: 244–250, 1973
9. Hempel CG: Introduction to problems of taxonomy, in Field Studies in Mental Disorders. Edited by Zubin J. New York, Grune & Stratton, 1961, pp 3–22
10. Kraepelin E: Psychiatrie: Ein Lehrbuch für Studierende und Arzte. Leipzig, Barth, 1915
11. Schneider K: Die Psychopathischen Personalichkeiten. Translation of the 9th ed by Hamilton MW. London, Cassell and Co, 1958
12. Jaspers K: General Psychopathology. Translated from the German 7th ed by Hoenig J, Hamilton MW. Manchester, Manchester University Press, 1963
13. Roth M: Psychiatric diagnosis in clinical and scientific settings, in Psychiatric Diagnosis: Exploration of Biological Predictors. Edited by Akiskal HS, Webb WL. New York and London, Spectrum Publications, 1978, pp 9–47
14. Garside R, Roth M: Multivariate statistical methods and problems of classification in psychiatry. Br J Psychiatry 133: 53–67, 1978
15. Johnstone EC, Owens DGC, Crow TJ: A CT study of patients with schizophrenia, affective psychosis, and neuritic illness, in Biological Psychiatry. Edited by Jansson B, Perris C, Struwe G. New York, Elsevier North Holland, 1981, pp 237–240
16. Roth M, Gurney C, Garside RF, Kerr TA: Studies in the classification of affective disorders. The relationship between anxiety states and depressive illness. I. Br J Psychiatry 121: 147–161, 1972
17. Gurney C, Roth M, Garside RF, Kerr TA, Schapira K: Studies in the classification of affective disorders. The relationship between anxiety states and depressive illnesses. II. Br J Psychiatry 121: 162–166, 1972
18. Kerr TA, Roth M, Schapira K, Gurney C: The assessment and prediction of outcome in affective disorders. Br J Psychiatry 121: 167–174, 1972
19. Mountjoy CQ, Roth M: Studies in the relationship between depressive disorders and anxiety states. I. Rating scales. J Affective Disord 4: 127–147, 1982
20. Mountjoy CQ, Roth M: Studies in the relationship of depressive disorders and anxiety states. II. Clinical items. J Affective Disord 4: 149–161, 1982
21. Roth M, Mountjoy CQ, Caetano D: Further investigations into the relationship between depressive disorders and anxiety states. Pharmacopsychiatria 15: 135–141, 1982
22. Brockington IF, Wainwright S, Kendell RE: Manic patients with schizophrenia or paranoid symptoms. Psychol Med 10: 665–675, 1980
23. von Zerssen D: Personality and affective disorders, in Handbook of Affective Disorders. Edited by Paykel ES. London, Churchill Livingstone, 1982, pp 212–228
24. Brown GW: Meaning, measurement and stress of life events, in Stressful Life Events: Their Nature and Effects. Edited by Dohrenwend BS, Dohrenwend BP. New York, Wiley, 1974

SECTION III

Regional Perspectives

7

DSM-III IN GERMAN-SPEAKING COUNTRIES

Peter Berner, M.D., Heinz Katschnig, M.D.,
and Gerhard Lenz, M.D.

At the time of writing of this article, the German translation of DSM-III was still in press (1).* A general evaluation of its acceptance by, and usefulness for, German-speaking psychiatrists was therefore not yet possible.

, Following a brief account of the historical development of diagnostic thinking in German-speaking countries, we shall present an empirical analysis of the relationship between DSM-III and German formulations of the concept of schizophrenia. In this comparison we draw on data from our own research on the functional psychoses, in which we used a "polydiagnostic approach" (2,3), i.e., simultaneous application of different diagnostic systems to one and the same research population, allowing, *inter alia*, a comparative nosology of different diagnostic formulations. We shall then consider the use of diagnostic systems in German-speaking countries, giving both a short historical overview and the results of a special survey carried out for this paper in all Austrian psychiatric inpatient units and in those of the Federal Republic of Germany, the German Democratic Republic, and Switzerland as well. Finally, we shall offer our views on the strengths and weaknesses of DSM-III.

Address correspondence to: Professor Peter Berner, Psych. Universitätsklinik, University of Vienna, Währinger Gürtel 74–76, A-1090 Wien, Austria

*To be published by Beltz-Verlag, D 6940 Weinhem, Federal Republic of Germany. See also Berner et al. (1).

GERMAN DIAGNOSTIC CONCEPTS AND DSM-III

Historical Overview of German Diagnostic Thinking

German psychiatry is one of the most important sources of modern scientific psychiatry. Since many elements of German psychiatric thinking can be found in DSM-III, a short historical outline of diagnostic thinking, from Kraepelin to the present, may be useful.

When Kraepelin (4) established, on the foundation laid by his French and German predecessors, the frame that still serves as reference for all considerations of psychiatric nosology, he used course of the illness and outcome as criteria for his classification. Although he did not explicitly specify obligatory symptoms for the disease entities in his system, his description of those diseases already contained nearly all the symptoms that have subsequently been used by other researchers as a matrix for the extraction of criteria for cross-sectional diagnosis.

Eugen Bleuler's (5) distinction between basic and accessory schizophrenic symptoms (see Annex 1) represents a first step toward an operational definition of diagnostic criteria. Bleuler abandoned Kraepelin's hypothesis of schizophrenia as a disease entity and replaced it with a pathogenetic one, stipulating that different etiologies could produce similar pathogenetic conditions and cause the appearance of the basic symptoms.

On the basis of Karl Jaspers's (6) fundamental outlines of general psychopathology, Kurt Schneider (7) drew up a hierarchical list of schizophrenic symptoms that distinguished between disturbances of experience and disturbances in behavior. As the former are much easier to identify, Schneider—in contrast to Bleuler, whose basic symptoms are partially behavioral disturbances—based his diagnostic system essentially on them. The disturbances of experience are separated into first- and second-rank symptoms (see Annex 2).

Provided organic disease has been excluded, Schneider considered the diagnosis of schizophrenia established whenever first-rank symptoms were clearly present. He understood his diagnostic assignments as a psychopathological classification, without claiming any pathogenetic or nosological connotations. But this assumption is only partly true, as he takes for granted that schizophrenia is an endogenous illness. Another theoretical problem in Schneider's diagnostic methods is his adherence to Jaspers's hierarchical principle. This principle, as applied to distinguishing between affective psychoses and schizophrenia, maintains that in the presence of both schizophrenia and affective symptoms, the latter are deprived of diagnostic value.

Bleuler's school follows the hierarchical principle, but in a "milder form": only when schizophrenic symptoms occur *simultaneously* with manic-depressive ones does the former diagnosis predominate; when they appear in an alternating fashion, the diagnosis is modified accordingly.

In German-speaking countries, diagnostic habits have generally, up to now, followed either Bleuler's or Schneider's lines of assignment. Neither one has developed clear-cut rules for applying their criteria in the form of diagnostic algorithms. In Vienna the criteria for defining schizophrenia have been put into a diagnostic algorithm. These research criteria (8) (see Annex 3), called "axial syndromes," on the one hand are based on the importance attributed by Bleuler to thought disorders and affective depletion for the diagnosis of schizophrenia and, on the other hand, take into account Janzarik's concept of the "basic dynamic constellations in endogenous psychoses," which is one of the most creative contributions to modern Germany psychopathology.

Janzarik (9) understands by "dynamic" a fundamental realm embracing affectivity and drive. He suggests that in states of "dynamic instability," perception, volition, and the experience of ego-boundaries may be impaired. These conditions may therefore be considered as the source of first-rank symptoms and of some of Bleuler's basic symptoms. As, according to Janzarik, dynamic instability may appear in abnormal conditions of various origins—frequently, for instance, in rapidly changing manic-depressive mixed states—the differential-diagnostic value of the above-mentioned symptoms is questioned.

The Viennese research criteria for functional psychosis are based on the following hypotheses:

1. The basic disturbances of schizophrenic illness consist of formal thought disorder, as revealed through speech and affective blunting. Such disturbances are also seen in organic illnesses of somatic or toxic origin, but do not occur in affective or psychogenic disorders.

2. Some of Bleuler's basic symptoms (ambivalence, depersonalization, derealization) and Schneider's first-rank symptoms are an expression of dynamic instability, a condition devoid of nosological specificity. These symptoms can therefore not be used to distinguish between schizophrenia and other psychotic disorders.

3. Affective disorders are expressed not only by typical manic and depressive states but also by states of hostile tension (dysphoria) and often by rapidly alternating mixed states. The characteristic symptoms of all of these thymopsychic disorders have consequently been included in the diagnostic criteria for affective disorders. Here the presence of biorhythmic disturbances is obligatory.

The axial syndromes for functional psychoses contain only symptomological criteria, and no mutually excluding elements. Should a patient present a semiology suggesting both cyclothymia and schizophrenia, it would be concluded—semiologically, not nosologically speaking—that he was suffering from a schizoaffective disorder. It is hypothetically assumed that disturbances of purely psychogenic origin do not present symptoms pertaining to the affective (cyclothymic) or schizophrenic axial syndromes. Hence, no excluding criteria have been established for such disturbances. In order to present the Viennese concept, its diagnostic criteria for schizophrenia are listed in Annex 3.

DSM-III and the Definition of Schizophrenia According to Bleuler, Schneider, and the Viennese Criteria: An Empirical Comparison

In a research project on the classification and course of the functional psychoses carried out at the Psychiatric Clinic of the University of Vienna since 1978 (by Berner, Gabriel, Katschnig, Küfferle, and Lenz), several diagnostic systems have been applied simultaneously in diagnosing 200 psychiatric inpatients admitted for the first time with a diagnosis of a functional psychosis. DSM-III was among the eight diagnostic formulations of schizophrenia used in a "polydiagnostic approach," first developed by Katschnig and co-workers* in a research project on the classification of depression (2,3). The simultaneous assignment of patients to diagnostic classes according to both DSM-III and formulations used in German-speaking countries—Bleuler's definition of schizophrenia, Schneider's first-rank symptoms, and the Viennese criteria (endogenomorphic-schizophrenic axial syndrome by Berner [11] see also Berner et al. [10])—provided the possibility of analyzing the relationships between DSM-III and typical German diagnostic formulations.

A first comparison (see figure 1) reveals that Schneider's first-rank symptoms pick up the greatest number of schizophrenic patients, and that the difference between the widest definition and the narrowest (three of Bleuler's four "A"s) is more than fivefold. Defining schizophrenia by the presence of at least one of the six basic symptoms of Bleuler (12) (see also Berner et al. [1]. Appendix 2) also allocates a large number of patients (91) to the category of schizophrenia. In contrast, DSM-III schizophrenia appears to be a rather narrow concept, with 49 patients receiving this diagnosis. If the time limit of 6 months is disregarded, i.e., if DSM-III schizophreniform disorders are included, the concept is broadened, and includes 80 patients. On the other hand, if Bleuler's diagnosis of schizophrenia is restricted to the presence of at least 2, or even 3, of the famous 4 "A"s (13,14), only 53 and 22,

---

*Katschnig H, Brandl-Nebehay A, Fuchs-Robetin G, Seelig P, Eichberger G, Strobl R, Sint PP: Lebensverändernde Ereignisse, Psychosoziale Dispositionen und Depressive Verstimmungszustände. Ein Beitrag zur Frage der Entstehung und der Klassifikation der Depression. Research Report, Psychiatric Clinic, University of Vienna, 1981

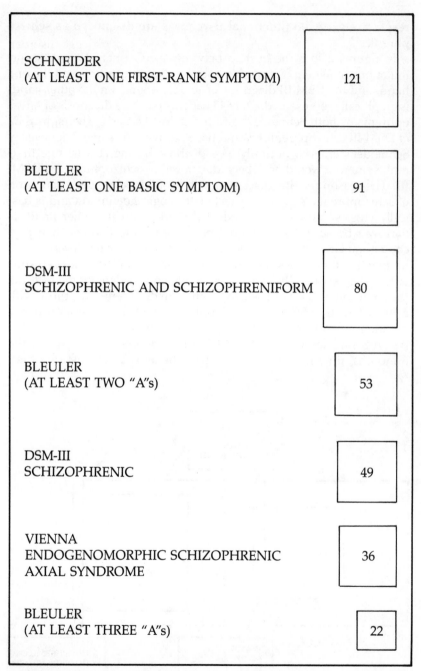

FIGURE 1. Number of Patients Diagnosed as Schizophrenic According to 7 Different Diagnostic Formulations among 200 First Admissions for Functional Psychosis to 2 Mental Hospitals in Vienna

respectively, of 200 functional psychoses are diagnosed as schizophrenic.

In figures 2 to 5 the overlap between the German diagnostic formulations of Bleuler, Schneider, and the Viennese criteria, on the one hand, and the DSM-III diagnosis of schizophrenia, on the other hand, is graphically represented. Only 43 patients receive a diagnosis of schizophrenia by both Schneider's and the DSM-III criteria. Therefore, 88% of DSM-III schizophrenics would have received the same diagnosis by Schneider's criteria, but only 36% of those having at least one first-rank symptom would have been diagnosed as schizophrenic by DSM-III. The reason for this discrepancy is twofold: Schneider's definition of schizophrenia is a purely psychopathological definition and is basically cross-sectional. The DSM-III definition, on the other hand, is narrower because it requires the presence of criteria other than psychopathological ones (e.g., "deterioration from a previous level of functioning") and excludes patients with a duration of the illness episode of less than six months. This is proven to some extent by the fact that the inclusion of "DSM-III schizophreniform disorders" (i.e., those with a full DSM-III definition of schizophrenia with the exception of the duration criterion of 6 months) produces a much greater overlap between Schneider and DSM-III: 60.3% (as opposed to only 36% if the 6 months' time limit is used) of the patients with at least one first-

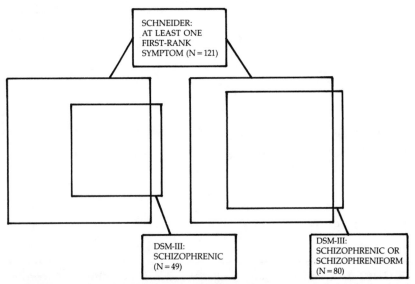

FIGURE 2. Overlap between DSM-III Concept of Schizophrenic/ Schizophreniform Disorders and Schneider's Concept

rank symptom receive either a "schizophreniform" or a "schizophrenic" diagnosis according to DSM-III.

Defining schizophrenia by the presence of at least one of the six basic symptoms of Bleuler yields a rather large group of 91 schizophrenic patients (see figure 3). Only 45% of them would also receive a DSM-III diagnosis of schizophrenia. The same reasons for this discrepancy probably apply here as in the DSM-III–Schneider comparison. If, however, the narrowest of Bleulerian definitions proposed in the literature (13, 14) is used, the picture is the reverse: only 22 of our 200 patients meet the criteria of at least 3 "A"s, and only 34, 7% of DSM-III schizophrenics would also conform to the narrow Bleulerian diagnostic formulation. If the time criterion of 6 months is dropped, 21 of 22 "narrow" Bleulerian cases would also be diagnosed as "schizophrenic" or "schizophreniform" by DSM-III standards. As the DSM-III definition more or less explicitly contains five of the six basic symptoms of Bleuler, this is quite understandable.

Using the rather narrow definition of the Viennese criteria (11. Appendix 3) yields 36 cases of schizophrenia, which are all included in the DSM-III formulation if the criterion of 6 months' duration is disregarded (figure 5). As thought disorders are the basic, necessary condition for a diagnosis of schizophrenia according to the Viennese criteria, and as they are also included in the DSM-III definition (al-

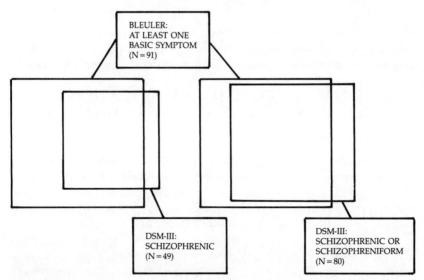

FIGURE 3. Overlap between DSM-III Concept of Schizophrenic/Schizophreniform Disorders and Bleuler's Concept (at Least One "Basic Symptom")

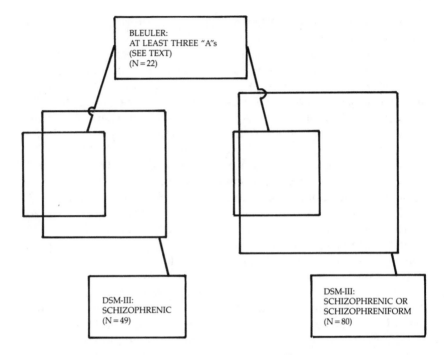

FIGURE 4. Overlap between DSM-III Concept of Schizophrenic/ Schizophreniform Disorders and Bleuler's Concept (at Least Three of the Four "A"s)

though they are regarded as important in DSM-III only if they occur together with other symptoms), this situation is not very astonishing.

THE USE OF DIAGNOSTIC CLASSIFICATION SYSTEMS IN GERMAN-SPEAKING COUNTRIES

Historical Overview

Systematic use of a diagnostic classification system has existed in Germany since 1930, when Wilmanns introduced the so-called diagnostic system of Würzburg (Würzburger Diagnosenschema). This system has been in use until very recently, having been slowly superseded by the International Classification of Diseases (ICD).

In the mid-1960s the Würzburg system came to be gradually regarded as less useful, because two-thirds of the diagnostic categories were concerned with organic brain disorders and because the categories of the system were mutually exclusive. The German Society of Psychiatry and Neurology therefore established a commission for classification and diagnosis in order to draw up a proposal for a new and modern

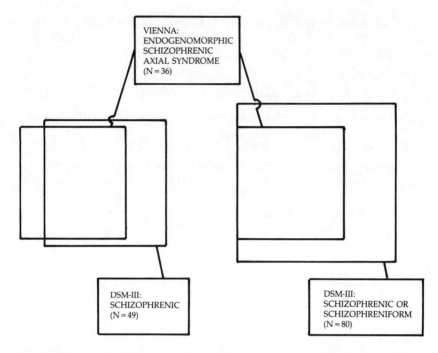

FIGURE 5. Overlap between DSM-III Concept of Schizophrenic/ Schizophreniform Disorders and the Viennese Criteria

diagnostic system. Following an earlier attempt at revising the Würzburg system by Häfner and Kisker (15), a proposal for a new system was published in 1966 by Helmchen, Hippius, and Meyer (16). The authors stressed the possibility and necessity of using the diagnostic categories they proposed not in the sense of disease entities, but in the sense of syndromes, thus enabling the diagnosing psychiatrist to use several categories simultaneously.

This early paper presents a clear multiaxial orientation, considered as providing a significant contribution to the revision of the seventh edition of the International Classification of Diseases. However, as the German Society for Psychiatry and Neurology could not provide any empirical data comparing their system with the ICD, these ideas were not taken into consideration for the eighth edition of the ICD, which was published in 1967. The German Society for Psychiatry and Neurology more or less reluctantly then recommended the general use of ICD-8 in German psychiatric institutions. ICD-8 was published together with this recommendation in the most prominent German psychiatric professional journal, *Der Nervenarzt*, in January 1970 (17.). ICD-8 was also published in book form (18), along with the international glossary. Since then, ICD-8 has been introduced into most psychiatric institutions in German-speaking countries, most of which subsequently changed to ICD-9, published in 1980 (19).

A Questionnaire Survey among Inpatient Institutions in Austria, the FRG, the GDR, and Switzerland

In a questionnaire survey conducted in preparation for this article, of 257 questionnaires sent out to psychiatric hospitals and psychiatric units in general hospitals in Austria, the Federal Republic of Germany, the German Democratic Republic, and Switzerland, 176, i.e., 68.5%, were returned (table 1). Eighty-five percent of the respondents reported that they were currently using ICD-9. The actual figures for each country are presented in table 2.

As far as DSM-III was concerned, only 9 of the 176 institutions returning the questionnaire reported that they were currently using,

TABLE 1. Number of Questionnaires Sent Out and Returned

Country	Number of Questionnaires Sent Out	Number of Questionnaires Returned
Austria	17	13 = 76%
Federal Republic of Germany	161	129 = 80.1%
German Democratic Republic	53	12 = 22.6%
Switzerland	25	22 = 88%
Total	257	176 = 68.5%

TABLE 2. Use of ICD in German-Speaking Countries

Country	Reported Use of ICD	% of All Questionnaires Sent Out	Returned
Austria	13	76.5	100
Federal Republic of Germany	109	67.7	84.5
German Democratic Republic	7	13.2	58.3
Switzerland	21	84	95.5
Total	150	58.4	85.2

or had already used, DSM-III (table 3). In the German Democratic Republic, not a single user was identified. In the Federal Republic of Germany, 7 of 129 respondents indicated that they were using DSM-III, mostly for research purposes. In Switzerland a single institution of the 22 sending back the questionnaire indicated limited use of DSM-III for research purposes. In Austria, apart from the authors of this article, no one was using DSM-III.

We provided the possibility for making comments in the questionnaire. The general attitude among the respondents who knew about DSM-III seemed to be slightly critical. The main argument against its introduction as a general diagnostic system was that, now that the International Classification of Diseases had been officially introduced, with great effort, and had even recently been changed from the eighth to the ninth edition, the introduction of a new diagnostic system would only create confusion. In some comments this state of affairs was regretted, as the respondents valued the multiaxiality of DSM-III. Some said that DSM-III was too complicated for routine purposes.

STRENGTHS AND WEAKNESSES OF DSM-III

Since the German translation of DSM-III had not yet appeared when we prepared this contribution, our evaluation of its strengths and weaknesses, based not on practical experience, but on our own research, must be limited to theoretical considerations. DSM-III presents an advantage over ICD-9 in that it strives toward operational definitions and thus increased reliability. Also, its multiaxial design seems to make it superior to the International Classification of Diseases. The main problems with DSM-III are rooted in its compromise character.

A closer look at the axes reveals several drawbacks. There is, for

TABLE 3. Use of DSM-III in German-speaking Countries

Country	Reported Use of DSM-III	% of All Questionnaires Sent Out	Returned
Austria	1	5.9	7.7
Federal Republic of Germany	7	4.4	5.4
German Democratic Republic	—	—	—
Switzerland	1	4	4.6
Total	9	3.5	5.1

example, a great imbalance with respect to the effort that seems to have been expended on making the content of the different axes operational. Axis IV (severity of psychosocial stressors) and axis V (highest level of adaptive functioning past year) are rather poorly defined in comparison with axes I and II (see below), which obviously received most of the attention of the task force working on DSM-III. It is very doubtful whether any reliable information about "severity of psychosocial stressors" can be recorded with the DSM-III instructions, given the methodological complexities of eliciting life stress (20). The same holds for "highest level of adaptive functioning." Furthermore, because of the rather vague definitions of the areas covered by axes IV and V, an overlap between them cannot be excluded.

Axis I, supposed to represent "clinical syndromes," in reality contains most of the classic psychiatric disease entities, thus blurring the distinction between a syndromatological and a nosological approach, with notable exceptions: DSM-III does not contain, for instance, a category of "neuroses," thus avoiding the confusion usually created by the different etiological connotations of this term. Apart from this, the "syndromes" of, for example, the functional psychoses contain many nonpsychopathological criteria, through which they gain a nosological status. Hence, for schizophrenia the advantages of multiaxiality cannot be made use of as the psychopathological syndrome is contaminated by time criteria—which should be on an independent axis—and by a criterion of "social functioning," for which a separate axis (V) already exists.

The efforts to provide operational definitions are hampered by the compromises made among various diagnostic schools and theories that were established for the elaboration of DSM-III and that represent several weak points in the system. Furthermore, in the view of German psychiatry, some important new developments in psychopathology, for instance, the research on rapidly changing manic-depressive mixed states (9, 21–24), have not been taken into account. This becomes especially evident when analyzing the DSM-III criteria for functional psychoses:

1. The symptomatic diagnostic criteria for schizophrenia, for instance, contain a large number of Schneider's first- and second-rank symptoms and Bleuler's basic and secondary symptoms. As only one of the symtoms enumerated under A 1–5 must be present, the reasons for the diagnostic attributions of the particular cases remain blurred, and are finally not more explicit than the mere clinical use of Bleuler's or Schneider's diagnostic methods. DSM-III tries to counterbalance this by introducing affective symptoms as excluding criteria (D), thus reversing Jaspers's hierarchical principle. The full depressive or manic syndrome, however, is required. Consequently, rapidly alternating manic-

depressive mixed states may still be erroneously attributed to schizophrenia. Certainly, the weight given to the deterioration from previous level of functioning (B) and to chronological criteria (C and E) may prevent a certain number of such errors, but cannot exclude them (as affective mixed states may very well last longer than 6 months, frequently have an onset before age 45, and show general deterioration compared with the previous level of functioning).

2. Jaspers's hierarchical rule is reversed in item D of the criteria for schizophrenia, but, on the other hand, is abandoned for the diagnosis of schizoaffective disorders. The reasons given for the maintenance of this category (comments on 295.70 and item C of the criteria for mania and major depression) do not take into account that affective disorders may lead to mood-incongruent delusions, which can—simply because of the reaction of significant others to the patient—persist beyond remission of the affective disorders. Generally speaking, German psychiatry thinks that the weight put on mood-incongruent delusions or hallucinations as excluding criteria for major affective disorders is exaggerated.

CONCLUSIONS

In our view, the main strength of DSM-III is its multiaxialty. Its main weakness is its compromise character, which counterbalances not only the efforts at standardization but also the multiaxial design itself. Although for the purposes of health statistics a worldwide common diagnostic system is desirable, we do not think that this should be accomplished at the expense of clarity and an openness to new developments. Useful as DSM-III might be for purposes of health statistics, we do not think it a diagnostic classification system to be recommended for research. This is in line with our general thinking about the use of diagnostic systems for research, which recommends the simultaneous application of several individual diagnostic systems in a given research project rather than the use of a single system. We have termed this the "polydiagnostic approach."

We have shown that such a polydiagnostic approach is feasible in psychiatric research (3, 10).* In order to promote this approach in psychiatric research, we have compiled 24 diagnostic formulations for the functional psychoses currently in use around the world (1). No single system available so far can claim superiority over the others. This is true also for DSM-III. Better a more cumbersome polydiagnostic approach than the disadvantages of a compromise!

---

*See also Katschnig et al., op. cit.

REFERENCES

1. Berner P, Gabriel E, Katschnig H, Lenz G, Koehler K, Simhandl Ch, Wallner-Damm W: Diagnostic Criteria for Schizophrenic and Affective Psychoses. Washington, DC, APA Press, 1983
2. Berner P, Katschnig H: Principles of "multiaxial" classification in psychiatry as a basis of modern methodology, in Methodology in Evaluation of Psychiatric Treatment. Edited by Helgason T. Cambridge, Cambridge University Press, 1983
3. Katschnig H, Berner P: The Poly-Diagnostic Approach in Psychiatric Research. Geneva, World Health Organization, 1983
4. Kraepelin E: Psychiatrie. Leipzig, Barth, 1899
5. Bleuler E: Dementia praecox oder Gruppe der Schizophrenien, in Handbuch der Psychiatrie. Edited by Aschaffenburg G. Leipzig and Vienna, Deuticke, 1911. Reprint: Munich, Minerva Publikations, 1978. English edition: Dementia Praecox or the Group of Schizophrenias, translated by Zinkin J. New York, International Universities Press, 1950.
6. Jaspers K: Algemeine Psychopathologie. Berlin, Springer, 1913
7. Schneider, K: Clinical Psychopathology, translated from the 3rd edition of Klinische Psychopathologie (1950) by Hamilton MW, Anderson EW. New York, Grune & Stratton, 1959
8. Berner P: Der Lebensabend der Paranoiker. Wien Z Nerv Heilk 27: 115–161, 1969
9. Janzarik W: Dynamische Grundkonstellationen von endogenen Psychosen. Monographie aus dem Gesamtgebiet der Neurologie und Psychiatrie. Berlin–Göttingen–Heidelberg, Springer, 1959
10. Berner P, Katschnig H, Lenz G: The poly-diagnostic approach: A method to clarify incongruences between different classification systems of the functional psychoses. Psychiatric Journal of the University of Ottawa, 1982
11. Berner P: Psychiatrische Systematik. Berne, Huber, 1977, 1982
12. Bleuler E: Lehrbuch der Psychiatrie, 9th ed. Berlin– Göttingen, Springer, 1955
13. Landmark I: A manual for the assessment of schizophrenia. Acta Psychiatr Scand 65, Supplement 298, 1982
14. Bleuler M: Schizophrenia, in The Schizophrenic Syndrome, edited by Cancro R. London, Butterworth, 1971
15. Häfner H, Kisker KP: Ein psychiatrisch-klinisches Diagnosenschema (Revision des Würzburger Schemas). Nervenarzt 35: 34–38, 1964
16. Helmchen H, Hippius H, Meyer JE: Ein neues psychiatrisches Diagnosenschema. Nervenarzt 37: 115–118, 1966
17. Deutsche Gesellschaft für Psychiatrie und Nervenheilkunde: Mitteilungen der Kommission für Klassifikation und Diagnosenschema. Nervenarzt 41: 50–52, 1970
18. Degkwitz R, Helmchen H, Kockott G, Mombour W: Diagnosenschlüssel und Glossar psychiatrischer Krankheiten. Deutsche Ausgabe der internationalen Klassifikation der Krankheiten der WHO: ICD, 8. Revision, und des internationalen Glossars. Berlin–Heidelberg–New York, Springer, 1971
19. Degwitz R, Helmchen G, Kockott G, Mombour W: Diagnosenschlüssel und Glossar psychiatrischer Krankheiten. Deutsche Ausgabe der internationalen Klassifikation der Krankheiten der WHO: ICD, 9. Revision, Kapitel V. Berlin–Heidelberg–New York, Springer, 1980

20. Katsching H (ed): Life Events and Psychiatric Disorders—Controversial Issues. Cambridge, Cambridge University Press (in press)
21. Mentzos S: Mischzustände und mischbildhafte phasische Psychosen. Stuttgart, Enke, 1967
22. Carlson GA, Goodwin FK: The stages of mania. A longitudinal analysis of the manic episode. Arch Gen Psychiatry 28: 221–223, 1973
23. Nunn CMH: Mixed affective states and the natural history of manic-depressive psychosis. Br J Psychiatry 134: 153–160, 1979
24. Berner P: Unter welchen Bedingungen lassen weitere Verlaufsforschungen noch neue Erkenntnisse über die endogenen Psychosen erwarten? Psychiatr Clin (Basel) 15: 97–123, 1982

Annex 1

BLEULER'S CRITERIA FOR DIAGNOSING SCHIZOPHRENIA

Basic or Fundamental Disturbances

Formal thought disorders
Disturbances of affect
Disturbances of the subjective experience of the self
Disturbances of volition and behavior
Ambivalence
Autism

Annex 2

KURT SCHNEIDER'S CRITERIA FOR DIAGNOSING SCHIZOPHRENIA

First-Rank Symptoms

Audible thoughts (*Gedankenlautwerden*)
Voices arguing and/or discussing
Voices commenting
Somatic passivity experiences
Thought withdrawal, thought insertion, and other experiences of influenced thought
Thought broadcasting
Delusional perceptions
All other experiences involving imposed volition, imposed affect, and imposed impulses

Annex 3

VIENNESE CRITERIA FOR DIAGNOSING SCHIZOPHRENIA

Endogenomorphic—Schizophrenic Axial Syndrome

A **Incoherence** without marked pressure of speech, marked retardation of thinking, or marked autonomous anxiety
(at least one of the following symptoms required)

 1 Blocking
Sudden cessation in the train of thought; after a gap the previous thought may be taken up again (*a*) or may be replaced by a different thought (*b*)

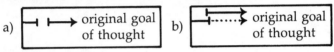

 2 Derailment
Gradual (*a*) or sudden (*b*) deviation from the train of thought without gap

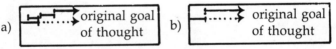

 3 Pathologically "Muddled" Speech
Fluent speech, for the most part syntactically correct, but the elements of different thoughts (which, for the patient, may belong to a common idea) get muddled together

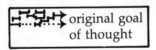

B **Cryptic Neologisms**
(the patient does not explain their private meaning)

C **Affective Blunting**
(without evidence of marked depression, tiredness, or drug effect)

This term includes flatness of affect, emotional indifference, and apathy. Essentially, the symptom involves a diminution of emotional response.

> Definitive : A and/or B present
> Probable : Only C present

8

THE USE OF DSM-III IN BELGIUM

Paul Cosyns, M.D., Marc Ansseau, and
Daniel P. Bobon, M.D., Ph.D.

Belgium, a country of approximately 10 million inhabitants, can usefully be divided, for the study of psychiatric practices and trends, into two main areas: the Dutch-speaking northern part, which is sensitive to Anglo-Saxon and Dutch influences, and the French-speaking southern part, where the French influence predominates. Both areas have been influenced by German psychiatry. In the small but independent Grand Duchy of Luxembourg, both French and German influences prevail; this area will be considered in conjunction with the French-speaking southern part of Belgium.

In this latter part of the country, diagnostic concepts of classic French psychiatry have always held sway. The textbook by Ey, Bernard, and Brisset (1) and the dictionary edited by Porot (2) are the main reference books. The Dutch-speaking area refers to the classic works by Mayer-

Address correspondence to: Paul Cosyns, M.D., Universitair Psychiatrisch Centrum St. Jozef, Leuvensesteenweg 517, B-3070 Kortenberg, Belgium

The authors wish to thank the participants in the round-table discussion held in Brussels on 22 October 1982 on DSM-III: R. de Buck and J. P. de Vigne (Hôpital Brugmann, Université Libre de Bruxelles); H. d'Haenen (Service de Psychiatrie, Vrije Universiteit Brussel); P. Linkowski (Hôpital Erasme, Université Libre de Bruxelles); Ch. Pull (Service de Psychiatrie, Centre Hôpitalier de Luxembourg); M. Servaes (Academisch Ziekenhuis, Universitaire Instelling Antwerpen); M. van Moffaert (Academisch Ziekenhuis, Rijks Universiteit Gent). The views expressed in this paper are, however, those of the authors.

The authors also wish to thank Mrs. Malbrecq and Mrs. Cazier for secretarial assistance and Mr. M. P. Harvey for helping with the translation.

127

Gross, Slater, and Roth (3) and Kaplan, Freedman, and Sadock (4) and to Dutch and German authors of a more phenomenological approach. Some members of the profession still adhere to a psychoanalytic viewpoint, but this tendency is more dominant in the southern, French-speaking area.

In view of these professional and cultural differences, it is understandable that the use of DSM-III has spread more readily in the northern part of Belgium, and is still used very little in the French-speaking area.

In clinical and, above all, biological research, the Research Diagnostic Criteria (5) are frequently employed in the selection of homogeneous samples of mental patients. DSM-III has been introduced too recently to be applied for research purposes. The ninth revision of the International Classification of Diseases (ICD-9) is the officially recognized nosological system for medical problems, including mental disorders; and traditional French psychopathological concepts are quite common therein (6).

Other clinical investigation systems, such as that of the French Institut National de la Santé et de la Recherche Médicale (INSERM) (7) and the Present State Examination and Catego systems (8), are used by a minority. With regard to syndromes, the Association for the Study of Methodology and Documentation in Psychiatry (Arbeitsgemeinshaft für Methodik und Documentation in der Psychiatrie—AMDP) scale (9, 10), of German origin, has developed considerably in the last few years. Quite recently, two Integrated Lists of Taxonomic Evaluation Criteria (Liste Intégrée des Critères d'Evaluation Taxonomique—LICET) rating scales have been developed by Pull (11) for classifying patients according to several systems, including DSM-III.

PROFESSIONAL REACTIONS TO DSM-III

To determine the reactions of Belgian psychiatrists to DSM-III, we interviewed several psychiatrists who are using this classification and organized a round-table discussion on the topic with specialists from various Belgian universities and from Luxembourg (see the acknowledgments). The present contribution is based on the information thus obtained. Owing the above-mentioned cultural characteristics of Belgium, we shall consider the two areas of the country separately.

Dutch-speaking Belgium

In the Dutch-speaking area, DSM-III has been generally well accepted. Two universities of a total of four are including it as part of their academic program, mainly at the postgraduate level. Psychiatrists working in the leading nonacademic psychiatric hospitals have also displayed interest in DSM-III and have broached the possibility of switching from ICD-9 to DSM-III for the registration of medical data. They have been attracted to DSM-III by its principal strength, namely, a model diagnosis based on defined operational criteria, which allows psychiatry to emerge from a traditional semantic vagueness in which though everyone may use the same nosological terms, they have different meanings according to the particular school or culture. DSM-III's diagnostic approach is revolutionary in psychiatry, and such a sharply differentiated reference tool does not exist in any other medical discipline. This standardization of diagnosis should improve communication among psychiatrists, create a common system of reference among various psychiatric centers, and permit more accurate statistical analysis of information.

We know of 26 hospital psychiatric departments that, at least in 1983, intend to use DSM-III for the registration of their patients. This represents more than 70% of the psychiatric beds in the northern area of Belgium. Computer compilation of DSM-III diagnostic data for affiliated centers can be done by the central administrative service (Administratie Centrum Caritas, Heverlee, Belgium), which can provide logistic and educational support. Spitzer and Williams visited Belgium in 1981 to train psychiatrists in the use of DSM-III, and the central service has also organized a training program for affiliated hospitals intending to use the new system.

Translation of the "Mini D" into Dutch has greatly helped spread the use of DSM-III for the diagnosis of inpatients in clinics (12). It is not yet much in use in private practice or for outpatients. General practitioners and specialists in other branches of medicine are not familiar with the new concepts, and sometimes not with the new terminology, so psychiatrists prefer to use traditional diagnostic descriptions in communicating with them.

French-speaking Belgium

Some basic DSM-III diagnostic concepts are far removed from the French nosological way of thinking; the DSM system introduces a completely different approach to psychiatric diagnosis, which meets considerable resistance in the French-speaking part of Belgium. Though a French translation of DSM-III, done under the supervision of P. Pichot (Paris), is expected to be available in 1983, this will not guarantee in-depth understanding of DSM concepts. ICD-9 is more compatible with the French way of conceptualizing mental disorders.

Bobon (6) has pointed out some of the incompatibilities between the two systems, among them the following:

1. Several ICD codes are not included in DSM-III. For example, of seven reactional psychoses, four are absent from DSM-III, including

reactive mania and reactive psychotic depression; unipolar mania is subsumed within bipolar disorder; neurasthenia is subsumed by dysthmic disorder.

2. Some categories use the same code in the two classifications, but refer to different morbid entities. For example, DSM-III speaks of "dysthymic disorder" or "depressive neurosis," not of "neurotic depression," and defines it, among others, as "a chronic [two years' duration] disturbance of mood . . . not of sufficient severity and duration to meet the criteria for a major depressive episode . . . ." This seems to imply that there is only a quantitative, not a qualitative, difference between an endogenous and a neurotic depression.

3. The same disorders are described by four-figure codes of which the fourth digit is not always compatible with ICD-9. For instance, bipolar depression is 296.3 in ICD-9 and 296.5 in DSM-III.

EXPERIENCE AND EVALUATION OF DSM-III

General Criticisms

All diagnostic systems, whatever their nature, have, apart from their advantages or even their necessity, inherent dangers, of which the least is freezing clinical reality behind fixed labels. The undeniable strength of DSM-III compared with other systems lies in its presenting defined operational diagnostic criteria, but the improvement in the interrater reliability has possibly resulted in decreased validity of certain DSM concepts.

Being descriptive and supposedly atheoretical, DSM-III should not replace existing psychiatric knowledge. There is a real danger that new generations of physicians or psychiatrists will think only in terms of DSM-III diagnoses. Mere knowledge of DSM's diagnostic criteria can give the illusion of a thorough knowledge of psychopathology. The same applies to other professional groups, such as lawyers, who are also interested in DSM-III as it relates to criminology: lawyers and others involved in legal proceedings may now, through knowledge of DSM-III criteria, think they have acquired an understanding of psychopathology.

When etiopathogenic criteria are taken into account, some DSM-III diagnoses present difficulties. For example, although the clinical picture can be exactly the same, a major depressive episode can be assigned to different categories depending on whether its etiology is somatic (organic affective syndrome) or not (affective disorder).

DSM-III reflects, in certain aspects, American culture and the habits of American physicians. In Belgium, physicians give much more importance to family psychiatric history, to environmental influences, and to the patient's social and cultural background. These are practically ignored in DSM-III, which remains firmly centered on observable symptoms during an interview.

To an outside observer, DSM-III, with its lists of standard criteria, which should be understood by psychiatrists of all origins, can seem simplistic. Those who use it stress, on the other hand, its enriching nature in the elaboration of a diagnosis. DSM-III forces one to check systematically an important number of symptoms. This invites the psychiatrist to ask new questions, or to envisage new alternatives. But it can be difficult to have to choose between the presence or absence of a criterion when, as is often the case, an intermediary level is met in clinical reality. Also, the list of diagnostic criteria sometimes lacks distinctness, and it is obvious that all of the individual criteria do not have the same clinical relevance.

The Multiaxial System

The multiaxial system obviously seem advantageous compared with other nosological systems. In practice, however, axes I and II are often the only ones used. In emergency cases or in ambulatory consultations, the diagnosis is generally limited to axis I because of lack of time and of information to complete the other axes. Certain participants in our round-table discussion found axes IV and V too unsophisticated compared with the complexity of axes I and II, whereas others regretted the absence of axes relating to therapeutic aspects or psychodynamic concepts.

The axis location of some diagnostic categories is controversial. For example, cyclothymic disorder and dysthymic disorder are put on axis I, as clinical syndromes, when they could just as well have been put on axis II, personality disorders. The elaboration of a decision tree for axis II would be useful.

Problematic Diagnostic Categories

Several psychiatric concepts used in Belgium present difficulties in terms of DSM-III classification. Here are some examples:

1. "Paraphrenia" (characterized by a very prolific imaginative delusional state but good adaptation to daily reality) and "chronic hallucinatory psychosis" (persistent hallucinatory activity with delusional moods, but without the development of a deficit state) must be classified as paranoid schizophrenia.

2. "Bouffée délirante," a transitory delusional state, might be included under "schizophreniform disorder," "atypical psychosis," "acute paranoid disorder," or "brief reactive psychosis."

3. Neurotic depression, a classic French concept assuming a pathological personality, has a completely different meaning from dysthymic disorder.

4. Involutional melancholia has lost its specificity, and is included in unipolar major depression.

Moreover, some DSM-III diagnostic categories present difficulties. Two examples are the antisocial personality, inappropriately restricted to law-breaking behavior, and paranoid disorders, restricted to persistent delusions of persecution or delusional jealousy, which excludes erotomaniac delusions, among others.

CONCLUSION

French-speaking psychiatrists are much more resistant to DSM-III than the Dutch-speaking ones, who practice mainly in northern Belgium, where the new system has spread rapidly. Even those who use DSM-III will require another year before they will be able to judge whether the strengths and promises of the new system meet expectations.

We share the hope of Dongier and Lehmann (13) that in a few years DSM-IV and ICD-10 will merge in the adoption of diagnostic criteria that will show improvements over those of DSM-III.

REFERENCES

1. Ey M, Bernard P, Brisset Ch: Manuel de psychiatrie. Paris, Masson, 1978
2. Porot A (ed): Manuel alphabétique de psychiatrie, 5th ed. Paris, Presses Universitaires de France, 1975
3. Mayer-Gross W, Slater E, Roth M: Clinical Psychiatry. London, Baillère, Tindall & Cassel, 1969
4. Kaplan HI, Freedman AM, Sadock BJ: Comprehensive Textbook of Psychiatry. Baltimore, Williams & Wilkins, 1980
5. Spitzer RL, Endicott J, Robins E: Research diagnostic criteria. Arch Gen Psychiatry 35: 773–783, 1978
6. Bobon DP: Description et comparaison de la révision de deux classifications des maladies mentales: la CIM-9 (ICD-9) et le DSM-III. Acta Psychiatr Belg 80: 846–863, 1980
7. Institut National de la Santé et de la Recherche Médicale (INSERM). Section Psychiatrie: Classification française des troubles mentaux. Paris (1968). Bulletin de l'Institut National de la Santé et de la Recherche Médicale, 24: Supplement to No. 2, 1969
8. Wing JK, Cooper JE, Sartorius N: Guide pour un examen psychiatrique. Translated by Timset-Berthier M, Bragard-Ledent A. Bruxelles-Liège, Mardaga, 1980
9. Bobon DP (ed): Le système AMDP, 2nd ed. Bruxelles-Liège, Mardaga, 1981
10. Guy W, Ban TA: The AMDP System. Berlin, Heidelberg, New York, Springer, 1982
11. Pull CB, Pull MC, Pichot P: LICET-5, une liste intégrée de critères d'éval-

uation taxonomique pour les psychoses non affectives. J Psychiat Biol Therap 1:33–37, 1981

12. Beknopte Handleiding bij de Diagnostische Criteria van de DSM-III. Swets en Zeitlinger, BV Lisse, 1982
13. Dongier H, Lehmann H: Nouveaux systèmes de classification diagnostique: DSM-III et ICD-9, in Encylopédie médico-chirurgicale. Psychiatrie. Paris, Editions Techniques, 1982, p. 37065 A10

9

DSM-III IN CANADA: THE VIEWPOINT OF ACADEMIC PSYCHIATRISTS

Mary-Louise Engels, M.A., A. Missagh Ghadirian, M.D., and Maurice Dongier, M.D.

> Physicians think that they do a lot for a patient when they give his disease a name.
>
> Immanuel Kant

Canadian psychiatry, although markedly influenced by U.S. psychiatry, likes to view itself as maintaining some degree of autonomy, both conceptually and in practice. Its links with European psychiatry, particularly British and French, may be at times significant enough to counterbalance the American connection. For instance, most psychiatric department chairmen of the 16 Canadian medical schools are European trained, certainly a much higher proportion than in the United States. In addition, psychiatrists immigrating to Canada from all parts of the world are less subject to the pressures of the "melting pot" than are those moving to the United States. The existence of such countervailing influences on the Canadian scene could logically lead to differences in diagnostic habits and in the selection of diagnostic tools for teaching and research. It may not be a chance observation that the few papers published by Canadian authors about DSM-III, and expressing some reservations about it, have come from European-trained academics (1–4).

In practice, most Canadian provinces have approved the ninth edition

Address correspondence to: Maurice Dongier, M.D., Professor and Chairman, Department of Psychiatry, McGill University, 1033 Pine Avenue West, Montreal, Quebec, H3A 1A1, Canada of the International Classification of Diseases (ICD-9) as their official classification, and statistical data must be provided accordingly.* The Canadian Psychiatric Association has made no official endorsement;† the Royal College of Physicians and Surgeons, which grants specialists' certificates and oversees postgraduate training, recommends that candidates be trained in the use of DSM-III and ICD-9. DSM-III has made its appearance in the most recent Canadian textbooks of psychiatry (5, 6), both of which are in French. The first of these provides a French translation of the DSM-III classification system in outline form; the second also summarizes the major principles behind the new system and the advantages of the multiaxial approach.

All this being said, what has been the impact of DSM-III on Canadian academic psychiatrists? In order to explore this question, we carried out a survey, during 1982, on the occasion of two meetings: the American Psychiatric Association meeting in Toronto in May, and the Canadian Psychiatric Association meeting in Montreal in September.

METHOD

Eighty academic psychiatrists from universities across Canada‡ contributed to our survey by means of semistructured interviews and/ or a written questionnaire. Interviews were carried out with numbers of faculty in approximate proportion to the number of trainees in each of the universities. No notable geographic or linguistic (English versus French) differences were apparent within the sample.

The following questions were asked:

1. Are you involved in teaching: medical students? psychiatric residents?
2. Do you use DSM-III in: undergraduate teaching? postgraduate teaching? clinical research?

---

*Manitoba and Alberta use the Clinical Modification of ICD-9 (ICD-9-CM).
†RW Junek: The DSM-III in Canada: A survey report to the Scientific Council of the Canadian Psychiatric Association (unpublished). See also the chapter in the present book.
‡We had access to teachers at the 16 Canadian medical schools: University of British Columbia (Vancouver); University of Calgary; University of Alberta (Edmonton); University of Saskatchewan (Saskatoon); University of Manitoba (Winnipeg); University of Western Ontario (London); McMaster University (Hamilton); University of Toronto; Queen's University (Kingston); University of Ottawa; Université de Montréal; McGill University (Montreal); Université de Sherbrooke; Université Laval (Québec); Dalhousie University (Halifax); Memorial University (St. John's, Newfoundland).

3. Which DSM-III axes are regularly used:

		UG	PG	CR
Clinical syndromes	I			
Personality disorders	II			
Physical disorders	III			
Psychosocial stressors	IV			
Adaptive functioning	V			

UG = undergraduate teaching; PG = postgraduate teaching; CR = clinical research.

4. What are the most improved diagnostic categories in DSM-III?
5. What are the diagnostic categories most in need of improvement?
6. What reservations would you have about the use of DSM-III?
7. More detailed comments?

Whenever feasible (in 47% of our sample), we personally interviewed psychiatrists known to us as highly involved in teaching and/or research, weaving the inquiry around the questions formulated above. By this means we aimed to elicit more lively and detailed replies and to obviate some of the well-known limitations of the questionnaire method. Respondents who were not interviewed completed and returned the questionnaires during the conferences, or subsequently by mail.

RESULTS

Present Use of DSM-III in Teaching and Research

Information from 73 respondents was recorded regarding their current use of DSM-III. Of this number, 53 were engaged in undergraduate teaching, 63 in postgraduate teaching, and 39 in clinical research.

As indicated by table 1, DSM-III has crossed the border, and is employed, by an overwhelming majority of the teachers and researchers sampled, as a tool for the identification of clinical mental syndromes (axis I). Use of axis II, personality disorders, is also widespread. To

TABLE 1. Percent of Respondents Using DSM-III Axes Regularly in Teaching and Research

	Under-graduate	Post-graduate	Research
Axis I. Clinical syndromes	91	97	97
Axis II. Personality disorders	70	78	61
Axis III. Physical disorders	53	56	41
Axis IV. Psychosocial stressors	36	48	5
Axis V. Adaptive functioning	38	41	26

date, researchers appear least captivated by axes IV and V. As might be expected, fullest utilization of all five axes occurs in the postgraduate training of residents; but even at the undergraduate level, considerable use is made of the complete multiaxial system.

What Are the Most Improved Diagnostic Categories in DSM-III?

For the most part, judgments concerning the most improved diagnostic categories (table 2) were recorded without comment. A few elaborations were provided, however. For example, a number of respondents listed personality disorders as both "most improved" and "most in need of improvement," suggesting that certain of these categories met with more approval than others. Antisocial and borderline personality disorders were both singled out as improved subtypes. Among the organic mental disorders, dementias in the senium and presenium and the dementia/delirium/amnestic syndromes were considered clarified in DSM-III. Investigators mentioned the excellence of the section on anxiety disorders for research purposes; and the description of phobias, in particular, was said to be an advance. Attention deficit disorders and developmental disorders of childhood were specified as "most improved" among the childhood disorders.

What Are the Diagnostic Categories Most in Need of Improvement?

In contrast to the terse responses regarding the most improved categories, those related to the respondents' dissatisfactions (table 3) included some lively elaboration. Critics of the classification of personality disorders made the following points: These categories are neither well described, mutually exclusive, nor practically useful. They lack the requisite phenomenological description, psychodynamic component, and research support. "Borderline," in particular, was judged to

TABLE 2. Most Improved Diagnostic Categories (Recorded as Percent of 127 Responses)

Affective disorders	31
Schizophrenic disorders	22
Personality disorders	15
Organic mental disorders	10
Anxiety disorders	8
Disorders of infancy, childhood, and adolescence	3
Other (somatoform, paranoid, psychosexual, neurosis, substance use, factitious)	11

TABLE 3. Diagnostic Categories Most in Need of Improvement
(Percent of 100 Responses)

Personality disorders (total)		39
Subtype unspecified	30	
Borderline	9	
Disorders formerly classified as "neurosis" (total)		28
Neurosis (subtype unspecified)	7	
Dysthymic Disorder	7	
Somatoform disorder		
Subtype unspecified	5	
Hysteria/Briquet's syndrome	4	
Anxiety disorder	5	
Schizophrenia (total)		12
Subtype unspecified	6	
Schizoaffective	4	
Schizophreniform	2	
Disorders of infancy, childhood, and adolescence (total)		6
Subtype unspecified	4	
Conduct disorder	2	
Affective		5
Organic mental disorders		5
Other (psychosexual, paranoia, eating disorders, mixed)		5

be poorly defined, overly complex, not validated, and psychody-namically vacuous.

A second major set of disagreements pertained, predictably, to the "dismantling of the neuroses," which a number of respondents characterized as premature and highly controversial. "Dysthymic disorder" was considered a confusing, heterogeneous category, and an inadequate replacement for "neurotic depression" and/or "depressive personality." The abandonment of the exogenous/endogenous, neurotic/psychotic polarities in the classification of depression was not readily accepted by some psychiatrists. Despite the problematic nature of these dichotomies, they were felt to point to a clinically important distinction that is now most inadequately represented in DSM-III. Lack of enthusiasm was also evinced for the fractionation of "hysteria" into syndromes without apparent link with each other, especially for the new "conversion disorder" (hysterical neurosis, conversion type/Briquet's syndrome) among the somatoform disorders. DSM-III's approach to these disorders has been analyzed in two recent Canadian publications (3, 4). These works note particularly the gratuitous departure of DSM-III from its atheoretical stance in implying psychological causation for conversion disorder without consideration of possible organic factors in its etiology.

Schizophreniform disorder, a broadly used concept, particularly in Scandinavia and in France (acute delusional psychosis; *la bouffée délirante*), obviously lacks clearly established diagnostic criteria. Several respondents found it arbitrary and unpleasant to rely solely on the duration criterion for differentiating it from schizophrenia.

DSM-III's concept of paranoid disorders was faulted for its almost total neglect of the European literature on the subject. Munro (2) has proposed a "paranoid spectrum" classification, which might facilitate the understanding, diagnosis, and treatment of paranoid illnesses.

Critics described the section on the organic mental disorders as overextended and lacking in clarity, especially the complicated division into organic brain syndromes and organic mental disorders. The sections on organic delusional, personality, and affective syndromes were characterized as confusing, and those related to substance-induced intoxication and withdrawal, as superfluous. Simplification would be achieved, it was suggested, by defining the syndrome on axis I, and the underlying disease on axis III (1).

What Reservations Would You Have about the Use of DSM-III?

Responses to the question about reservations in using DSM-III were mainly of two kinds, conceptual and practical. Conceptual objections focused on the perceived shortcomings of DSM-III as a formal classification system and as a diagnostic tool. Practical drawbacks cited were that DSM-III is now incompatible with ICD-9 and unwieldy to use in clinical settings.* Since this was a write-in section that did not lend itself to tabulation, a composite rendering of the 80 respondents' views will be presented in summary form.

DSM-III is inadequate as a formal classification system. DSM-III emphasizes reliability at the expense of validity, and the external validation of the categories is a major task for the future development of psychiatric nosology. Present categories are too refined and rigid, necessitating too many "undifferentiated" diagnoses. The new system is overelaborate and overinclusive, with idiosyncratic selection of criteria. Finally,

---

*The approximate frequency of each of these classes of objections was as follows: 1) inadequate classificatory system, 25%; 2) inadequate diagnostic tool, 50%; 3) incompatible with ICD-9, 15%; 4) unwieldly, 5%; 5) unclassified, 5%.

DSM-III represents a political compromise and thus loses its credibility as a scientific document.

DSM-III is inadequate as a diagnostic tool. DSM-III has important deficiencies as a diagnostic system. The attempt to be atheoretical is artificial, and is not consistently carried out (1, 3, 4). The course of illness is not sufficiently considered, and the focus on symptomatology is conceptually limited. Categories that appear watertight on the pages of DSM-III prove to be porous in clinical practice. At present, DSM-III is probably most suitable for research, secondarily so for teaching, and least appropriate for clinical practice.

The greatest shortcoming of DSM-III is its focus on categorization, not conceptualization. The overemphasis on rigid operationalization and the mechanistic application of criteria tend to short-circuit clinical thinking. Its operational formulations create the illusion of greater certainty than in fact exists, and may foster rigid, static, and reified psychiatric concepts. The seemingly clear-cut definitions and diagnostic decision trees oversimplify the process of clinical judgment, conveying the misleading impression that psychiatric diagnosis is an unambiguous enterprise. This apparent rigor of the new system has a seductive appeal for students, whose learning of the more subtle skills of clinical assessment, thinking, and decision making may be jeopardized if DSM-III is taught in a "cookbook" fashion. The exclusion of psychodynamic formulations from DSM-III and its neglect of humanistic approaches to complex and ambiguous realities further reflect a regrettably arid concept of psychiatric diagnosis. DSM-III is "a gigantic defense against diagnostic problems in psychiatry."*

As the foregoing summaries suggest, critics of DSM-III's conceptual approach to diagnosis regret that the quest for reliability, operational rigor, and completeness has overshadowed concern for validity, clinical flavor, and psychodynamic understanding. "DSM-III is like a bikini— it shows you everything but the essentials."

DSM-III conflicts with ICD-9. The introduction of the new classification system has engendered confusion and inconsistency because of the present use of ICD-9 in Canada. DSM-III is not internationally recognized, current record-keeping is geared to ICD-9, and it is difficult to adapt axes IV and V to present computerized systems. Other medical specialists have to be educated about DSM-III, and general hospitals are reluctant to introduce it, as it does not include medical, surgical, and obstetrical diagnoses. It is of limited use for transcultural research

---

*Comments in quotation marks are direct quotations from our respondents.

since it does not contain some important classifications, such as "neurasthenia," that are internationally employed.

DSM-III is complex and unwieldy. It has been insufficiently recognized that the use of the new classification requires a considerable degree of clinical sophistication. DSM-III is of intimidating size and complexity. The five axes are time-consuming and inconvenient to employ in the time-pressured realities of daily clinical practice.

CONCLUSIONS: CONTRIBUTIONS OF DSM-III

The questionnaire results up to this point have suggested that Canadian academic psychiatrists make extensive use of DSM-III, but express numerous conceptual and practical reservations about it, reflecting in part the persisting impact of Canada' European diagnostic heritage and the current sway of ICD-9 in Canadian hospital settings.

To conclude on a positive note, numerous advantages were ascribed to DSM-III in the replies to the final question and during the interviews. Once more the "composite voice" will be heard.

DSM-III is the clearest and by far the most reliable system available, and is thus an excellent research tool. The multiaxial system is an important advance, particularly the recording of personality disorders on axis II, which draws attention to and stimulates the simultaneous assessment of personality disturbances and mental syndromes. DSM-III has also contributed to improvement in teaching and clinical practice. The criteria are clearer, the phenomenology is comprehensive, and the descriptions of the diagnostic process in the decision trees facilitate instruction and clinical use. In the teaching of medical students, DSM-III makes an effective case for the complexity of mental disorders and for the efforts of psychiatrists to be objective. The new classification also constitutes an important language of communication between psychiatrists and other mental health professionals. It has, for example, been successfully employed as a unifying conceptual model in the teaching of emergency psychiatry to nurses and social workers.*

DSM-III is flawed, but many of its limitations are simply veridical reflections of the state of the art in psychiatry today. Thus, although it will require further revision as medical science develops, DSM-III nonetheless represents an important step forward. Already "there has been a great improvement in diagnostic behavior among students, residents and even, more slowly, among psychiatrists themselves."

---

*C Lamarre, D Thomson: The teaching of emergency psychiatry to nurses and social workers. Paper presented at the October 1982 Canadian Psychiatric Association Meeting, Montreal.

REFERENCES

1. Hoenig J: Nosology and statistical classification. Can J Psychiatry 26: 240–243, 1981
2. Munro A: Diagnosis and treatment of paranoid disorders. Perspectives in Psychiatry: 1(2): 1–5, 1982
3. Dongier M, Lehmann H: Nouveaux systèmes de classification diagnostique: DSM-III et ICD-9, in Encyclopédie médico-chirurgicale. Psychiatrie. Paris, Editions Techniques, 1982, p. 37065 A 10
4. Dongier M: Briquet and Briquet's syndrome viewed from France. Can J Psychiatry (in press)
5. Duguay R, Ellenberger H (eds): Principes pratiques de psychiatrie. Montréal, Chenelière et Stanke; Paris, Maloine, 1981
6. Lalonde P, Grunberg F: Psychiatrie clinique; Approche contemporaine. Chicoutimi, Gaëtan-Morin, 1981

10

DSM-III IN CANADA

R. Wade Junek, M.D., F.R.C.P.(C)

CLASSIFICATION SYSTEMS IN CANADA

Unlike the American Psychiatric Association, the Canadian Psychiatric Association (C.P.A.) does not officially endorse the use of one diagnostic classification system. As a result, at least three systems have been commonly in use: the ninth edition of the International Classification of Diseases (ICD-9), the Clinical Modification of that classification (ICD-9-CM), and the *Diagnostic and Statistical Manual of Mental Disorders* published by the American Psychiatric Association, now in its third edition (DSM-III). There are, however, a few organizations and individuals who use a locally developed system, or no system at all. Locally developed systems are found in university training programs, and those who use no system are private practitioners who find that a well-constructed psychodynamic formulation is much more important to them than a diagnostic label.

The use of the three "standard" systems has arisen from differing needs of various organizations, primarily government statistics-col-

Address correspondence to: R. Wade Junek, M.D., F.R.C.P. (C), Clinical Psychiatrist, Atlantic Child Guidance Centre, Halifax Branch, Garden Park, 1464 Tower Road, Halifax, Nova Scotia, B3H 4L4, Canada

A version of this paper was published as the DSM-III in Canada: a survey. *Canadian Journal of Psychiatry* 28: 182–187, 1983

lecting agencies and university training programs. The federal government's major collector of such information is Statistics Canada, but each province and territory also collects data. With the exception of Alberta and Manitoba, all the provinces and territories—and Statistics Canada—use ICD-9, published by the World Health Organization. Alberta employs the services of the Professional Activity Study, which uses U.S.-based computers; hence, it uses ICD-9-CM. Manitoba prefers ICD-9-CM to facilitate hospital morbidity studies.

University training programs are influenced by several factors. Canada has always enjoyed the benefits of a close European connection, and many departments of psychiatry have members who have trained abroad or who have immigrated from Europe; similarly, many members have trained in the United States. All are influenced by the massive amount of literature and research generated in both areas. Directors of training programs want to meet the needs of psychiatric residents (to whom the axes and criteria of DSM-III are very appealing), their respective hospitals, government data-collecting organizations (which have already mandated other systems), and the various professional licensing bodies and associations (none of which endorses any particular system). Despite this profusion of pressures and regulations, general trends are emerging, as will be noted later in this report.

CLASSIFICATION SYSTEMS

A few comments about classification systems in general may contribute to understanding the variation found in Canada. Feinstein (1) and Temkin (2) have reviewed some of the history of classification systems and noted that their purposes and construction have always been fertile areas for controversy, even the need for a classification having been questioned until recent times. The 1976 review by Blashfield and Draguns (3) of the purposes of psychiatric classification best laid this latter controversy to rest. They summarized the purposes under five headings:

1. Communication. Without a common nomenclature, scientists lack a basic means of communication.

2. Information retrieval. As a means of organizing information within a scientific area, a classification system should permit efficient information retrieval.

3. Description. A classification system provides a basis for describing important similarities and differences among psychiatric patients. If the diagnostic groupings are homogeneous, a diagnosis should furnish a reasonably accurate summary of a patient's important characteristics.

4. Prediction. There are points of contact between the uses of a classification for descriptive and for predictive purposes. Information

about past and currently observable symptoms enters into the descriptive value of a system. The predictive value extends also to treatment, prognosis, and prevention.

5. Theory. Classificatory terms should be viewed as extensions of scientific concepts, and must meet three basic criteria; they must (*a*) possess clear criteria for application that can be stated in terms of publicly ascertainable concepts; (*b*) specify the concepts used in a theory within a given scientific discipline; and (*c*) lend themselves to empirical validation in terms of reliability, coverage, and descriptive and predictive value. In most classification studies, it is the reliability that is evaluated.

These purposes suggest the characteristics that should be considered in assessing any classification system. The first two indicate the need for a system to be universally used in order to reduce problems. Wing (4) also has noted the need for a standardized glossary and descriptions to enable effective communication and reliable scientific studies.

Unfortunately, a statement by Feinstein (1) about the eighth edition of the International Classification (ICD-8) probably still holds true for ICD-9 and ICD-9-CM: "On the few occasions where the actual usage of the ICD was specifically checked, the variability among users was so great as to suggest that the domain of vital statistics was intellectually moribund." He commented that though the medical model of disease fosters a classification based on etiology, the ICD taxonomy has no such logic: it is a confusing polyglot, assembled from antiquity to modern times, and includes terms about morphology, biochemical entities, physiological abnormalities, microbial agents, symptom clusters, eponyms, symptoms, and habits.

This paper reports the results of a survey that suggest that some of the reluctance of Canadian psychiatrists to endorse a particular classification system may well be related to each system's inadequacies in meeting the purposes outlined above.

THE SURVEY

The introduction of DSM-III, first in draft versions, then in final form, in 1980, reawakened many of the controversies about classification in Canada. As a result, a survey (5) was conducted to obtain answers to a number of questions.

1. What classification systems were Canadian psychiatrists using before the advent of DSM-III, and what have they used since its introduction?

2. What systems were being used in training programs?

3. Do Canadian psychiatrists favor continuing the policy of not endorsing a particular system?

4. What is the reaction of Canadian psychiatrists to DSM-III?

5. What recommendations would Canadian psychiatrists make to those responsible for producing an ICD-10?

By March 1981, 26.3% (n = 529) of the members of the C.P.A. had responded to these questions. The geographic distribution and years in practice of the psychiatrists who returned the questionnaires closely matched those previously determined by a manpower survey (6). The only significant difference was that the Province of Quebec was underrepresented, perhaps because only an English-language version of the questionnaire had been distributed.

Use of Classification Systems

Systems used in the past. Respondents were asked to rank in order of preferred usage the classification systems they had employed in the past. The results of this ranking are presented in table 1, which shows only the first three preferences and the "not ranked" choices. If no ranking was given, it indicated that the particular system was seldom used; thus, a high "not ranked" percent appears in the table for some systems, and the frequently used systems have a relatively low percent in the "not ranked" category.

Unfortunately, by mistake DSM-III (available in draft versions since 1977) was included in answers to this question. For the 60 respondents who listed it as first choice, the second choice may represent pre-DSM-III usage. Second choices were ICD-9, 25%; ICD-9-CM, 18.8%; DSM-III, 50.2%; unknown, 6.0%.

Future plans. A similar question was asked of respondents with respect to the system they would choose to use in the future. The results are

TABLE 1. Rank Order of Systems Used in the Past: Percent of Respondents Making Each Choice

Classification System	1	2	3*	Not Ranked
ICD-9	28.5	12.1	7.8	46.5
ICD-9-CM	6.4	11.3	7.9	68.8
DSM-II	25.9	20.2	7.9	39.9
DSM-III	11.3	9.8	9.5	60.5
None	1.7	1.3	0.4	89.2
Don't know	0.8	0.6	0.8	91.1
No response	25.4			

*4th and 5th ranks have not been included here and in table 2.

given in table 2. There was a significant association between increased familiarity with DSM-III (see table 4) and its selection as the system for future use.

It is interesting to note that despite a choice of responses to cover all possibilities, including not knowing what system had been used ("Don't know"), a large percentage of respondents left both the first and the second questions unanswered. These are recorded as "No response."

Use of Classification Systems in Training Programs

Fifteen of Canada's 16 postgraduate psychiatric training programs (P.P.T.P.s) provided information about the classifications they used. For the past, the figures were: ICD-9, 2; ICD-9-CM, 5; DSM-II, 7; and a local system, 1. In future, the envisioned use is: ICD-9, 3; ICD-9-CM, 3; DSM-III, 8; continuing use of a local system, 1. It was noted for one program, however, that though use of ICD-9-CM was mandated, DSM-III was preferred.

The C.P.A. Policy of "Nonendorsement"

The C.P.A.'s policy of not endorsing the use of any one system was approved by 39.7% of the respondents; 54.8% wanted to change this policy; 5.5% did not answer the question. Despite only a slim majortiy who supported a change in policy, when the issue of whether other organizations should endorse one system was raised, a much larger number replied yes. Table 3 summarizes the results of this question by relevant professional groups (the Royal College is the licensing body for specialists, and the Medical Council is responsible for licensing all M.D.s in Canada).

Respondents who thought that one system should be recommended were asked to rank in order of preference the systems they would advocate

TABLE 2. Rank Order of Choice of Systems for Future Use: Percent of Respondents Making Each Choice

Classification System	1	2	3	Not Ranked
ICD-9	16.3	11.2	6.0	61.8
ICD-9-CM	5.5	10.0	5.3	74.9
DSM-II	2.3	8.1	4.2	77.3
DSM-III	42.0	13.8	4.2	36.1
None	2.3	1.5	0.2	90.0
Don't know	2.1	0.4	0.4	90.9
No response	29.5			

TABLE 3. Recommendation to Use One Classification System: Percent of Respondents Giving Each Answer

Organization	Yes	No	No Response
Royal College	68.6	22.7	8.7
Medical Council of Canada	65.2	25.0	9.8
Statistics Canada	78.6	13.2	8.1
P.P.T.P.*	71.8	19.7	8.5

*Postgraduate psychiatric training programs

be endorsed by each of the professional groups. As might be expected, the rank orderings were similar for each organization. Approximately half recommended DSM-III as their first choice; 10%, ICD-9; and 5%, ICD-9-CM. About 35% did not rank any system, in some cases because they believed that they did not know enough about any of the specific systems.

Written comments elaborated on the problem of whether or not to endorse one system. Those favoring the present policy were concerned that endorsement of one system might impede creativity in research and clinical work by encouragiang dogmatic thinking. They thought that psychiatrists should be familiar with more than one system and be allowed flexibility. They did not believe that any system had enough interrater reliability to permit its exclusive use. Others noted that no association should dictate what system should be used, that the C.P.A. should only encourage the use of one system, not endorse it.

There were more comments favoring endorsement of one particular system. The most commonly expressed desire was simple: Let us have just *one* system, for research, epidemiology, communication, and teaching. Some were concerned that the use of many systems usually produced more confusion than flexibility, and noted further that endorsing one system did not preclude familiarity with others. It was even suggested that Canada should produce its own system, although it was recognized that the country had neither the manpower nor the resources to do so.

Those who did not choose sides on this issue also offered comments. Their concern was that psychiatrists were becoming more preoccupied with labeling than with treating and that this preoccupation was hindering the production of good, dynamic formulations about the individual human being.

Reactions to DSM-III

A general question was asked to gain some idea of the degree of familiarity that respondents had with DSM-III, with the following results:

	Percent
Heard about but have not seen it	10.0
Glanced at a copy	18.7
Have studied it in detail	31.4
Have studied it and used it in practice	24.8
Have studied it and attended a workshop on its use	10.4
No answer or no familiarity	4.7
	100.0

It can be seen that 33.4% had little or no familiarity with DSM-III. Many of these respondents did not answer the other questions that required some familiarity with DSM-III; on other questions, as previously noted, the extent of a respondent's familiarity with the new system affected his or her answers (e.g., regarding choice of a system for future use).

Two questions were asked to elicit the respondents' general impression of DSM-III and what they thought would be its impact on psychiatric practice in Canada. The results are presented in table 4. If we eliminate from consideration those who did not respond to these questions, 70.8% gave a 1 or 2 (favorable) rating to DSM-III, and 72.5% gave a 1 or 2 (beneficial) rating concerning its anticipated impact.

Again, written comments gave some notion of the thinking behind the answers.

On the negative side, some respondents pointed out that the basic concepts in DSM-III were not well researched. The work was characterized as "consensus psychiatry," and a fear was expressed that dogma would replace science. The DSM-III's standardization might lead to

TABLE 4. Rating of DSM-III According to a Five-Point Scale: Percent of Respondents Selecting Each Rating

General Impression

Favorable				Unfavorable	No Response
23.8	28.5	13.8	3.8	4.0	26.1

Effects on Psychiatric Practice

Beneficial				Detrimental	No Response
26.8	26.1	14.1	3.2	2.8	28.0

required treatment methods, suffocate research and creativity, and lessen benefits to patients. The details introduced too many neologisms and idiosyncrasies, and the system was generally unsuitable for the needs of private practice and discouraged an emphasis on good psychodynamic formulations. Certain areas were seen as inadequately covered or even neglected, particularly recent biological advances, neurological factors, and the familial and interpersonal aspects of psychiatry especially relevant to child psychiatry. In the most unfavorable reactions, DSM-III was perceived as cumbersome, awkward, arbitrary, complex, unusable rubbish—and profoundly boring.

On the positive side, there was appreciation of several features of DSM-III relevant to the very purposes of classification outlined earlier. Communication would improve with more uniformity in diagnosis. The multiaxial system, use of diagnostic criteria, and the phenomenological approach were frequently singled out for praise. Many who regarded the system favorably saw its use as best for epidemiology, instruction, statistics, research, and computerization. The systematic definitions, even if "wrong," at least allowed for scientific testing. They found the system useful yet flexible and an aid to self-discipline and improved diagnostic skills. Frequently, much of the approval was summed up in the two words "best yet." As an antidote to the strong reactions against DSM-III, there were expressions such as "How did I get along without it!" and "Greatest advance since Kraepelin!"

Pragmatists noted that much of the psychiatric literature is dominated by the Americans, and, like it or not, Canadians must realize that this dominance will persist. DSM-III will be a tremendous influence.

Toward an ICD-10

In preparation for the eventual production of an ICD-10, questions were asked about whether some of the basic concepts of DSM-III should be considered for incorporation in it. The results are given in table 5, and indicate that a considerable number of respondents did not answer these questions (the 33.4% who had little familiarity with DSM-III probably accounted for a large part of this nonresponse).

DISCUSSION

Policy of the C.P.A.

As noted earlier, the C.P.A.'s policy is not to endorse any of the three classification systems in common use. Medical students and psychiatric residents are expected to be familiar with more than one system. The C.P.A. policy is frequently updated, but barely more than half (54.8%) of the survey respondents advocated actually changing it.

TABLE 5. Recommendations for an ICD-10: Percent of Respondents Giving Each Response

Recommendation	Yes	No	No Response
1. Increase the number of coded disorders, allowing more specificity	74.3	11.9	13.8
2. Use a multiaxial system	69.2	11.9	18.9
—Similar to that of DSM-III	66.0	12.5	21.6
3. Use criteria of inclusion and exclusion	78.3	5.7	16.1
—Similar to those in DSM-III	69.0	9.5	21.5

On the other hand 65.2%–78.6% of the respondents would support recommending a single system for other affected organizations.

The consequence of the C.P.A.'s not endorsing one classification system is the variable use of all three systems across Canada. As it now stands, C.P.A. policy allows for flexibility and does not, of course, prevent the gradual emergence of one system as the dominant choice.

DSM-III

The results of the survey reported here indicate that DSM-III has already had an impact on psychiatrists in Canada. Most of them have studied it in detail, and 42.0% rank it first as the system to use in the future (versus only 16.3% who chose the next highest, ICD-9). Similarly, it is recommended as the system of choice for various relevant organizations. It is the first choice of half the postgraduate psychiatric programs in Canada, and is considered important to learn in the rest. When general impressions of DSM-III are compared with specific recommendations for an ICD-10, it is apparent that the basic concepts of the former are strongly favored.

CONCLUSIONS

The developers of DSM-III clearly saw the manual in an evolutionary context, as a "still frame in an ongoing process." One respondent perhaps best illustrated its evolutionary component in stating: "Right or wrong, the systematic definitions of the DSM-III provide a system that can be scientifically tested." The importance of scientific methodology to a classification system has been pointed out by Hampel (7) and by Blashfield and Draguns (3). DSM-III is recognized as a significant step in moving classification from the political to the scientific realm. Indeed, the methodology of description in the manual may be its most significant and longest-lasting contribution.

Canadian psychiatrists, though they have pointed out its weaknesses, have generally welcomed DSM-III.

REFERENCES

1. Feinstein AR: A critical overview of diagnosis in psychiatry, in Psychiatric Diagnosis. Edited by Rakoff VM, Stancer HC, Kedward HB. New York, Brunner/Mazel, 1977
2. Temkin O: The history of classification in the medical sciences, in Classification in Psychiatry and Psychopathology. Edited by Katz MM, Cole JO, Barton WE. Chevy Chase, Md: US Department of Health, Education, and Welfare, 1968
3. Blashfield RK, Draguns JG: Toward a taxonomy of psychopathology: The purpose of psychiatric classification. Br J Psychiatry 129: 574–583, 1976
4. Wing JK: The limits of standardization, in Psychiatric Diagnosis. Edited by Rakoff VM, Stancer HC, Kedward HB. New York, Brunner/Mazel, 1977
5. Junek RW: The DSM-III in Canada: A survey. Can J Psychiatry (in press)
6. El Guebaly N, Leichner P: Psychiatric manpower in Canada: The 1980 surveys. Can J Psychiatry 27:486, 1982
7. Hampel CG: Aspects of Scientific Explanation. New York, The Free Press, 1966

11

FRENCH PERSPECTIVES ON DSM-III

Pierre Pichot, Julien Daniel Guelfi, M.D., and Jerome Kroll, M.D.

The appearance of DSM-III constitutes an important date in the history of psychiatric nosology and, more generally, in the development of those fundamental theoretical models upon which our concepts of mental disorders rest. Its importance is all the greater because the initiative for its production comes from the United States, whose influence on world psychiatry, if only for reasons of medical demography, has become considerable since the end of World War II. French psychiatrists, like doubtless many other European psychiatrists, have been struck by the major conceptual departure that DMS-III represents, not only in relation to DSM-II (which was practically unknown in France and, in any case, was very close to the eighth revision of the International Classification of Diseases [ICD-8]) but, especially, in relation to previous diagnostic usages of American psychiatry. The latter, particularly under the influence of the psychodynamic school, had shown a profound disinterest in, even hostility toward, the very idea of nosology, preoccupied as it was more with the "mechanisms" than with the observation and description of symptoms.

In France, as in Europe in general, a stereotype had developed, no doubt excessive and caricatural, of psychiatry in the United States in which a disdain for the clinical approach, a lack of interest and great

Address correspondence to: Professeur Pierre Pichot, Clinique des Maladies Mentales et de l'Encéphale, 100, rue de la Santé, 75674 Paris Cedex 14, France

This article was translated by Jerome Kroll, M.D.

incompetence in observation and description of symptoms, and a laxity in nosology reigned supreme. This was exemplified by an uncritical extension of the diagnosis of schizophrenia, particularly in epidemiological studies, to the point where the boundaries between normality and pathology dissolved. This point of view can be summarized by the judgment of the Norwegian psychiatrist Langfeldt (1), who, following a stay of ten months in the United States in 1954–1955, commented, "After a sufficiently long acquaintanceship with American psychiatric institutes, one cannot help but be discouraged . . . in particular with their almost complete disregard of ordinary descriptive diagnosis and prognosis."

HISTORICAL BACKGROUND

It is impossible, in view of its duration and complexity, to describe the evolution of the French tradition of nosography. It begins at the end of the 18th century with Bossier de Sauvages; it is truly inaugurated around 1800 by Pinel; and it finds its classic expression in Esquirol's *Treatise on Psychiatry* (1838). The conceptions of Esquirol and his students dominated French psychiatry and, indirectly, world psychiatry for a long time, to around 1880. It is necessary to note, however, to put the matter simply, that French psychiatry had at this time three different models that, to a certain extent, contradicted each other.

The first was that of Pinel and Esquirol, which can be described as syndromic. Nosological categories had been based essentially on empirical observation of actual symptoms, and there was no preconceived theory behind the classes. Even though the authors took into consideration numerous etiological and pathogenic hypotheses, these barely influenced the nosology. The philosophy underlying this position was best expressed by Esquirol (2) in 1838 in the preface to his *Treatise:*

> The work that I offer to the public is the result of forty years of study and observation. I have observed the symptoms of mental illness; I have studied the behavior, the habits, and the needs of the insane, in whose midst I have spent my life . . . immersing myself in the facts, I have approached them by what they have in common with each other. I write about them as I have seen them. I have rarely sought to explain them, and I have not let myself become attached to systems that have always seemed to me more appealing in their brilliance than useful in their applications.

To this clinical, descriptive, and syndromic nosology another orientation was to be opposed. In 1822 A. L. J. Bayle (3) published his treatise *Research on Mental Illnesses*, which was supplemented by his later works. He described general paralysis as a single illness characterized by a specific etiology (inflammation of the arachnoid membrane) and by a series of symptoms evolving in three distinct phases, each of which was defined by a specific clinical picture. Bayle's model was to have a fundamental influence on the evolution of nosological concepts. In effect, he sought to isolate a mental "illness" whose characteristics were superimposed on those physical illnesses that were then being discribed within the framework of the clinico-anatomical method. In doing this he repudiated the syndromic model and thought that, at the level of symptoms, illness was characterized by a particular sequence of manifestations. Even if one leaves aside the etiological problem, there was a fundamental disagreement between the "cross-sectional" symptomatic model of Esquirol and the "longitudinal" one of Bayle. This found expression in interminable discussions in the 19th century between partisans of the two points of view.

In 1857, B.A. Morel (4) published his *Treatise on Physical, Intellectual, and Moral Degeneration in the Human Species*. He sought to show that a great number of mental illnesses were caused by the action of external toxic, psychological, and social pathogenic factors whose effects on the nervous system were transmitted by heredity. He argued that this "tendency toward degeneration" became worse over successive generations, manifesting itself in different clinical pictures of increasing severity.

It is necessary to emphasize certain essential features of Morel's work. Unlike his predecessors, he suggested that nosology required a theoretical base in etiology, furnished by the "doctrine of degeneration." It is true that one of the criteria in defining general paralysis as a single illness had been its etiology, the inflammation of the meninges, but this was a matter of an anatomical-pathological finding and not, as Morel postulated, a general theoretical hypothesis. Morel's work thus introduced into French (and world) psychiatry a third orientation.

The subsequent evolution of psychiatry was characterized by attempts to synthesize these three points of view. The model of Bayle, which can be described as medical, was an ideal; but despite all the anatomic-pathological research, specific lesions, except in mental disorders of gross organic etiology, such as the dementias, could not be found.

In the absence of a demonstrable anatomic-pathological basis for the identification and delimitation of mental illness, 19th-century psychiatrists found it necessary to look to the characteristic course as a way of defining an illness, as was done with general paralysis. An example of this was the principle formulated by Jean-Pierre Falret (5) in 1864:

> What it is necessary to investigate is the course and the different phases of actual types of mental illness, many of which are still unknown to this day, but which study will permit us to discover. The idea of a natural form implies in effect a predetermined course, and, reciprocally, the idea

of a natural course presupposes the existence of a natural type of illness, with a particular course. Therein resides, we believe, the most fruitful direction for progress in our specialty.

The isolation by Falret and Baillarger of what we today call manic-depressive psychosis was the first accomplishment of this nosological perspective.

This approach was followed by Kahlbaum in his work of 1863 (6) and in his description of catatonia in 1874 (7). It came to be the basis of Kraepelin's nosology, beginning with the fifth edition (1896) of his treatise (8), in the preface to which he states:

> In the development of this work, the present edition constitutes the final, decisive step from the symptomatic conception to the clinical conception of mental illness. This transformation in viewpoint, for which practical concerns have shown me the necessity more and more strongly, is characterized above all by the delimitation and grouping of pathological pictures *(Krankheitsbilder)*. Everywhere the importance of external signs of illness have had to yield to points of view that give prominence to the conditions of appearance, course, and termination. All the pure syndromes *(Zustandsbilder)* have thus disappeared from nosology.

The present French nosological tradition rests largely on the movement that developed between about 1890 and World War I, in which the central figure was Magnan (9). This tradition was characterized by Magnan's efforts to construct a nosolgical system that borrowed elements from Esquirol's syndromic tradition, Bayle's medical model, and Morel's theoretical concepts of degeneration. However, the parallel development of Kraepelinian nosology, the prestige of which was growing, led to compromises. The ideas of Kraepelin were only partially accepted, and some specifically French categories persisted—categories derived directly from Magnan (e.g., *les bouffées délirantes des dégénérés* [transitory delusional states of degeneracy] or the idea of *déséquilibre mental* [mental imbalance]) or indirectly from him (e.g., *délires chroniques* [chronic delusional states]). The developments of this crucial epoch have been described by Pichot (10).

The nosological system thus established before World War I has remained essentially stable. True, after the war Bleuler's schizophrenia was substituted for Kraepelin's dementia praecox, but this substitution affected only the terminology and the utilization of Bleuler's "enduring symptoms" *(Dauersymptome)* or "fundamental symptoms" *(Grund-symptome)* to confirm the diagnosis, without, however, changing the relatively conservative boundaries of the nosological framework, which remained limited as much by the *bouffées délirantes* as by the *délires chroniques*. (This position explains why Kurt Schneider's "first-rank symptoms," which characterize for the French tradition certain chronic delusional states, particularly chronic hallucinatory psychoses, as much as, if not more than, schizophrenia, have not been accepted in France, as a recent survey of French psychiatrists has shown.)

On the other hand, some limited additions have been made to the traditional nosological scheme by the adoption of diagnostic categories borrowed from foreign schools between the two wars, such as Kretschmer's hypersensitive delusional states, the pseudoneurotic form of schizophrenia, and the borderline states more recently derived from the influence of American psychiatry, and, in this last case, the growing influence of psychodynamic points of view.

The trends that have emerged since 1914 have not had a major effect on the original points of view. Thus, the "organodynamic doctrine" developed by H. Ey (11–13), which played a notable role in the '50s despite its declared intention to establish a nosology on a new theoretical basis of the nature of psychopathology, has had only a very small effect on the nosological structure. Similarly, the psychodynamic tendencies that have had a diffuse influence (very late by comparison with the United States) have had very limited influence in this area.

If one wished to sum up the French psychiatric tradition, one might say that it has been marked since Esquirol by an attachment to a clinical descriptive approach. The many successive influences, such as the doctrine of degeneration of the 19th century or the psychodynamic influence that today is of psychoanalytic inspiration, have never truly crowded out this orientation. The establishment of a diagnosis based on careful observation of current symptoms, the precursors of the illness, and the clinical course is now generally considered fundamental. (It is probable that this attitude has been reinforced by the system of competitive examinations for obtaining a post as resident in psychiatry and as a specialist, which includes the writing of an essay on an established nosological system and/or the study of an illness; the report must include a discussion of diagnostic, prognostic, and treatment issues.) Moreover, it is obvious that the French psychiatric tradition is characterized by a conservative attitude toward a system that it has developed autochtonously, a point that has been confirmed in recent studies. The reason probably ought to be sought less in "national character" than in the considerable age of this tradition and the complexity of its evolution, nosology being, in the final analysis, the expression of the whole of the conceptual system that undergirds psychiatry. In a situation in which new concepts have not demonstrated their superiority in an obvious manner in terms of prognosis or course of treatment, the French tradition is likely to maintain the system it has constructed; if it has adopted without difficulty the division of manic-depressive psychosis into a unipolar and a bipolar form, it has refused to include within the concept of schizophrenia *les bouffées délirantes* and *les délires chroniques*.

The French attitude regarding the World Health Organization's International Classification of Diseases (ICD) is characteristic: it has never been adopted in France. An official French classification for statistical purposes, now in use, was developed in 1968 by a committee reflecting, to some extent, the mainstream of French psychiatric opinion. It was published by the Institut National de la Santé et de la Recherche Médicale—INSERM (14). Although it attempted to be compatible with ICD-8, it deviated considerably, maintaining, for example, separately from schizophrenia the *bouffées délirantes* and the *délires chroniques*. This system is the one that is obligatorily used for the annual statistics of the public mental hospitals. In the investigation we recently made among professors of psychiatry in France, that is to say, among the psychiatrists best informed with regard to the international literature and most open to new approaches, this attachment to tradition was confirmed. The principal reason ought to be sought in the fact that French tradition adopted, between 1900 and 1913, and has retained, certain diagnostic categories, the principal ones being summarized below.

SOME SPECIFICALLY FRENCH DIAGNOSES

Bouffée Délirante

The *bouffée délirante* (transitory delusional state), described for the first time in 1896 by Legrain (15), a student of Magnan's, is, in its pure form, characterized by the following criteria:

1. It is a "psychotic" condition (in the sense of DSM-III).
2. The onset is abrupt, without any evident cause, or at most with a minor precipitating factor.
3. The characteristics of the delusion must be present from its beginning. The delusion has various themes, and is not systematized; it is polymorphous and experienced intensely; the patient has a deep delusional conviction. It can be accompanied by hallucinations, but these are of only secondary importance, and may not be present at all.
4. The delusional state may coexist with abnormalities of awareness and mood; it may be associated with a certain amount of confusion; it may be accompanied by symptoms of anxiety, depression, and mania; the symptomatology is characterized by its polymorphism and its instability over time.
5. There are no accompanying somatic problems.
6. The spontaneous evolution moves toward recovery, which can often occur rapidly, "in a few hours, a few days, or several weeks." There are no residual symptoms. The transitory delusional state can occur as a single episode, or the subject may have several episodes in the course of his life, separated by intervals completely free of symptoms.

7. It appears among subjects who present with a fragile personality, for which Magnan used the term "degenerated," in the context of his own time. This is, in effect, more a position of principle than of a notion easily definable idea in terms of objective symptoms. Grossly, the "degeneration" shows up in a permanent condition as a personality disorder.

Since the initial description by Magnan of the transitory delusional state of degeneracy, the French tradition has evolved in distinguishing:

1. The "pure" transitory delusional state (type Magnan).

2. The "reactive" transitory delusional state, with a similar course and symptoms, but coming after intense psychological stress.

3. The "schizophrenic" transitory delusional state. This involves a developing diagnosis: a subject whose initial diagnosis is transitory delusional state in whom the course, after a few months, tends toward residual symptoms characteristic of schizophrenia.

4. Certain authors (although opinion is not unanimous on this point) speak of a "symptomatic" transitory delusional state, which has the same characteristics, but in which an organic cause, particularly a toxic one, has been found.

DSM-III categorization. All the "true" transitory delusional states can be included under DSM-III code 295.40, schizophreniform disorder, or, if the duration is less than two weeks, under 298.90, atypical psychosis. Moreover, true transitory delusional states and schizophreniform psychoses are very closely related, though the latter concept does not include several of Magnan's criteria (presence of pathology of mood, the development of confusion, and the presence of an underlying fragile personality, among others). The corresponding category for the "reactive" transitory delusional state is brief reactive psychosis, 298.80, in which the duration is less than two weeks. When the duration is between two weeks and six months, there may be a resemblance to 298.30, acute paranoid disorder, but the latter does not mention polymorphism of the symptoms.

On the whole, DSM-III (unlike ICD-9) has introduced some categories, *distinct from schizophrenia*, that are considered by French psychiatrists to reflect an aspect of their tradition. (In the French version of the ICD-9—CIM-9, the term *bouffée délirante* appears as a translation of the English "acute paranoid reaction"—298.3, but the ICD-9 description is more akin to that of the reactive transitory delusional state, not the "true" delusional state.)

Délires Chroniques

The traditional concept of *délires chroniques* (chronic delusional states) was established at the beginning of this century. French tradition distinguishes, among the states of chronic development:

—Schizophrenia. This is defined above all by the presence of the principal symptoms (*Hauptsymptome-Dauersymptome*) of Bleuler, primarily by the dissociation (*Spaltung*) also referred to as disintegration—of the personality and of a general manner characterized by negative symptoms.

—Chronic delusional states. These are defined by the existence of a chronic psychotic state (as in DSM-III) without clear dissociation of the personality.

In practice, French tradition excludes from schizophrenia a considerable proportion of the cases customarily diagnosed in international psychiatry as paranoid schizophrenia. The chronic delusional states are divided schematically into three major categories:

1. *Systematic delusional states without hallucinations.* These are characterized by: the coherent character of the delusion; the existence of an essentially interpretive mechanism; the absence of hallucinations, or at least their contingent character.

They comprise the following varieties: (*a*) delusions of the interpretive type of Sérieux and Capgras (16); these correspond mainly to Kraepelin's description of paranoia, though the criteria may be less restrictive; (*b*) sensitive-type delusions, or sensitive paranoia, which corresponds to Kretschmer's description of hypersensitive paranoia; (*c*) romantic and vindictive delusions, which differ from the first two types in the manner of development of the delusion: there is an initial belief ("I have been the object of an injustice"; "She has wronged me"; "He loves me"), and all the subsequent beliefs develop to "prove" the initial postulate, whereas in the other two varieties (also often called "paranoiac") there is a progressive extension of themes (for example, in the delusion of persecution, the persecutors become progressively more numerous, as do the motives for the persecution, ideas of grandeur appear, etc.).

The French tradition describes subvarieties of these romantic and vindictive delusional states such as: litiginous delusions (Kraepelin's *Querulantenwahn*—querulousness); the delusion of inventors; the "passionate idealists" (found particularly among certain social reformers and among the authors of attacks against political and other personalities); delusions of jealousy (Jaspers's *Eifersuchtwashn*); and delusions of pure erotomania (described in France by de Clérambault (17, 18]), consisting of romantic delusions in a restricted sense.

2. *Chronic hallucinatory psychosis (19, 20).* This is defined by:

(*a*) The existence of hallucinations, which have a predominant place in the symptomatology. French tradition describes them under the term "triple mental automatism" (de Clérambault), comprising 1) sensory and sensitive automatisms (mainly auditory hallucinations, but also visual, gustatory, olfactory, and cenesthetic); 2) ideational-verbal automatisms (thoughts spoken aloud, hearing commentaries on one's thoughts, thought-echoing, theft and divination of thought); and 3) psychomotor automatisms, which are more rare (sensations of imposed movement and verbal utterances).

It is to be noted that "mental automatism," which is the central positive element of the diagnosis, contains practically all the first-rank symptoms that Kurt Schneider considers pathognomonic of schizophrenia, whereas in the French tradition chronic hallucinatory psychosis is completely distinct from schizophrenia.

(b) The existence of delusional ideas, most often of persecution, but also grandeur.

(c) The preservation of lucidity and intellectual capacity, contrasting with the importance of the delusional and hallucinatory syndrome (this is a fundamental criterion distinguishing it from schizophrenia).

3. *Chronic paraphrenic delusional states, or delusions of imagination.* Much less frequent than the other two categories (the proportion among admissions to psychiatric hospitals is approximately as follows: systematized delusions, 5; chronic hallucinatory psychosis, 4; paraphrenic delusions, 1), these are defined by the following criteria: the presence of paralogical thinking of a magical type; fantastic and megalomaniacal themes of the delusions; mechanisms essentially of confabulation, with very few interpretations or hallucinations; and paradoxical preservation of adaptation to reality, contrasting with the fantastic character of the delusions.

Unlike the case with regard to ICD-9, in which, for example, paraphrenia, 297.2, can eventually be assimilated with the French chronic hallucinatory psychosis, there is a fundamental discord here between the French tradition and DSM-III.

Categories 297.10 and 297.30 (paranoia, shared paranoid disorders) would cover only a small part of the French systematic delusional states without hallucinations; in fact, the DSM-III categories are even more restrictive than the true paranoia of Kraepelin in including only two themes, persecution and jealousy. The chronic hallucinatory psychoses have some criteria partially analagous to schizophrenic disorders (A1–A5, C), but the criteria A6 and B do not agree. The same is true for chronic paraphrenic delusions (criteria A2 and C, but not B). In fact, by definition, criterion B (deterioration) does not apply to chronic delusional states, although the notion of "deterioration from a previous level of functioning" is in certain cases difficult to interpret. In other words, except for a small number of nonhallucinatory systematic delusional states, the group of French chronic delusional states would have to be placed in the residual category "atypical psychosis," which is hardly satisfactory, given the fact that of the admissions to French mental hospitals, for 100 diagnoses of schizophrenia (all types considered together) there are 50 diagnoses of chronic delusional psychoses.

Under these circumstances, it is not surprising that in our study of 25 psychiatrists who responded to the question "What diagnostic concept seems to you to be lacking in the DSM-III classification?" 12 mentioned chronic delusional psychoses in general; 4, chronic hallucinatory psychoses; and 4, chronic paraphrenic delusional states—that is, 20 of 25 respondents mentioned all or part of this French category. In contrast, only four psychiatrists mentioned transitory delusional states, and yet it is possible that the lack of that response was due more to the nature of the terminology than to the concept, inasmuch as schizophreniform disorders are perceived as having the greater analogy or similarity.

Mental Imbalance

The diagnostic concept *déséquilibre mental* (mental imbalance) was introduced by Magnan. Insofar as it made use of Morel's "doctrine of degeneration," it established a category of patients, the "degenerate" ones, who, on the one hand, were characterized by their predilection to develop acute psychiatric symptoms (the most typical being the transitory delusional state) and, on the other hand, presented with a permanent state of signs of illness, "stigmata." The stigmata, which in the literature of the time were referred to as "the degenerated mental state," comprised separate elements that were later attributed to specific pathological syndromes (phobias, obsessions, and conditions classified in DSM-III as "impulse control disorders" and "psychosexual disorders") and anomalies that correspond to the current group of personality disorders. Magnan had postulated that the nervous-system anomaly underlying the stigmata of "degenerate" persons was an "imbalance" between the spinal cord, the posterior brain, and the anterior brain, and he introduced the term *imbalanced* as a synonym for *degenerated*.

The French conception of personality disorders has evolved from this point of departure, incorporating categories of varied origins. Nevertheless, even at the present time, the personality disorder 301.78, antisocial personality disorder, continues to be called in France "mental imbalance" or, in certain cases, through contamination by the German terminology, "psychopathic imbalance." But apart from this problem of vocabulary, one cannot say that an absolutely specific French tradition exists in this area of personality disorders. It is distinct, for example, from the German tradition typically presented by Kurt Schneider. In fact, in the area of personality disorders there is considerable heterogeneity of ideas according to country. This heterogeneity explains the responses in our investigation to the question "Which diagnostic categories of DSM-III appear to you difficult of application or inapplicable in France?" Of 22 responses, 10 concerned personality disorders either in their entirety (6) or of a particular type: schizotypal, 2; passive aggressive, 1; avoidant, 1.

FRENCH REACTIONS TO DSM-III

It is difficult to make a judgment concerning the reaction of French psychiatrists to DSM-III. It is necessary to note, first, that at the present time DSM-III is available only in English. The problems of importation have resulted in a very high price, and the book is difficult to obtain.

Our survey was addressed to 80 professors, generally heads of departments. Forty-one did not respond; 2 indicated that they knew nothing about DSM-III; 8, that they knew it existed, but did not have a copy of it in their department; and 29, that they knew of it and possessed a copy. Despite the uncertainty about the reasons for not responding, one must acknowledge that among the professors, fewer than half knew enough about DSM-III, two years after its appearance, to express an opinion. It is evident that, for other French psychiatrists, the proportion is considerably less. Extending interest in DSM-III is tied to the availability of a French translation.

It can be predicted with great probability that whatever the ultimate interest that DSM-III is likely to awaken, the likelihood of its official adoption is practically nil. It suffices to note that up until now, ICD-8 and ICD-9 have not been officially adopted, despite the fact that in their general philosophy they are much closer to French practices than is DSM-III. The production of the INSERM classification in 1968 is evidence of the reluctance of French psychiatrists to abandon the concepts they have developed. The French nosological system has, in the course of its development, included categories of foreign origin without difficulty, but the adoption of DSM-III *in toto* would be a matter of a very different nature. It is possible and probable that DSM-III will be used in parallel with other systems.

At the present time, in our inquiry into the question "Outside of the statistical figures that the public services are obliged to furnish to the administration, which system, or systems, of diagnostic classification do you use *most often* in your psychiatric practice?" the 37 responses are distributed as follows:

INSERM	25
ICD-8/ICD-9	10
DSM-III	10
Others	5

In phrasing the question, we took into account the fact that all the psychiatric services have to furnish their statistics each year in terms of the INSERM classification. One can say with certainty that about one in eight university departments of psychiatry utilize DSM-III in practice, although, from all evidence, not exclusively. More precise indications are given by the answers to two other questions.

"Does DSM-III seem to be of interest to you?"

	Yes	No	No response
For clinical service	23	9	5
For teaching	25	8	4
For research	30	3	4

"Do you personally use DSM-III?"

	Yes	No	No response
For clinical service	20	9	8
For teaching	18	12	7
For research	22	9	6

The above figures can give the impression of more frequent use, but it is rather a matter of occasional utilization that represents, at a maximum (use for research purposes), only one-fourth of the questionnaires sent.

Concerning the future use of DSM-III, it is probably necessary to take into account the following considerations.

1. When European pharmaceutical companies request physicians to conduct a clinical trial, they tend more and more to require the use of DSM-III, perhaps in parallel with another system such as that of INSERM. The reason is that these companies hope eventually to obtain authorization to enter the American market by performing the clinical trials in Europe, and they think that the use of DSM-III will be a factor in acceptance by the FDA.

2. Many French researchers intend to publish their experimental work in the journals that appear in the United States. They think that the use of DSM-III will further understanding of their results by American readers. To the question in our investigation "If you have actually had any research programs in which DSM-III was used, indicate the title of this program," 19 psychiatrists of 37 indicated that they had at present one or more research programs (a total of 26 programs) utilizing DSM-III. Seventeen of the projects are of a clinical-biological nature (concerning affective and schizophrenic disorders), and nine are epidemiological and/or clinical studies.

These two factors evidently concern a limited number of psychiatrists. It can be assumed that when a French translation of DSM-III becomes available, its influence will be much greater and more widespread than it is at present. But it is impossible to predict which of its fundamental principles and/or particular categories will be accepted. It is necessary to bear in mind that the Kraepelinian nosology, despite its considerable prestige, has never been completely incorporated in France. It is necessary to consider also the role that nonscientific factors can play. (In our investigation, 6 of 27 psychiatrists resented the American origin of DSM-III, marked by utilization of a terminology, concepts, and a vocabulary to which French physicians are not accustomed. One psychiatrist regretted more specifically "the total absence of consideration of European concepts, notably French ones, because of the lack of true international collaboration.")

We think that in fact one of the difficulties that will impede the adoption of DSM-III in France is its "agnostic" character, particularly the absence of reference to any psychopathological concept (in the European sense of that word) throughout the manual. (For example, six of our respondents criticized it for not having "a structural perspective"). A further difficulty is that DSM-III is confined to a descriptive symptomatic approach (phenomenological, in the American sense of the term), no attempt being made to take etiological-pathogenic theories into account. (One psychiatrist remarked that "the publicity surrounding DSM-III runs the risk of giving people the false impression that it represents the position of all of American psychiatry.")

In the final analysis, the ramifications of this problem will be able to be judged only when a French translation permits easy access to DSM-III. The translation of DSM-III into the French language was carried out in 1982 by a working group initiated and coordinated by Dr. J.D. Guelfi, along with Drs. P. Boyer, J. F. Henry, A. Lisoprawsky, C.B. Pull, M.C. Pull, and G. Welsh. The consultant to the translation, Professor Bourgeois, has reviewed the whole text. The general supervision of the Italian, French, and Spanish translations has been carried out by P. Pichot. It will appear in 1983. The working group has encountered relatively few real difficulties in the translation with the exception of certain terms that have a different sense in French and in English (a particular example being "paranoid") and of certain typically American expressions the literal translation of which would have been difficult to understand or ambiguous for the French psychiatrist.

The translation team has, however, chosen to remain as faithful as possible, in a quasi-systematic manner, to the American text, feeling free to exercise this option or to offer an alternative more meaningful for the French specialist through use of brief footnotes.

The most important difficulties have to do not so much with literal translation as with the style used in DSM-III. At times the multiple repetition of certain terms makes reading the French text difficult. These systematic repetitions have, however, almost always been maintained in the French translation, inasmuch as they correspond to a deliberate attitude of the American authors. This translation certainly meets expectations.

Indeed, even if only a limited number of French psychiatrists, mainly in universities, have any precise acquaintance with DSM-III, its existence is known to a great many doctors because of references at various scientific meetings to its existence, its principles, and certain of its aspects.

To continue with our evaluation of DSM-III, we again refer to responses to our survey. To the question "Do the following orientations seem to you important in order to make progress in knowledge of psychopathology?" the following responses were given:

	Yes	No	No response
1. The importance of a nonambiguous description of symptoms by precise definitions.	31	2	4
2. The importance of a return to a purely descriptive classification.	15	17	5
3. The importance of a delineation of symptoms or of syndromes and of underlying personality traits, simultaneously and independently recorded on different axes.	32	0	5
4. The importance of a delineation of symptoms or syndromes and of other additional concomitant pathology (of a nonpsychiatric nature), recorded simultaneously and independently on their different axes.	27	4	6
5. The importance of a delineation of symptoms or syndromes and of precipitating events (psychosocial stressors) in a person's life preceding the disorder, recorded simultaneously and independently on a different axis.	28	3	6
6. The necessity of a quantification of symptoms in psychiatry.	25	8	4
7. The necessity of quantification in psychiatry of the degree of social adaptation before the appearance of the disorder.	21	9	7

To the question "What, according to you, is the greatest weakness of DSM-III?" the responses (given by 32 psychiatrists) were often multiple. Besides the already noted references to the "too American" nature of DSM-III (6), these criticisms were made: absence of reference to psychopathological theories (5); practical difficulties in using DSM-III (5); excessive importance given to toxic disorders and sexual disorders by comparison with neurotic disorders (5). But without doubt the most fundamental criticisms focused on the system of diagnostic criteria, on the procedure consisting of requiring that a minimal number of criteria be present, ending with obtaining the same diagnosis with different combinations, hence with heterogeneity of groups. Two of the psychiatrists even added that this technique makes DSM-III an "artificial creation" that is accompanied by "a radical misunderstanding of a psychic reality treated as a quantifiable substance."

In conclusion, we should like to present some personal reflections concerning the evaluation of DSM-III, coming to terms with the principles upon which it rests. The title itself, which contains the expression *mental disorders* (not, like ICD-9, *mental diseases*), is indicative of the general attitude of systematic agnosticism that permeates DSM-III. To a certain extent, it is a matter of a pre-Kraepelinian attitude (that is, one much closer to Esquirol than to Kraepelin, who, as noted above, thought in 1896 that he had made psychiatry take a decisive step in forming nosology based upon "illness pictures" instead of syndromes, which were previously used). But except for some categories (organic mental disorders, substance use disorders, acute reactive psychosis, adjustment disorders), etiology is never incorporated into the diagnosis. The refusal to use the adjective *endogenous* to designate a particular depressive syndrome (the substitution of "melancholia," which is, with hysteria, a diagnostic term linked to an etiologic hypothesis that is the most ancient in the history of psychiatry, appears at least curious in this perspective!) is significant in this respect. The nosology of DSM-III, as contained in axes I and II, even if in certain cases it incorporates in its criteria certain aspects of the course (duration, etc.), is above all syndromic. A European reader can only conclude that this systematic attitude is a reaction against the psychoanalystic etiological-pathogenic hypotheses that were dominant in the United States in the preceding period, to the detriment of clinical description. But it is necessary to note that this attitude ends up preferentially using the first-rank symptoms of Kurt Schneider for the diagnosis of schizophrenic disorders and isolating this piece of his work from the whole of the psychopathological system that this author developed, based on Jaspers's distinction between process and development (the somatogenic hypothesis).

It should be recognized that this etiologic-pathogenic "agnosticism" goes against the current of a trend, inaugurated in the middle of the 19th century, that has always sought to base nosology on theoretical concepts (whether on the idea of illness defined by anatomic lesion or, by default, the clinical course and end state, as according to Kraepelin; or according to the physiological-anatomic hypotheses of Meynert, Wernicke, or Kleist; the general biological ones, such as those of Morel and Magnan; or the psychopathological ones in different perspectives, such as those of Bleuler, Jaspers, Kurt Schneider, and Freud). One may, following one's own orientations, either salute the courage that has necessitated total rejection of a tradition that has lasted more than a century, or well regret this iconoclastic zeal, which risks the loss of much of importance that has been gained.

The multiaxial system is intimately linked with this agnosticism, since it winds up recording the syndromes (axis I), the personality disorders (axis II), and the variables that, in uniaxial systems, are necessarily incorporated into the diagnosis, without offering hypotheses or inferring causal relations among these syndromes, traits, and variables. If one accepts the "agnostic" attitude and wishes, at the same time, not to lose information (particularly for research purposes), the multiaxial system is the sole solution possible. At a general level, one could reproach it only for being a part of DSM's atheoretical approach. On a practical level, on the other hand, it is a great burden, since the number of possible theoretical combinations is considerable (the number of categories in axis I times the number of categories in axis II times the number of categories in axis III, etc.). It appears difficult to use correctly outside of a research structure. (The argument that one can be satisfied using axes I and II is acceptable only if one is able to resign himself to using a nosology that is almost purely syndromic.)

The use of diagnostic criteria appears as a transposition to clinical diagnosis, on the one hand, of the psychological technique of scaling and, on the other hand, of methodological preoccupations in the construction of items of rating scales, or, finally, of the experience with programs of computer diagnoses. The fundamental problem that their use poses is the existence of the principle of scaling in order to reach a determination of discrete categories. The mental tests and the personality inventories that utilize this technique rest on the hypothesis that the dimension one measures is a continuous variable and that the intensity of this variable is expressed in the number of dependent behaviors expressed (for example, the number of items to which the subject responds "yes" in a questionnaire on anxiety is considered proportional to the intensity of his anxiety), whatever the behaviors may be. But in the technique of diagnostic criteria, the hypothesis is that one has discrete categories (the subject either *has* or *does not have* a schizophrenic disorder; it is not a matter of a variable continuum). In these conditions, DSM-III has introduced the notion of a "critical level." In the diagnosis of major depressive episode, the scale includes 8 items, a score of 4 being the critical level; subjects receiving the same diagnosis can have 4, 5, 6, 7, or 8 items present (the combination is of no importance), but not just 2. The justification for this technique is not evident, and it is certain that psychiatrists (even if they are not familiar with the theory of scaling) will intuitively resent this difficulty.

Many other remarks could be made concerning DSM-III. One may, for example, pose the question "What reasons can be given for placing mental retardation on axis I, but specific developmental disorders on axis II?" This renders categorization impossible in the case of schizophrenia with retardation (*Propfschizophrenie*), a schizophreniform disorder, or a brief reactive psychosis in a subject presenting with "mild mental retardation" when there have been relatively frequent episodes.

Although it has been confirmed by numerous repetitions that the criteria of the categories have been defined by the empirical results of experimental research, one may think that despite this claim, certain decisions have been arbitrary (a French psychiatrist has asked why, for antisocial personality disorder, criterion 4 is positive if the subject has had ten sexual partners or more in a year, but not if he has had only nine!). One may wonder, on the other hand, if certain decisions (e.g., the almost total incorporation of schizoaffective disorders within the affective disorders and, at the opposite pole, the very restrictive nature of the criteria for schizophrenic disorders) do not stem as much from a reaction against the earlier prevailing attitude in American psychiatry as from consideration of decisive experimental arguments.

In conclusion, we believe that, whatever reservations one may have concerning DSM-III, it constitutes an accomplishment of great importance for the development of psychiatry. Inasmuch as it conflicts with customary usage (as in the use of the word *neurosis*) and with strongly established theoretical positions, it will certainly stimulate fruitful discussion and doubtless experimental work, to verify or refute its conceptions. From this point of view, its confrontation with traditional French psychiatric nosology can be considered of particular interest.

REFERENCES

1. Langfeldt G: Scandinavia, in Contemporary European Psychiatry. Edited by Bellak L. New York, Grove Press, 1961.
2. Esquirol JED: Des Maladies mentales considerées sous les rapports médical, hygienique, et médico-legal. Paris, 1838
3. Bayle ALJ: Recherches sur les maladies mentales. Paris, 1822
4. Morel BA: Traité des dégénérescences physiques, intellectuelles et morales de l'èspece humaine. Paris, Bailliere, 1857
5. Falret JP: De la folie circulaire. Bulletin de l'Academie de Médicine 19: 382, 1854.
6. Kahlbaum KL: Die Gruppierungen der psychischen Krankheiten und die Einteilung der Seelenstorungen. Danzig, 1863
7. Kahlbaum KL: Die Katatonie oder das Spannungsirresein. Berlin, 1874
8. Kraepelin E: Psychiatrie. Ein Lehrbuch für Studierende and Aerzte, 5th ed. Leipzig, Johann Ambrosius Barth, 1896
9. Magnan V, Legrain M: Les Dégénérés (etat mental et syndromes episodiques). Paris, Rueff et Cie, 1895
10. Magnan V, Sérieux P: Le Délire chronique à l'évolution systematique. Paris, Gauthier Villars/Georges Masson, 1893
11. Pichot P: The diagnosis and classification of mental disorders in French-speaking countries: Background, current views and comparison with other nomenclatures. Psycholog Med 12: 457–492, 1982

12. Ey H, Bernard P, Brisset C: Manuel de psychiatrie, 4th ed. Paris, Masson et Cie, 1974
13. Ey H: Hughlings Jackson's principles and the organodynamic concept in psychiatry. Am J Psychiatry 118: 673–682, 1962
14. Ey H: Outline of an organo-dynamic conception of the structure, nosography, and pathogenesis of mental diseases, in Psychiatry and Philosophy. Edited by Natanson M. New York, Springer, 1969
15. Institut National de la Santé et de la Recherche Médicale. Section Psychiatrie: Classification française des troubles mentaux. Bulletin de l'Institut National de la Santé et de la Recherche Médicale 24, Supplement to No. 2, 1969
16. Legrain M: Du Délire chez les dégénérés (doctoral thesis). Paris, Librairie A. Deshaye et E. Lecrosnier, 1886
17. Serieux P, Capgras J: Les Folies Raisonnantes. Le Délire d'interpretation. Paris, Felix Alcan, 1909. (See review of this book in English in American Journal of Insanity 64: 182.)
18. Clérambault G de: Oeuvre psychiatrique (2 vols). Paris, Presses Universitaires de France, 1942
19. Baruk H: Delusions of passion, in Themes and Variations in European Psychiatry. Edited by Hirsch SR, Shepherd M. Charlottesville, Va, University Press of Virginia, 1974
20. Ballet G: La psychose hallucinatoire chronique. Encephale 6: 401–411, 1913
21. Ballet G: La psychose hallucinatoire chronique et la désagregation de la personnalité. Encephale 8: 501–508, 1913

ADDITIONAL READINGS

1. Boyer P, Guelfi, JD, Pull, CB: Nosologie et psychométrie des dépressions, in La Maladie dépressive. Paris, Ciba, 1983
2. Brugnon S: Contribution à l'étude des personnalités pathologiques (doctoral thesis). Paris, 1982
3. Dongier M, Lehmann H: Nouveaux systèmes de classification diagnostique: DMS III et ICD 9, in Encyclopédie Médico-chirurgicale. Psychiatrie. Paris, Editions Techniques, 1982, p. 37065 A 10
4. Ellenberger HF: Le problème des classifications psychiatriques, in Précis pratique de psychiatrie. Edited by Duguay R, Ellenberger HH. Paris, Maloine, 1981
5. Guelfi JD: Psychiatrie de l'adulte. Paris, Ellipses Marketing, 1983
6. Guelfi JD, Boyer P, Geberowicz B, Remey-Levi Strauss B: Dépressions. Actualisation clinique et aspects pratiques. Paris, Brillant, 1982
7. Overall JE: Des critères pour le diagnostic de dépression, in La symptomatologie dépressive. Enregistrement et évaluation. Edited by Pichot P, Pull CB. Rueil-Malmaison, Geigy, 1981
8. Pichot P: Classification des dépressions : orientation actuelle et perspectives d'avenir, in Symposium Deparon (démexiptiline). Edited by Guelfi JD, Pichot P, Sutter JM. Amsterdam, Excerpta Medica, 1981
9. Pichot P: Actualités du concept de dépression. L'Encéphale 7: 307–314, 1981

10. Pichot P, Guelfi JD, Pull CB: Sémiologie de la dépression, in Encyclopédie médico-chirurgicale. Psychiatrie. Paris, 1980, p. 37 110 A10 12
11. Pull, CB: Classification psychiatrique. Etat actuel et perspectives, in Précis de psychiatrie. Edited by Koupernik C, Loo H, Zarifian E. Paris, Flammarion, 1982
12. Pull CB, Pull MC: Des critères de diagnostic pour la schizophrénie, in Actualités de la schizophrénie. Edited by Pichot P. Paris, Presses Universitaires de France, 1981
13. Pull CB, Pull MC, Pichot P: LICET-S: une liste intégrée de critères d'évaluation taxonomique pour les psychoses non affectives. J Psychiat Biol Therap 1: 33–37, 1981

12

DSM-III AND ITALIAN PSYCHIATRY

Giovanni B. Cassano and Carlo Maggini

Most Italian psychiatrists, both in their daily practice and in scientific research, use diagnostic concepts, despite the strong criticisms, over the last 20 years, from colleagues with a psychodynamic or sociocultural orientation, who accuse them of analyzing the disease rather than the individual patient (1). The effect of such criticisms has been to make psychiatric opinion less convinced of the value of diagnosis. Moreover, the introduction of psychopharmacological drugs has helped to undermine diagnostic concepts that had been accepted for decades.

In Italy, phenomenological studies (*daseinsanalyse*) have emphasized the relationship between man and his environment. This line of thought has produced a much more profound and comprehensive transformation of Italian psychiatry than did psychoanalysis*. Some of its extreme adherents have ended up condemning psychiatry, denying that mental disorders have any biological or genetic foundation, and rejecting the value of a diagnostic or psychopathologic approach to mental disturbance.

Nevertheless, diagnosis in Italy has remained an irreplaceable methodological tool in clinical work: every psychiatrist has always been

Address correspondence to: Profesor Giovanni B. Cassano, Universitá degli Studi di Pisa, Cattedra di Clinica Psichiatrica II, Ente Ospedaliero di Pisa, Via Roma, 67, 56100 Pisa, Italy
*Gozzano M: Prolusione al Congresso "La Societá e le Malattie Mentali." Roma 20–22 giugno, 1968

175

aware that only after symptom and diagnostic problems have been clarified can the patient be considered in his personal uniqueness.

The ideology of the antipsychiatry movement was one of the factors that led to passage of the Italian Mental Health Act of 1978. Significantly, four years later there was to be a growing revival of interest in the diagnosis and classification of mental illness in Italy (2). In particular, the extensive use of pharmocotherapy in community care stimulated research on diagnosis and classification.

GENERAL EVALUATION OF DSM-III

DSM-III, which entails a significant revaluation of medico-diagnostic procedures, reached Italian psychiatry just when the antidiagnosis polemics were beginning to subside. Unexpectedly, a new interest has begun to emerge in various psychiatric schools that previously were hostile to a diagnostic approach (2). This renewed interest derives from awareness of the need for a more rigorous semiological and descriptive assessment of mental disorders.

Since the advent of pharmacological treatment, the role of the psychiatrist has changed: psychiatrists used to be observers who simply watched a mental disorder take its natural course; now, however, Italian psychiatrists encounter a growing number of patients with mild, incomplete, chronic, or residual symptoms that may be at an early or late stage of evolution, see subsyndromic pictures, and have to uncover masked and atypical psychopathological symptoms in order to treat patients effectively with drugs (3). Thus, the traditional classifications have become inadequate for investigators, practicing psychiatrists, and those involved in education alike. The traditional criteria for diagnosis are ill defined, and the categories have not been clinically validated; a new common language capable of improving communication among psychiatrists is needed in Italy as in other countries.

In this particular situation, DSM-III offers a set of well-established operational diagnostic criteria that may be applied in attempting to identify and validate new diagnostic categories and in selecting patients for specific therapies. Italian psychiatrists—especially those in research—will welcome the viewpoint adopted by DSM-III, though it is likely that its many innovative features and new diagnostic concepts will hinder its widespread adoption.

The multiaxial approach represents a concrete attempt to make a global evaluation of the patient's condition; this will surely be considered a significant advance when compared with previous classification systems, which were restricted to labeling diagnostic categories. The fact that DSM-III is based on a multiaxial system should allow it to overcome sterile theoretical conflicts between biological and psycho-social approaches, which tend to take a radical form in Italy.

The omission from DSM-III of some of the most widely used categories, such as neurosis, neurotic depression, endogenous depression, and schizophrenia simplex, will not be accepted rapidly or easily, because they are deeply embedded in the cultural background of Italian psychiatrists. Giving up such diagnostic concepts will not be a painless process, and will not occur without vigorous opposition. Moreover, there may be strong resistance to the introduction of completely new diagnostic categories, such as schizotypal personality disorder, cyclothymic and dysthymic disorders, and somatoform disorders. And abandoning an etiological basis to classification has meant the elimination of clinical concepts that are still regularly used by Italian psychiatrists, who may understandably experience such changes as revolutionary and as an imposition of, or intrusion by, North American thought and culture.

The scientifically grounded, atheoretical approach adopted in DSM-III may generate a sense of loss and disorientation in psychiatrists who rely largely on psychoanalytical, sociological, or biological models for understanding psychopathology. It is hard to determine to what extent the clinician should be deprived of theoretical models, some of which have been considered of practical use even though their validity has not been objectively demonstrated.

One of the most important characteristics of DSM-III is its diagnostic criteria, which are presented in a largely unambiguous and well-defined fashion and mark a great advance. Nevertheless, some traditionalist psychiatrists may consider such criteria too complex and involved; others may see them as reductive and simplistic; and still others may view them as a threat to their "indispensable clinical sense." By introducing a quantitative assessment of symptoms, DSM-III goes against traditional psychiatric evaluation, which is qualitative and empathic (4). The operational diagnostic criteria will inevitably give rise to criticism and lead to disputes, but they will offer Italian psychiatrists an effective set of diagnostic models with a strict semantic delimitation. It has to be borne in mind, however, that such diagnostic criteria are closely linked with clinical experience and are subject to future change.

Excessive concern with the diagnostic process seems an impediment to obtaining thorough knowledge of the patient, though it is recognized that the diagnostic process is no more than the initial phase of the clinician–patient relationship and that such criticism can be made of any diagnostic system.

Psychiatrists may find the number of diagnostic categories provided by DSM-III confusing and worrisome. The manual seems to be much more than a simple statistical tool, yet does not claim to be a clinical textbook. Proper understanding of the operational aspects of this instrument will make it clear that its use will not result in applying a large number of diagnoses to a single patient with unusual features. In fact, its strictly defined criteria aim to make it possible to give a syndromic or categorical diagnosis at a high hierarchical level; the less relevant categories are recorded only when the major ones have been ruled out. Thus, fear of excessive fragmentation of psychopathological features is unwarranted. For instance, a diagnosis of hypochondriasis within somatoform disorders may be made only if the symptom picture "is not due to any other mental disorder such as Schizophrenia, Affective Disorder, or Somatization Disorder."

In its philosophy and structure, DSM-III appears to the clinician as an evolving tool in which the classifications and the large number of diagnostic categories may be continually brought up to date, or even radically modified, on the basis of sound clinical and scientific data. All the material presented may be considered operational models that should undergo further validation in various countries.

REACTIONS TO SPECIFIC CATEGORIZATIONS

DSM-III's atheoretical approach imposed the elimination of the term *neurosis*; all the psychopathological phenomena previously classified under this heading have been reclassified separately as anxiety, somatoform, dissociative, or psychosexual disorders, depending on purely descriptive clinical features.

Within this classification, anxiety disorders play an important role. They are sharply isolated from other neurotic disorders, and they are described in a clear-cut way that offers a unified, global description through a cross-sectional and longitudinal analysis. This approach to anxiety disorders has an obvious practical validity, as it enables treatment to be differentiated and adapted to each individual category.

DSM-III provides an opportunity to test the separation of anxiety disorders from, or their connection with, depression. Patients commonly labeled "neurotic" may well suffer from depression or panic disorder. Actually, recent data suggest that panic disorder is more frequently associated with depression than with a generalized anxiety condition (5). It has to be determined whether panic attacks trigger depressive episodes, if they are just an early manifestation of unipolar or bipolar disorders, or if the depression that often follows panic disorder is a secondary phenomenon. Once their etiological connotations have been removed, as in DSM-III, anxiety disorders become a well-defined diagnostic class that can be investigated from different standpoints.

Among the really innovative aspects of DSM-III, its unified approach to and expansion of the area of affective disorders warrant special consideration, and should be welcomed. Its method of classification on the basis of the description of symptoms and course, free from any etiological inference, reflects a laudable effort to maintain scientific objectivity, and should bring immediate practical advantages to the investigation of therapeutic and epidemiologic issues.*

In DSM-III the expansion of the category of affective disorders is due mainly to: 1) its recognition of affective disorders with psychotic symptoms not congruent with mood, which may be considered revolutionary in North America, but not in Europe; 2) the limitations it places on the use of a diagnosis of schizoaffective disorder, which can be given only after schizophrenic and schizophreniform disorders and unipolar and bipolar affective disorders with incongruent psychotic symptoms have been excluded; and 3) its new categories of cyclothymic and dysthymic disorders, including neurotic depression, minor affective syndromes, chronic affective disorders, and subaffective personality disorders.

Affective disorders are classified according to acute and chronic course, mono- and bipolarity, and typical and atypical symptoms and course. The categories of dysthymic and cyclothymic disorders make it possible to consider and include those depressive syndromes that, because of a nonepisodic course and a low degree of severity, are usually excluded from the category of affective disorders. The DSM-III emphasis on the evolution and course of this illness is, we believe, fundamental if the various features of depressive pathology are to be recognized and correctly evaluated.

Unlike cyclothymic disorder, dysthmyic disorder appears to form an unduly large category, including some heterogeneous features that could have been more clearly identified and defined while leaving them within the domain of affective disorders. An expansion of this area within a unified framework is clinically indicated for the future, and should be a real step forward in understanding, and valuable in dealing with, the affective disorders.

Removal of the concept of reactive depression from affective disorders and placing it among adjustment reactions require clinicians to make a more rigorous analysis of the temporal relation between environmental events and types of mood change. This omission of the endogenous/reactive dichotomy may encounter some opposition in Italy, where, as a legacy of classic nosology, endogenous depression is still contrasted with reactive depression in many professional circles, on

---

*GB Cassano, C Maggini: Delimitazione diagnostica e clinica degli stati depressivi. Paper presented at the 35th National Meeting of the Italian Society of Psychiatry, Cagliari, Italy, October 1982

the basis not only of etiological but also of symptomatologic, prognostic, and therapeutic criteria (6).

One major clinical advantage offered by DSM-III is its clear-cut delimitation of the area of affective disorders from the areas of organic mental disorders and reactive disorders. A diagnosis of adjustment disorder clearly implies the rejection of a purely psychological etiology for depression and mania. The category "organic affective syndrome" appears to be poorly defined; here a somatic etiology must be clinically ascertained. The clinician is supposed to be able to assess the etiological relation between an affective disturbance and "specific organic factors" such as thyroid dysfunction. Similarly, for the category "other unspecified substance affective disorder," etiological significance is attributed to drugs such as alpha-methyldopa, reserpine, and hallucinogens when the affective disturbance follows the ingestion of a drug and there is no personal and family history of affective disorders. The multiaxial approach should make it possible to be less dogmatic in these cases and to defer establishing etiological links between organic factors and affective disorders. For these categories it is, surprisingly, assumed that there is clear-cut clinical evidence of a purely organic affective syndrome, although the physiopathological basis is still not sufficiently known to exclude other etiologies. Though in other sections DSM-III keeps strictly to an atheoretical approach, in this one it paves the way for etiological inferences on the basis of vague chronological and anamnestic criteria.

The separation between substance use disorders and substance-induced organic mental disorders insofar as alcohol is concerned appears to be clinically relevant. This distinction is particularly valuable in allowing one to distinguish between alcohol dependence and the clinical syndromes due to acute and chronic alcohol intoxication. The diagnostic criteria for alcohol abuse and alcohol dependence will draw the attention of clinicians to the most widespread and detrimental effects, which can be treated before irreversible brain damage has been done.

The tendency for the range of true schizophrenic pathology to become narrower is being strengthened in Italy, as elsewhere, by the efficacy of antidepressive treatments and by the short- and long-term effects of neuroleptic drugs. Most of the acute forms of schizophrenia and some of the psychoses that were previously called "schizoaffective" are now diagnosed as affective disorders. This trend is clearly in agreement with DSM-III, in which the diagnosis of major affective disorder with "mood-incongruent psychotic features" is given a higher priority than that of schizophrenic or schizophreniform disorders.

The diagnostic problem of acute nonschizophrenic psychosis has been provisionally solved in DSM-III simply by considering the duration of the evolution of an episode: if it is less than two weeks, atypical psychosis is diagnosed; if less than six months, schizophreniform disorder; and if more than six months, schizophrenic disorder. This procedure has been adopted after an extensive examination of the literature that led to the conclusion that no other valid differential criteria were currently available (4). Though pragmatic, these diagnostic distinctions appear to be an oversimplification hard to reconcile with traditional clinical concepts.

One of the main advantages introduced by the multiaxial approach is the prominence given to personality features, which should be reported on axis II. This implies an accurate definition of personality traits, with the introduction of terms new to European psychiatrists, such as schizotypal personality disorder.

Some major problems are evident in the attitude of the developers of DSM-III toward borderline states:

1. Confusion and disagreement may arise from use of the term *borderline personality disorder* to represent a single diagnostic entity when up to now the term *borderline* has implied a heterogeneous group of disorders that are on the boundary of other well-recognized conditions.

2. It is not clear what conditions "border on" borderline personality disorder. Previously, schizophrenia was one of those conditions; but according to DSM-III, schizotypal personality disorder, not borderline personality disorder, is related to schizophrenia.

3. The nosological position of schizotypal personality disorder is inconsistent. If this category is a part of the schizophrenic spectrum (7), why is it included within the section entitled "Personality Disorders," when the personality affective disorders such as cyclothymic and dysthymic disorders are included within the class of affective disorders? The definition of this category is in line with the current tendency of North American psychiatry to circumscribe the diagnosis of schizophrenia, which was too widely employed in the past, and to enlarge the realm of affective pathology. In Italy the concept "borderline" is used to refer to a variety of clinical pictures on the border of schizophrenia, neurosis, manic-depressive psychosis, and personality disorders without a clear syndromal connotation.

CONCLUSIONS

DSM-III has met the need to supersede previous classification systems. As we have stressed, it has made a resolute attempt to reject the introduction of dogmatic etiopathogenetic concepts. Nevertheless, some categories, such as organic affective syndromes, narcissistic personality, and dissociative disorders, appear to contain unproven etiologic assumptions. The atheoretical approach may account for some oversimplifications, such as the distinction between major and other specific affective disorders and the arbitrariness of the distinction between schizotypal and borderline personality disorders.

Some of the proposed categories appear to be the result of negotiated solutions aiming to reconcile different orientations in the absence of clear-cut empirical data. But any classificatory system inevitably has some shortcomings and gaps that leave it open to criticism.

On the whole, the proposed models respond to current clinical reality, and can be considered to arise from a well-planned initiative that has required years of commitment and work by many groups of outstanding clinicians and researchers. The diagnostic criteria of DSM-III, in particular, will be of great help in clinical-diagnostic and therapeutic activity.

Apart from any criticisms that can be made, the idea behind DSM-III has already influenced the Italian scientific community, as was evident at the 35th National Meeting of the Italian Society of Psychiatry, held in Cagliari in October 1982. DSM-III will stimulate an enormous amount of clinical investigation and speculative work in Italy. Its impact will inevitably reach the educational level and will affect the clinical training of medical students and specialists in psychiatry. It will also have an important influence in other areas, such as medical psychology and sociology. There are indications that DSM-III is already making headway in both psychiatric and nonpsychiatric domains. For instance, a recently published volume written for general practitioners, *Depression in Medicine*, edited by G.A. Fava and L. Pavan (8), uses a classification derived largely from DSM-III.

DSM-III represents an important advance in psychiatric diagnosis. It is to be hoped that it will be widely accepted in Europe; this would make for improved scientific communication and greater uniformity in the diagnostic definition of patients selected for clinical, therapeutic, and epidemiologic studies (9).

With the reservations noted above, we believe that DSM-III, some of whose basic concepts stem from the European nosologic tradition, will be welcomed in Italy, where fundamental Kraepelinian concepts still play an important role in the clinical training of psychiatrists.

REFERENCES

1. Cargnello D: Nosografia delle depressioni, in Le Sindromi Depressive. Edited by Fazio C. Torino, Minerva Medica, 1960, pp 47–71
2. Sarteschi P, Maggini C: Psichiatria. Parma, Goliardica Editrici, 1982
3. Maggini C, Cassano GB: La depressione. Aspetti sintomatologici e diag-

nostici attuali, in La Condizione Depressiva. Edited by Cassano GB. Milan, Masson Italia Editori, 1982, pp 151–159

4. Dongier M, Lehmann H: Nouveaux systèmes de classification diagnostique: DSM-III et ICD-9, in Encyclopédie médico-chirurgicale. Psychiatrie. Paris, Editions Techniques, 1982, p. 37065 A 10

5. Dunner DL: Anxiety disorders and depression. Bulletin of the International Committee for the Prevention and Treatment of Depression, No 8, p 8, Winter 1982

6. Sarteschi P, Cassano GB, Maggini C: Nosografia della depressione, in La Condizione Depressiva. Edited by Cassano GB: Milan, Masson Italia Editori, 1981, pp 39–53

7. Kendler KS, Gruenberg AM, Strauss JS: An independent analysis of the Copenhagen sample of the Danish adoption study of schizophrenia. II. Relationship between schizotypal personality disorders and schizophrenia. Arch Gen Psychiatry 38: 986–987, 1981

8. Fava GA, Pavan L: Depressione in Medicina. Bologna, Patron Editore, 1982

9. Dotti A: La nosografia degli stati depressivi da Kraepelin al DSM-III. Rivista di Psichiatria 17: 38–55, 1982

13

DSM-III IN JAPAN

Yutaka Honda, M.D.

JAPANESE PSYCHIATRY: HISTORICAL BACKGROUND

The history of psychiatry in Japan dates back for about 1,300 years. In 701 the national law Taiho Ritsuryo described *ten* ("paroxysmal attacks") and *kyo* ("behavioral abnormalities"); and another law, Yohro Ritsuryo, in 718 decreed exemption of taxes for the physically and mentally disabled and guiltlessness or reduction of penalty for crimes committed by the mentally disabled.

In the early days Japanese medicine as a whole was strongly influenced by the ancient Chinese "Kampo" medicine, which became deeply rooted in the soil of Japan. "Kampo" medicine assumed a wholistic approach to illness and placed special emphasis in somatic *sho* ("syndromes") on either positive or negative signs. Treatments consisted mainly of administration of combinations of herbs. Toward the end of the Edo period (1603–1867), "Kampo" medicine reached its zenith.

At about this same time, medical texts on psychiatry began to be published. The famous books of the day included *Ippondo Gyoyo Igen* [Medical essays] (1), by Shutoku Kagawa (1683–1755), published in

Address correspondence to: Yutaka Honda, M.D., 2-7-9 Kugenuma-matsugaoka, Fujisawa City, Kanagawa-ken, 251, Japan

1807, which described precise mental symptoms and 30 observed cases of anorexia and constipation; *Tenkan-kyo Keiken-hen* [Experiences with psychoses] (2), by Ken Tsuchida, published in 1819, which described 61 of his own clinical cases of various psychoses; *Ryoji Chadan* [A teatime chat about treatments], by Gensen Tamura, published in 1808; and *Toho-hen* [Guide to treatment with emetics] (3), by Kanae Kitamura, published in 1817, covering 23 of his own cases. These books described mental symptoms mostly in terms of behavioral abnormalities, with less emphasis on the psychopathology of subjective mental symptoms.

The end of the Edo period was also important in the history of Japanese medicine, because of the gradual introduction of European, especially Dutch, medicine into the country, under very strict governmental controls. Soken Homma (1803–1872) described clinical records of mental patients in his book *Naika Hiroku* [Secret notes on internal medicine] (4), which was published in 1864 and was modeled after European medicine.

Following the Meiji restoration, in 1868, a radical political transition from the feudalistic Edo Shogunate period to modern Japan, Western medicine was officially adopted, and German medicine was systematically introduced. This produced drastic changes in Japanese medicine. The old Chinese "Kampo" school rapidly lost its influence and continued to be practiced only among a limited number of specialists, who were not officially recognized as qualified medical doctors. But some of the terms used in the "Kampo" medicine to describe mental symptoms persisted in psychiatric terminology, and are still in use today (5)—e.g., *utsu* ("depression"), *kommei* ("stupor"), *kembou* ("amnesia"), *shinkisho* ("hypochondriasis"), *sakuran* ("confusion"), and *tenkan* ("epilepsy").

In 1877 a German doctor, Erwin Baelz (1849–1913), came to Japan and started to teach Western medicine, including psychiatry, at the Tokyo Medical School, forerunner of the present University of Tokyo Faculty of Medicine. Hajime Sakaki (1857–1897) went to Europe and studied psychiatry under Westphal and Virchow in Germany and became the first professor of psychiatry at the Department of Psychiatry, Faculty of Medicine, University of Tokyo, in 1886.

Sakaki's pupil Shuzo Kuré (1866–1932) studied under Emil Kraepelin and became the second professor of psychiatry at the University of Tokyo, in 1901. He taught Kraepelin-school German psychiatry and trained many psychiatrists for 25 years. Kuré is considered the founder of modern psychiatry in Japan. Many of his pupils taught psychiatry in various parts of Japan and formed a dominant school of psychiatry. At present there are about 80 universities with a psychiatric department in Japan, and it can be said that most of these departments have been influenced by the teachings of Kuré, and still use German terminology in describing mental symptoms.

In parallel with the general social trend of rapid absorption of Western cultures into the country, Japanese psychiatrists eagerly studied and assimilated various types of Western psychiatry, especially German, French, and British; and after World War II, American psychiatry was also introduced. Thus, Japanese psychiatry became a mixture of the various psychiatric schools of the world.

Among the many Western psychiatrists whose works have been translated into Japanese and have had a significant influence on Japanese psychiatry, the following names are especially familiar to Japanese psychiatrists: W. Griesinger, J.M. Charcot, K.L. Kahlbaum, J.H. Jackson, H. Maudsley, R. Krafft-Ebing, C. Wernicke, I.P. Pavlov, E. Kraepelin, S. Freud, E. Bleuler, P. Janet, A. Hoche, A. Meyer, K. Bonhoeffer, A. Adler, C.G. Jung, K. Birnbaum, K. Kleist, L. Binswanger, K. Jaspers, K. Horney, E. Minkowsky, K. Schneider, E. Kretschmer, H.S. Sullivan, J. Zutt, and H. Ey.

On the other hand, some original clinical concepts and treatments have emerged in Japan. These include Morita therapy for obsessive-compulsive *shinkeishitsu* ("nervosity"*) patients (6), originated by Takemasa Morita (1874–1938); *shuchaku-kishitsu* ("immodithyme temperament"*) (7), a premorbid personality of a depressive type, described by Mitsuzo Shimoda (1885–1978); genetic study of atypical psychosis (8), undertaken by Hisatoshi Mituda (1910–1979); and *seikatsu rinsho*, a living-learning therapy for schizophrenic patients (9), devised by Hiroshi Utena (1913–) and his group of psychiatrists at Gumma University.

Because of the mixture of psychiatrists with different orientations in Japan, various psychiatric diagnoses and terminologies have been freely used, depending on the particular viewpoint of each psychiatrist. The resulting confusion has been especially noticeable in dealing with borderline areas and atypical cases.

JAPANESE DIAGNOSTIC CONCEPTS AND DSM-III

Although no systematic diagnostic criteria or classifications of mental disorders have originated in Japan, the major trend in Japanese psychiatry can be classed as somewhere near the German school, with a biological orientation. Most of the Japanese textbooks of psychiatry have adopted a classification that includes endogenous, exogenous, and psychogenic mental disorders and have described many subtypes

---

*These terms will be further explained and discussed in a later section.

under these three major categories according to the possible etiology of the disease. The philosophical or psychological theories concerning the etiology of mental disorders are usually mentioned in these textbooks, and special terminologies are explained. Psychoanalysis, existential analysis, and schools with other theoretical bases have been introduced into Japan and aroused much interest, but they have not been used as standards of diagnostic classification. It can be said that the influence of descriptive German psychiatry still persists in Japanese psychiatry. In this regard, DMS-III, which emphasizes objective description of mental symptoms, including adoption of Schneider's first-rank symptoms for the diagnosis of schizophrenia, appears to be acceptable to the majority of Japanese psychiatrists.

Recently there have been increasing opportunities for Japanese psychiatrists to participate in international meetings, and they recognize the need to use internationally communicable diagnostic terms and criteria if they are to be able to exchange information with psychiatrists from other countries.

The ninth revision of the International Classification of Diseases (ICD-9) has been translated into Japanese by Masaaki Kato, superintendent at the National Institute of Mental Health, and has been adopted as the official diagnostic classification by the Ministry of Health and Welfare. But the use of ICD-9 in the daily practice has been very limited, possibly because some people are not quite satisfied with the non-operational diagnostic criteria of ICD-9.

REACTION OF JAPANESE PSYCHIATRISTS TO DSM-III

When the draft of DSM-III appeared in 1978, several Japanese psychiatrists paid special attention to this new classification. In 1980, when DSM-III was completed and published, many Japanese psychiatrists started to study it. Among them, Saburo Takahashi and his group of psychiatrists at the Shiga University of Medical Sciences were the earliest to translate DSM-III into Japanese, to try to apply DSM-III diagnostic criteria to Japanese patients, and to discuss the usefulness and weaknesses of the new system. Their activities have been published serially under the title "Clinical applications of DSM-III diagnostic criteria and their limitations" in 17 issues (10–26) of the *Japanese Journal of Clinical Psychiatry* [Rinsho Seishin Igaku], from October 1980 to April 1982.

There has been a tremendous response to this serial publication, and a growing interest in DSM-III has arisen among a wide range of mental health professionals in Japan. In April 1981, Yomishi Kasahara, Professor of Psychiatry at Nagoya University, gave a presidential lecture, under the title "On DSM-III, new diagnostic criteria in America" (27), at the 77th Annual Assembly of the Japanese Society of Psychiatry and Neurology. This lecture also stimulated the spread of DSM-III in Japan.

In December 1981, a research group on the application of DSM-III diagnostic criteria and their limitations was organized with the support of a grant-in-aid from the Ministry of Education and Cultural Sciences. The chairman of the research group was Saburo Takahashi, Professor of Psychiatry at the Shiga University of Medical Sciences, and the organizing members of the group included representatives of six other universities: Ryo Takahashi, Professor of Neuropsychiatry, Nagasaki University; Nariyoshi Yamaguchi, Professor of Neuropsychiatry, Kanazawa University; Nobukatsu Kato, Professor of Neuropsychiatry, Kyoto Prefectural University of Medicine; Takuro Noguchi, Professor of Neuropsychiatry, Saitama Medical School; Hajime Kazamatsuri, Professor of Psychiatry, Teikyo University; and Yutaka Honda, of the Department of Neuropsychiatry, University of Tokyo. This research group conducted a joint field trial of DSM-III with Japanese mental patients. The interrater reliability (28) on axis I diagnoses of 326 adult patients was an overall kappa of 0.70, which was similar to the results obtained in the United States field trial (29). Details of the results of this study are reported by Koichi Hanada and Saburo Takahashi elsewhere in this volume.

The results on a 9-item questionnaire distributed by Saburo Takahashi and Koichi Hanada (30) to 103 participants in the DSM-III field trials were as follows: 83% of 69 respondents considered the addition of DSM-III significant; 84% recognized the multiaxial approach as useful; 60% considered coding personality disorders on axis II adequate; and 55% answered yes, and 19% no, to the question "Is DSM-III applicable as it is in Japan?"

The second year of research of this group was focused on an interinstitutional reliability study, which was conducted by circulating color videotaped records of 14 actual patients prepared by the 7 participating psychiatric departments. As the third-year project, an interrater reliability study of axis I diagnoses of child and adolescent patients is now being conducted.

Along with the progress of this research group, a Japanese Committee on International Diagnostic Criteria in Psychiatry (JCIDCP) was organized, in May 1981. The members include about 100 representative psychiatrists from 36 universities and 4 psychiatric facilities. The organizing committee consisted of the seven organizing members of the research group on Application of DSM-III Diagnostic Criteria and Their Limitations. The chairman of JCIDCP has been Saburo Takahashi, of the Shiga University of Medical Sciences, and the general secretary, Yutaka Honda, of the University of Tokyo.

In late 1981, Dr. Robert L. Spitzer, Chairperson of the Task Force on

Nomenclature and Statistics of the American Psychiatric Association, and Dr. Janet B. W. Williams, text editor of DSM-III, visited Japan. An evening of lectures was held in Tokyo on 31 October. Titles of the lectures were: "Background and major achievements of DSM-III," by Dr. Spitzer (31), and "A multiaxial approach to diagnosis," by Dr. Williams (32). More than 300 psychiatrists from the Tokyo area attended the lectures. Dr. Spitzer and Dr. Williams delivered two more lectures, in Osaka and Nagoya. On 1 November 1981 the first annual meeting of JCIDCP was held in Tokyo; its theme was "The application of DSM-III in Japan." The first presentations were "Overview of DSM-III in the USA," by Dr. Spitzer (33) and "Field Study of DSM-III in the USA," by Dr. Williams (34). From the Japanese side, three papers were read on a second topic, "Clinical application of DSM-III in Japan" (28, 35, 36). Four papers were then read on the third topic, "Conventional psychiatric diagnoses in Japan and DSM-III" (37–40), followed by two papers (41, 42) on the fourth topic, "Other international diagnostic criteria and DSM-III." About 80 members from various parts of Japan participated in heated discussions. The proceedings of this meeting and the lectures by Drs. Spitzer and Williams were published in detail in Volume 11, No. 2, 1982, of the *Japanese Journal of Clinical Psychiatry*, under a special title, "Topics Concerning DSM-III" (28, 31–42).

In April 1982, DSM-III became the theme of a symposium at the general assembly of the Japanese Society of Psychiatry and Neurology in Kyoto. It was also one of the topics of symposia at the World Psychiatric Association Regional Meeting at Kyoto International Conference Hall in April 1982. Dr. Andrew E. Skodol, of the New York State Psychiatric Institute, participated in this symposium. Later, he gave two seminars, one in Kyoto (43) and another in Tokyo (44), based on the *DSM-III Case Book*, of which he was one of the authors. In his Tokyo seminar, Dr. Skodol explained the classification and the principles of treatment of psychosexual disorders, which the audience found very interesting. Although research reports on psychosexual disorders have been few in Japan, interest in this area has been growing since the introduction of DSM-III.

On 6 November 1982, the second annual meeting of the JCIDCP was held. Six papers on clinical experiences in using DSM-III, the Research Diagnostic Criteria (RDC), and the Present State Examination (PSE) were presented, following which Ryo Takahashi, of Nagasaki University, gave a special lecture entitled "Recent topics on diagnostic criteria in psychiatry in the world." Case presentations and discussions, with the aid of videotape recordings, were given by Saburo Takahashi, of the Shiga University of Medical Sciences, on interrater discrepancies.

A two-day teaching seminar on DSM-III was held 12–13 February 1983, in Tokyo, for general mental health professionals.

TRANSLATION OF DSM-III INTO JAPANESE

The *Quick Reference to the Diagnostic Criteria from DSM-III* (Mini-D) was translated into Japanese by Saburo Takahashi and Koichi Hanada, of the Shiga University of Medical Sciences, and Akira Fujinawa of Kyoto University, and was published in March 1982 by Igaku Shoin, Ltd., Tokyo (45).

DSM-III Training Guide, by Linda J. Webb, Carlo C. DiClemente, Edwin E. Johnstone, and others was translated into Japanese by Makoto Shimizu, of Jikei Medical University, and was published in January 1982 by Seiwa Shoten Publishers, Tokyo (46).

DSM-III Case Book, by Robert L. Spitzer, Andrew E. Skodol, Miriam Gibbon, and Janet B. W. Williams, was translated into Japanese by Saburo Takahashi, Koichi Hanada, Yutaka Honda, and several other members of the faculties of both the Shiga University of Medical Sciences and the University of Tokyo. It was published in March 1983 by Igaku Shoin Ltd., Tokyo (47).

Some controversies have arisen about how to translate important terms in DSM-III. The term *disorder* was initially translated by Saburo Takahashi and his group as *byo*, which implies disease. This translation became the subject of heated discussion among organizing members of JCIDCP and Drs. Robert L. Spitzer and Janet B. W. Williams at the dinner meeting after the first meeting of the JCIDCP. There are three choices for a Japanese translation of *disorder*: *shogai, sho,* and *byo*. Most people agreed that none of these three Japanese terms was acceptable as the sole term for *all* mental disorders in the Japanese language meaning of the term. Dr. Spitzer stressed that the translated term for *disorder* should not imply etiology, and that the same term should be used throughout the classification. After two hours of heated discussion, *shogai* was adopted as the term for *disorder*, and extensive changes were made in the galley proofs of the Mini-D translation (48–50).

Other points of discussion concerning the translation of DSM-III included the term for *major depression*. This was translated by Saburo Takahashi as *dai-utsubyo: major* was translated as *dai*, meaning "large," or "big," which was initially considered strange, but was later considered appropriate in view of the pervasiveness of the depressive state covered by major depression. Here the translation of *depression* was *utsubyo*, an established Japanese term containing *byo*, implying disease. The term *utsubyo* is very popular and acceptable in the Japanese language, and there was no reason to avoid using it. The same use of *-byo* at the end occurred in the translation of *schizophrenia, atypical psychosis,* and other terms. This lack of harmony was caused partly by the inconsistent use of *disorder* and *psychosis* in DSM-III.

EVALUATION OF DSM-III IN JAPAN

The introduction of DSM-III into Japan has been rapid, and has had a significant impact on Japanese psychiatry. Since DSM-III has been officially adopted by the APA, and is the diagnostic classification used routinely in clinical practice and mental health activities all over the United States, it carries considerable weight, and has attracted the interest of many mental health personnel in Japan (51–55). The clear description of clinical syndromes and the adoption of operational criteria are easy for Japanese psychiatrists to understand and appear to fit the cultural climate of Japanese psychiatry.

Some of the psychiatrists of the older generations, who have been accustomed to using traditional diagnoses, have shown reluctance to use the unfamiliar DSM-III terminology and diagnostic criteria. Psychiatrists of the younger generations are picking up DSM-III with relatively less resistance. As a matter of fact, the information on all of the five axes of DSM-III are necessary in making diagnoses and planning treatment in ordinary clinical practice, and has long been utilized tacitly by most psychiatrists. The clear framing of these important clinical aspects as a multiaxial system in DSM-III is useful for grasping the total picture of a patient systematically, and is also helpful in ensuring that no aspects are left out.

With regard to the evaluation of each axis, axis I categories of DSM-III are, generally speaking, clear and easy to use. But some points have been raised in the clinical application of DSM-III to Japanese patients.

1. The concept of major depression is too wide, and is more like a depressive state than a clinical entity.

2. The so-called "negative" symptoms of schizophrenia, such as blunted affect, decrease in initiative, autism, social isolation, etc., are not given enough weight in the diagnostic criteria for schizophrenic disorder.

3. There are no diagnostic criteria for atypical psychosis.

4. There is no category for puerperal psychoses, which require special psychiatric attention and care.

5. A group of mental disorders, popularly known in Japan as *taijin-kyofu* ("anthropophobia"), is not covered by DSM-III. *Taijin-kyofu* is fear of a situation in which the patient, without an awareness of what he is doing, gives unpleasant feelings to people around him. The patient complains of varying worries, originating in his physical condition, such as fear of body odor (*taishu-kyofu*), in which the patient believes that he emits rank odors from his body, often from his axilla, mouth, anus, or genital area, etc.; or fear of glancing (*shisen-kyofu*), in which the patient believes that he glances at other persons around him unintentionally and gives others unpleasant feelings; or fear of ugly facial expressions (*shubo-kyofu*,

"desmorphophobia"), such as grinning, or showing the whites of the eyes; or fear of thinking aloud (*dokugo-kyofu*); etc.

An illustration of *taijin-kyofu* follows: A 48-year-old unmarried woman presented with a chief complaint of "thinking aloud unconsciously and hurting the feelings of other people around her." She lives with her 78-year-old mother, 43-year-old unmarried brother, a bank employee, and 37-year-old unmarried sister, a government employee. After graduation from senior high school, with a good record, she worked as an assistant teacher at a primary school for three years, then as a clerical employee for five years, a cartographer for six years, and a clerk for a construction company for three months. Afterward she stayed at home, doing house-work, and sometimes engaged in part-time jobs irregularly.

The patient's past history revealed no particular physical and mental disorders. In personality she was characterized as reserved, prudent, conscientious, and tender in sentiment. She has not been overly sociable, but has had some friends and worked earnestly in her jobs. She has been somewhat unyielding in her inner spirit, but has always adapted to circumstances. She has been sensitive to the feelings of other people and desired to be accepted by those around her.

In the past five years, her brother has started to think aloud while bathing at home, which the patient disliked and feared that she might someday do the same thing. When she was 45 years of age, she felt that she must have thought aloud, spoken ill of other people unconsciously, and hurt other people's feelings. As evidence of her thinking aloud, she said that she has received several telephone calls in which no one has spoken, made by somebody who knows her habit of thinking aloud and who has attempted to evoke her habit while she was holding the phone receiver. When a new collector of her bills appeared, she reasoned that it was the result of her thinking ill aloud of the previous collector in front of him, although she has no memory of doing so.

The patient believed that her habit of thinking aloud was known to everybody in the vicinity of her house, and she hesitated to go out shopping, fearing that people would avoid her or look back or turn their heads away from her. Whenever she left the house, neighbors would come out of their houses and stand at their gates or on the street watching her, a "queer woman." She said that she was never aware of thinking aloud or of speaking ill of others consciously. In spite of the assurance of her sister that the patient never thought aloud at home, she insisted that she often thought aloud even at home and that her sister was a "foggy head" and simply unobservant. When she complained about her habit of thinking aloud, she had tears in her soft eyes, and wanted to die rather than live under such miserable and painful conditions. The facial expressions and the emotional contact of the patient were soft and gentle. The patient's judgment was normally intact, except for the un-realistic fear of thinking aloud. In spite of her fear of other people, she kept on working, both at home and at part-time jobs.

After one year of treatment with trifluoperazine and diazepam, the intensity of the patient's fear gradually decreased, and she started to admit that she did not think aloud at home anymore; but her belief that she though aloud outside the house persisted, but with less intensity and frequency.

Patients with *taijin-kyofu* are rather frequent in Japan, and there is a considerable literature on this condition. Most investigators in Japan classify it as a neurosis, akin to obsessive-compulsive neurosis. The emotional contact, social functioning, outcome, and personality of the patient are well maintained, and are obviously different from those of schizophrenia. But the patient never admits that his or her worries are excessive or unreasonable. The patient has an unrealistic belief that he or she is doing harm to other people by hurting their feelings and feels bad about it. This is contrary to the psychopathology of the idea of persecution often observed in psychotic patients, in which they feel that other people are going to harm them.

Itaru Yamashita, Professor of Psychiatry at Hokkaido University, a well-known investigator of *taijin-kyofu*, commented in his monograph on the subject (56) that there is a common psychopathology in *taijin-kyofu* and hypochondriasis. In hypochondriasis physical sensations are interpreted as proof of a serious somatic disease. A hypochrondriac patient complains of a serious disease with an affirmative attitude and confidence, in spite of logical reassurance by a physician. In *taijin-kyofu*, trivial actions such as coughing, laughing, or turning the head and accidental behaviors of other people are experienced by the patient as proof that he or she is hurting the feelings of other people as a result of a physical defect, and develops a firm, delusional belief in spite of the assurance of family members and physicians. In hypochondriasis, the self as a physical existence, and in *taijin-kyofu*, the self as a social existence, are in jeopardy and are a source of anxiety, which shows a tendency to develop from fear to delusional belief.

In DSM-III, hypochondriasis is classified as a somatoform disorder. The diagnostic criteria for hypochondriasis include:

> A. The predominant disturbance is an unrealistic interpretation of *physical signs or sensations* as abnormal, leading to preoccupation with the fear or belief of having a serious *disease*.
> B. Thorough physical evaluation does not support the diagnosis of any *physical disorder* that can account for the *physical signs or sensations* or for the individual's unrealistic interpretation of them.
> C. The unrealistic fear or belief of having a *disease* persists despite medical reassurance and causes impairment in social or occupational functioning. [Emphasis added.]

Yamashita points out that if the phrase "physical signs or sensations" is replaced by "actions and behaviors of people around the patient" and "disease" or "physical disorder" is replaced by "physical defect that causes unpleasant feelings to the other people," these descriptions might well become the diagnostic criteria for *taijin-kyofu*. He thinks that *taijin-kyofu* should be classified in a new category of "sensitive state" or "sensitive disorder."

Although *taijin-kyofu* is common in Japan, it is not clear whether it is found in the United States or in European countries. A personal communication has indicated that there is a similar condition in Taiwan. In Japan, a thickly populated, narrow island where the traditional life of the people has been agricultural, one has to live in harmony with other people, and tends to be sensitive to the feelings of others. The social phobia of DSM-III is essentially not applicable, because the patient with *taijin-kyofu* never admits that his fear is excessive or unreasonable. If this unrealistic belief is judged as a delusion, with gross impairment of reality testing, *taijin-kyofu* must be classified as a special type of nonschizophrenic delusional disorder, possibly as an atypical psychosis in the present DSM-III. In any case, a new axis I category may be necessary for *taijin-kyofu*.

With regard to axis II, the types of personality disorders described in DSM-III are rather unfamiliar to Japanese psychiatrists. In the field trial of DSM-III made in Japan, axis II diagnoses were made in only 14% of the cases. The newly introduced schizotypal personality disorder is understandable and useful. Avoidant, narcissistic, and borderline personality disorders, however, appear to reflect the American influence of psychoanalysis.

Some of the personality disorders commonly observed in Japan are not found in DSM-III. One is *shinkeishitsu* ("nervosity"), described by Masatake Morita, characterized by perfectionism and hypochondriacal tendencies, and considered a premorbid personality of obsessive-compulsive neurosis. Another is *shuchaku-kishitsu* ("immodithyme temperament"), described by Mitsuzo Shimoda, characterized by excessive conscientiousness and thoroughness, and considered a premorbid personality of depression. The criteria for compulsive personality disorder in DSM-III are close to, but somewhat different from, these Japanese personality disorders.

With regard to axis III, it is sometimes difficult to judge if some autonomic symptoms, such as sleep disturbances, sexual dysfunctions, changes of body weight, etc., are to be classified as axis III symptoms or dealt with as axis I symptoms.

Judgment of the level of psychosocial stressors on axis IV is not easy. As Dr. Spitzer commented in the discussion at the first JCIDCP meeting in 1981, the effect of a particular stressor is influenced by individual vulnerability and by the duration of the stress.

Axis V is also difficult to judge with confidence. The criteria of what is optimum social functioning and social adaptation are somewhat different in Japan, and the American examples are not readily applicable to Japanese cases.

Other limitations in the clinical use of DSM-III include the lack of criteria for judging the presence or absence of critical symptoms. This often causes serious ambiguity in making critical decisions in reaching a final diagnosis according to DSM-III.

DSM-III AND NEUROPSYCHIATRY

When DSM-III was applied to Japanese patients in our field trials, we excluded patients with epilepsy, narcolepsy, and neurological disorders without manifest mental symptoms. In daily clinical practice, however, we often encounter symptomatic psychoses, toxic psychoses, epilepsies, mental disorders associated with altered consciousness, narcolepsy, periodic somnolence, and various types of sleep and vegetative disorders, and must treat them. These patients constitute a wide borderline area between psychiatry and neurology. When we see psychotic patients, we commonly examine electroencephalograms (EEGs), computerized tomography (CT), eye ground, etc., and we frequently find mild changes in central nervous system functioning, e.g., a patient with schizophrenic mental symptoms sometimes shows minor EEG abnormalities, such as increased slow-wave components, 6 and 14 positive spike activity, or minor paroxysmal discharges. Are these findings to be noted on axis III as associated somatic symptoms, and is an axis I diagnosis of schizophrenic disorder justified in this case? Or should the axis I diagnosis be changed to organic hallucinosis and organic delusional syndrome, with an axis III diagnosis of epileptic EEG abnormality?

DSM-III intentionally renounced etiological classification and adopted a principle of classification by clinical mental syndromes. But this principle was not observed in the classification of organic mental disorders and substance use disorders, in which etiological classification was adopted. This inconsistency in principle causes various problems in diagnosing patients in the borderline area between psychiatry and neurology. It is surprising that general paresis, which occupied a very important position in clinical psychiatry some 30 years ago, has now disappeared completely from the list of DSM-III diagnoses. The same thing has happened with regard to epilepsy. For Japanese psychiatrists who are actually treating such patients, more precise neuropsychiatric diagnostic criteria for these pathological conditions are needed. It may be necessary and desirable to adopt etiological criteria for those categories for which they have been scientifically established.

To make the situation more complicated, there are some symptoms that are acceptable both as mental symptoms and as somatic symptoms, e.g., hypersomnia, headache, vertigo, and other vegetative symptoms. Appendix E of DSM-III, the diagnostic classification of sleep disorders, as proposed by the Association of Sleep Disorders Centers and the Association for the Psychophysiological Study of Sleep, is presented without any explanation. Among sleep and arousal disorders are classified excessive somnolence, insomnias, changed sleep-wake rhythms, and parasomnias. But their relationship with DSM-III is not clear.

Such sleep-related clinical syndromes are very often found in our clinical patients, and we need operational criteria for classifying them. But there is no diagnostic category for even simple insomnia in DSM-III. Only sleep-walking disorder (307.46) and sleep terror disorder (307.46) are listed, as axis I categories. On the other hand, insomnia and hypersomnia are included as axis I symptoms in the criteria for major depressive episode, dysthymic disorder, generalized anxiety disorder, post-traumatic stress disorder, and so on. Disturbance of the sleep-wakefulness cycle, with insomnia or daytime drowsiness, is included in the axis I criteria for delirium. Hypnagogic hallucinations are primarily mental symptoms, and are observed in catatonic schizophrenia and in other conditions, but are not listed in DSM-III. Also, there are no categories for periodic somnolence, periodic altered consciousness, periodic moodiness, and narcolepsy, which are usually treated by psychiatrists in Japan. Should we classify insomnia, hypersomnia, and parasomnias as signs of organic brain syndromes and note them on axis III? Provision of a new category of "biologically grounded mental disorders" for these borderline categories may be a future topic of discussion.

In the United States and European countries, neurology is now separated from psychiatry; and disorders with somatic symptoms, including EEG abnormalities and sleep disorders, are no longer the subject matter of psychiatry and are no longer treated by psychiatrists. It seems that as new somatic evidence develops for a particular mental disorder, after earnest biological research, the disorder is chased out of psychiatry. It will be an unhappy consequence if psychiatry becomes a garbage pit of scientifically confirmed mental conditions. On the contrary, it is necessary to evaluate biological findings in mental disorders from the viewpoint of neuropsychiatry, since mental disorders and central nervous system functions are inseparable and constitute neuropsychiatric disorders.

It is clear that patients in the borderline area between psychiatry and neurology require precise diagnosis and treatment by specialists with knowledge of both psychiatry and neurology. Integration of both the biological and the mental aspects of our patients will be an important step forward for the psychiatry of tomorrow.

REFERENCES

1. Shutoku Kagawa: Ippondo Gyoyo Igen (1807) [Medical essays], in Goshi Iseido Sosho Series. Tokyo, Shibunkaku Publishers, 1970 (in Jpn)

2. Ken Tsuchida: Tenkan-kyo Keiken-hen (1819), translated by Tsuneo Osuga and Susumu Yokoi. Seishin Igaku [Clinical Psychiatry] 20(4): 445–460, 1978 (in Jpn)
3. Kanae Kitamura: Toho-hen (1817) [Guide to treatment with emetics], in Goshi Iseido Sosho Series. Tokyo, Shibunkaku Publishers, 1970 (in Jpn)
4. Soken Homma: Naika Hiroku (1864) [Secret notes on internal medicine]. Kinsei Kampo Isho Shusei 22. Tokyo, Meicho Shuppan, 1979 (in Jpn)
5. Genshiro Hiruta: Psychiatry in the Edo period. Part 1. Concepts of illness. Jpn J Clin Psychiatry 11:39–47, 1982 (in Jpn)
6. Collected Works of Masatake Morita, vol 1–7. Edited by Takehisa Kohra, Kenshiro Ohara, and Shiro Nakagawa. Tokyo, Hakuyosha Ltd., 1974–1975 (in Jpn)
7. Mitsuzo Shimoda: On manic-depressive illness. Yonago Medical Journal, March 1950 (in Jpn)
8. Hisatoshi Mitsuda: Clinical Genetics in Psychiatry—Problems in Nosological Classification. Tokyo, Igaku-shoin Ltd., 1967 (in Jpn)
9. Seikatsu-rinsho [Living-learning therapy of schizophrenics]. Edited by Hiroshi Utena. Tokyo, Sozo Shuppan Ltd, 1978 (in Jpn)
10. Saburo Takahashi, Hideo Yamane, Koichi Hanada et al: Clinical application of DSM-III diagnostic criteria and their limitations. Part 1: From DSM-II to DSM-III. Jpn J Clin Psychiatry 9:1097–1105, 1980 (in Jpn)
11. Michihiko Nakamura, Saburo Takahashi, Hideo Yamane et al: Clinical application of DSM-III diagnostic criteria and their limitations. Part 2: Affective disorders. Jpn J Clin Psychiatry 9: 1243–1251, 1980 (in Jpn)
12. Koichi Hanada, Saburo Takahashi, Hideo Yamane et al: Clinical application of DSM-III diagnostic criteria and their limitations. Part 3: Schizophrenia. Jpn J Clin Psychiatry 9: 1379–1385, 1980 (in Jpn)
13. Saburo Takahashi, Hideo Yamane, Koichi Hanada et al: Clinical applications of DSM-III diagnostic criteria and their limitations. Part 4: Psychotic disorders not elsewhere classified. Jpn J Clin Psychiatry 10: 109–114, 1981 (in Jpn)
14. Koichi Hanada, Keizo Ino, Saburo Takahashi et al: Clinical application of DSM-III diagnostic criteria and their limitations. Part 5: Paranoid disorders. Jpn J Clin Psychiatry 10:235–240, 1981 (in Jpn)
15. Keizo Ino, Saburo Takahashi, Hideo Yamane: Clinical application of DSM-III diagnostic criteria and their limitations. Part 6: Anxiety disorders. Jpn J Clin Psychiatry 10: 349–356, 1981 (in Jpn)
16. Saburo Takahashi, Hideharu Iida, Hidoe Yamane et al: Clinical application of DSM-III diagnostic criteria and their limitations. Part 7: Adjustment disorder. Jpn J Clin Psychiatry 10: 487–493, 1981 (in Jpn)
17. Michihiko Nakamura, Saburo Takahashi, Hideo Yamane et al: Clinical application of DSM-III diagnostic criteria and their limitations. Part 8: Somatoform disorders, dissociative disorders, and factitious disorders. Jpn J Clin Psychiatry 10: 609–618, 1981 (in Jpn)
18. Saburo Takahashi, Hideo Yamane, Koichi Hanada et al: Clinical application of DSM-III diagnostic criteria and their limitations. Part 9: Psychosexual disorders. Jpn J Clin Psychiatry 10: 703–711, 1981 (in Jpn)
19. Saburo Takahashi, Motohiro Tsuji, Hideo Yamane et al: Clinical application of DSM-III diagnostic criteria and their limitations. Part 10: Organic mental disorders. Jpn J Clin Psychiatry 10: 861–874, 1981 (in Jpn)
20. Saburo Takahashi, Hideo Yamane, Koichi Hanada et al: Clinical application of DSM-III diagnostic criteria and their limitations. Part II: Personality

disorders. Jpn J Clin Psychiatry 10: 1009–1020, 1981 (in Jpn)
21. Noribumi Iwase, Saburo Takahashi, Hideo Yamene et al: Clinical application of DSM-III diagnostic criteria and their limitations. Part 12: Substance use disorders. Jpn J Clin Psychiatry 10: 1135–1144, 1981 (in Jpn)
22. Saburo Takahashi, Koichi Hanada, Hideo Yamane et al: Clinical application of DSM-III diagnostic criteria and their limitations. Part 13: V codes for conditions not attributable to a mental disorder that are a focus of attention or treatment, and additional codes. Jpn J Clin Psychiatry 10: 1269–1278, 1981 (in Jpn)
23. Masataka Ohta, Masahiko Saito, Hiroshi Kurita et al: Clinical application of DSM-III diagnostic criteria and their limitations. Part 14: Developmental disorders, with special reference to so-called "childhood schizophrenia." Jpn J Clin Psychiatry 10: 1387–1408, 1981 (in Jpn)
24. Hiroshi Kurita, Masataka Ohta, Yasuo Shimizu et al: Clinical application of DSM-III diagnostic criteria and their limitations. Part 15: In what category can "school refusal" be classified? Jpn J Clin Psychiatry 11: 87–95, 1982 (in Jpn)
25. Yasuo Shimizu, Masatake Ohta, Hiroshi Kurita et al: Clinical application of DSM-III diagnostic criteria and their limitations. Part 16: Behavioral disorders; minimal brain dysfunction syndrome and juvenile delinquency. Jpn J Clin Psychiatry 11: 385–395, 1982 (in Jpn)
26. Michihiko Nakamura, Saburo Takahashi, Hideharu Iida et al: Clinical application of DSM-III diagnostic criteria and their limitations. Part 17: Physical disorders of childhood or adolescence, with special reference to anorexia nervosa and Tourette's syndrome. Jpn J Clin Psychiatry 11: 527–536, 1982 (in Jpn)
27. Yomishi Kasahara: On DSM-III, a new diagnostic criteria in America. Psychiatr Neurol Jpn 83: 607–611, 1981 (in Jpn)
28. Koichi Hanada, Saburo Takahashi: DSM-III field trials in Japan—Interrater reliability among psychiatrists from seven university hospitals. Jpn J Clin Psychiatry 11: 171–181, 1982 (in Jpn)
29. Diagnostic and Statistical Manual of Mental Disorders, 3rd ed. Washington, DC, American Psychiatric Association, 1980, Appendix F.
30. Saburo Takahashi, Koichi Hanada: DSM-III field trials in Japan—Questionnaires to the field trial participants. Jpn J Clin Psychiatry 11: 1471–1479, 1982 (in Jpn)
31. Spitzer RL, Williams JBW, Skodol AE: DSM-III: Background and major achievement. Jpn J Clin Psychiatry 11: 137–141, 1982 (translated by Yuji Okazaki and Yutaka Honda into Japanese)
32. Williams JBW: The multiaxial system of DSM-III: A comprehensive approach to evaluation. Jpn J Clin Psychiatry 11: 143–149, 1982 (translated by Yuji Okazaki and Yutaka Honda into Japanese)
33. Spitzer RL, Williams JBW, Skodol AE: DSM-III An overview of the classification. Jpn J Clin Psychiatry 11: 151–164, 1982 (translated by Yutaka Honda and Yuji Okazaki into Japanese)
34. Williams JBW: The DSM-III field trials: Rationale and results. Jpn J Clin Psychiatry 11: 165–168, 1982 (translated by Yutaka Honda into Japanese)
35. Michio Takemura: Analysis of interrater discrepancies in DSM-III diagnosis. Jpn J Clin Psychiatry 11: 183–188, 1982 (in Jpn)
36. Yutaka Honda: Application of DSM-III diagnostic criteria to narcoleptics with hallucinatory paranoid states. Jpn J Clin Psychiatry 11: 239–246, 1982 (in Jpn)

37. Nariyoshi Yamaguchi: Conventional diagnosis of schizophrenia in Japan and DSM-III. Jpn J Clin Psychiatry 11: 189–196, 1982 (in Jpn)
38. Takashi Maeshiro, Ryoichi Toyoshima, Hiroshi Motomura et al: Conventional diagnosis of affective disorders in Japan and DSM-III. Jpn J Clin Psychiatry 11: 197–203, 1982 (in Jpn)
39. Itaru Yamashita: Conventional diagnosis of neurosis in Japan and DSM-III. Jpn J Clin Psychiatry 11: 205–212, 1982 (in Jpn)
40. Nobukatsu Kato, Tadashi Noto, Toshiaki Tadai et al: Alcoholic psychoses in Japan and DSM-III. Jpn J Clin Psychiatry 11: 213–220, 1980 (in Jpn)
41. Ken-ichi Hiramatsu: Application of RDC, DSM-III, and ICD-9 to depressive patients. Jpn J Clin Psychiatry 11: 221–228, 1982 (in Jpn)
42. Yoshibumi Nakane, Yasuyuki Ohta, Shun-ichiro Michitsuji et al: Application of PSE and DSM-III to the same group of patients. Jpn J Clin Psychiatry 11: 229–238, 1982 (in Jpn)
43. Saburo Takahashi: DSM-III Case Book seminar by Dr. Andrew E. Skodol in Kyoto. Journal of the Japanese Association of Psychiatric Hospitals 1(7): 25–27, 1982 (in Jpn)
44. Yutaka Honda: A seminar evening on DSM-III Case Book by Dr. Andrew E. Skodol—Recent trends in the diagnosis and treatment of psychosexual disorders in the United States. Journal of the Japanese Association of Psychiatric Hospitals 1(7): 23–25, 1982 (in Jpn)
45. Quick reference to the Diagnostic Criteria from DSM-III. Washington, DC, American Psychiatric Association, 1980. Translated by Saburo Takahashi, Koichi Hanada, and Akira Fujinawa into Japanese. Tokyo, Igaku-shoin Ltd, 1982
46. Webb LJ, DiClemente CC, Johnstone EE, et al: DSM-III Training Guide. New York, Brunner/Mazel, 1981 Translated by Makoto Shimizu into Japanese. Tokyo, Seiwa Shoten Publishers, 1982
47. Spitzer RL, Skodol AE, Gibbon M, Williams JBW: DSM-III Case Book. Washington DC, American Psychiatric Association, 1981. Translated by Saburo Takahashi, Koichi Hanada, and Yutaka Honda into Japanese. Tokyo, Igaku-shoin Ltd, 1983
48. Yutaka Honda: Closing remarks for the serial publications of "Clinical application of DSM-III diagnostic criteria and their limitations"—Review of a year and a half and the future problems. Jpn J Clin Psychiatry 11: 647–648, 1982 (in Jpn)
49. Saburo Takahashi: Clinical application of DSM-III diagnostic criteria and their limitations. What we acquired from the serial publications. Jpn J Clin Psychiatry 11: 648–650, 1982 (in Jpn)
50. Saburo Takahashi: DSM-III and the nomenclature of mental disorders. Seishin Igaku [Clinical Psychiatry] 24:244–245, 1982
51. Yutaka Honda: On DSM-III. Journal of the Japanese Association of Psychiatric Hospitals 1(2): 3–8, 1982 (in Jpn)
52. Saburo Takahashi: Reliability of diagnosis in psychiatry. Journal of the Japanese Association of Psychiatric Hospitals 1(2): 9–12, 1982 (in Jpn)
53. Masaaki Kato: On DSM-III and ICD-9. Journal of the Japanese Association of Psychiatric Hospitals 1(2): 13–15, 1982 (in Jpn)
54. Yutaka Honda: On DSM-III. Mind and Society 37:74–79, 1983 (in Jpn)
55. Yutaka Honda: Significance of DSM-III. Japanese Journal of Physical Therapy and Occupational Therapy 17(3): 261, 1983 (in Jpn)
56. Itaru Yamashita: Taijin-kyofu [anthropophobia]. Tokyo, Kanehara Shuppan Publishers, 1977 (in Jpn)

ADDITIONAL READINGS

1. Hanada K: New diagnostic criteria for depressive disorders. Japanese Journal of Neuropsychopharmacology 4: 213–221, 1982 (in Jpn)
2. Hanada K, Takahaski S: Diagnostic reliability of atypical psychosis according to DSM-III and the conventional system. Jpn J Clin Psychiatry 11: 479–485, 1982 (in Jpn)
3. Hanada K, Takahashi S, Honda Y, et al: Multi-institutional field trial of DSM-III in Japan and diagnosis of endogenous psychoses. Psychiat Neurol Jpn 84: 794–799, 1982 (in Jpn)
4. Kasahara H, Onda M. Ito H, et al: Diagnosis of mild depressive state by various diagnostic criteria. Psychiat Neurol Jpn 84: 779–786, 1982 (in Jpn)
5. Maruta T: Diagnostic and Statistical Manual III (D.S.M. III): The new diagnostic criteria in USA psychiatry. Clinical Psychiatry 20: 1145–1149, 1978 (in Jpn)
6. Minagawa K: Therapeutic diagnosis for child and adolescent patients, and DSM-III vs. GAP. Psychiat Neurol Jpn 84: 779–786, 1982 (in Jpn)
7. Ohno Y, Okonogi K, Minagawa K, et al: Some problems of DSM-III in diagnosing borderline cases. Psychiat Neurol Jpn 84: 787–793, 1982 (in Jpn)
8. Saito M: Concept and classification of alcoholism: A comparison of ICD-9 and DSM-III. Jpn J Clin Psychiatry 11: 285–294, 1982 (in Jpn)
9. Takahashi R: International collaborative studies on depressive disorders—With reference to diagnostic classification. Clinical Psychiatry 22: 1263–1274, 1980 (in Jpn)
10. Takahashi S, Tohara S: Classification and diagnosis of alcoholic mental disorders. 1. Alcohol-induced organic mental disorders. Jpn J Clin Psychiatry 12: 63–73, 1983 (in Jpn)
11. Takahashi S, Tohara S: Classification and diagnosis of alcoholic mental disorders. 2. Nonorganic mental disorders as complications of alcohol dependence and abuse. Jpn J Clin Psychiatry 12, 1983 (in press) (in Jpn)
12. Tatsunuma T: Destiny of classification of mental disorders. Clinical Psychiatry 25: 4–5, 1983 (in Jpn)

14

PSYCHIATRIC DIAGNOSIS
IN THE NETHERLANDS

Gerolf A.S. Koster van Groos, M.D.

Nationwide consensus of opinion on psychiatric diagnosis has never existed in the Netherlands; every school of psychiatry has had its own criteria, terms, and concepts. After a period of rejection and neglect of diagnosis in psychiatry, there is now a growing interest in its practice. The "alienation" from diagnosis was strongly influenced by the ideas of Karl Menninger and Thomas Szasz, and strongly promoted in the Netherlands by the Dutch psychiatrist Jan Foudraine. The involvement of social workers in psychiatric care further diminished the significance of traditional medical practices such as establishing a diagnosis. At the same time, an "antidiagnostic" spirit was evident in statements by several political parties, the press, and other media. During this period a "psychiatric diagnosis" at best took the form of a literary exposition about a patient that specifically avoided the use of psychiatric labels.

Since there is no typical Dutch psychiatry, the theory and practice of psychiatry in the Netherlands have been characterized by eclecticism. Some clinics have been particularly oriented toward French etiologic-pathogenetic concepts; others, toward a German nosological approach; and still others, toward various psychodynamic theories.

Address correspondence to: Gerolf A. S. Koster van Groos, M.D., Hoog Beugt 5, 5473 KN Heeswijk-Dinther, The Netherlands

PREDOMINANT SCHOOLS OF PSYCHIATRY IN THE NETHERLANDS

Among the early influences on Dutch psychiatry were the theories of psychopathology of Karl Birnbaum, E.A.D.E. Carp, and H.C. Rümke. Nearly all mental health workers were influenced by the structure-analysis theory of Birnbaum (1). According to this view, symptoms in a given case were arranged in a hierarchy, some indicating structural changes in the personality, and some representing a reaction of the personality to a changed internal or external environment.

Carp (2) viewed psychopathology as due to either a disintegration or a disregulation of a basic personality structure. The structure of the personality, according to him, consists of five interrelated aspects: character, psychomotor activity, temperament, drives, and intelligence. In psychotic conditions, a disintegration of the personality structure occurs; in what Carp termed "psychopathic states," there is disregulation, i.e., the basic structure is maintained, but the five aspects become unbalanced. For Carp a diagnosis consisted of a determination of the presence of disintegration or disregulation and a judgment, in the latter case, concerning the particular aspect of the personality that was out of balance with the others.

Rümke (3), a professor in Utrecht, also had considerable interest in nosology. He believed that a diagnosis should provide an explanation for the origin of a particular person's psychological state. He considered pathogenesis a complicated matter, because there was no single cause for mental syndromes. Rümke therefore proposed, following Birnbaum, a hierarchical system of causal factors and attempted, in each case, to understand the contributions of various biological and psychological factors and their interrelationships. Under his system, a diagnosis was an individualized conceptualization, i.e., each patient was best described according to an individualized formulation. Rumke was responsible for introducing into Dutch psychiatry the notions of Kretschmer's multidimensional diagnosis, an emphasis on the form as well as the content of psychological disturbance, and the hierarchical development theories of Hughlings Jackson.

H. R. Kraus (4) viewed mental disorders as in a constant state of change. He therefore cautioned against the search for static disease entities and advocated the multidimensional and structure-analytic approaches as a way of monitoring the continually changing courses of mental disorders. H. M. van Praag (5), on the other hand, influenced Dutch psychiatry's attitude toward diagnosis by introducing the idea of a need for a standardized typology of psychiatric disorders that could be reliably used for the purposes of pharmacotherapeutic research. He pointed out that only with such a system could rigorous drug studies on comparable patient groups be replicated.

In recent years, Kuiper (6), at the University of Amsterdam, has advocated multicausal diagnosis, but acknowledged that traditional systems are very obscure. Kuiper recognized that there were several kinds of potentially meaningful diagnostic systems: a simple description of a patient's symptoms, a classification of syndromes, a prognostic system based on an understanding of differences in course of illness, or a system based on factors causing illness. He also recognized that, in the 1970s, diagnostic practices unsystematically combined all of these approaches, and that this contributed to the difficulties in arriving at a suitable classification system.

In 1971, R. M. Silbermann (7), also at the University of Amsterdam, introduced his own classification system, based on descriptive symptoms and syndromes. His CHAM system (Consistent, Hierarchical, Arbitrary, Monothetic) is depicted in table 1.

In a book called *The New Psychiatry*, published in 1978, Lit (8) criticized contemporary classification systems based on psychiatric symptoms. He questioned the scientific merit of such classifications, since he viewed symptoms not as objective phenomena, but rather as communications subject to influence by context. Thus, a psychiatric examination influences the behavior it is designed to evaluate, and symptoms are considered important depending on the theoretical school to which the psychiatrist belongs. Traditional diagnostic systems are therefore unreliable and useless (9). Lit proposed a systems-analytic approach to classification based on the ideas of Von Bertalanffy. A healthy human being is conceptualized as a system for processing information with the properties of openness, ordered oneness, hierarchical structure, adaptive self-stabilization, and adaptive self-organization. *Illness* is a general term for the loss of system properties, and *therapy*, a term for the rehabilitation of system properties. Lit's diagnostic schema is outlined in table 2.

The introduction of an official classification of mental disorders occurred in the Netherlands in 1967. The Geneeskundige Hoofdinspectie voor de Geestelijke Volksgezondheid (the Medical Chief-Inspectorate of Mental Health) adopted the eighth revision of the International Classification of Diseases (ICD-8) for use in psychiatric hospitals. The psychiatric departments of the universities joined in its use in 1970. In 1978 there was a switch to the ninth revision (ICD-9). The general hospitals, including the psychiatric wards, started with the Hospital Adaptation of the International Classification of Diseases, Adapted (H-ICDA) in 1968, which was replaced in 1980 by the Clinical Modification of ICD-9 (ICD-9-CM).

TABLE 1. The CHAM-System of R. M. Silbermann (7)

1. Coma	
2. Subcoma	
3. Soporous state	—Disturbed consciousness
4. Twilight state	
5. Delirious state	
6. Stuporous state	—Stupor
7. Paranoic hallucinatory state	—Hallucinations
8. Hallucinatory state	
9. Paranoic state	
10. Manic state	—Delusions
11. Melancholic state	
12. Amnesic state	—Amnesia
13. Amnesic confabulatory state	
14. Confusional state	—Confusion
15. Agitated state	—Disinhibition
16. Depressive state	—Depression
17. Agitated depressive state	
18. Anxious state	—Anxiety
19. Behavioral abnormality	—Behavioral abnormality
20. Hyperaesthetic emotional state	—Affective instability
21. "Observation"	

THE INTRODUCTION OF DSM-III IN THE NETHERLANDS

In the summer of 1981, a group of biologically oriented psychiatrists, realizing the problems presented by the absence of a uniform diagnostic system in the Netherlands, became interested in DSM-III. In March

TABLE 2. Diagnostic Schema of A.C. Lit (8)

Theory of the Healthy Human	Terms Used in Psychiatry
2.0 A human being is a system for processing information with the following properties:	
2.1 Openness	
2.1.1 Input of information	Perception
2.1.2 Storing and processing of information	Apperception
	Memory
	Learning/thinking
2.1.3 Output of information	Speaking/writing
	Acting
	Expressing
2.1.4 Information cycles	Affective contact
	Emotional involvement
	Interest and sympathy
2.2 Ordered oneness	Integration of psychological functioning
2.3 Hierarchical structure	
2.3.1 Intrasystem hierarchy	Cell/organ/organ systems
	Endocrine system
	Central nervous system
	Limbic system
2.3.2 Internally active system	Self-consciousness
	Personality
	Affectivity
	Biography
2.3.3 Intersystem hierarchy	Couple
	Family
	Relatives
	Community
	Religious community
2.4 Adaptive self-stabilization	
The preservation of the existing stability in varying circumstances	Stress/adaptation
2.5 Adaptive self-organization	
The ability to change function and structure in varying circumstances	Aptitude
	Growth/development
	Learning/life phase

Theory of the Ill Human	Therapy
3.0 Being ill is the generally used term for loss of system properties	4.0 Therapy is the generally used term for the rehabilitation of system properties
3.1 Loss of openness	4.1 Recovery of openness
3.1.1 Diseases of the senses and the brain	4.1.1 Ophthalmology, otology, neurology
3.1.2 Illusions/hallucinations Amnesia, thought disorders	4.1.2 Multidisciplinary
3.1.3 Aphasia/agraphia/mutism Psychomotor disorders Inhibition	4.1.3 Speech-training Activating therapies Expression by movement
3.1.4 Blunted affect Autism Apathy	4.1.4 Individual, group, and sociotherapy
3.2 Loss of order and oneness e.g., schizophrenic disorders	4.2 Recovery of ordered oneness; multidisciplinary
3.3 Loss of hierarchical structure	4.3 Rehabilitation of hierarchical structure
3.3.1 Symptomatic psychosis, endocrine psychosis, organic psychosis, disorders in vitality	4.3.1 Internal medicine, endocrinology, neurology, biological psychiatry
3.3.2 Neuroses Personality disorders Developmental disorders	4.3.2 Individual psychotherapy
3.3.3 Relation disorders Estrangement Doubt/anxiety/delusions of sin	4.3.3 Sexual/couple/family therapy Sociotherapy Activating therapy Social work Ministration

Theory of the Ill Human	Therapy
3.4 Loss of adaptive self-stabilization	4.4 Rehabilitation of adaptive self-stabilization
Anxiety—tension—aggression conflicts—stress—diseases	Psychopharmacology psychotherapy (individual, group, social, activating)
3.5 Loss of adaptive self-organization	4.5 Rehabilitation of adaptive self-organization
Hereditary disorders Early acquired adjustment disorders Mental retardation—partial ability	Optimum use of other system properties Multidisciplinary
Psychoses in adolescence Psychoses in involution Psychogenic psychoses Sociogenic psychoses	

1982, they invited Drs. Robert Spitzer and Janet Williams to conduct a two-day conference on DSM-III. This meeting was attended by all Dutch teachers of psychiatry. At the present time, neither the Vereniging voor Psychiatrie (Dutch Psychiatric Association) nor the Hoofdinspectie voor de Geestelijke Volksgezondheid can officially speak in favor of the acceptance of DSM-III, but a committee has been formed to decide which classification system should be acknowledged and promoted in our country.

As a first step toward evaluating DSM-III, the Dutch committee on DSM-III translated the *Quick Reference to the Diagnostic Criteria from DSM-III*. The translation was edited by Drs. F. van Ree and G. A. S. Koster van Groos and titled *Beknopte Handleiding bij de Diagnostische Kriteria van de DSM-III*.

An early problem involved translating new terms, which in some cases became neologisms in the Dutch language. The translators tried to closely approximate the English with Dutch equivalents, even when this resulted in the construction of rather "bad-looking" words. A general problem was the seemingly inconsistent use of the terms *disorder*, *illness*, *disturbance*, and *syndrome*. It was decided to follow the text of DSM-III as closely as possible and use the terms *illness* and *disturbance* only for organic syndromes and/or known pathophysiologic processes.

Among the specific terms that caused difficulty was *melancholia*, which was translated as "with vital features," since in the Netherlands "vital" depression corresponds to the DSM-III concept of major depression with melancholia. In the Netherlands *melancholia* conveys the meaning of endogenous and psychotic depression. Another term presenting difficulty was *mental retardation*, which translated into Dutch suggests too strongly that the disorder is curable. The Dutch term for "feeblemindedness" was substituted. The term *major* in "major depression" also caused considerable problems, since it is not a common word other than in its use in music theory. Therefore, a Dutch word meaning "in-a-more-restricted-sense" was used to modify the term *depression* (10).

Certain cultural differences also presented difficulties in translation, particularly in the section on psychosexual disorders. For example, in its discussion there, DSM-III adopts a male point of view, as in the term *effeminate homosexuality* and in the description of "transvestism."

EXPERIENCE IN THE USE OF DSM-III

At the present time DSM-III is in use, or its use is being considered, in a growing number of psychiatric hospitals and some university clinics. The DSM-III committee organized two training conferences in 1982 to introduce the system. More workshops are planned. Currently, approximately 25% of Dutch psychiatrists have been brought into contact with the system.

In October 1981, a conference on DSM-III was held under the auspices of the Committee on Biochemical and Neurophysiological Research of the National Hospital Council; the lectures presented at that conference have been published (11). Articles on DSM-III have also been published in the *Monthly Magazine for Mental Health* and in the *Dutch Journal of Psychiatry*. An introduction to DSM-III will soon appear in the *Dutch Medical Journal*. Two articles deserve special mention: van Praag's article on the diagnosis of depression according to DSM-III (12), which also was translated and appeared in *Comprehensive Psychiatry*, and an article by Slooff and co-workers on functional nonaffective psychoses (13). DSM-III was recently used for the first time in a doctoral thesis by a Dutch psychiatrist, R. J. van den Bosch, who studied attentional correlates of schizophrenia (14).

EVALUATION OF DSM-III

The DSM-III system offers the possibility of clearer and more comprehensible classification. The reliability of clinicians using the system will grow with experience and further refinement of the diagnostic criteria. By emphasizing diagnosis by specified criteria, DSM-III brings the process of arriving at a diagnosis more into focus. It should help bring the recent period of neglect of issues of psychiatric diagnosis in the Netherlands to an end.

Yet, the system is not faultless, according to the Dutch psychiatrists who have written about it. Lit (15) has been quite critical of DSM-III, claiming it is based on outdated theories of psychiatric disorder. More specifically, Slooff and co-workers (13) raise a number of objections to the DSM-III differential diagnosis of psychotic disorders. They question the rationale for dividing acute paranoid disorders, lasting longer than one week, but less than six months, from the more chronic disorder paranoia, which lasts six months or more. They object to the DSM-III concept of schizophrenia, which they find too broad in that nearly all cases of chronic psychosis are diagnosed as schizophrenia, including some that most Dutch psychiatrists would diagnose as chronic paranoia or chronic psychogenic psychosis. Other Dutch psychiatrists think that having a maximum duration of two weeks for brief reactive psychosis will impede the use of this category. Some also argue that the residual subtype of schizophrenia is more likely an aspect of the course of the disorder than a special symptomatic subtype. Other residual states, such as those due to a prolonged stay in a psychiatric hospital that are characterized by social deprivation (in the Dutch language, this is called "hospitalization syndrome") are not classifiable according to the DSM-III system.

Van Praag's recent review articles discuss current conventions in the diagnosis of depression and the DSM-III approach from the perspectives of Dutch psychiatry. Van Praag takes issue with the validity of many of the current dichotomous concepts of depression, including the primary/secondary, the unipolar/bipolar, the psychotic/neurotic, and the endogenous/reactive. He praises DSM-III for officially recognizing that:

1. Major depressions can be precipitated by stress, and are not necessarily etiologically "endogenous."

2. Major depressions can occur in people with other mental disturbances, including alcoholism and personality disorder; and the nature of the depression in these cases is not different from those with no additional psychopathology, although the total symptom picture is more complicated.

3. Both major depressions characterized by vegetative symptoms and those that are not so characterized can be recurrent.

Van Praag also, however, raises a number of objections to the DSM-III classification in this area. He cannot understand why organically induced (i.e. drug-induced, or due to a viral infection) depressions are not classified as affective disorders. In his own diagnostic schema, etiology is a separate designation for all depressive syndromes, and the syndromal diagnosis is made on the basis of symptoms alone. Van Praag also objects to the DSM-III criterion that allows any four of eight associated symptoms of depressions to indicate a full depressive syndrome; he thinks that the implication that these eight symptoms of the depressive syndrome are of equal importance is doubtful.

Van Praag considers the diagnoses covering milder depressive syndromes inadequate to account for a wide range of depressions seen in clinical practice. He sees the category "cyclothymic disorder" as a potential diagnosis for people who may have mild recurrent depressions. The criteria, however, for cyclothymic disorder require that mild depressive and hypomanic phases alternate more or less continually for a period of two years or more. The patient who develops a mild depressive episode not related to stress cannot be classified under this scheme. Similarly, the person who has recurrent, but infrequent, mild depressions or mild recurrent depressions without hypomanic phases does not meet these or any other criteria in DSM-III. Van Praag suggests that separate dimensions of severity and frequency be added to all affective disorder diagnoses in an attempt to resolve these problems.

The definition of dysthymic disorder, in van Praag's opinion, falls short on two points. First, although the existence of a separate category for milder depression with criteria that include symptoms corresponding only in part to those of a major depression suggests that depressions differ both quantitatively (i.e., in severity) and qualitatively (i.e., in symptom type), the actual definition of dysthymic disorder suggests that severity is the only relevant factor (plus duration) in the differential diagnosis. This, in van Praag's view, represents a lost opportunity. He feels the duration requirements are also restrictive, since there is no explanation of why patients with an intermittent course can have an interepisode interval of only a couple of months and since there is no way to classify patients with dysthymic features and longer, symptom-free intervals.

Finally, van Praag questions the "adjustment disorder with depressed mood" category. He does not like it for several reasons:

1. It is defined in negative terms (the absence of a full depressive syndrome).

2. The maladaptive indicators apply equally to all depressions and therefore have no specific value.

3. Adjustment disorders in normal personalities following ordinary psychosocial stressors are very rare, he has found.

In conclusion, although admitting to a number of reservations about the DSM-III approach to depression, van Praag expresses appreciation for the advances, which far outweigh his criticism. He states that DSM-III creates order out of the prevailing chaos in this diagnostic area in many ways. He recommends a three-dimensional approach to classifying depressions that independently rates symptoms, etiology, and course.

DIAGNOSTIC CATEGORIES COMMONLY USED IN THE NETHERLANDS THAT ARE NOT IN DSM-III

Specific diagnostic categories used frequently in the Netherlands for which there are no clear DSM-III counterparts include psychogenic psychosis, hysterical psychosis, degeneration or disintegration psychosis, and psychasthenic personality. I shall discuss each of these briefly.

Psychogenic psychosis develops in normal personalities following psychological trauma and has a course with different phases. The first phase is a typical premorbid state that is characterized by feelings of tiredness, irritability, tearfulness, anxiety, worry, inadequacy, uneasiness, insecurity, mild suspiciousness, and the inability to cope. Then comes an intermediate or latent phase, following the traumatic event, that lasts a variable period, seldom less than two weeks, and often five or six weeks (similar to an incubation period for a contagious disease). The psychotic phase then appears. The psychosis often has many features suggesting an organic mental disorder (for example, a change in level of consciousness, such as reduced awareness). The final phase, the reconvalescence phase, develops after the resolution of the psychotic symptoms, usually within a few days to a week after they have appeared, but occasionally not until months after the onset of the psychosis. Characteristically, the psychotic symptoms disappear entirely. The DSM-III category of brief reactive psychosis comes close to the concept of psychogenic psychosis, but the absence of a latency period and a premorbid phase with increasing psychopathology would exclude most patients with psychogenic psychosis. In both diagnoses, the psychotic phase tends to resolve within two weeks.

The patient with a hysterical psychosis typically has alternating periods of psychotic and normal experience. Visual hallucinations are prominent among the symptoms. There are alterations in the level of consciousness and denial of certain aspects of reality. For example, a patient may deny that her parents are really her parents. Affect is expressed by means of gestures, with the intention of forcing the environment to fulfill the individual's desires and needs. A woman with a hysterical psychosis might open her skirt or blouse in order to express a sexual wish, or might curl up in a corner in order to express the need to be taken care of. The needs expressed are often unrealistic, but the thoughts are well ordered. Conversion symptoms such as fugue states and poriomania (wandering about in a reduced state of consciousness in search of someone) are frequent. For this syndrome an alternative term might be *dissociative psychosis*.

Another category used in the Netherlands for which there is no clear DSM-III counterpart is degeneration or disintegration psychosis. This is a psychosis in which paranoid features and hallucinations predominate. The patient does not hold to the delusions with the same tenacity as is seen in schizophrenia. The patient characteristically appears to be "playing with" objective reality: experiencing the significance of people and things in various symbolic ways, as in an allegory. A chair is not a chair, but an altar; nonetheless, it can be sat on. The mood can be depressed or despairing, but not with the intensity of a psychotic depression. Sometimes feelings of happiness or elation can develop after recovery from the psychosis. Often there is a sense of mysticism and rapture with strong religious overtones. The duration of these psychoses is short, ranging from a few days to several weeks and rarely lasting more than three to four months. Recovery is complete; frequently patients indicate that they feel better than ever.

Finally, the Dutch concept of psychasthenic personality disorder deserves mention. Psychasthenia is a basic personality type—an expression of constitution. The patient experiences fluctuations in energy and vitality, but frequently expresses tiredness, particularly mental tiredness. Commonly there is a mild tic disorder, usually around the eyes or other facial muscles. There is low frustration tolerance; the patient gets upset if his or her need to be taken care of is frustrated, and may complain of headache, an inability to think clearly, and the need to go to bed. The patient sometimes has mild phobic symptoms, depersonalization, or derealization. The patient experiences anxiety when unable to make up his or her mind, or when feeling uncertain about a direction to take. The French term *caractère scrupuleux inquiet* has been used to describe these people, because of their feeling that things are always wrong and need to be made right—a feeling that causes considerable worry and leads to fatigue. People with psychasthenic personality disorder frequently use stimulants such as caffeine, alcohol, and nicotine.

CONCLUSION

Although it is difficult to compare DSM-III with the current diagnostic system in the Netherlands, owing to the absence of any single system that is generally accepted by Dutch psychiatrists today, I have attempted to present a history of psychiatric diagnosis and the impact of DSM-III. It should be clear that for many clinicians and researchers in the Netherlands the decrease in emphasis on diagnosis that had developed and the lack of any coherent and integrated system that was widely used were considered a liability. This accounts for the considerable interest shown in DSM-III within the first few years of its publication.

DSM-III has been criticized from the various theoretical perspectives current in Dutch psychiatry, but this criticism will undoubtedly spur further interest in and empirical investigation of the DSM-III system. Clinicians and researchers see in DSM-III an opportunity to bring psychiatrists together by means of a common diagnostic language. Since the lack of usefulness of the ICD-9 is recognized in the Netherlands, the possibility exists that the Dutch government and the Dutch Psychiatric Association will decide to adopt DSM-III officially.

REFERENCES

1. Birnbaum K: Der Aufban der Psychose: Grundzüge der Psychiatrischen Strukturanalyse [The Construction of Psychosis: Principal Characteristics of Psychiatric Structure-Analysis]. Berlin, Springer Verlag, 1923
2. Carp EADE: Medische Psychologie en Pathopsychologie [Medical Psychology and Pathopsychology]. Amsterdam, Scheltema & Holkema, 1951
3. Rümke HC: Psychiatrie I [Psychiatry I]. Amsterdam, Scheltema & Holkema, 1954
4. Kraus G: Leerboek der Psychiatrie [Textbook of Psychiatry]. Leiden, Stenfert Kroese, 1968
5. van Praag HM: Een Kritisch Onderzoek naar de Betekenins van Monoamine Oxydase-Remming als Therapeutisch Principe bij de Behandeling van Depressies [A Critical Investigation of the Importance of Monoamine Oxidase Inhibition as a Therapeutic Principle in the Treatment of Depressions]. Nijmegen, Janssen, 1962
6. Kuiper PC: Hoofdsom der Psychiatrie [Principles of Psychiatry]. Utrecht, Bijleveld, 1973
7. Silbermann RM: CHAM: A Classification of Psychiatric States. Amsterdam, Excerpta Medica, 1971
8. Lit AC: Nieuwe Psychiatrie: Een Systeembenadering [New Psychiatry: A System Approach]. Leiden, Stenfert Kroese, 1978
9. Rooymans HGM: Oordeel en Vooroordeel in de Psychiatrische Diagnostiek [Judgment and Prejudice in Psychiatric Diagnosis]. Groningen, van Denderen, 1969
10. Van Ree F, Koster van Groos GAS: Beknopte Handleiding Bij de Diagnostische Kriteria van de DSM-III [Quick Reference to the Diagnostic Criteria from DSM-III]. Lisse, Swets & Zeitlinger, 1982
11. Verslag Contactpersonendag 1981: Bulletin 14:89–120, 1981

12. Van Praag HM: Een transatlantische visie op diagnostiek van depressies volgens de DSM-III. Tijdschrift voor Psychiatrie 24: 470–496, 1982 [Published in USA as: A transatlantic view of the diagnosis of depressions according to the DSM-III. Compr Psychiatry 23: 315–338, 1982]
13. Slooff CJ, Giel R, Wiersma D, et al: De classificatie van de functionele nietaffectieve psychosen [The classification of functional nonaffective psychoses]. Tijdschrift voor Psychiatrie 24: 454–469, 1982
14. Van den Bosch RJ: Attentional Correlates of Schizophrenia and Related Disorders. Lisse, Swets & Zeitlinger, 1982
15. Lit AC: Over het classificeren in de psychiatrie. Tijdschrift voor Psychiatrie 23: 5–21, 1981

ADDITIONAL READINGS

1. Bakker JB: Het assensysteem van de DSM-III [The axis system of DSM-III]. Bulletin 14: 100–104, 1981
2. Giel R: Waarom een diagnostische classificatie? [Why a diagnostic classification?]. Bulletin 14: 95–99, 1981
3. Hoencamp E: Neurose en DSM-III: antipolen? [Neurosis and DSM-III: antipoles?]. Bulletin 14: 110–114, 1981
4. Koster van Groos GAS: Invoering van het DSM-III systeem in de psychiatrische kliniek [Introduction of DMS-III in the psychiatric clinic]. Bulletin 14: 118–120, 1981
5. Nolen, WA: Controversen in de classificatie van depressies [Controversies in the classification of depressions]. Bulletin 14: 115–117, 1981
6. Schnabel P: Review of the Diagnostic and Statistical Manual of Mental Disorders (DSM-III). Maandblad voor de Geesteliijke Volksgezondheid [Monthly for Community Mental Health] 37: 688–690, 1982
7. Slooff CJ, Giel R, de Jong A, Wiersma D, et al: Classificatie van functionele niet-affectieve psychosen [Classification of functional nonaffective psychoses]. Bulletin 14: 105–109, 1981

15

SCANDINAVIAN PERSPECTIVES ON DSM-III

Nils Retterstøl, Dr. Med., and Alv A. Dahl, M.D.

By the term *Scandinavia* we shall here refer to Denmark, Finland, Iceland, Norway, and Sweden. These countries, which have a rather scattered population of 23 million people, are closely related in culture and language, except for Finland, whose language is quite different from the others'.

Until World War II Scandinavian psychiatry was strongly influenced by German psychiatry, especially by Kraepelin. Freud's influence was late to arrive and did not really take hold until after the war. Generally speaking, Scandinavian psychiatry may be said to have been largely somatically and constitutionally oriented up to that time, but later became increasingly psychodynamically oriented, leaning more toward American and British than French psychiatry and retaining its contact with the German-speaking Middle-European countries. Finland and Norway have been especially strongly oriented toward psychodynamic concepts and practice, whereas Sweden and Denmark have been more under the influence of biological psychiatry. In all of the Scandinavian

Address correspondence to: Professor, Dr. Med. Nils Retterstøl, Gaustad Hospital, Gaustad, Oslo 3, Norway

The authors would like to thank the following Scandinavian colleagues for supplying information for this paper: Professor K. Achté, Helsinki; Professor T. Helgason, Reykjavik; Professor M. Mellergaard, Copenhagen; Professor J. O. Ottosson, Gothenburg; Professor Niels Reisby, Aarhus; Professor M. Åsberg, Stockholm; Associate Professor L. von Knorring, Umeå; and Dr. Med. Per Bech, Hillerød.

countries, however, most psychiatrists will profess themselves "eclectic."

During the past 20 years social psychiatry has entered the psychiatric scene in all the Scandinavian countries. Psychiatry is now highly socially oriented, as befits the development of the Scandinavian welfare states.

The most important research contributions of Scandinavian psychiatry have come from studies of heredity and constitutional factors and, during recent decades, from epidemiological studies and follow-up investigations of various clinical groups. The Scandinavian countries have a small, reasonably stable, and easily accessible population. Their registration systems are advanced, from both a domiciliary and a medical point of view; they have central statistical registers of great reliability on a wide variety of subjects—e.g., psychoses, twins, cancer, suicide, etc.

Official national diagnostic systems were previously used, but the eighth revision of the International Classification of Diseases (ICD-8) has been the official system in the Scandinavian countries since 1969. Its acceptance, however, has met with difficulties among Scandinavian psychiatrists, particularly with regard to diagnosing the reactive psychoses, a diagnosis made in Scandinavia far more frequently than elsewhere. The ninth revision of the International Classification (ICD-9) has not been officially adopted except in Iceland (personal communication, Helgason, 1982), partly because of doubt about whether it represents an advance over ICD-8. Since the Scandinavian countries have national registers of the mentally ill, they hesitate to change their diagnostic procedures too often, because of all the complications this entails. For instance, the code numbers are quite different in ICD-9 and ICD-8, which means that comparing data coded by the two classifications would be extremely difficult. Moreover, introducing a new electronic coding system would be very expensive. This is the main reason why most Scandinavian health authorities still stick to ICD-8 and await ICD-10, which is expected to be influenced by DSM-III.

The multiaxial diagnostic model in international psychiatry has its origins in the work of the Scandinavian psychiatrists Essen-Möller and Wohlfahrt (1); it was further developed by Essen-Möller (2) and Ottosson and Perris (3), and is used by many Scandinavian psychiatrists in their daily practice. The axes commonly employed in addition to the main descriptive diagnosis are a personality diagnosis (describing in a few words the most prominent character features of the patient) and a situational diagnosis (noting briefly the main precipitating factor in the mental illness). A routine diagnosis might, for example, read: Neurosis (anxiety type) in an insecure and timid woman with marital problems. If applicable, problems with alcohol might also be mentioned, in parentheses.

RELATIONSHIP OF SCANDINAVIAN DIAGNOSTIC CONCEPTS TO DSM-III

Reactive Psychosis

The Scandinavian concept of reactive psychosis has its roots in German psychiatry, but later was elaborated by Scandinavian psychiatrists. The term *psychogenic psychosis*, which was previously used for what we now call reactive psychosis, goes back to 1894, to the German psychiatrist Sommer (4). In Continental psychiatry the term *erlebnisbedingt* was also used. Of importance for further conceptualization of this disorder are the criteria for "genuine reaction" developed by the German psychiatrist Karl Jaspers (5) and the studies of the Danish psychiatrists Wimmer (6) , Strømgren (7, 8), and Færgeman (9, 10) and the Norwegian psychiatrists Retterstøl (11,12) and Noreik (13).

In Norway reactive psychoses were originally called "constitutional psychoses" (14), the main emphasis being on the abnormal premorbid personality and constitution that predispose to the development of the psychoses. In Denmark the same condition was labeled "psychogenic psychoses," the focus being on the psychological stresses that trigger the psychosis. In all the Scandinavian countries the common label for these psychoses is now *reactive psychoses*, indicating that these disorders are reactions to external stresses most of which exacerbate psychological conflicts, but can also be a combination of psychological, social, and somatic stresses, as in puerperal psychoses or psychoses related to surgery.

A reactive psychosis is now defined as a psychosis in which the development of the disorder seems understandable in terms of the affected person's constitutional background and personality development within a life situation that fosters a mental disturbance in that specific person at that particular time in his or her life. In making this diagnosis the clinician tries very hard to elicit information on the personality development and life pattern of the patient and then considers how the disorder relates to these factors and the external stress.

In practice, it is usual to find that most of Jaspers's criteria for a "genuine reaction" are met. The psychosis generally bears a temporal relationship to an acute mental trauma, the content of the psychotic symptoms reflects a traumatic experience, and the course of the psychosis is usually benign. The psychotic symptoms generally disappear after treatment of relatively short duration (weeks or months), especially when the traumatic experiences are dealt with and the life situation is changed for the better or becomes better accepted.

In making a diagnosis one must bear in mind that quantitative measurement of psychic traumas is impossible. One has to take the background of the individual's personal development into account. To one person a severely traumatic situation may at a particular time be up-setting; at another time, or to another person, the same situation may be of no importance at all. In order to label a psychosis *reactive*, the psychic trauma must be considered of such significance that the psy-chosis would not have occurred in its absence. There must be a temporal connection between the trauma and the onset of the psychosis. These are *psychoses*, and should be distinguished from neuroses in that the patient has no insight into his or her disorder and no understanding that the symptoms (e.g., delusions) are of a morbid nature.

Even though psychogenesis seems probable in the reactive psy-choses, other possible causal factors cannot be excluded. Particular mention must be made of the importance of somatic factors, above all, physical conditions that reduce the patient's general psychic resistance, e.g., surgery, severe physical disorders, and sensory defects. Many cases of reactive psychosis are precipitated in a hospital setting.

The onset of a reactive psychosis is usually acute; thought content tends to center on the emotional trauma; preservation of good emo-tional contact is characteristic. In most cases the patient regains a normal level of functioning after some weeks or months.

Longitudinal studies indicate that the reactive psychoses can clearly be distinguished from manic-depressive psychosis and schizophrenia on the basis of symptoms and course. In a long-term (5–18 years) follow-up investigation of a large series of delusional patients, Retterstøl (11,12) demonstrated that clinical and social outcomes were favorable in 70%–80% of the patients who, on discharge from the University Psychiatric Clinic in Oslo, were diagnosed as having had a reactive psychosis; in contrast, the rate for those with a diagnosis of schizophrenia was only 18%–30%. Studies by Færgeman (9, 10) and Noreik (13) also point to a much better course in patients diagnosed as suffering from reactive psychosis than in those with a diagnosis of schizophrenia.

Although there seems to be some overlap with manic-depressive psychosis (affective disorders), genetic studies indicate that reactive psychosis is so distinct as to warrant a separate diagnostic category, a point emphasized by McCabe and Strømgren (15,16).

Lifetime expectancy for developing a reactive psychosis in Denmark and Norway is 1%, which is the same as the rate for schizophrenia and manic-depressive disorders, the two other groups of functional psychoses (8).

In DSM-III reactive psychoses would be diagnosed among the group of psychotic disorders not elsewhere classified, which includes schiz-ophreniform disorder (the Scandinavian term will be discussed later), brief reactive psychosis, schizoaffective disorder, and atypical psy-chosis. But DSM-III specifies that only a psychotic syndrome of less than two weeks' duration that follows a significant psychosocial stressor should be classified as "brief reactive psychosis" (298.80), i.e., a small proportion of the group covered by the Scandinavian concept. Scandinavian psychiatrists regard the DSM-III concept as too narrow. It seems artificial to limit the duration to two weeks and to label disorders of more than two weeks' duration (with a similar symptom picture and pathogenesis) "schizophreniform." As previously pointed out, one must also bear in mind the relativity of a psychic trauma, which must always be evaluated againt the background of the premorbid personality and the person's life situation.

The Scandinavian concept of reactive psychoses would involve a great many cases diagnosed in DSM-III as schizophreniform disorder (295.40) and schizoaffective disorder (295.70). If these groups and the group of paranoid disorders (297) are included, most of the psychoses diagnosed in Scandinavia as reactive psychoses are covered.

Though Scandinavian psychiatrists regard the DSM-III system as a step forward in comparison with ICD-8, they think that further consideration should be given to the classification of the reactive psychoses in DSM-IV.

Schizophreniform Psychoses

The concept of schizophreniform psychoses was introduced in the Scandinavian literature by Langfeldt (17,18), whose research demonstrated that a rough line could be drawn between a nuclear group of schizophrenics and a second group that had a better spontaneous prognosis. Because this latter group had, as a predominant feature, presenting symptoms similar to true or nuclear schizophrenia, Langfeldt chose the label *schizophreniform*. The symptoms were frequently found to be rich in pathoplastic trends and occasionally were mixed with traits from other forms of psychosis, such as manic-depressive psychosis. In 1961 Langfeldt stated that the group of schizophrenias should be divided into two subgroups: *typical schizophrenias*, and *schizophreniform psychoses*. He added that the latter included a number of cases of uncertain diagnosis, often with mixed symptoms, and that some of these cases later turned out to be nuclear schizophrenia whereas others belonged to other nosological entities, most often the reactive psychoses.

As it now stands, the term *schizophreniform psychosis* is frequently used by Scandinavian psychiatrists to indicate a psychosis that over the long term usually turns out to be a reactive psychosis or a schizophrenia (when diagnosed retrospectively).

Schizophreniform psychosis can be defined as follows: The symptoms are acute and episodic rather than chronic, often developing in previously well-adjusted persons; they are frequently precipitated by problems of living or by organic factors. Consciousness is often mildly clouded. The patient may display affective symptoms. Recovery from the episode is usual, though there may be recurrent relapses in some cases, and the illness may take a more chronic course. There is some evidence of a relationship between schizophreniform psychosis and primary affective disorders. Many of the schizophreniform psychoses in the long run turn out to have been a reactive psychosis, which should then retrospectively be rediagnosed as *reactive psychosis, schizophreniform type*.

In practice in his clinic, Langfeldt gave a separate label to disorders of this type, indicating doubt as to whether the case was that of a true schizophrenia, a reactive psychosis, or something else.

In a study by Retterstøl (11,12), 78 delusional patients diagnosed as having schizophreniform psychoses by Langfeldt, 173 diagnosed as suffering from reactive psychoses, and 52 diagnosed as schizophrenic were compared after 5–18 years of follow-up. On the basis of Langfeldt's discharge diagnoses, it was determined that 81% of the patients with the reactive psychoses had a favorable course, compared with 61% of those with schizophreniform symptoms and only 23% of those with "true" schizophrenia. Thus, in terms of course there is a continuum from the reactive psychoses, through the schizophreniform psychoses, to true or nuclear schizophrenia.

Several entities included in the DSM-II concept of schizophrenia are excluded from the DSM-III classification (19), among them schizophreniform disorder, now bearing the code 295.40 and included in the psychotic disorders not elsewhere classified. These categories have been separated from schizophrenia because of research evidence that they may be associated with a greater likelihood of emotional turmoil and confusion, a better prognosis, a tendency toward acute onset and resolution, more likely return of the patient to his or her premorbid level of functioning, and no increased frequency of schizophrenia among the patient's relatives.

Langfeldt (20) has criticized the DSM-III concept of schizophreniform disorder, but we think it is in many ways close to the view of later Scandinavian researchers. The DSM-III concept does, however, seem too narrow in its restriction of the illness to cases in which the symptoms have lasted from two weeks to six months and the essential symptoms are identical with those of schizophrenia. Langfeldt has suggested, and we agree with him, that schizoaffective disorder (295.70) might well be incorporated in the schizophreniform group (295.40).

Schizophrenia

The Scandinavian concept of schizophrenia is stricter than that employed in most European countries, and definitely more so than that prevailing the Anglo-American literature. Contrary to the schizophreniform psychoses, schizophrenia is often referred to as "nuclear schizophrenia," "process schizophrenia," or "nonremitting schizophrenia." It usually has an insidious onset and course. Characteristically there are delusions and hallucinations in a clear sensorium, often intermittent, and blunted, shallow, or inappropriate affect and disordered thinking, with loosening of associations. The disorder involves personality changes, autistic preoccupation, influence phenomena, and depersonalization symptoms.

The Scandinavian concept of schizophrenia is more in line with Continental European than with American or Russian traditions. This was demonstrated by the International Pilot Study of Schizophrenia (21). In seven of the nine regional centers involved in the project, including London, Prague, and Aarhus (Denmark), the local psychiatrists all had basically the same concept of schizophrenia. In the Moscow and Washington centers, however, a considerably broader concept prevailed. It is important to keep this in mind when scientific results from the United States and Europe are compared.

In 1976 Rawnsley (22) published an interesting study in which he compared the diagnoses given to a series of 30 patients by groups of psychiatrists from 5 different countries—Denmark, Norway, Sweden, the United Kingdom, and the United States. A clear tendency emerged for American psychiatrists to diagnose schizophrenia where European psychiatrists diagnosed depression, obsessional disorders, or paranoid psychosis, and for Scandinavian psychiatrists to diagnose reactive psychosis where British and American psychiatrists tended to diagnose a neurotic illness.

The DSM-III definition of schizophrenia eliminates several entities that previously were included in the DSM-III concept and in earlier American diagnostic tradition. Syndromes that look like schizophrenia but have lasted less than six months are termd schizophreniform psychoses. For this reason, Scandinavians welcome the DSM-III system, as it seems to offer a narrower concept of schizophrenia, one more in line with the Scandinavian concept.

Paranoid Disorders

Paranoid symptoms or features occur in many mental disorders, and paranoid psychoses therefore do not constitute a diagnostic entity in Scandinavian psychiatry. Nevertheless, in most of the official national classifications, and also in the ICD system, the term *paranoid states* is applied to psychoses, not classifiable as schizophrenia or affective psychoses, in which delusions of a fairly fixed, elaborate, and systematized nature, especially of being persecuted or treated in some special way, are the main symptom.

In DSM-III the paranoid disorders include: paranoia (297.10), a chronic disorder with systematized delusions; shared paranoid disorder (297.30);

acute paranoid disorder (298.30) (with a duration of less than six months), a category that permits the identification of the most common form of paranoid disorders, which is of acute onset and brief duration; and atypical paranoid disorders (297.90). In the DSM-III system, an opening is made for the large group of patients included in the Scandinavian follow-up studies (Retterstøl's studies [11,12] on paranoid and paranoiac psychoses, Johanson's [23] on mild paranoia, and Astrup's [24] on benign functional psychoses). It may be added that many of the patients diagnosed as having reactive paranoid disorders in Retterstøl's study would be classifiable under the DSM-III group 298.30, but could not be classified under the DSM-III category brief reactive psychosis (298.80), as the criterion for duration (less than two weeks) is too stringent. As indicated above, we should like the latter group to be assigned a less strict time limit, and we should strongly suggest that acute paranoid disorder remain in the classification, perhaps as a subgroup of brief reactive psychosis, if the time limitation is extended to six months.

Although the DSM-III system has incorporated many of the diagnostic groups made explicit by the systematized Scandinavian follow-up studies, there is still need for further elaboration in this area. An obvious weakness of DSM-III is that the term *paranoid disorders* is restricted to persistent persecutory delusions and delusional jealousy. Ideas of self-reference, hypochondriac delusions, and psychoses with delusions concerning sex, grandeur, etc., might well have been included. Therefore, we propose an expansion of the concept of paranoid disorders in DSM-IV.

Affective Disorders

In Scandinavia the term *affective disorder* has usually been identified with the concept of manic-depressive disorder, unipolar or bipolar type. DSM-III does not refer to the affective disorders as psychoses (25), which is not in accord with Scandinavian traditions; it does, however, make the unipolar–bipolar distinction, which is Scandinavian practice (26). The Scandinavians will miss "reactive psychotic depressions," a common type of psychosis and of depression, for which the ICD-8 supplies a code number: "298.0: Other psychosis, reactive depressive psychosis."

Psychoses are not distinguished from neuroses in the DSM-III system, in which neurotic disorders are classified only according to their main clinical manifestation. This lack of distinction between neurosis and psychosis is, from a Scandinavian viewpoint, one of the greatest limitations of DSM-III. The distinction, which is usually clear and consistent, though there are some borderline cases, is very important for practical forensic-psychiatric reasons. Only when a patient is psychotic is involuntary admission to a mental hospital legally permitted; and when a criminal is psychotic, he or she cannot be punished for his or her act ("the biological forensic system," common in parts of Scandinavia).

In DSM-III the spectrum concept of affective disorders is favored instead. This leads to the removal of a neurosis (dysthymic disorder) and a personality disorder (cyclothymic disorder) from their traditional groups in ICD-8 and grouping them together according to the new spectrum concept. It could be argued that DSM-III puts too much emphasis on the descriptive similarities of disturbances at the cost of acknowledging the different pathogenetic factors in these two disorders.

Neurosis

Neurosis is a well-established diagnostic category in Scandinavian psychiatry. The term came into use in the present century, mainly following Freud's works. In Scandinavia, however, the term *neurosis* is used mostly in a descriptive sense, as is the practice in ICD-8/9; the neuroses are therefore classified according to the dominant symptom. Symptom neurosis is commonly distinguished from character neurosis, the latter being generally defined according to Vanggaard (27):

> Character neurosis is a form of neurosis where neurotic symptoms are few or absent, but the patient shows character traits which give him an abnormal inhibition or restriction in his abilities for natural display. These inhibitions and these restrictions will limit his ability to utilize his intellect, emotions, fantasy and drives, and they will also limit his abilities to live closely together with others, and to establish and keep satisfactory intimate emotional contact with others.

These various character traits can have patterns that correspond to the personality disorders described under category 301 in ICD-8/9. According to the Scandinavian view, neuroses are either character neuroses or symptom neuroses. Neurotic symptoms almost invariably involve pathological character traits. In the ICD-8 classification the Scandinavian concepts of neurosis are thus coded either under 300 (the symptom neuroses) or 301 (the character neuroses).

According to ICD-8/9, hysterical neurosis includes both hysteria and conversion neurosis. The depersonalization syndrome has been used in Norway for the classification of syndromes close to the DSM-III category borderline personality disorder because of the disturbed identity and sense of self.

The key difference between neurosis and psychosis is faulty reality testing. A psychosis is also considered to affect a greater part or the total personality of the patient. Generally, a patient with a neurosis has a feeling of illness and suffering, and may seek help, whereas a psychotic patient usually does not consider his or her psychotic symptoms to be of a morbid nature.

Exclusion of neurosis as a category is one of the most controversial features of DSM-III, and certainly is one of the points in conflict with Scandinavian concepts. The ICD-8/9 class "neurosis" is now spread over five sections of DSM-III—affective disorders, anxiety disorders, somatoform disorders, dissociative disorders, and psychosexual disorders. The points of view on neurosis described in the introduction to DSM-III (pages 9–10) do not correspond to two of the aims of DSM-III as stated on pages 2–3, namely, to maintain compatibility with ICD-9 and to avoid the introduction of new terminology and concepts that break with tradition.

The descriptive definition of neurosis given on pages 9–10 in DSM-III can be subscribed to by Scandinavian psychiatrists. However, the DSM-III definition of neurotic disorders introduces a viewpoint on course—that neuroses are long-standing disorders—and a prognostic view—that the course if positively affected by treatment—that contrast with Scandinavian views, which see neuroses as conditions that can be of short or long duration and that often improve or "heal" without treatment. In fact, only two of the disorders considered neurotic according to the DSM-III definition have a duration criterion (i.e., dysthymic disorder and transvestism). The DSM-III definition of neurotic disorders implies that there are effective treatment approaches that can change their course. In Scandinavia one makes such a statement more cautiously.

From a Scandinavian viewpoint much of what the DSM-III task force wanted, namely, an atheoretical descriptive approach to neurosis and inclusion of newly described neurotic disorders, could have been achieved by definitions of criteria and expansion of the neurosis section of the ICD-9.

The political implications of DSM-III's abandonment of neurosis have been cleary stated by Skodol and Spitzer (25). It was important to do away with the psychoanalytic concept of neurosis, and that was most easily done by giving up the term completely. Obviously, this was an important decision for American psychiatry. But what will the cost be internationally? Kendell (28) says that the World Health Organization is like a convoy that does not move faster than its slowest member. The point of a convoy is that it is more protected from attack and destruction than the ship that sails alone. By abandoning the term *neurosis* American psychiatry seems to be willing to take that risk.

Depressive neurosis is the most common type diagnosed in Scandinavia. But with the DSM-III criterion of two years' duration for dysthymic disorder, many Scandinavian cases will fall somewhere between that diagnosis and adjustment disorder with depressed mood. There seems to be no DSM-III category for depressive disorders between these two categories. The category of adjustment disorder is seldom used in Scandinavia, although it is listed in ICD-8.

The placement of depersonalization syndrome in the chapter on dissociative disorders seems to us a wise one. The depersonalization syndrome was seldom thought to be in accord with the common Scandinavian definition of neurosis. The inclusion of post-traumatic stress disorder in DSM-III is also certainly welcomed. This type of disorder, formerly called "compensation neurosis," has been studied extensively by Eitinger (29) in Norway. In contrast to the DSM-III concept, however, in Scandinavian usage the stress can be minimal, and the disorder is often observed after a mild physical illness or injury. The category of psychosexual disorders in DSM-III is really excellent, and integrates new findings in a very satisfying way, far better than is done in ICD-8/9.

In summary, from the Scandinavian point of view, the exclusion of the term *neurosis* from DSM-III seems dubious. The international literature on neurosis from now on will probably have to live with two sets of diagnoses, the DSM-III and the ICD-8/9 ones, for some time to come. The Norwegian concept of neurosis is in practice close to the "neurotic disorders" in DSM-III, but, as noted above, there are some conceptual differences.

Personality Disorders

The Scandinavian concept of personality disorders has several roots. The close contact with Germany psychiatry made it natural that Scandinavia would be influenced by Germany's dominating trends. Kraepelin's concepts of temperament, with identification of the autistic and cyclothymic types related to the major psychoses (30), are well known. Kurt Schneider's important empirical investigations on psychopathic personalities (31) have also had a persistent impact. Sjöbring's work (32) on constitution is an original Scandinavian contribution to typology, which has had little influence outside Sweden. Kretschmer's contributions (33) in this area were much appreciated, especially with regard to the hypersensitive personality and the connection between body type and character type. During the last 40 years, however, there has been a reaction against the mainly descriptive use of personality disorders. Dynamic views, influenced particularly by psychoanalytic points of view, have gained favor.

All of these trends meet in the current Scandinavian distinction between personality and character. This view is based on the concept that personality is composed of more than character, that temperament, intelligence, and constitution have to be included. These factors overlap, so the personality is more than the sum of its components as they are formed individually in each person. Currently, Scandinavians prefer the term *character neurosis* for many of the conditions that in DSM-III are called personality disorders. This viewpoint does not imply a psychoanalytic understanding of the development and dynamics of the character; it can easily be combined with an empirical approach, in the tradition of Schneider.

During the last few decades there has been a trend favoring a focus on character and character neurosis rather than personality disorder. In Scandinavia there has been a tradition of calling "character neuroses" those conditions in which a psychogenic, milieu-determined pathogenesis could be identified, and to keep the term *psychopathy* for personality disorders of more endogenous, constitutional types, often associated with outwardly directed aggression. However, this separation into constitutional, genetically determined conditions and more milieu-determined ones is very difficult in practice.

It is uncommon for Scandinavian psychiatrists to make a fourth-digit diagnosis of type of personality disorder. The guidelines provided by the Norwegian Directorate for Health for use of the ICD-8 classification simply states: "Classification in subgroups is so controversial that each hospital is left free in this regard." When the health authorities five years later summed up the Norwegian experience with the ICD-8 classification, the directorate concluded that subgroups of personality disorders were used to only a small extent. This can be explained by the Norwegian tradition of a triaxial diagnosis, as mentioned earlier. In our personality descriptions, the types of personality disorder listed in ICD-8 are seldom used; rather, such terms as *sensitive, weak,* or *immature personality* are more apt to be employed. In Scandinavia at present, personality disorders according to ICD-8 are rarely diagnosed except for diagnosing the antisocial personality, the psychopath.

The DSM-III section on personality disorders is, then, covered in the Scandinavian tradition by the diagnostic terms *character neurosis* and *personalitas pathologica,* meaning mainly antisocial personality disorder. The concept of character neurosis is applied descriptively to indicate patterns of traits outside the normal variation that may cause the individual and/or society suffering. In its present use this concept does not imply any specific etiology, particularly not unconscious conflicts per se, even if the condition is supposedly related to early defense mechanisms arising from a strict upbringing. At the moment it seems unlikely that the concept of character neurosis will disappear or be replaced in Scandinavia by more systematic use of the subtypes of personality disorder.

From a Scandinavian vantage point, several aspects of the axis II concept of personality disorder in DSM-III seem noteworthy. First of all, the DSM-III approach calls for systematic evaluation of personality traits in all cases. This seems to be a timely and very important contribution, especially for planning treatment.

However, several problems can also be seen. The DSM-III personality disorder section largely follows the ten subgroups of personality disorders in ICD-8/9, which basically go back to Schneider's empirically derived subgroups. But DSM-III seems to lack a consistent view of the *severity of the psychopathology*. Dependent personality disorder, for example, comes dangerously close to describing a traditional female role in Scandinavian society, which has been challenged during the feminist liberation movement, but which still seems pervasive. On the other hand, histrionic personality disorder is clearly described as much more severe than the ordinary hysterical character disorder commonly described in Scandinavian psychiatry.

There seems also to be a problem concerning the *separation* of the various personality disorders. It is admitted that schizotypal and borderline personality disorders often overlap, as originally pointed out by Spitzer, Endicott, and Gibbon (34). But patients with a hysterical disturbance so severe as to warrant a diagnosis of histrionic personality disorder generally also have a disturbed sense of identity, which makes the separation from borderline personality disorder difficult. Similarly, the differences between the schizoid and the schizotypal personality disorders seem very small in actual clinical practice.

This critique obviously is related to a fairly general critique of the whole operational criteria approach taken in DSM-III—the problems that arise from arbitrarily set cutoff levels, and the equal importance of all criteria (symptoms).

The concept of spectrum disorders has had considerable success during the last decade. In the DSM-III classification one senses an ambivalent stance toward this. The well-established affective personality has been taken out of the personality disorder section and placed among the affective spectrum disorders under a new name: cyclothymic disorder. The schizophrenic spectrum disorders, however, are not treated in the same way. The schizotypal and schizoid personalities are classified under personality disorders. The schizophreniform disorder is placed among psychotic disorders not classified elsewhere, and only the more severe "schizophrenia" is classified under "schizophrenic disorder." This way of classifying schizophrenia spectrum disorders is quite confusing, and is an apparent contrast to the spectrum approach in the section on affective disorders.

Organic Mental Disorders

DSM-III lists six organic brain syndromes. *Delirium* and *dementia*, as defined in DSM-III, are terms used in Scandinavia. We seldom isolate the amnestic syndrome, which is generally seen as a part of delirium or dementia. Korsakoff's syndrome is rare, in both alcoholic and non-alcoholic conditions. Organic delusional syndrome and organic hallucinosis diagnoses are accepted in Scandinavia, but often are simply called "organic psychosis." The organic affective syndrome, the organic personality syndrome, withdrawal, and intoxication are usually not listed as organic conditions because in Scandinavia we adhere to the concept of organic psychosis, and these last four brain syndromes are not considered psychotic and therefore are not categorized as organic mental disorders. They are, however, often seen as a part of Eugen Bleuler's *Organisches Psychosyndrom*, which involves disturbances in affect and personality. Withdrawal and intoxication are commonly viewed as a part of substance abuse disorders.

Another difference is that the term *confusion* is often used in the description of organic mental disorders in Scandinavia, but is not used in DSM-III, where the term *disorientation* comes closest to it.

For Scandinavian psychiatrists it is important to stress that even if a diagnosis of organic psychosis is given, psychogenic factors are not ruled out. On the contrary, one is always looking for precipitating factors in the patient's life situation (social isolation, death of close relatives, etc.) in an organic psychosis just as in the reactive psychoses.

Substance Use Disorders

Scandinavian psychiatrists have given considerable attention to substance use disorders in the last two decades. Several follow-up studies concerning the treatment and prognosis of young drug abusers have been published. An overview of the Scandinavian perspective has been presented (35). In these studies the definitions of drug abuse and drug dependence have followed ICD-8/9. In Scandinavia the term *drug dependence* is interpreted according to the World Health Organization definition and includes psychic (or mental) or physical dependence (or both combined).

The Scandinavian definition of substance use disorder is somewhat different from the principles applied in DSM-III. In Scandinavia one of the main features in substance use disorders is the *strong compulsion* to take the drug to develop the euphoria that follows the intake of the substance. Physical dependence with tolerance phenomena is not seen as a *conditio sine qua non*. Dependence-producing drugs such as cannabis, LSD, and amphetamine cause little or no physical dependence, yet they are strongly dependence producing (psychic). The classification of intoxication and withdrawal as organic mental disorders rather than substance use disorders seems somewhat artificial since all the phenomena seen in substance use disorder can be said to be connected with the substance's effects on the brain. Thus, intoxication and withdrawal are generally diagnosed in Scandinavia as actual substance use disorder.

REACTION OF SCANDINAVIAN PSYCHIATRISTS TO DSM-III

There has been much interest in DSM-III in all the Scandinavian countries. A symposium at Gaustad Hospital, Oslo, in 1980, at which Drs. Spitzer and Williams introduced the system to Scandinavian psychiatrists, bore witness to this interest and produced positive reactions. The DSM-III system was also discussed at the 19th Nordic Congress, in Uppsala, Sweden, in 1979. The Nordic Psychiatric Cooperation Committee (under the auspices of the five Scandinavian countries) has taken the initiative to cooperate on a Scandinavian level in using DSM-III in addition to the official diagnostic system, but no results are yet available. DSM-III is used in many research projects, probably in most projects in which diagnostic labeling is an important part of the study. This is the case in all five countries, but less so in Denmark and Iceland, according to personal information we have received from Mellergaard, Reisby, and Helgason (all in 1982). Achté (personal communication, 1982) has reported that much use is made of DSM-III in research in Finland, and the whole of the manual has been translated into Finnish, by Fuhrman, Lønnquist, and Huttunen. Many research projects using DSM-III are under way in Norway and Sweden.

From discussions with several academic psychiatrists and younger colleagues, we have gained the impression that DSM-III has been welcomed in Scandinavia as a step forward in psychiatric classification. The greatest advantage is the multiaxial coding, which seems clinically relevant and easy to use. Another advantage is that the system in some ways brings American psychiatry closer to European concepts and establishes strict criteria for differentiation of disorders. Nevertheless, the system seems more appropriate for communicaton generally and for epidemiological purposes and psychiatric research than for more dynamic, clinical, everyday work. The phenomenological and operational approach seems to many clinicians too complicated for routine clinical use.

Elimination of the diagnosis of neurosis is strongly questioned, as is also the lack of a more psychodynamic and psychotherapeutic approach in the entire DSM-III sytem. There is some concern that comparisons among categories of patients may be made more complicated by this five-axial system.

GENERAL ISSUES

The creation of DSM-III involved some very impressive work. The wide circulation of various drafts and the field trials indicate an openness to a democratic and pragmatic process that to many Scandinavians confirms the best traditions of American culture. The willingness of the American Psychiatric Association to accept a diagnostic manual based on operational descriptive criteria reveals a desire to seek progress in the complicated area of classification. In view of all this, it may seem presumptuous to make critical comments; however, there are some that seem important to note for the sake of future advances in the classification of mental disorders.

In the introduction to DSM-III ten different goals of the new classification are listed. Most of these have to do with research and clinical aims. One wonders if perhaps the problems of criterion variance and interrater reliability of psychiatric diagnostic systems may not have been overemphasized in the preparation of DSM-III. These are very important questions for research, but probably much less so for the clinician. What the clinician loses is a certain flexibility in making diagnoses. This stems from several features of the manual:

1. The diagnostic criteria in DSM-III are based on three types of data: descriptive symptoms, severity, and duration. Such criteria create boundary problems—e.g., one or more days' duration can change the diagnosis from one disorder to another.

2. Descriptive criteria are mostly given equal value, so that clinicians weighing various symptoms may, because of their experience, easily get lost in a mechanical addition of the symptoms registered. In this connection, one may wonder about the statement that the specific diagnostic criteria in DSM-III are *guides*. It is not at all clear to what extent each clinician can use his own judgment in relation to this guide, or if DSM-III is to be regarded as a body of laws.

3. The basic concept of DSM-III is that it does not assume that each mental disorder is a discrete entity with sharp boundaries between it and other mental disorders and between it and no mental disorder. Thus, DSM-III takes the position that there are only quantitative, not qualitative, differences between, for example, schizophrenia and no mental disorder. Most Scandinavian psychiatrists would disagree with this view.

4. The manual states that DSM-III classifies disorders that individuals have. Multiple classifications are thus made possible, so that a person can be diagnosed as having several different mental disorders. In Scandinavia it has been a common tradition that patients should have one diagnosis at a time, even though several diagnoses may be considered; a choice of principal diagnosis has to be made. ICD-9 offers the same

possibility as DSM-III, that of registering all diagnoses and thus making a principal diagnosis according to the study one is doing or according to what brought the patient to the mental health service.

A main feature of DSM-III that obviously is an improvement compared with ICD-8/9 is the persistence of an atheoretical, descriptive attitude that leads to a comprehensive picture of the manifestation of mental disorder. The excellent glossary helps considerably in clarifying various nebulous concepts as the clinician considers what the patient says or how he or she behaves. The introduction of decision trees is also a help in making a diagnosis and clearly indicates that DSM-III is a classification system that takes into account the fact that we are on the threshold of the computer age, which will certainly change time-honored diagnostic practice enormously.

Though opinions differ and many are skeptical, most Scandinavian psychiatrists who have made themselves acquainted with the DSM-III system have a positive feeling, some even an enthusiastic one, about it. All look forward to the improvements that will doubtless come with DSM-IV. We extend our congratulations to the American Psychiatric Associaton for contributing this original and carefully worked out stimulus to progress in international psychiatry.

REFERENCES

1. Essen-Möller E., Wohlfahrt S: Suggestions for the amendment of the official Swedish classification of mental disorders. Acta Psychiatr Scand, Supplement 47, 1947, pp 551–555
2. Essen-Möller E.: Suggestions for further improvement of the international classification of mental disorders. Psychol Med 1:308–311, 1971
3. Ottosson JO, Perris C: Multidimensional classification of mental disorders. Psychol Med 3:238–243, 1973
4. Sommer R: Diagnostik der Geisteskranken. Vienna, Urban & Schwarzenberg, 1894
5. Jaspers K: Allgemeine Psychopathologie. Berlin, Springer, 1913
6. Wimmer A: Psykogene Sindssygdomsformer. Copenhagen, Jacob Lunds Boghandel, 1916 (in Danish)
7. Strømgren E: Episodiske psykoser. Copenhagen, Munksgaard, 1940 (in Danish)
8. Strømgren E: Atypische Psychosen. Reaktive (psychogene) Psychosen, in Psychiatrie der Gegenwart. Forschung und Praxis. Klinische Psychiatrie, I. Berlin, Springer, 1972, pp 141–152
9. Færgeman PM: De psykogene psykoser. Copenhagen, Munksgaard, 1945 (in Danish)
10. Færgeman PM: Psychogenic Psychoses. London, Butterworths, 1963
11. Retterstøl N: Paranoid and Paranoiac Psychoses. Springfield, Ill, Thomas, 1966

12. Retterstøl N: Prognosis in Paranoid Psychoses. Springfield, Ill, Thomas, 1970
13. Noreik K: Classification of Functional Psychoses, with Special Reference to Reactive Psychoses. Oslo, Universitetsforlaget, 1970
14. Langfeldt G: Lærebok i klinisk psykiatri. Oslo, Aschehoug, 1951 (in Norwegian)
15. McCabe MS: Reactive psychoses. Acta Psychiatr Scand, Supplement 259, 1975
16. McCabe MA, Strømgren E: Reactive psychoses: A family study. Arch Gen Psychiatry 32:447, 1975
17. Langfeldt G: The prognosis in schizophrenia and the factors influencing the course of the disease. Acta Psychiatr Neurol Scand, Supplement 13, 1937
18. Langfeldt G: The Schizophreniform States. A Catamnestic Study Based on Re-examination. Copenhagen, Munksgaard, 1939
19. Spitzer RC, Williams JPW: Classification of mental disorders and DSM-III, in Comprehensive Textbook of Psychiatry, 3rd ed, vol 3. Edited by Kaplan HI, Freedman AM, Sadock BJ. Baltimore, Williams & Wilkins, 1980
20. Langfeldt G: Definition of "schizophreniform psychosis." Am J Psychiatry 139:703, 1982
21. World Health Organization: The International Pilot Study of Schizophrenia, vol 1. Geneva, World Health Organization, 1973
22. Rawnsley K: An international diagnostic exercise, in Proceedings of the Fourth World Congress of Psychiatry. Amsterdam, Excerpta Medica Foundation, 1976, vol 4, pp 2683–2686
23. Johanson E: Mild paranoia. Acta Psychiatr Scand, Supplement 77, 1958
24. Astrup C: Benign Functional Psychoses, 1983 (in press)
25. Skodol AE, Spitzer RL: DSM-III: Rationale, basic concepts, and some differences from ICD-9. Acta Psychiatr Scand 66: 271–281, 1982
26. Perris C: A study of bipolar (manic-depressive) and unipolar recurrent depressive psychosis. Acta Psychiatr Scand, Supplement 42, 1966, pp 9–188
27. Vanggaard T: The concept of neurosis. Acta Psychiatr Neurol Scand, Supplement 136, 1959, pp 116–136
28. Kendell RE: The Role of Diagnosis in Psychiatry. Oxford, Blackwell, 1957
29. Eitinger L: Concentration Camp Survivors in Norway and Israel. Oslo, Universitetsforlaget, 1964
30. Kraepelin E: Psychiatrie: Ein Lehrbuch, 8th ed. Leipzig, Barth, 1913
31. Schneider K: Die psychopatischen Persönlichkeiten. Vienna, Deuticke, 1923
32. Sjöbring H: Personality structure and development. A model and its application. Acta Psychiatr Scand, Supplement 244, 1973
33. Kretschmer E: Körperbau und Character. Berlin, Springer, 1925
34. Springer RL, Endicott J, Gibbon M: Crossing the border into borderline personality and borderline schizophrenia. Arch Gen Psychiatry 36:17–24, 1979
35. Retterstøl N (ed): Drug Issues: The Scandinavian Perspective of Drug Issues. J Drug Issues 10: 401–521, 1980

16

THE IMPACT OF DSM-III
ON CHINESE PSYCHIATRY

Tao Kuo-Tai, M.D., and Yan Shan-Ming, M.D.

As soon as DSM-III appeared, this outstanding work was introduced into China. The *Quick Reference to the Diagnostic Criteria from DSM-III* was translated into Chinese in 1981, under the guidance of Professor Tao Kuo-Tai; and this Chinese version has been widely distributed among Chinese psychiatrists. Some of the classic case reports, with modern diagnoses, from the *DSM-III Case Book* have also been translated, and have been published in the Chinese medical journal *Foreign Medicine* (Section: Psychiatry), in which a review article on the major achievements of DSM-III has also been published (1).

Recently at our national and local academic meetings on various aspects of psychiatry, DSM-III, its approach and its definitions of mental disorders, has frequently been referred to or heatedly discussed. At a national Symposium on Schizophrenia, sponsored by the Chinese Medical Association and held in November 1981 at Soozhou City, Professor Robert Spitzer and Dr. Janet Williams were invited to deliver a series of lectures on DSM-III, which stimulated further interest in this work.

RESPONSE TO, AND USE OF, DSM-III
BY A GROUP OF CHINESE PSYCHIATRISTS

In August 1982, a questionnaire on the response to, and use of, DSM-III was sent to 54 senior psychiatrists at 23 psychiatric centers in

Address correspondence to: Tao Kuo-Tai, M.D., Professor of General & Child Psychiatry, Nanjing Neuropsychiatric Institute, 264 Kwangchow Road, Nanjing, People's Republic of China

235

various parts of China. All of the questionnaires were returned; and although it is difficult to evaluate the responses precisely, the views of these experienced psychiatrists may be considered representative of those of a significant proportion of Chinese mental health specialists. The responses are summarized in the accompanying table.

As this table indicates, the psychiatrists generally displayed keen interest in DSM-III and reacted favorably to it. Most of our respondents had studied and used the manual; it had been applied in both research work and routine clinical practice. The multiaxial diagnostic approach and the detailed diagnostic criteria were much appreciated. Generally speaking, the concept and classification of schizophrenia, schizophreniform disorder, schizoaffective disorder, and paranoid disorder were accepted. There seemed to be general recognition that DSM-III would have a significant influence on Chinese psychiatry in diagnosing and classifying mental disorders.

CHINESE PRACTICES IN LIGHT OF DSM-III CONCEPTS AND CRITERIA

Major Psychoses

In China most of the inpatients in mental hospitals have been cases of the major psychoses, and these disorders have therefore been the main concern of Chinese psychiatrists. We have tended to have a quite narrow concept of affective disorders, with the result that most of our inpatients (about 80%) have been diagnosed as schizophrenic and fewer than 5% as suffering from affective disorders. Recently, as we have become familiar with the Langfeldt school (2, 3), the St. Louis approach (4) and its successor, DSM-III, and the work of Michael Alan Taylor's group (5–8), we have begun to examine and reevaluate our diagnostic concepts concerning the major psychoses. We have begun to realize that admissions for manic-depressive illness are actually far more numerous than we have thought, and that cases of schizophrenia are, in fact, much less frequent than they have commonly been diagnosed (9, 10).

A national symposium on the affective disorders is being planned; this represents the first time that these disorders have been accorded such importance. This is in agreement with the current trend in world psychiatry and marks definite progress for Chinese psychiatry.

A Chinese investigator, Zhang Mingyuan (11), in 1982 in Shanghai reviewed the charts of inpatients and rediagnosed, according to DSM-III criteria, 100 cases in which the discharge diagnosis had been schizophrenia. He found that 74 cases were diagnosable as schizophrenia (a concordance rate of 74%); but 13 cases met DSM-III criteria for affective disorders; 7, for schizophreniform disorders; 5, for paranoid

Responses of 54 Chinese Psychiatrists to Multiple-choice Questionnaire on DSM-III

Questions	Responses

1. You and colleagues in your unit have studied DSM-III
   a. systematically and thoroughly — 11
   b. generally or routinely — 41
   c. not at all — 2

2. In your unit, DSM-III has been
   a. used or consulted for diagnosis — 51
   b. never used — 3

3. If DSM-III was used, it was for
   a. research work — 22
   b. daily clinical work — 13
   c. both — 16

4. You consider the multiaxial evaluation*
   a. useful for research — 12
   b. useful for routine clinical work — 8
   c. useful for both — 30
   d. not useful for either — 1

5. You consider the explicit diagnostic criteria
   a. highly valuable and very useful — 30
   b. useful or helpful — 24
   c. not useful or helpful — 0

6. In DSM-III a narrow concept and strict definition of schizophrenia are offered. This is good for identifying a relatively homogeneous group. You are
   a. fully in agreement with this — 34
   b. partially in agreement — 20
   c. not in agreement — 0

---

*Three responses unavailable.

Questions	Responses

7. In DSM-III, a six-month duration of illness is required for a diagnosis of schizophrenia. You are
   a. fully in agreement with this — 18
   b. partially in agreement — 29
   c. not in agreement — 7

8. In DSM-III schizophreniform disorder is introduced. You are
   a. fully in agreement with this — 30
   b. partially in agreement — 13
   c. not in agreement — 11

9. In DSM-III paranoid disorders are classified as being separate from schizophrenia and other classes of disorders. You are
   a. fully in agreement with this — 42
   b. partially in agreement — 11
   c. not in agreement — 1

10. In DSM-III schizoaffective disorder is classified as separate from either schizophrenia or affective disorders. You are
    a. fully in agreement with this — 31
    b. partially in agreement — 20
    c. not in agreement — 3

11. In DSM-III a simple type is no longer included under schizophrenia; it is classified as personality disorder. You are*
    a. fully in agreement with this — 4
    b. partially in agreement — 17
    c. not in agreement — 31

12. In DSM-III the term *hysteria* has been eliminated; the concept of hysteria has been divided into a number of disorders. You are
    a. fully in agreement with this — 7
    b. partially in agreement — 19
    c. not in agreement — 28

---

*Two responses unavailable.

Questions   **Responses**

13. In DSM-III the term *neurasthenia* has been
    eliminated. You are
    a. fully in agreement with this   11
    b. not in agreement   43

14. In diagnosing neurotic disorders, do you
    use the DSM-III classification and con-
    cepts, or do you still adhere to the old
    ones?*
    a. DSM-III fully in use   3
    b. partially in use   27
    c. adhere to old concepts   23

15. Overall evaluation: In terms of psychiatric
    diagnosis and classification in China, do
    you think DSM-III has exercised
    a. very marked influence   11
    b. marked influence   43
    c. minimal or no influence   0

disorders; and 1, mental retardation. If similar studies were conducted in other psychiatric centers in China, the discrepancies between our clinical diagnoses and ones according to DSM-III criteria would, we think, be comparable with those revealed by this investigator.

As a result of the modern diagnostic approach, a first draft of diagnostic criteria for schizophrenia was made available in 1981; though these criteria are tentative, this work represents a first attempt to draw up such criteria in China and reflects our endeavor to standardize our diagnostic practice. The draft incorporates many of the advantages of DSM-III and other modern classifications; it contains both inclusion and exclusion criteria, and is closely modeled after its predecessors, especially DSM-III.

Because of differences in cultural background and conceptual influences on our psychiatry, opinions concerning the DSM-III definition of schizophrenia varied among the respondents to our questionnaire. Most of them considered it premature to exclude the simple type from the main body of schizophrenia and thought it somewhat unnecessary to change the traditional nomenclature of hebephrenia. Since the Chinese government's policy on health care gives priority to prevention and

---

*One response unavailable.

emphasizes early identification and treatment of any disease, the DSM-III requirement of six months' duration for a diagnosis of schizophrenia is difficult for many Chinese psychiatrists to accept. A minimum duration of three months has been adopted in our criteria; though this is inadequate for excluding a diagnosis of "acute schizophrenia," it is much longer than the two weeks required in the Research Diagnostic Criteria (RDC). In addition, because there is some evidence of a probability of the occurrence of schizophrenia in middle age, some Chinese psychiatrists question the validity of an age limit of 45.

Neuroses

The neuroses are frequently diagnosed in the outpatient departments of both general and mental hospitals in China. The influence of the Pavlov school and of the traditional system of classification of these disorders (especially the Russian system) has been profound. For example, neurasthenia is often diagnosed in China. Today, some Chinese investigators insist that neurasthenia warrants classification as an independent syndrome; others, applying DSM-III criteria, argue that all cases of neurasthenia can be diagnosed as other disorders; and the debate on this issue continues.*

Generally, most of the respondents to our questionnaire think that abolishing terms such as *neurosis* and *hysteria* and eliminating these disorders from the classification are changes that are too premature and drastic to be accepted. They still hold to traditional concepts of the neuroses, including the notion that there may be some constitutional predisposition to certain clinical features or traits associated with this group of disorders.

Childhood Mental Disorders

In Chinese child mental health care, two conditions are accorded particular attention: mental retardation and attention deficit disorder.†

We accept the DSM-III criteria for the diagnosis of mental retardation. But as we are a country with a vast territory and an enormous population, the cultural backgrounds of people in various areas and in different economic strata vary widely, which makes the evaluation of intelligence very difficult. Studies on the application of intelligence tests in China are under way. It is recognized, however, that the usefulness of such tests is restricted and conditioned by many factors; and it

---

*Liu Xiehe, Yang Quan; [Rediagnosis in a group of neurasthenic patients using DSM-III criteria]. Presented at National Symposium on Neurosis, sponsored by the Department of Psychiatry, Sichuan Medical College, Chengdu City, 1982
†Tao Kuo-Tai: [Some child mental health problems in China]. Lecture at WHO Workshop on Psychosocial Aspects of Primary Health Care, Beijing, 1983

seems to us inappropriate to rely very heavily on such measurements for diagnostic purposes. In our clinical practice we follow ICD-9 (12), which holds that the assessment of intellectual level should be based on whatever information is available, including clinical evidence and adaptive behavior, in addition to psychometric tests. An I.Q. serves only as a guide, and should not be applied rigidly.

One of the present authors (Tao Kuo-Tai), using DSM-III criteria, rediagnosed a group of 100 child outpatients originally diagnosed as having attention deficit disorder with hyperactivity according to Nanjing criteria. The concordance rate was 63%, which indicated that the concept of this disorder in Nanjing was broader than that of DSM-III. It is interesting to note that 85% of the cases that met DSM-III criteria had most of the symptoms of the "inattention" category, i.e., had the first four of the five items listed under "inattention." In contrast to this, only a single symptom in each of the categories of impulsivity and hyperactivity was present in 85% of the cases that met DSM-III criteria. In other words, clinical manifestations with respect to impulsivity and hyperactivity were less uniform and less identical with those across the entire sample of cases than those with respect to inattention. This may indicate that the criteria in DSM-III are well constructed and are adequate enough for selection of a relatively homogeneous group of cases; it may also demonstrate that the term for this disorder adopted in DSM-III is justified.

We should like to suggest that there is need for some improvements. Rating symptoms as present or absent may often be difficult. For instance, "easily distracted" has to be judged according to the child's age and the situation in which he finds himself, and such judgments may not be very reliable.

The definition of childhood onset pervasive developmental disorder is also of particular interest to us. Using DSM-III criteria, one of us (Tao Kuo-Tai) rediagnosed 20 cases originally diagnosed as schizophrenia (13), with these results: 1 case of infantile autism, 11 cases of schizophrenia, and 8 cases of pervasive developmental disorder. These last 8 patients, with age at onset of the illness between 30 months and 12 years, did not have delusions, hallucinations, incoherence, or marked loosening of associations. The definition of this disorder provided by DSM-III facilitates differentiating this condition from schizophrenia. We are aware, however, that distinguishing between these two conditions, by means of clinical judgment, in children under seven years of age may be unreliable. The relationship between the two conditions is still unclear, and needs to be further explored.

CONCLUSION

Though all the concepts and views on various subjects embodied in DSM-III are not accepted by Chinese psychiatrists, they greatly appreciate the major achievements of their American colleagues and the initiative and pioneering spirit displayed in the preparation of this classification of mental disorders. We believe that this work will have a profound influence on the development of psychiatry throughout the world.

REFERENCES

1. Yan Wenwei: [On the Diagnostic and Statistical Manual of Mental Disorders (3rd ed)]. Foreign Medicine, Section: Psychiatry (Changsha, China) 1:5–9, 1981 (in Chinese)
2. Langfeld G: The prognosis in schizophrenia and the factors influencing the course of the disease. Acta Psychiatr Neurol Scand, Supplement 13, 1937
3. Langfeld G: The Schizophreniform States. Copenhagen, Munksgaard, 1939
4. Feighner JP, Robins E, Guze SB, Woodruff RA, et al: Diagnostic criteria for use in psychiatric research. Arch Gen Psychiatry 26: 57–63, 1972
5. Taylor MA: Schneiderian first-rank symptoms and clinical prognostic features in schizophrenia. Arch Gen Psychiatry 26: 64–67, 1972
6. Abrams R, Taylor MA, Gaztanaga P: Manic-depressive illness and paranoid schizophrenia. Arch Gen Psychiatry 31: 640–642, 1974
7. Abrams R, Taylor MA: Catatonia: A prospective clinical study. Arch Gen Psychiatry 33: 579–581, 1976
8. Taylor MA, Abrams R: The prevalence of schizophrenia: A reassessment using modern diagnostic criteria. Am J Psychiatry 135: 945–948, 1978
9. Yan Shan-Ming, Chen Deyi, Taylor MA, et al: Prevalence and characteristics of mania in Chinese inpatients: a prospective study. Am J Psychiatry 139: 1150–1153, 1982
10. Yan Shan-Ming, Xiang Dezhao, Taylor MA, et al: Modern diagnosis of schizophrenia and major affective disorders in Chinese psychiatric inpatients: a reassessment of admission prevalence. Am J Psychiatry (in press)
11. Zhang Mingyuan, Zhou Tianxin, Wang Zucheng: Evaluation of American diagnostic criteria for schizophrenia. Chinese Journal of Nervous and Mental Disease (Guangzhou, China) 8(3): 162–164, 1982 (in Chinese)
12. World Health Organization: International Classification of Diseases, 9th Revision. Geneva, World Health Organization, 1977
13. Tao Kuo-Tai, Yu Lian, Qiu Jinghua: Diagnostic criteria of childhood schizophrenia and pervasive developmental disorders. Chinese Journal of Neurology and Psychiatry (Beijing, China) (in press) (in Chinese)

17

A LATIN-AMERICAN PERSPECTIVE ON DSM-III

Renato D. Alarcon, M.D., M.P.H.

Hailed by many as America's single most relevant contribution to world psychiatric nosology, the third edition of the American Psychiatric Association's *Diagnostic and Statistical Manual of Mental Disorders (DSM-III)* deserves the attention and praise it has already generated and the close scrutiny and testing accorded any new diagnostic instrument. DSM-III represents the historical culmination of a long process that involved a general realization of taxonomic deficiencies and a concomitant radical change in attitudes toward the essence, purposes, and designing of classification systems (1,2).

For the most part, the objections raised so far against DSM-III reflect the views of Anglo-Saxon observers (3). It has, however, also been received with cautiousness and even some skepticism by Western European, non-English-speaking psychiatrists, who have been more closely associated with the *International Classification of Diseases, 9th Revision (ICD-9)*, officially introduced in 1979 (4).

It may be premature to try to assess the impact of DSM-III on the psychiatric practices in most developing countries. One can surmise, however, that DSM-III will create a great deal of interest, if for no other reason than the undeniable American influence in vast parts of the

Address correspondence to: Renato D. Alarcon, M.D., M.P.H., University Hospital, Three North, Room 390, University Station, Birmingham, Alabama 35294

A version of this chapter originally appeared in the *American Journal of Psychiatry* 140: 102–105, 1983.

Third World. Latin American psychiatry is perhaps the most solid and active among these countries, and some of its observations deserve special mention.

Many Latin American psychiatrists will warmly welcome the evidence that, at last, phenomenological, descriptive psychiatry, practiced for a long time in Latin America, has officially entered the privileged circles of U.S. psychiatry. They will also welcome the improvement in diagnostic language that DSM-III brings and the tight research design that its criteria make possible. These advances should facilitate comparative studies in which cultural factors can be independent variables. The great success of multinational studies on schizophrenia (6) and depression (7) has demonstrated the importance of such studies.

SOME CRITICISMS

The social notions underlying the identity struggle of Latin American psychiatry (8) are much more than a declarative, rhetorical ideology: they are facts of clinical import that go beyond a particular etiological theory or school of thought, and must therefore guide the clinician's approach to his or her patient. Thus, most of the comments that a Latin American perspective could generate with respect to the new system have to do with the reliability and applicability of the criteria themselves. Some of the areas thus addressed are the following.

Personality Disorders

DSM-III users will have to keep in mind Frances's cogent remarks on the personality disorders section (9), particularly the still low reliability levels, the trait-state and trait-role dilemmas, and the limitations of the categorical approach. The old conceptual shibboleth somewhat simplistically encompassed by the notions of predisposition and specificity still haunts present-day nosologists, however. Latin American clinicians have always striven to characterize specific personality patterns or traits underlying major diagnostic conditions, e.g., schizoid type portending schizophrenia, cyclothymic pattern preceding manic-depressive illness, hysterical personality supporting conversion neuroses (10). DSM-III comes close to subscribing to these clinical relationships, although it rightly falls short of assuming them fully, awaiting clinical refinements and field testing.

The categorical approach becomes somewhat blurred by the clustering criterion, in what amounts to only quantitative differences among some of the disorders. The clearest example is the schizoid-schizotypal continuum. Schizotypal personality features are specifically described as "not severe enough to meet the criteria for schizophrenia," while the social interactions encompass, in fact, the typical schizoid style.

The same comment can be applied to what looks like the avoidant-dependent continuum. The new challenges of borderline and narcissistic disorders will be as intriguing to Latin American clinicians as they are to their U.S. counterparts.

From the Latin American perspective there may be some disappointment over the elimination of the hysterical personality disorder and its (incomplete) replacement by the term *histrionic*. In spite of its pejorative connotation ("hysterical" may be only slightly more socially undesirable than "dependent," however), the former label encompassed a set of behaviors, dispositions, interactions, and traits that are hardly conveyed by the new term, which seems only to emphasize the antics to which patients with this diagnosis are prone. To say that the explanatory paragraphs restate the previous criteria means only that the new choice is unfortunately incomplete indeed. As for the label "compulsive," pure phenomenologists might have solidly argued in favor of using the term *anancastic*, which, like *hysterical*, represents a well-established clinical set (11) that is perhaps much more seasoned and revealing than some of the new, unproven labels, i.e., "avoidant," "narcissistic," and "borderline."

The fears stressed by Frances (9) with regard to the eventual abuse of the label "antisocial personality disorder" for people "growing up in rough and deprived areas" could blatantly materialize when applied to many otherwise average Latin American patients. Traditional political instability can only add more risks to the use of this label. Vast segments of the Latin American population, a young population indeed, may acquire or use some of the behavior described in the diagnostic criteria as the only way to social survival (12). We should not forget that, in some countries, failure to accept social norms has been elevated to the category of a collective enterprise. Latin American psychiatrists, one may suspect, will question even the use of the prefix *anti*, in order to underline their lack of oppositional or adversarial views. Decades ago they also renounced the use of the term *psychopath* simply because Kurt Schneider applied it to all types of abnormal personalities (13). For lack of a better term they would have liked to have kept the old word *sociopath*.

There is, in the American subcontinent, a keen awareness of new nosological developments, particularly in the area of affective disorders, that can still make the once broad concept "antisocial" even narrower (14). In addition, future improvements in this section (perhaps in DSM-IV) may confirm some of Schneider's predictions regarding subclassifications or subcategories of personality disorders, with both therapeutic and prognostic implications.

The Cultural Dimension

In the midst of renewed controversy, the notions of culture and cultural factors in mental illness appear as ideas whose time may not yet have come. They relate to psychiatric diagnosis in two ways: as factors in the clinical appraisal of patients and as determinants of the so-called psychocultural disorders, a growing category of mental and behavioral disturbances (15). Admittedly, DSM-III deals with well-known, well-established mental disorders as it purports to introduce homogeneity and clarity into the diagnostic process. No one could deny, however, that an implicit aspiration of the new nomenclature is to reach all the strata of the patient population and to achieve acceptance the world over. This ecumenical objective becomes even more mandatory in a multicultural country such as the United States, where an increasing number of minorities (by 1990 perhaps 20% of the U.S. population will be of Latin origin) impose themselves upon the system and force it to work flexiby or risk premature obsolescence. In fact, it may not be an exaggeration to affirm that these factors will enjoy increasing frequency in years to come, as the influx of new immigrants persists and the use of diverse labels such as "hysterical psychoses" (16), "hysteroid dysphoria" (17), or even the "-like" or "-form" disorders and the atypical disorders continues to mushroom. If we add the well-known categories of psychocultural or folkloric syndromes in different parts of the world, their relevance becomes even more evident.

Latin American psychiatry holds a respectable position in the areas of transcultural and cross-cultural psychiatry. As a result, distinct phenomenological descriptions and diagnostic discussions have been universally accepted (18). According to Wittkower (19), the clinical issues related to psychocultural disorders have to do with frequency, symptomatology, and treatment. Some transcultural psychiatric findings seem to confirm the assertion that diagnostic labels developed and employed in advanced countries are not necessarily applicable to so-called primitive societies. Other comparative studies, however, show essential similarities among well-defined disorders (20, 21). The key to a complete diagnostic terminology would be the inclusion of provisions that would allow consideration of these factors and syndromes under the heading of "disorders not elsewhere classified," the axis V codes, or some other specifically suitable section. Nowhere in DSM-III does one find such a possibility.

The main objection to the inclusion of cultural criteria or of psychocultural syndromes as such in a nomenclature like DSM-III is the atheoretical character of the manual, with the implicit assumption that their adoption would be the equivalent of recognition of an etiological set. The overwhelming evidence of cultural psychiatric literature, however, is that cultural factors are a substantial part of every disorder, not just a descriptive, picturesque component. In fact, many of the DSM-III assumptions, including the classification of axis IV events or axis V scores, have a strong cultural implication. What is lacking in the system, from a Latin American perspective, is the explicit recognition of psychocultural categories or cultural criteria—or both—to aid in the identification of crucial categories and in the description of clusters of symptoms. Eventual alternatives for countries outside the United States that would like to consider using DSM-III or adaptations of it might be the design of an additional axis incorporating these criteria, adequate assignment of the known categories to the existing headings, and the correlative additions to the differential diagnoses. Even within the United States, all this may later become a historical and clinical necessity.

Axes IV and V

A safe prediction (from the Latin American point of view) with regard to axes IV and V is that, although their underlying philosophical bases are sound and amply justifiable, the typology and severity of the stressors and the composition and appraisal of the actual adaptive functioning will have to be substantially explored and radically redefined. This prediction stems from evaluation of the socioeconomic and cultural background of the vast majority of the Latin American population, the different degree and even the quality of the stressors, and the peculiar means of adjustment to such stressors and to their surrounding circumstances, such as length of exposure, social networks, and culturally determined beliefs.

The examples given in DSM-III illustrate these dramatic differences quite well. Psychosocial stressors and adaptive functioning will be of an entirely different order of magnitude from those defined in DSM-III in countries with a high degree of illiteracy; few educational opportunities; high levels of unemployment; substantial numbers of illegitimate children, transient families, and children of broken homes; polarization of social groups, with small middle classes; scarce leisure opportunities; uncertain retirement prospects; and productivity and economic performance guided by distant forces. It is a real challenge for Latin American and Third World psychiatrists to develop scales that, by implementing axes IV and V and thus assuring the comprehensiveness of their diagnostic efforts, reflect, with accuracy and objectivity, the reality of these areas in the bulk of their patient population.

CONCLUSION

Many other aspects of DSM-III probably deserve careful analysis from a Latin American vantage point. The categories of adjustment, somatoform, factitious, and substance abuse disorders are both attractive and intriguing. In some cases this may be so simply because of lack of awareness of novel (or rebaptized) diagnostic categories; in other cases, because of the inclusion of seemingly magnified nosological entities with "trial balloon" purposes; in still others, because of the omission of clinical pictures familiar to psychiatrists south of the Rio Grande.

Be that as it may, DSM-III's incursion into world psychiatry is as much a challenging stimulus as it is a real test for the influence and consistency of American psychiatry.

REFERENCES

1. Ottoson JO, Perris C: Multidimensional classification of mental disorders. Psychol Med 3:238–243, 1973
2. Cooper AM, Michels R: Book review, APA: Diagnostic and Statistical Manual of Mental Disorders, 3rd ed. Am J Psychiatry 138:128–129, 1981
3. Kendell RE: Book review, APA: Diagnostic and Statistical Manual of Mental Disorders, 3rd ed. Am J Psychiatry 137:1630–1631, 1980
4. World Health Organization: International Classification of Diseases, 9th Revision (ICD-9). Geneva, World Health Organization, 1973
5. Delgado H: Curso de psiquiatr, Barcelona, Editorial Cientifico-Medica, 1969
6. World Health Organization: The International Pilot Study of Schizophrenia, vol 1. Geneva, World Health Organization, 1973
7. Jablensky A, Sartorius N, Gulbinat W, et al: A report from the WHO collaborative study on the assessment of depressive disorders. Acta Psychiatr Scand 63:367–383, 1981
8. Alarcon RD: Hacia una identidad de la psiquiatría Latinoamericana. Bol Of Sanit Panam 81:109–121, 1976
9. Frances A: The DMS-III personality disorders section: a commentary. Am J Psychiatry 137:1050–1054, 1980
10. Alarcon RD: Hysteria and hysterical personality: how come one without the other? Psychiatr Q 47:258–275, 1973
11. Forssman H: The anancastic syndrome. Acta Psychiatr Scand 39:208–217, 1963
12. Lewis O: Five Families. New York, Basic Books, 1959
13. Schneider K: Clinical Psychopathology. New York, Grune & Stratton, 1959
14. Akiskal HS: Subaffective disorders: dysthymic, cyclothymic and bipolar II disorders in the"borderline realm." Psychiatr Clin North Am 4:25–46, 1981
15. Yap RM: Classification of the culture-bound reactive syndromes. New Zealand Journal of Psychiatry 1:172–179, 1967
16. Langness LL: Hysterical psychosis: the cross-cultural evidence. Am J Psychiatry 124:143–152, 1967
17. Klein DF, David JM: Diagnosis and Drug Treatment of Psychiatric Disorders. Baltimore, Williams & Wilkins, 1969
18. Seguin CA: Introducción a la psiquiatría folklórica. Acta Psiquiatr Psicol Am Lat 20:301–334, 1974

19. Wittkower ED, Termansen PE: Transcultural psychiatry, in Modern Perspectives in World Psychiatry. Edited by Howells JG. New York, Brunner/Mazel, 1971
20. Odejide AO: Cross-cultural psychiatry: a myth or reality. Compr Psychiatry 20:103–109, 1979
21. Mezzich JE, Raab ES: Depressive symptomatology across the Americas. Arch Gen Psychiatry 37:818–823, 1980

18

SPANISH PSYCHIATRY AND DSM-III

Juan López-Ibor, Jr., M.D., and
José M. López-Ibor, M.D.

Although, as of this writing, a Spanish translation of DSM-III is not yet available, the manual is well known in the more important psychiatric research and teaching centers of Spain, being used mostly for research purposes. At the 1981 Congress of the Sociedad Española de Psiquiatría and the 1982 Congress of the Sociedad Española de Psiquiatría Biológica, DSM-III diagnostic criteria were used in several of the presentations on clinical research. Moreover, the Grupo para el Progreso de la Psiquiatría (Group for the Advancement of Psychiatry) in 1982 organized a round table on "Current Nosological Criteria in Psychiatry" to discuss personal experiences with DSM-III and the ninth revision of the International Classification of Diseases (ICD-9) and the possible integration of nosological criteria specific to Spanish psychiatry into these established classifications.

Familiarity with DSM-III among the most elite psychiatric groups in Spain has been furthered by interest, in the last few years, in biological approaches to psychiatry and clinical research and by increasing use of the Research Diagnostic Criteria (RDC), which have only recently been translated into Spanish (1), but which have been used by some researchers since at least 1977.

Address correspondence to: Juan López-Ibor, Jr., M.D., Clinica Lopez Ibor, Av. Nueva Zelanda, 44, Puerta de Hierro, Madrid (35), Spain

HISTORICAL BACKGROUND

The above developments should be considered within a historic perspective (2), which should aid understanding of the position of Spanish psychiatry among other schools of psychiatry. Briefly stated, modern Spanish psychiatry reflects the influence of both the French and the German schools, but has been trying to regain its former quality in provision of psychiatric services, which was very high from the 16th century until about the 19th century, when it began to diminish. Spanish psychiatry has always been very eclectic, and has not had much difficulty in assimilating some very different approaches. In the period between World Wars I and II, Kraepelin's thinking exerted a very strong influence, and Freud began to be known. (It is worth noting that the first translations of Freud from the German were into Spanish.) At the same time, the neurohistological school of Ramon y Cajal, which had great scientific prestige, became very influential.

Following our civil war, in the late 1930s, phenomenological psychiatry developed extensively, especially in university centers. This had various important consequences. One was that Spanish psychiatrists, being less dynamically oriented than their North American counterparts, and having always been more interested in clinical description and in diagnosis and classification, began to make extensive use of Kurt Schneider's criteria for the classification of the basic forms of mental illness and for the diagnosis of the various syndromes, especially in schizophrenia. These criteria are still widely used in Spain. Spanish psychiatrists (e.g., Ruiz Ogara [3]) long ago spoke out for diagnosis based on overt symptoms, not on inferences about psychodynamic constructs.

CURRENT DIAGNOSTIC PRACTICES

Many Spanish psychiatrists have been using the successive editions of the ICD; but others have preferred, for a long time, to use their own diagnostic concepts or those of a particular school. In a desire to unify concepts, some of us have, for more than 15 years, been recording two diagnoses for each patient—the first in accordance with the ICD, and the second, according to our own concepts.

We have, for example, had great difficulty in finding an adequate place for *timopatía ansiosa*, a clinical entity, described by López Ibor in 1949 (4, 5), that clinically presents in the form of a neurosis, but that does not have a psychodynamic origin, a criterion assumed at that time to be necessary for the diagnosis of a neurosis. The cardinal feature of *timopatía ansiosa* is a special form of anxiety, called vital anxiety, which is endogenous and therefore related to the depressive disorders.

From this starting point, research has evolved toward the view that in all neuroses there is a core of vital anxiety (6) and that many psychosomatic disorders are affective equivalents or masked depressions (7,8). We think that recent developments in clinical psychiatry, in particular DSM-III, are fully compatible with these, already old, ideas of Spanish psychiatry.

MERITS AND FLAWS OF DSM-III

During the previously mentioned round table on "Current Nosological Criteria in Psychiatry," Spanish psychiatrists expressed their opinions of DSM-III; some were positive, but others stressed its limitations. North American psychiatrists from Torrejon Air Base, who were familiar with the systematic use of DSM-III in daily practice (something quite different from using it for research purposes with selected patients), also participated in the discussions.

DSM-III, which was field tested and modified extensively before final publication, is based on a pure description of symptoms and clinical data, precisely defined. It assumes the possibility of a description of psychopathological manifestations devoid of theoretical considerations regarding etiology. This possibility is not accepted by everyone since it can be argued that a phenomenon can be described only from a specific perspective. It is indeed true that the positivist, medical model has demonstrated its importance in psychiatry, but it does have some limitations. In the case of a descriptive nosology, it is necessary to define the specific context, scientific or social, in which the symptoms present themselves. For example, among the anxiety disorders, DSM-III lists as panic disorder (300.01) attacks of panic that occur unpredictably, without pointing out that "unpredictable" is a relative concept, and therefore what is "panic" in one context is not in another (9).

In relation to this last point, it should be noted that DSM-III reflects only a specific level of development of psychiatric knowledge, and that it will doubtless change in the future. Its present emphasis on symptoms and concrete clinical facts, omitting fundamental theoretical concepts about pathogenesis, is evident in the decision to eliminate the neuroses as a diagnostic class that had not only theoretical but also clinical validity. The psychoanalytic hypotheses about neuroses are inadequate, and to have abandoned them in DSM-III was a positive move; but the neurotic symptoms scattered about in many DSM-III diagnostic classes do not reflect clinical reality.

Recent efforts at classification of mental disorders endeavor, among other things, to resolve the problem of interrater reliability. At the same time, for research purposes an attempt is made to avoid false positives. These efforts, however, are achieved at the cost of validity and an increase in the number of cases that are included in residual categories. The first problem, that of validity, is alleviated in DSM-III by its multiaxial system, but the second one persists, particularly as it applies to clinical practice. In some cases it is difficult to find the appropriate category, e.g., mild cases of anorexia nervosa in which the essental disturbance in body image is present, but the associated symptoms necessary for the diagnosis are not.

Multiaxial diagnosis is very much esteemed by psychiatrists in Spain. It has been adopted in a nationwide study of the mental problems of patients with toxic oil syndrome (10) and in the development of a unified clinical record, used widely in different centers in Spain for research, teaching, and clinical care (11). It should be borne in mind that Birnbaum's concept of structural diagnosis (12) and Kretschmer's concept of polydimensional diagnosis (13) have been known and applied in Spain for a long time, especially with regard to affective disorders.

The inclusion of axis III in the DSM-III multiaxial system is seen in Spain as most appropriate. According to recent epidemiological research, almost 40% of patients in need of psychiatric care present somatic disturbances not previously diagnosed. Moreover, in general hospitals the psychiatrist must consider the diagnosis of somatic illnesses in giving comprehensive care. We think that other specialists should also have the benefit of this experience with DSM-III and that they should develop a multiaxial system for somatic disorders that includes psychiatric diagnosis, or even the present axes I, II, IV, and V of DSM-III.

CONCLUSIONS

As a whole, DSM-III is viewed by Spanish psychiatrists as a psychiatric achievement of the first rank, marking a frontier between two ages, the old and the new. The "old" psychiatry, which was born and grew up during the 19th century, was based on a nosology modeled on classification procedures appropriate to botany. The "new" psychiatry approaches nosology with very different methods, in particular:

1) The use of objective standards of definition of nosological categories. These standards have been confirmed by clinical experience, and are not contaminated by untested hypotheses. Thus, terms very much used by, and quite dear to, psychiatrists, such as *neurosis* and *psychosis,* must be sacrificed in favor of less ideology-laden words, such as *disorders, major* or *minor.* The great stress put on symptoms and objective clinical data is positive when it compels psychiatrists to refer constantly to clinical reality rather than to the doctrines or opinions of "great masters."

2) The use of operational diagnostic criteria that permit very high interrater reliability.

3) The adoption of a multiaxial system.

4) A method of field testing and use of empirical research that has made possible the development of a classification suitable for general use by psychiatrists in the United States and in many other countries.

We Spanish psychiatrists do not believe that the American Psychiatric Association (APA) is going to rest on its laurels and the admiration of the rest of the countries of the world. We suggest that in the future the APA might well consider:

—adopting a wider, interactive or phenomenological, concept of symptoms, one that includes the context in which they develop;

—increasing the validity of the diagnositc criteria in a way that will facilitate international communication of psychiatric knowledge and improve everyday clinical care;

—studying in depth the relationship among the five DSM-III axes. It is possible that psychiatry is not yet ready for *multidimensional* classifications and has to be satisifed with *multiaxial* evaluation, but the goal of a truly multidimensional classification should not be abandoned.

Many psychiatrists are interested in the new paths DSM-III has opened and await with interest the results of international research using this classification and studying its relationship to widely used systems such as ICD-9. There are still important problems to be solved, among them the link of diagnosis to prognosis and to treatment. With regard to the first—the link of diagnosis to prognosis—Kendell (15) and López Ibor and colleagues (16) have studied the factors that contribute to instability or change in the diagnosis of mental patients over time, a common experience. Axis V of DSM-III already contains a germ of this approach to prognosis, but it might be useful to widen its scope in the future.

REFERENCES

1. Spitzer RL, Endicott J, Robins E: Research Diagnostic Criteria (RDC). Criterios Diagnosticos de Investigación. Barcelona, Hoescht, 1982
2. López Ibor JJ, López-Ibor JJ Jr: Historia de la psiquiatría Española, in Psiquiatría. Edited by Ruíz Ogara C, Barcia D, López-Ibor JJ, Jr. Barcelona, Toray, 1982, vol I, pp 28–42
3. Ruíz Ogara C: Corrientes del pensamiento psiquiátrico, in Psiquiátría. Edited by Ruíz Ogara C, Barcia D, López-Ibor JJ, Jr. Barcelona, Toray, 1982, vol I, pp 42-58
4. López Ibor, JJ: La Angustia Vital. Madrid, Paz Montalvo, 1950

5. López Ibor, JJ: Basic anxiety as the core of neurosis. Acta Psychiatr Scand 41:329-332, 1965

6. López Ibor, JJ: Las Neurosis como Enfermedades del Animo. Madrid, Gredos, 1966

7. López-Ibor, JJ, Jr: Los Equivalentes Depresivos. Madrid, Paz Montalvo, 1972 (2nd ed, 1976)

8. López-Ibor, JJ, Jr: Clinical aspects of depressive equivalents in psychiatry (Part I), in Proceedings of the V World Congress of Psychiatry. Amsterdam, Excerpta Medica, 1972, pp 644-652

9. Barcia D: Las psicósis esquizo-afectivas en el DSM-III. Actas Luso Esp Neurol Psiquiatr (in press)

10. Soria J, Muñoz PE, Santo-Domingo J, López-Ibor, JJ, Jr, Cañas, F: Aspectos psiquiátricos del síndrome tóxico, in Symposium Nacional Síndrome Tóxico. Madrid, Ministerio de Sanidad y Consumo, 1982

11. López-Ibor JJ, Jr: Manual de la Historia Clínica Unificada (HCU). Madrid, Garsi, 1982

12. Birnbaum K: Der Aufbau der Psychose. Grundzüge der psychiatrischen Strukturanalyse. Berlin, Springer, 1923

13. Kretschmer E: Constitución y Carácter. Barcelona, Labor, 1947

14. Giner J: Las esquizofrenias y los trastornos de personalidad en el DSM-III y en la C.I.E. 9a. ed. Actas Luso Esp Neurol Psiquiatr (in press)

15. Kendell RE: The stability of psychiatric diagnoses. Br J Psychiatry 124:352-356, 1974

16. López-Ibor JM, Calcedo A, Castro JM, Jimenez F, Conde L: La inestabilidad del diagnostico en psiquiatría y su relación con los re-ingresos. Actas Luso Esp Neurol Psiquiatr 4:11-16, 1975

SECTION IV

Empirical Studies and Future Directions for Research

19

AN AUSTRALIAN STUDY REFLECTING ON THE RELIABILITY AND VALIDITY OF AXIS II

Graham Mellsop, M.B.Ch.B.(Otago), D.P.M., F.R.A.N.Z.C.P., M.R.C.Psych., M.D.(Melb.) and Frank T. N. Varghese, M.D., B.S., B.Sc., F.R.A.N.Z.C.P.

Disorders of personality have long been a controversial area of psychiatry. A survey of Australian psychiatrists (1) showed that although they spent 25% of their time working with patients they considered had personality disorders, there was little agreement on the concept of personality disorder as an illness or a deviation from the normal, or on the criteria for diagnosis. Clinicians who treat people who have personality disorder as the primary problem find the plethora of available classifications of personality disorder of little help. The absence of a widely accepted concept of personality disorder and poor diagnostic reliability have frustrated the development of research on the natural history and the efficacy of treatment procedures of these disorders (2,3).

The advent of DSM-III appears to present a significant advance. First, its separation of the "illness" categories (axis I) from the more longitudinally consistent aspects of the patient (axis II) means that diagnostic arguments need no longer be on an either/or basis. Second, the provision of specified diagnostic criteria offers hope of greater reliability. Third, the specific personality disorders (i.e., subcategories) included are more in keeping with current clinical trends. Fourth, in a move toward a more natural, Linnaean classification, these subcategories are

Address correspondence to: Professor Graham Mellsop, Department of Psychological Medicine, Wellington Clinical School of Medicine, University of Otago, Wellington Hospital, Wellington, New Zealand conceptualized as grouping into three clusters characterized by eccentricity, emotionality, and anxiety (4,5).

Preliminary field trials for axis II of DSM-III demonstrated that levels of agreement between pairs of raters for separate interviews varied considerably for the specific personality disorders, but for personality disorder as a class were represented by an overall kappa coefficient of 0.54 (6). In order to examine the reliability of the types of personality disorder and the specified diagnostic criteria, a number of studies were undertaken in Melbourne. These studies also examined the validity of the proposed axis II clusters and their relationship to objective personality tests. This report is an account of work completed to date.*

RESEARCH AIMS

Reliability (Project A)

The first aim of our study was to assess, under the conditions of ordinary clinical practice, the reliability of certain aspects of the second axis of DSM-III, in particular, the diagnostic reliability of: (1) the presence or absence of a personality disorder, (2) the particular subcategories (specific personality disorders), and (3) the individual specified diagnostic criteria.†

Validity

The second objective was to assess the relationship between the axis II subcategories and the dimensions underlying the broad category of personality disorders (projects A and B).

PROCEDURE

For the study (A) reflecting on reliability, 3 psychiatrists from different Melbourne psychiatric hospitals were each to admit 25 patients into the study on a "catch-as-catch-can" basis, as in the DSM-III field trials. The patients were required to be between 18 and 40 years old. Those diagnosed as suffering from schizophrenia, organic brain disorders (according to DSM-III criteria), or mental deficiency were ex-

---

*Unpublished details of this work are reported in two theses submitted to the University of Melbourne: AJ Hicks: The reliability of psychiatrists' diagnosis of personality disorders using the criteria presented in DSM-III and the classification of personality disorders; and S Brown-Greaves: The relationship between personality disorder categories on DSM-III and MMPI and CPI profiles. An initial account of one aspect has been published elsewhere (7).

†Not referred to further in this report.

cluded from the study. Patients were not excluded if they presented a difficult diagnostic problem or had no diagnosis on axis II.

The admitting psychiatrist was allowed to take as much time as necessary to ensure that the selection criteria were met and to consider the diagnoses on axes I and II. The second and third psychiatrists interviewed the patients on consecutive days and concentrated only on information they regarded as relevant to axis II. The order of the psychiatrists' assessments of patients was randomly varied. Each psychiatrist was free to use any interview technique he pleased, in order to make the study as close to ordinary clinical practice as possible. They were, however, required to be familiar with DSM-III, to mark a schedule containing the axis II criteria, and to make their diagnosis on that basis only.

Levels of agreement are calculated using the weighted kappa coefficient (8).

To reflect on the second set of aims, those concerned with validity, clustering and factor analytic techniques were to be applied to the data, where appropriate, to test the validity of the proposed clusters (4,5).

In a second project (B), subjects were referred for inclusion if the psychiatrists in charge of their case considered they might have a personality disorder. They were then seen by the senior author. If he confirmed the (category) diagnosis of personality disorder, using the criteria of axis II of DSM-III, then the subject was accepted into the study. Patients were *not* accepted into this study if they had *any* diagnosis on axis I.

Of the 76 subjects obtained in this fashion, 44 were also part of project A, above, the other 32 being part of a commencing longitudinal study. The 76 patients were subsequently seen by a co-worker, who had the patients each complete a Minnesota Multiphasic Personality Inventory (MMPI) and a California Personality Inventory (CPI). All MMPI response sheets were scored to yield kappa corrected t-scores for each subject on the three validity scales L, F, and K and the ten standard clinical scales Hs, D, Hy, Pd, Mf, Pa, Pt, Sc, Ma, and S; cluster analysis was used to generate three cluster groups, this being the number suggested in DSM-III.

The computer program HGROUP, from the Veldman (9) series of programs, was used to perform a hierarchical analysis.

RESULTS

Reliability

Over a period of 9 months, 74 patients were admitted into the first study. For various reasons, a few (n = 9) were able to be seen by only two of the psychiatrists. Twenty-four patients received only one personality disorder diagnosis, 40 received more than one, and 10 received no personality disorder diagnosis. The kappa coefficients can be seen in table 1.

For the broad category of personality disorder, the results for all possible combinations of assessors were compared with each other and with the results obtained in the DSM-III field trails. No significant differences were found.

The kappa coefficients for the specific types of personality disorder are displayed in table 2. No more than chance agreement occurred for the categories atypical, mixed, other, and schizoid.

The presence or absence of any personality disorder was determined more consistently than specific subtypes were diagnosed, except for the antisocial subtype (kappa − 0.49).

The sex ratios in the seven most frequently encountered subtypes

TABLE 1. Kappa Coefficients of Agreement among Three Psychiatrists on Various Groupings

Psychiatrists	Number of Patients	Kappa
A/B/C	65	0.41
A/B	66	0.34
A/C	70	0.58
B/C	65	0.38

TABLE 2. Kappa Coefficients of Agreement among All Three Psychiatrists on Personality Disorder Subtypes

Category	Number of Times Diagnosis Was Made	Kappa
Antisocial	15	0.49
Dependent	29	0.4
Paranoid	8	0.35
Borderline	33	0.29
Histrionic	35	0.23
Avoidant	34	0.23
Compulsive	5	0.2
Schizotypal	30	0.19
Schizoid	3	0.01
Passive-aggressive	1	—
Narcissistic	0	—
Atypical/mixed/other	33	− 0.05

are noted in table 3. Males were in a minority (32%) in the total sample. They were overrepresented in the categories schizoid, schizotypal, and antisocial. Females were diagnosed more frequently as having histrionic, borderline, avoidant, and dependent personality disorders.

Rater bias was evident in a number of areas, some specific personality disorders being "favored" by individual assessors. Forty-nine percent of all diagnoses of atypical, mixed, and other personality disorder were made by one psychiatrist-assessor, 59% of all borderline disorders were diagnosed by a second assessor, and 50% of all diagnoses of an antisocial personality disorder came from the third assessor.

Validity

In order to examine the possible underlying structures of the personality disorder category, factor analysis of the items making up the 11 specific personality disorders was undertaken, but only in cases where there was some agreement about the presence of a personality disorder. Only subjects seen by all three assessors and judged by at least two as warranting a diagnosis of personality disorder were included (n = 48).

When 11 factors were extracted, using principal components analysis, it was quite clear that only the first 4 were meaningful. Beyond these we seemed to have what Cattell (10) has described as factorial letter or scree. None of the four factors corresponded exactly to any of the DSM-III categories of personality disorder.* However, factor 1 consisted principally of items from the antisocial category, and some of these items loaded very highly. Factor 2 appeared to describe people who

TABLE 3. Male and Female Percentages in Axis II Subtypes Containing More than Three Patients

Axis II Subtypes	Male	Female
Schizoid	67	33
Schizotypal	52	48
Histrionic	26	74
Antisocial	63	37
Borderline	32	68
Avoidant	35	65
Dependent	12	88
Total sample	38	62

---

*A more complete report is in preparation: A Hicks, G Mellsop, F Varghese, S Joshua: The validity of the DSM-III subcategories of personality disorder (unpublished).

lacked the ability to express emotion and had withdrawn from society. Factor 3 appeared to be the opposite of factor 2 and covered the "over-emotional." Factor 4 contained only a few items and appeared to describe the narcissistic character.

Since the DSM-III criteria sometimes overlap and the subtypes can in no way be considered orthogonal, oblique rotations were attempted as well as the varimax rotation. Again, no factors totally corresponded to the proposed DSM-III clusters, but the prominent factors included an antisocial subcategory, a histrionic cluster, and a paranoid-schizoid cluster. A three-factor solution (varimax and oblique) contained one subtype that could be clearly labeled antisocial, one that was dominated by items from the paranoid, schizoid, and schizotypal subtypes, and one that was characterized by "emotionality." Thus, there was some support here for DSM-III's suggestion that the subtypes schizoid, schizotypal, and paranoid formed a cluster that could be called eccentric. However, the other two clusters (emotional and anxious) were not evident. In fact, two subtypes that make up the emotionality cluster (antisocial, histrionic) seemed to be clearly dominant in different factors.

A further attempt to see if three DSM-III clusters were the basis of our personality disorder diagnoses was made by factor analyzing the DSM-III axis II subtypes, as opposed to the individual criterion items. It was possible to extract four factors. The factorial solutions (principal component, varimax, oblique) indicate a very strong grouping of the paranoid, schizoid, and schizotypal subtypes. The avoidant and dependent subtypes were also consistently grouped, as were histrionic and borderline, and narcissistic and passive-aggressive. Antisocial personality disorder seemed to be associated negatively with the avoidant and dependent subtypes. These groupings strongly supported the paranoid, schizoid, schizotypal clustering, but only partially supported the other clusterings. For the final factor analysis, the subtypes were scored for each patient (3,2,1,0) according to the number of psychiatrists who judged each as present. The results still showed the strong linkage of the paranoid, schizoid, and schizotypal subtypes; but the other subtypes were not grouped in any way that supported the three proposed clusters.

In the second project, using the MMPI data as a base, cluster group I of the 76 personality-disordered patients contained 26 (24 male, 2 female) subjects; cluster group II, 16 (2 male, 14 female); and cluster group III, 34 (5 male, 29 female).

The MMPI profiles of the three derived cluster groups are shown in the figure. The F values of the analysis of variance (ANOVA), demonstrating the effective statistical separations achieved by the clustering, appear in table 4.

MMPI Profiles of the Derived Clusters

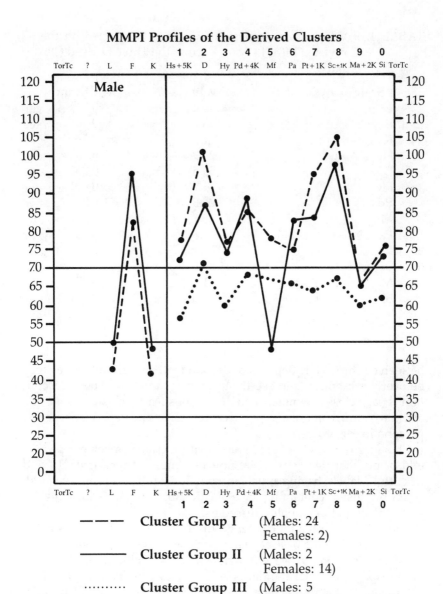

— — —	**Cluster Group I**	(Males: 24 Females: 2)
————	**Cluster Group II**	(Males: 2 Females: 14)
··········	**Cluster Group III**	(Males: 5 Females: 29)

When the traditional "cookbook" approach to interpreting MMPI profiles (11–13) was used, very different descriptions were found to apply to each group. The highly elevated 8–2 profile of group I has been described as being typical of people who may be anxious, agitated, tense, jumpy, and confused and may be seen as avoiding socialization and having chronic incapacitating symptoms. Such people may also

TABLE 4. F Values from Analysis of Variance Conducted on the K-Correlated MMPI t-Scores across the Three Derived Cluster Groups

t Scale	F Value	Significance
L	3.4	0.04
F	28.7	0.001
K	1.8	0.16
Hs	20.9	0.001
D	53.5	0.001
Hy	14.7	0.001
Pd	26.5	0.001
Mf	46.1	0.001
Pa	18.8	0.001
Pt	127	0.001
Sc	88.6	0.001
Ma	1.3	0.27
Si	22.0	0.001

be seen as chronically depressed, despondent, and irritable. They may be overly self-critical and see themselves as suffering. These descriptions bear a close resemblance to the anxious/fearful cluster, consisting of the avoidant, compulsive, passive-aggressive, and dependent specific personality disorders.

Cluster group II's 8–4 profile has been described as being typical of odd or peculiar people who are nonconforming, angry, irritable, and resentful—labels having much in common with the proposed odd/eccentric cluster, containing the DSM-III subtypes paranoid, schizoid, and schizotypal personality disorders.

The 2–4 profile seen for cluster group III has been described as being typical of people who have been in trouble with the law or their families. They tend to be impulsive and unable to delay gratification, often have little respect for social standards, and display acting-out behavior involving alcohol abuse, arrests, and job loss. Following impulsive acts, they may seem guilty, remorseful, and even depressed. Suicide attempts are common. When not in trouble, these people tend to be energetic, sociable, and outgoing and often make good first impressions. They appear to be within the suggested emotionality/erractic cluster consisting of the histrionic, narcissistic, antisocial, and borderline specific disorders. Table 5 shows the actual personality disorder subtypes assigned to patients in the three MMPI clusters.

The means of the CPI raw scores are recorded in table 6. As the

TABLE 5. Percentage of MMPI-Derived Clusters with Particular DSM-III Personality Disorder Subtypes (Assigned by the Psychiatrist)

Psychiatrist's Diagnoses	Cluster Derived from MMPI		
	I	II	III
Paranoid Schizoid Schizotypal	30	9	11
Histrionic Narcissistic Antisocial Borderline	29	50	32
Avoidant Compulsive Pass-aggressive	36	29	43
Atypical Mixed Other	5	12	14
	100	100	100

differentiation among the three cluster groups was not marked, more detailed results are not reported here. There were some small, but significant, differences (e.g., on the "well-being" scale) that indicated that the people in cluster group III (antisocial/impulsive) were the "best adjusted." However, the differences among the groups were small, and the differences by sex were virtually negligible.

DISCUSSION

Reliability

The agreement among the three assessors (kappa = 0.41) for the presence or absence of a personality disorder was less than that between two psychiatrists in sequential interviews in the DSM-III field trials (kappa = 0.54). The difference is most likely accounted for by differences in the design of each study, most notably, the use of the same three psychiatrists for all of the subjects in the study, compared with many groups of two psychiatrists each seeing a few subjects in the field trials, and the broader data base available in the latter case. It needs to be emphasized that the data available to the rating psychiatrists were limited to what they elicited during a relatively brief,

TABLE 6. Means of CPI Scale Raw Scores for Cluster Groups I, II, and III Derived from the MMPI

| | Scores | | |
CPI Scales	Group I	Group II	Group III
Do	15.3	15	20.4*
Cs	11.9	10.2	16.7
Sy	14.8	14.5	17.8
Sp	25.2	28.2	24.7
Sa	17	17.7	16.6
Wb	19.5	18.5	26.1*
Re	21.2	17.1	20.9
Sc	23.3	22	28
Si	20.7	17.8	27.8
To	13.1	9.5	15.8
Gi	14.5	9.3	17
Cm	18.7	22	18.4
Ac	15.6	14.1	24.2*
Ai	15.5	10.7	16
Ie	27.8	22.2	28.6*
Py	7.7	8.1	9.5
Fx	10.4	7.4	11
Fe	19	19	20

*$P<0.01$, ANOVA.

single interview. This was assumed to simulate the often nonoptimal circumstances of clincial practice and thus to represent a severe test of the usefulness of DSM-III in that type of situation. The different experience and training of the three assessors may have been another contributing factor.

It should also be noted that as DSM-III provides no specific criteria for the diagnosis of the broad category "personality disorder," agreement about its presence or absence is only indirect. It depends on "agreement" that the patient has, or has not, a specific (or several different) personality disorder(s).

This study confirms the finding of the DSM-III field trials that there is relatively poor agreement on the diagnoses of specific personality disorder subtypes. The best agreement was obtained for antisocial personality disorder (kappa = 0.49). This is most likely because the criteria are more objective for this subtype, requiring information that can easily be checked by independent sources. The criteria do not require subjective judgments by the assessors, so interpretation variance is much less. Nevertheless, even with such criteria, rater bias was not eliminated entirely

The poor agreement on the subtypes atypical, mixed, and other personality disorders demonstrated that the provision of specific criteria is essential if agreement among assessors is required. None of the kappa levels on these disorders reaches what may be regarded as a scientifically acceptable level (i.e., 0.7) (8). The major ways of improving the system in this regard would clearly include the raters' obtaining more adequate information, standardizing its elicitation and recording, firming up the criteria, and, possibly, modifying the choice of available subtypes. In clinical work, little can be done about the variations in apparently factual answers given by the same patients at different times, or about the discrepancies in information from patients and relatives.

The preference of individual psychiatrists for particular diagnoses has been reported by others (3). The reasons for this may be related to differing interview procedures, so that information is variable, or due to diagnostic sets in the assessors. A standardized interview schedule, as suggested by Kendell (14), could eliminate this to some extent, but would not be practical in the ordinary clinical situation.

The sex difference observed in this study has also been noted by others (3,15). Whether this reflects rater bias or the actual distribution of personality disorders in the sample is an open question.

The levels of agreement for specific criteria are still being studied. Preliminary findings indicate that the subtype kappa levels could be markedly improved by eliminating or improving some items.

Validity

The results of factor analysis of the items making up the criteria for the 11 subtypes of personality disorder must be treated skeptically, because the number of items was more than the number of subjects. Some consistent trends may, however, be noted. There seemed to be a mutually exclusive relationship between antisocial behavior, on the one hand, and avoidant/dependent behavior, on the other. "Borderline" also appears to be mutually exclusive with avoidant/dependent behavior. This provides some support for the validity of the proposed DSM-III clusters emotionality versus anxiety. The grouping of histrionic and borderline factors is also consistent with this. The paranoid, schizoid, and schizotypal items and subtypes are certainly found together, and this datum offers support for the validity of the eccentricity cluster. However, the inconsistent and mixed findings require confirmation on a larger data base. Although a valuable beginning, the three proposed clusters may prove to be an oversimplification.

The attempt to define clusters based on the patients' responses to the MMPI and CPI again provided support for some aspects of the view that eccentricity/emotionality/anxiety are superordinate dimensions transecting the broad category of personality disorder. The MMPI did distinguish three groups that showed a number of characteristics consistent with the above. The configuration of the three validity scales L, F, and K was relatively consistent throughout the cluster groups, varying mainly with regard to the elevation of F. Such a configuration has been described as consistent with a disturbed population, a group of people who see themselves as having problems, but who may tend to exaggerate their symptoms.

The first cluster group consisted of persons who were variously described as anxious, highly strung, suicidal, suffering from sleep disturbance, and fearful. Such a group would seem to fit into the anxious or fearful cluster, encompassing the diagnoses of avoidant, dependent, compulsive, and passive-aggressive personality disorders. This group's profile differed from the remaining two most markedly in the increased elevation of three scales (8, 7, and 2) that all had t values greater than 90.

The patients in cluster group II seemed to form a second discrete group. These are the 8–2–4 people, who have been variously described as angry, irritable, resentful, paranoid, and schizoid. These characteristics seem to bear some resemblance to the proposed "eccentric" cluster, containing DSM-III diagnoses of paranoid, schizoid, and schizotypal personality disorders.

The remaining, mainly female, cluster group III is somewhat more difficult to classify. These patients' almost equal t-scores on codes 2 and 4 tend to point toward some of the antisocial traits described by Graham (11). However, the lower elevation would indicate that they are not overly socially deviant, but are more likely to have problems in terms of interpersonal (especially family) relationships, may be shy and withdrawn beneath a façade of competence, and may, in reality, be quite uncomfortable in social settings. Graham describes an F scale t-score of between 65 and 79 as being typical of people who, if relatively free of "serious" psychopathology, may be described as moody, restive, affectively restless, dissatisfied, changeable, unstable, curious, complex, opinionated, and opportunistic. Labels such as these would tend to point toward an emotionally erratic type of person. Thus, a tentative classification on the basis of MMPI profiles would place these patients in the emotionality cluster.

It was notable that subtype labels assigned by the psychiatrists did not correspond to the proposed clusters as well as the MMPI-derived clusters. This discrepancy may simply reflect the degree of unreliability of the personality disorder subtype diagnoses. Another important factor, however, may be the diagnosticians' use of a categorical "all or none" rating system. For instance, many patients may have given sufficient particular information to be included in an MMPI-derived cluster, but may have just missed out on inclusion in that category using the DSM-III criteria.

Differentiation among the three cluster groups by CPI profiles was nowhere as pronounced as that achieved with the MMPI. Nonetheless, small differences in elevation and significant differences on some scales (notably Wb) were found, indicating some differences in the functioning of the three groups. As determined by the MMPI analysis, cluster group III, although having some difficulties of both an internal and interpersonal nature, was shown by the CPI to be the best adjusted of the three: cluster groups II and I were both more disturbed than group III. The differences among the three groups were small, however, and sex differences were virtually negligible. It must be remembered that the imbalance in numbers made this analysis tentative. Given sufficient and comparable numbers, clustering of CPI profiles would have been the ideal procedure.

CONCLUSION

Axis II has a degree of interjudge reliability, even under suboptimal conditions, that suggests that it represents a significant contribution to psychiatric classification. Its reliability can probably be markedly improved by refinement of the items used for subtype assignment.

Attempts to improve the usefulness and validity of this axis should concentrate on pruning the number of subtypes and trying to define more basic dimensions along which personality-disordered patients can, ultimately, be assessed. The suggestion in DSM-III that "emotionally," "eccentricity," and "anxiety" are three basic clusters has received some support, and provides a beginning for a more rational classification of personality disorders.

REFERENCES

1. Berah E, Mellsop G: Personality disorders. Australian Journal of Psychiatry 16:85, 1982
2. Walton HJ, Presley AS: Use of a category system in the diagnosis of abnormal personality. Br J Psychiatry 122:269–276, 1973
3. Tyrer P, Alexander MS, Lichett D, et al: Reliability of schedule for rating personality disorders. Br J Psychiatry 135:168–174, 1979
4. Frances A: The DSM-III personality disorders section: A commentary. Am J Psychiatry 137:1050–1054, 1980

5. Vailliant G, Perry JC: Personality disorders, in Comprehensive Textbook of Psychiatry, 3rd ed. Edited by Kaplan HI, Freedman AM, Sadock BJ. Baltimore, Williams & Wilkins, 1980
6. Spitzer RL, Forman JBW, Nee J: DSM-III field trials: Initial interrater diagnostic reliability. Am J Psychiatry 136:815–817, 1979
7. Mellsop G, Varghese F, Joshua S, Hicks A:The reliability of axis II of DSM-III: A report of a clinical study. Am J Psychiatry 82:1360–1362, 1982
8. Cohen J: Weighted kappa: nominal scale agreement with provision for scaled disagreement or partial credit. Psychol Bull 20:213–219, 1968
9. Everitt BS: Cluster Analysis. London, Heinemann, 1974
10. Cattell RB: Handbook of Multivariate Experimental Psychology. Chicago, Rand McNally, 1966
11. Graham JR: The MMPI: A Protocol Guide. New York, Oxford University Press, 1977
12. Marks PA, Seeman W, Haller DL: The Actuarial Use of the MMPI with Adolescents and Adults. Baltimore, Williams & Wilkins, 1974
13. Gilberstadt H, Duker J: A Handbook for Clinical and Actuarial MMPI Interpretation. Philadelphia, WB Saunders, 1965
14. Kendell RE: An important source of bias affecting ratings made by psychiatrists. J Psychiatr Res 6:135–141, 1968
15. Warner R: The diagnoses of antisocial and hysterical personality disorders. An example of sex bias. J Nerv Ment Dis 166:839–845, 1978

20

MULTI-INSTITUTIONAL COLLABORATIVE STUDIES OF DIAGNOSTIC RELIABILITY OF DSM-III AND ICD-9 IN JAPAN

Koichi Hanada, M.D., and Saburo Takahashi, M.D., Ph.D.

In the practice of psychiatry it is essential to diagnose the patient precisely in order to plan treatment and assess prognosis. The validity of a diagnosis is tested by systematic approaches, including laboratory studies, follow-up studies, family studies, etc. (1). In clinical medicine, ensuring diagnostic reliability, i.e., the same patient's receiving the same diagnosis by different clinicians, is important for purposes of comparison and communication of research or therapeutic achievements. It has been recognized, however, that the diagnostic systems in psychiatry have not necessarily been reliable (2) and have varied among clinicians and countries (3). Inasmuch as the most frequent reason for diagnostic disagreement is inadequacies of nosology or lack of criteria (4), the use of the same specified criteria is absolutely essential for improving reliability. Since publication of Feighner and co-workers' study on the subject (5), diagnostic criteria for selecting homogeneous patient groups have been applied by biologically oriented researchers. The American Psychiatric Association's *Diagnostic and Statistical Manual of Mental Disorders*, 3rd edition (DSM-III) (6), published in 1980, provides specified diagnostic criteria for almost all mental disorders, which should improve reliability not only for research use but in daily practice as well.

Address correspondence to: Koichi Hanada, M.D., Lecturer of Psychiatry, Department of Psychiatry, Shiga University of Medical Science, Seta Tsukinowacho, Otsu 520–21, Japan

In Japan, until recently little attention has been paid to the standardization of psychiatric diagnosis, and each clinician has been accustomed to using his or her own nomenclature. Even the ninth revision of the International Classification of Diseases (ICD-9) (7) is not widely used in daily practice. Not satisfied with the current situation in Japan, we were encouraged by the publication of DSM-III and became interested in translating it into Japanese, hoping thus to unify our criteria of mental disorders. It seemed to us that if DSM-III could be proved to have good reliability, it would greatly improve the diagnostic system in Japan and serve educational, clinical, and research purposes.

We have conducted multi-institutional reliability studies of DSM-III and ICD-9, with the collaboration of seven Japanese university clinics. Our study is divided into two parts: the first consists of field trials using joint in-person interviews, and the second is a study using videotaped material.

INTERRATER RELIABILITY STUDY WITH JOINT INTERVIEWS

The purposes of this study were to examine the following issues:

1. Do the classification and diagnostic criteria of DSM-III ensure good diagnostic reliability?

2. Does clinical experience affect the reliability?

3. To what extent do the reliability and classification differ between DSM-III and ICD-9 as used in Japan?

Method

The clinicians who participated in this study were associated with seven university psychiatric departments, as indicated below:

	Number of Doctors	Number of Patients
University of Tokyo	25	85
Shiga University of Medical Sciences	8	54
Kanazawa University	18	50
Kyoto Prefectural University of Medicine	13	48
Saitama Medical School	13	38
Nagasaki University	11	38
Teikyo University	15	32
Total	103	345

Three of these clinics, those in Tokyo, Teikyo, and Saitama, are located in the Tokyo metropolitan area; two of them, in the central part of Japan, around Kyoto City (Kyoto and Shiga); and the other two, in provincial cities. Four of them are national institutions, one is prefectural, and two are private. The participants are all psychiatrists, with clinical experience ranging from 1 to 43 years.

The method of study basically followed that of the DSM-III field trials in the United States conducted by Spitzer and Williams (6,8), with some modifications, as follows:

1. DSM-III diagnostic criteria were translated into Japanese (9) and were distributed to each participant.

2. Several seminars using DSM-III for patient evaluation were conducted by one or the other of us at each institution.

3. In the evaluation sessions, two clinicians interviewed the same patient and completed the diagnostic forms independently. Each clinician was requested to note his or her evaluation according to both DSM-III (axes I and II) and ICD-9.

The subjects of the study were adult patients (18 years or older) seen at the psychiatric clinic of each institution. Three hundred and forty-five patients, 155 males and 190 females, were evaluated. The mean age was 38.5 (± 14.3) years; the oldest patient was 79. All were evaluated during their initial visit to the outpatient clinic of the hospital except 32 patients seen at Teiko University, who were evaluated at the time of new admission to the psychiatric ward. Of these patients, 330 were evaluated following a joint interview by 2 clinicians, and 15 were evaluated separately.

The study ran from January through September 1981. Reliability was expressed in terms of the kappa coefficient of agreement (2,10).

Results

Reliability of DSM-III diagnoses. Interrater reliability and frequency for each diagnostic category of DSM-III are shown in table 1. Values presented in the table were calculated from the assembled data, except in the cases of 19 patients for whom diagnosis was deferred by at least one of the paired clinicians. The overall kappa for the major classes of axis I diagnoses was 0.70, a value comparable with the result of previously reported (6) DMS-III field trials in the United States. The kappa was sufficiently high for organic mental disorders (0.91), paranoid disorders (0.85), and schizophrenic disorders (0.82); it was rather low in classes such as adjustment disorder (0.50), psychotic disorders not elsewhere classified (0.57), and personality disorder, on axis II (0.43). The diagnostic frequency was highest for affective disorders (27.9%); three major classes—schizophrenic disorders (16.4%), anxiety disorders (14.1%), and somatoform disorders (10.0%)—also showed high frequencies.

TABLE 1. Kappa and Frequency for Axes I and II DSM-III Diagnostic Classes

Diagnostic Class	Kappa	% of Sample
Axis I (N = 326)	0.70	
Disorders usually first evident in infancy, childhood, or adolescence	0.67	0.9
Organic mental disorders	0.91	5.4
Substance use disorders	0.78	2.8
Schizophrenic disorders	0.82	16.4
Paranoid disorders	0.85	3.2
Psychotic disorders not elsewhere classified	0.57	8.6
Affective disorders	0.73	27.9
Anxiety disorders	0.63	14.1
Somatoform disorders	0.61	10.0
Dissociative disorders	0.70	0.5
Psychosexual disorders	1.0	0.3
Factitious disorders	0.25	0.2
Disorders of impulse control not elsewhere classified	0.25	0.2
Adjustment disorder	0.51	6.7
Psychological factors affecting physical condition	0.18	1.1
V codes	0.49	1.8
No diagnosis on axis I	0.38	2.3
Axis II (N = 345)		
Personality disorder	0.43	13.8

Reliability of ICD-9 diagnoses. Because several different classification systems are used by different schools in Japan, ICD-9, which has been adopted as the official classification in all seven university hospitals, was used in this study. After excluding the cases with a deferred diagnosis, we obtained an overall kappa for 330 cases of 0.64 (table 2). This value was apparently lower than that for the DSM-III diagnoses. With ICD-9, the kappa was high for the major classes of organic psychotic conditions, alcohol and drug dependence or abuse, and schizophrenic psychoses; it was low for adjustment reaction, other nonorganic psychoses, and depressive disorder not elsewhere classified. The diagnostic frequency for schizophrenic psychoses was very high: 27.7%.

TABLE 2. Kappa and Frequency for Conventional Diagnosis According to ICD-9

Diagnostic Class (N = 330)		Kappa	% of Samples
290-4	Organic psychotic conditions	0.86	5.9
295	Schizophrenic psychoses	0.78	27.7
296	Affective psychoses	0.64	16.4
297	Paranoid states	0.53	2.3
298	Other nonorganic psychoses	0.30	5.5
300	Neurotic disorders	0.67	25.5
301	Personality disorders	0.59	2.6
303-5	Dependence and abuse of alcohol and drugs	0.80	2.3
306	Physical conditions arising from mental factors	0.25	1.4
307	Special symptoms or syndromes not elsewhere classified	0.74	3.6
309	Adjustment reaction	0.27	3.9
310	Specific nonpsychotic mental disorders following organic brain damage	0.70	0.5
311	Depressive disorder, not elsewhere classified	0.39	3.6
312	Disturbance of conduct not elsewhere classified	0.25	0.2
317-9	Mental retardation	0.86	1.1
	No mental disorder	0.50	0.6
	Total	0.64	

Clinical experience and diagnostic agreement. For the DSM-III diagnoses there was no significant correlation between the participants' years of clinical experience and the rate of diagnostic agreement (table 3). In this study, however, the pairs of clinicians were not randomized among participants and institutions. For the ICD-9 diagnoses the agreement rate for clinicians with 7–10 years of experience was lower than that for any other group (table 4).

Discussion

The finding of an overall kappa for axis I diagnoses equal to the value obtained in the U.S. study is evidence that DSM-III will also be

TABLE 3. Years of Experience and Rate of Diagnostic Agreement for DSM-III

	11–20	7–10	5–6	3–4	–2	Total
21 yrs-	0.50**	0.80	0.57	0.71	0.86	0.76
(14)*	(10)	(15)	(7)	(14)	(42)	(88)
11-20	0.69	0.71	1.0	0.79	0.69	0.71
(17)	(13)	(14)	(1)	(33)	(32)	(116)
7–10		0.73	0.50	0.70	0.65	0.70
(17)		(22)	(6)	(23)	(23)	(125)
5–6			0.83	0.90	0.63	0.73
(11)			(6)	(10)	(8)	(44)
3–4				0.63	0.78	0.73
(23)				(16)	(23)	(135)
–2					0.88	0.76
(21)					(8)	(144)

*Number of clinicians of each class of experience.

**Rate of diagnostic agreement (not kappa). Number of cases diagnosed is in parentheses.

TABLE 4. Years of Experience and Rate of Diagnostic Agreement for ICD-9 Diagnosis

	11–20	7–10	5–6	3–4	–2	Total
21 yrs-	0.60	0.71	0.29	0.64	0.88	0.74
(14)	(10)	(14)	(7)	(14)	(43)	(88)
11–20	0.75	0.79	1.0	0.79	0.75	0.75
(17)	(12)	(14)	(1)	(33)	(36)	(118)
7–10		0.41	0.83	0.70	0.64	0.60
(17)		(22)	(6)	(23)	(22)	(123)
5–6			0.86	0.50	0.63	0.65
(11)			(7)	(10)	(8)	(46)
3–4				0.75	0.77	0.72
(23)				(16)	(26)	(138)
–2					0.83	0.78
(21)					(6)	(147)

Legends are the same as for table 3.

useful in Japan. The fact that DSM-III exceeded the ICD-9 in reliability for the same patient group indicates that DSM-III can be a tool for improving the diagnostic system in our country. In some major classes, however, rather low reliability was demonstrated. For example, in order to make a diagnosis of adjustment disorder, which would be given to patients who might, according to ICD-9, be diagnosed as having a mild psychogenic reaction, clinicians must judge that the disorder is due to a psychosocial stressor and does not meet the criteria for other mental disorders. Such double judgments, based on descriptive criteria, on the one hand, and on etiological criteria, on the other, may result in unreliability for that diagnosis. Patients who according to ICD-9 were diagnosed as having a depressive reaction, in particular, received many different DSM-III diagnoses. Among the DSM-III psychotic disorders not elsewhere classified, atypical psychosis had poor reliability (0.31). This result may reflect the fact that there is no consensus concerning the diagnosis of so-called "atypical psychosis" in Japan, though the term has been very widely used.

In DSM-III, personality disorders are separated from axis I mental disorders and recorded on Axis II. This confused Japanese clinicians somewhat, as they have been accustomed to the ICD-9 system, in which personality deviations are alternatives to other disorders; hence, a very low kappa (0.43) was obtained. Several new, unfamiliar terms may have increased the confusion. Since diagnostic reliability of personality disorders was not good in phase 2 of the U.S. field trials (0.60), we must consider whether "personality" itself can be properly described (11). The frequency of personality disorders according to DSM-III (13.8%) was markedly higher than according to ICD-9 (2.6%). This result indicates that one of the purposes of the DSM-III multiaxial system, namely, to ensure that personality disorders are not overlooked when the patient has florid symptoms, is quite well understood in Japan. Personality disorders are, however, diagnosed significantly less often in Japan than in the United States.

Other outstanding features were noted when our results were compared with those reported in the U.S. study (6). For example, affective disorders were diagnosed most frequently in both countries, but the frequency was much higher in the United States, though the kappas were nearly the same in the two countries. Frequency and kappa for both substance use disorders and adjustment disorder were higher in the United States. "Neurotic disorders" were more frequently diagnosed in Japan. Frequency and kappa for schizophrenic disorders were similar for the two countries.

With ICD-9, the frequency of schizophrenia was much higher than with DSM-III, reflecting a broader concept of schizophrenia among Japanese psychiatrists. One of the interesting results of this study was that the frequencies of schizophrenia and affective psychoses in the ICD-9 diagnoses were virtually the reverse of those in the DSM-III diagnoses. This is partly because DSM-III criteria are narrower for schizophrenia and broader for affective disorders, and partly because the Japanese schools have focused mainly on the psychopathology of schizophrenia. The kappa was good for schizophrenia (0.78), but the DSM-III value for affective disorders (0.64) was a little lower.

The relationship between years of clinical experience and the agreement rate on the diagnoses was not clear. The low agreement rate on

ICD-9 diagnoses among clinicians with 7–10 years of experience may indicate two kinds of biases: (*a*) moderately experienced clinicians may tend to make too many diagnoses of categories in which they are interested; (*b*) clinicians who have had only a few years of experience may tend to be influenced by the structure of the interview set by the senior doctors with whom they are jointly interviewing a patient. DSM-III may limit bias, because of its clear descriptions and its novelty for all clinicians. Since we did not randomize the level of clinical experience in selecting our pairs of interviewers, further study will be needed to determine if there is any correlation between clinical experience and diagnostic reliability.

RELIABILITY STUDY USING A VIDEOTAPE APPROACH

Our previous field trials revealed that DSM-III had good diagnostic reliability in Japan. Some major classes, however, had low reliability. In order to improve overall reliability, it is necessary to investigate the source of the disagreement in these classes. Also, both the reliability coefficient and the frequency of each category were variable among the seven institutions (table 5), although all these university clinics were founded by staff from one school, and are thought to practice psychiatry on the basis of the same nosological concepts.

There are several possible reasons for these variances (12). For example, variability of the patients, particularly geographic variability, must be considered. Also, overall reliability is likely to be better when more patients who are easily diagnosable, "textbook cases" are included. Variability in the raters—in their background, clinical experi-

TABLE 5. Kappa and Frequency of Major Diagnoses at Each Institution in the Field Trials

Hospital	Patients	Kappa	Percent Sch	Aff	Anx	Som
Tokyo	81	0.75	17.9	24.7	22.8	10.5
Shiga	54	0.55	16.7	23.1	11.8	13.9
Kanazawa	48	0.76	20.8	16.7	1.0	14.6
Kyoto	45	0.56	17.8	27.8	16.7	6.7
Nagasaki	38	0.80	14.5	36.8	15.8	3.9
Saitama	32	0.68	10.9	23.4	10.9	14.1
Teikyo	28	0.88	12.5	58.9	16.1	1.8
Overall	326	0.70	16.4	27.9	14.1	10.0

Sch = Schizophrenic disorders; Aff = Affective disorders; Anx = Anxiety disorders; Som = Somatoform disorders.

ence, training, and orientation toward the study—may affect reliability as well. Differences in the amount of practice in using DSM-III are also a very important factor in reliability.

To explore the possibility of variance among the seven institutions and the source of disagreement, the second part of our reliability study involved the use of videotaped materials.

Method

The controller, Dr. A. Fujinawa, Kyoto University, was requested to select 14 categories from DSM-III and to allot 2 to each psychiatric department of the 7 institutions. The controller kept the key, and it was not opened until the end of the study. The 14 assigned categories were: 3 subtypes from affective disorders, including bipolar disorder, major depression, and other specific affective disorders; 2 from anxiety disorders; 2 from somatoform disorders; and 1 each from paranoid disorder, psychotic disorder not elsewhere classified, organic mental disorder, and personality disorder. Each institution was instructed not to give any information on an assigned case to other institutions until the conclusion of the study.

In accordance with the given assignment, each institution selected two patients who were willing to cooperate in our study and gave their consent for us to use videotaped interviews with them. Senior psychiatrists conducted the two videotaped interviews, which were then edited to 30 minutes. The interviews were not structured, but included questions necessary for DSM-III and ICD-9 diagnoses. Case vignettes less than two pages in length were also made for the two patients; these contained information on the patients' familial and personal history, history of the present illness, and physcial and laboratory findings. The videotapes and case vignettes were circulated for evaluation among the seven institutions.

Evaluations were made at each of the 7 institutions for 12 patients, the exclusions being the patients from their own institutions. Each participant was requested to evaluate the patients independently and to record his or her diagnosis according to both DSM-III, axes I and II, and ICD-9, without discussing the diagnosis or any other information with other raters; they were also requested not to defer their decision on diagnosis.

One hundred and forty raters participated in the study, and 1,187 evaluation forms were collected. Diagnoses made by raters whose clinical experience was less than a year (15 of the 140) were excluded from the following analyses, except for the correlation of clinical experience with reliability. Not all of the 125 raters attended every evaluation session for the 12 cases; hence, we wound up with 1,100 forms regarded as useful for further analyses.

This part of the study began in March and ended in October 1982. Kappa coefficients of agreement were calculated according to the Fleiss method (13).

Results

Diagnostic variance among institutions. For each case evaluated, no significant difference was observed in the frequencies of DSM-III axis I diagnoses among the seven institutions. On the diagnoses according to the ICD-9 classification, there were significant differences in the frequencies of diagnoses given to three cases (nos. 12, 32, and 71). Because of the design of the study, stipulating that the two cases that the particular institution had prepared for evaluation were not to be evaluated by the raters from that institution, the chances of evaluating any particular case were not completely the same for every institution. In order to compare the data among the seven with one another, some modifications were made, i.e., for the cases not evaluated at a certain institution, average values of frequency of the other six institutions were given. Frequency and reliability for the major classes of DSM-III axis I diagnoses for each institution after the modification had been made are presented in table 6.

The kappa was over 0.76 for every institution. At Nagasaki University, the frequency of anxiety disorders was lower and that of somatoform disorders was higher than the values for the other university clinics, but the differences were not significant.

Frequency of axis II diagnoses, after the same modification had been made, varied significantly among the seven institutions (table 7). Excluding personality traits, the total frequency of axis II diagnoses was 15.5%. Personality disorders were diagnosed more often at Tokyo

TABLE 6. Kappa and Diagnostic Frequency of Major Diagnoses on Axis I for Each Institution in Videotape Study

Hospital	Kappa	Org	Sub	Sch	Par	Psy	Aff	Anx	Som
Tokyo	0.772	7.2	9.0	22.9	5.4	7.2	21.7	15.7	12.7
Teikyo	0.818	6.4	8.7	20.6	7.3	6.9	21.6	17.9	11.9
Saitama	0.763	8.1	9.2	19.5	8.1	7.6	21.6	16.8	10.8
Kanazawa	0.768	5.8	8.0	22.2	5.8	8.4	19.9	15.4	14.1
Shiga	0.844	7.3	12.1	21.0	7.3	7.3	21.0	17.7	8.9
Kyoto	0.842	4.7	7.3	22.0	8.0	8.0	20.7	16.7	11.3
Nagasaki	0.845	5.4	10.8	21.5	6.2	5.4	22.3	10.0	16.2

Org = Organic mental disorders; Sub = Substance use disorders; Sch = Schizophrenic disorders; Par = Paranoid disorders; Psy = Psychotic disorders not elsewhere classified; Aff = Affective disorders; Anx = Anxiety disorders; Som = Somatoform disorders.

Original data modifed by method described in the text.

TABLE 7. Diagnostic Frequency of Axis II Diagnoses (Personality Disorders)

	%	
Tokyo	24.7*	(41/166)
Teikyo	12.4	(27/218)
Saitama	22.2**	(41/185)
Kanazawa	9.6**	(30/311)
Shiga	17.7	(22/124)
Kyoto	14.0	(21/150)
Nagasaki	13.1	(17/130)
Total	15.5	(199/1284)

*$p = 0.01$; **$p = 0.05$.

Original data modified by method described in the text.

TABLE 8. Kappa and Frequency for Axes I and II DSM-III Diagnostic Classes

Diagnostic Class	Kappa	% of Samples
Overall for axis I	0.798	
Organic mental disorders	0.589	6.1
Substance use disorders	0.729	9.2
Schizophrenic disorders	0.945	20.8
Paranoid disorders	0.879	6.5
Psychotic disorders not elsewhere classified	0.818	7.5
Affective disorders	0.927	22.1
Anxiety disorders	0.678	15.8
Somatoform disorders	0.542	12.6
Others	0.081	4.7
Personality disorders (axis II)	0.331	15.9

University and Saitama Medical School, and less often at Kanazawa University.

Overall diagnostic reliability. Reliability and frequency for each DSM-III diagnostic class were calculated from the 1,100 diagnoses given to the 14 cases (table 8). The overall kappa for the major classes of axis I was 0.798. Diagnostic reliability for schizophrenic disorders and affective disorders was very high, but the kappa was not very good for anxiety disorders, somatoform disorders, and personality disorders.

The kappa for ICD-9 diagnoses was 0.746, lower than that for DSM-III (table 9). Low values for kappa were shown for paranoid states and for other nonorganic psychoses, for which very good kappa values were obtained with DSM-III.

Diagnostic reliability and clinical experience. Raters were grouped into seven classes according to their years of clinical experience. As shown in table 10, those with clinical experience of less than five years apparently displayed lower diagnostic reliability than more experienced psychiatrists. In every class of clinical experience, the reliability of DSM-III diagnoses was better than that of ICD-9 diagnoses.

Diagnoses given to each case presented.
   1. Schizophrenic disorders (cases 11, 31, and 41)
   For every case of schizophrenic disorder, very good diagnostic agreement was shown for DSM-III (table 11). ICD-9 diagnoses given to these patients also showed good agreement (table 12). With regard to the subtypes, the paranoid type was most frequently assigned to all three cases. Although case 41 was prepared as one of the residual type by the videotape producers, 55% of the raters diagnosed it as paranoid.
   2. Other psychotic disorders (cases 22 and 32)
   DSM-III diagnoses for two cases of paranoia or atypical psychosis were in good agreement. More than 90% of the diagnoses were con-

TABLE 9. Kappa and Frequency for Conventional Diagnosis According to ICD-9

Diagnostic Class		Kappa	% of Samples
290-4	Organic psychotic conditions	0.704	7.9
295	Schizophrenic psychoses	0.833	23.4
296	Affective psychoses	0.829	20.2
297	Paranoid states	0.555	5.7
298	Other nonorganic psychoses	0.426	3.7
300	Neurotic disorders	0.745	26.5
304-5	Dependence and abuse of drugs	0.760	5.4
306	Physical conditions arising from mental factors	0.565	4.6
	Others	0.114	6.0
	Overall	0.746	

TABLE 10. Years of Experience and Reliability at Each Level of Experience

Experience, years	Kappa for DSM-III Diagnosis	Kappa for ICD-9 Diagnosis	Number of Reports
Under 1 year	0.770	0.643	87
1–2 years	0.752	0.689	277
3–4 years	0.726	0.710	249
5–6 years	0.835	0.787	85
7–10 years	0.890	0.717	206
11–20 years	0.843	0.808	173
21 and more	0.867	0.790	110

cordant. ICD-9 diagnoses, however, varied more widely, with a frequent diagnosis of schizophrenia. For case 22, a diagnosis of paranoia was given in more than 90% of the answers based on DSM-III, whereas a diagnosis of late-onset schizophrenia or paranoid schizophrenia accounted for a considerable number of the ICD-9 diagnoses. This means that the boundary between paranoia and schizophrenia has been unclear in Japanese conventional diagnosis.

DSM-III diagnoses of atypical psychosis accounted for 67% of those given to case 32. In the ICD-9 diagnoses for this case, psychogenic reaction or reactive psychosis dominated, but accounted for only 41% of all diagnoses; 23% of the raters noted only paranoid-hallucinatory state. This case was considered to be an organic mental disorder by several raters.

3. Affective disorders (cases 51, 61, and 71)

Cases 51 and 61 were of patients with major affective disorders. Diagnoses given to these two, according to both DSM-III and ICD-9, were in good agreement. Several raters regarded case 51 as an organic mental disorder.

Diagnoses given to case 71, presented as an example of dysthymic disorder, varied considerably, although almost all raters agreed that the patient suffered from an affective disorder.

4. Anxiety and somatoform disorders (cases 12, 42, 62, and 72)

These four cases were those representing various types of neurosis in the traditional sense. With regard to the two cases with clear symptomatology—case 62, conversion disorder, and case 72, obsessive-compulsive disorder—high agreement was achieved on both DSM-III and ICD-9 diagnoses. The DSM-III diagnoses for cases 12 and 42, with both anxiety and physical complaints, varied between anxiety disorder and

TABLE 11. DSM-III Diagnoses Given to Each Case

Diagnosis	Case Number													
	11	12	21	22	31	32	41	42	51	52	61	62	71	72
Organic mental disorders										1				1
Substance use disorders			54			4			8	70				
Schizophrenic disorders	76		31	2	79		71							
Paranoid disorders		1		68	2					1				
Psychotic disorders not elsewhere classified	2			3	1	75								
Affective disorders										1		1		
Major affective disorders									81		75		83	3
Other specific affective disorders									81		75		53	2
Atypical affective disorders										1			30	1
Anxiety disorders		39						46		7			10	
Somatoform disorders		31						23		11		69		81
Other diagnoses		13	1		1	4		8		16		6	3	3
Personality disorders	0	14	6	5	13	1		5	1	57	3	46	2	11
Total number of raters	78	80	69	73	84	83	71	73	88	80	75	75	86	85

TABLE 12. ICD-9 Diagnoses Given to Each Case

Diagnosis	Case Number													
	11	12	21	22	31	32	41	42	51	52	61	62	71	72
Organic psychotic conditions		1	65	2		7			5				5	2
Schizophrenic psychoses	75			17	77	13	65							
Paranoid states	2			51	4	2				1				
Other nonorganic psychoses				1		38								
Paranoid-hallucinatory state			1			19					73		60	
Affective psychoses									78	1	2		7	1
Depressive state								64		22		69	12	84
Neurotic disorders		30	1							56				
Drug dependence or abuse														
Physical conditions arising from mental factors		48						1						
Other diagnoses		6	1			1		1		17		5	3	
Total number of raters	77	80	67	71	81	82	65	66	83	71	75	73	86	85

somatoform disorder. The most frequent diagnoses given to these two cases at Nagasaki University Clinic were different, which represented an instance of interinstitutional disagreement, i.e., most of the raters there diagnosed these as somatoform disorders, whereas at the other six institutions the most common diagnosis was anxiety disorder. As the predominant feature in case 12 was episodes of hyperventilation, the most frequent ICD-9 diagnosis was hyperventilation syndrome. The DSM-III diagnosis for this case was either anxiety disorder or a somatoform disorder, depending on whether the rater regarded the episodes of hyperventilation as panic attacks or as conversion symptoms.

5. Other disorders (cases 21 and 52)

Case 21 developed hallucinations and delusions following repeated use of stimulants. On axis I of the DSM-III diagnosis, both organic mental disorder and substance use disorder should be recorded, according to the manual's instructions. Only 16 raters (23%) noted both diagnoses. The most frequent (73%) ICD-9 diagnosis was psychostimulant intoxication.

For case 52, presented as an example of histrionic personality disorder, it is of interest how often an axis II diagnosis was made. Fifty-seven raters (71%) made the diagnosis on axis II together with the axis I disorder. The frequency of personality disorder diagnoses was much higher with DSM-III than with ICD-9.

Case 62 was another patient who received a diagnosis of a personality disorder by more than half (61%) of the raters. A total of 16% of all the raters noted axis II diagnoses, for 14 patients.

Discussion

In the second part of our reliability study, using videotaped materials, very good reliability, 0.798, was achieved for overall DSM-III axis I diagnoses. (It should be noted that this was only the first attempt to investigate diagnostic reliability with videotaped material in Japan.) This result was better than that obtained in the first part of our study, with in-person interviews, and seems to reflect the methodological difference between the two substudies. In general, DSM-III served to reduce variability in diagnoses among the raters and thus improved diagnostic reliability. The overall kappa for the ICD-9 diagnoses, 0.746, was also satisfactory, although some disagreement in diagnoses was observed among the seven institutions.

The reliability of DSM-III diagnoses consistently exceeded that of the ICD-9 diagnoses made by raters of varying clinical experience. This result suggests that DSM-III is suitable for general use in Japan. The results also suggest, however, that several years of training are needed to make acceptable diagnoses, even using DSM-III. This view is supported by the finding that the reliability of ICD-9 diagnoses also improved in proportion to clinical experience.

Reliability of axis II diagnoses was poor; large interrater variance was observed in these diagnoses. The videotapes presented in the study generally contained little information about personality characteristics. Videotape editors in each institution seemed to pay less attention to depicting axis II disorders than to describing the clinical syndrome necessary for diagnosing axis I disorders. This tendency to overlook information on personality may be due to defects in our conventional training programs. Of course, it is very difficult to provide enough information in a short videotape to make precise diagnoses of personality deviations.

The reliability results for the major classes of disorder were generally consistent with those of the previous field trials. Diagnoses of schizophrenic disorders and major affective disorders had a high rate of agreement for both the DSM-III and the ICD-9 systems. Paranoid disorders and psychotic disorders not elsewhere classified achieved good reliability in DSM-III diagnoses, but rather poor ones according to ICD-9.

REFERENCES

1. Robins E, Guze SB: Establishment of diagnostic validity in psychiatric illness: its application to schizophrenia. Am J Psychiatry 126: 983–987, 1970
2. Spitzer RL, Fleiss JL: A re-analysis of the reliability of psychiatric diagnosis. Br J Psychiatry 125: 341–347, 1974
3. Kendell RE, Cooper JE, Gourlay AJ, et al: Diagnostic criteria of American and British psychiatrists. Arch Gen Psychiatry 25: 123–130, 1971
4. Ward CH, Beck AT, Mendelson M, et al: The psychiatric nomenclature. Reasons for diagnostic disagreement. Arch Gen Psychiatry 7: 198–205, 1962
5. Feighner JP, Robins E, Guze SB, et al: Diagnostic criteria for use in psychiatric research. Arch Gen Psychiatry 26: 57–63, 1972
6. American Psychiatric Association: Diagnostic and Statistical Manual of Mental Disorders, 3rd ed. Washington DC, American Psychiatric Association, 1980
7. World Health Organization: International Classification of Diseases, 9th Revision. Geneva, World Health Organization, 1977
8. Spitzer RL, Forman JBW, Nee J: DSM-III field trials: I. Initial interrater diagnostic reliability. Am J Psychiatry 136: 815–817, 1979
9. Takahashi S, Hanada K, Fujinawa A: Quick Reference to the Diagnostic Criteria from DSM-III (American Psychiatric Association) (Japanese translation). Tokyo, Igaku Shoin, 1982
10. Spitzer RL, Cohen J, Fleiss JL, et al: Quantification of agreement in psychiatric diagnosis. A new approach. Arch Gen Psychiatry 17: 83–87, 1967
11. Frances A: The DSM-III personality disorder section: A commentary. Am J Psychiatry 137: 1050–1054, 1980

12. Andreasen NC, McDonald-Scott P, Grove WM, et al: Assessment of reliability in multicenter collaborative research with a videotape approach. Am J Psychiatry 139: 876–882, 1982
13. Fleiss JL: Measuring nominal scale agreement among many raters. Psychol Bull 76: 378–382, 1971

21

THE DSM-III DIAGNOSES OF
NEW ZEALAND CHILDREN

John S. Werry, M.D., R. James Methven, M.B., Ch.B.,
Joanne Fitzpatrick, B.Sc., and Hamish Dixon, M.A.

Few data on the reliability and validity of diagnostic systems in children are available, and criticism of such systems is common (1,2). In its short history, DSM-III (3) has already produced four studies involving children (4–7).

Although the American Psychiatric Association's field trials in preparing DSM-III were promising, Cantwell and co-workers, in a study in which psychiatrists completed standardized diagnostic questionnaires on 24 actual case records covering a variety of conditions, found the overall rater agreement on diagnoses of children to be less than 50%. Agreement was, however, higher on certain categories and subtypes (psychosis, conduct disorders, attention deficit disorders, and mental retardation); and these investigators were encouraged by the results, especially since the raters were unused to using the DSM-III criteria.

A study by Strober and colleagues (7), from the same center as Cantwell, yielded an overall kappa of 0.74 and higher kappas in many categories. This study differed from the Cantwell group's (4,5) in that it used 1) a larger number of older subjects (N = 95; median age,

Address correspondence to: John S. Werry, M.D., Professor and Head, Department of Psychiatry, School of Medicine, University of Auckland, Private Bag, Auckland, New Zealand

This study was supported by the Medical Research Council of New Zealand and the Mental Health Foundation of New Zealand.
Portions of this paper are in press in the Journal of Abnormal Child Psychology.

around 15), 2) successive inpatient first admissions, 3) only two raters, 4) a joint interview situation, and 5) standardized methods of history taking and examination. The investigation provided frequency data on various diagnoses—an uncommon practice in child psychiatry (8). Because of the age group, well over half of the diagnoses were in the adult category (schizophrenia, personality disorders, affective disorder), and only conduct and eating disorders from the children's section attained double-digit percentage figures.

In testing the reliability and validity of a diagnostic system, it is important to control, to the extent possible, for contamination by errors in history taking, examination, and interpretation. In the study by Cantwell and colleagues, control was achieved by using case records, whereas Strober and associates used standardized interviews with both raters present. The former has the disadvantage of possible omission of critical data and preconceptions regarding a diagnosis by the writer of the history, and the latter is also subject to innuendo and biases.

Rutter and Shaffer (9) have been sharply critical of the field-trial studies of Spitzer and Williams on the grounds that geographic distribution, while appearing extensive, was limited to self-selected *pairs* of clinicians. They argue that the logistics of locating such pairs created an unspecified data base and a lack of formal control over the independence of the raters. This was further compounded by the fact that the clinicians were free to select their own cases. Rutter and Shaffer also point out that the Cantwell study, while showing good interrater reliability on the clear-cut major categories, demonstrated lack of agreement on both minor categories and more complex disorders.

Further, these writers allude to an (as yet) unpublished study of the ICD-9, involving 50 British child psychiatrists, that, using the case-history approach and many geographically separated raters, showed good interrater agreement for only the common major diagnostic categories of conduct disturbance, emotional disorder, and depressive condition and a marked loss of reliability in subcategorization. Along with others, such as Quay (2), they concluded that the DSM-III classification was grossly overrefined.

The present study differed from that of Cantwell and co-workers in that, for practical reasons, it had to be conducted as part of the usual clinical procedures of a psychiatric unit (i.e., live case presentations). It also has a much larger number of subjects (N = 195). It differs from the study by Strober and associates in that most of the children were not adolescent, and were seen in a routine case-presentation approach that lacked a standardized method of history taking and examination.

PROCEDURE

During the periods January 1978 through June 1980 and January 1981 through July 1981, children successively admitted to our inpatient unit were assigned a diagnosis by two or more of six clinicians (two senior psychiatrists, one Fellow in child psychiatry, one Fellow in behavioral pediatrics, and two psychologists). The diagnoses were made on the basis of the presentation of the case at ward rounds in the week of the patient's admission to the unit. The length of the presentation varied, but generally averaged about 15 minutes. When necessary, clarifications were made in response to queries about missing data or ambiguities in the data. Except in an occasional case, the presentation was made by a person not actually involved in assigning a diagnosis, and considerable care was taken in the presentation not to mention any diagnostic terms. When this did occur, the subjects were eliminated from the study. The number of diagnosers per child ranged from two to four (usually two or three) and varied according to absences, staffing changes in the unit, and, mostly, the punctiliousness of the diagnosers in completing their sheets. Demographic data were collected routinely, but often not completely, as part of the registration procedure. The length of time the patient stayed in the inpatient unit was also recorded routinely, for administrative purposes.

The study began with the penultimate draft of DSM-III, and was completed with the published version. The differences in the two versions with regard to disorders affecting children are minor, and did not greatly influence the results.

The unit, which is the only inpatient psychiatric facility for children in New Zealand, is situated within the main campus of the principal teaching hospital in Auckland (population, 800,000), and is adjacent to both the medical school and the pediatric section of the university hospital. Referrals to the unit come equally from the pediatric division of the hospital and from family doctors. Hospitalization is entirely free, under the government health insurance scheme. The staff of the unit consists of a multidisciplinary team of 2 senior child psychiatrists, 2 rotating psychiatric residents, 2 rotating pediatric residents, 1 clinical psychologist, 2 social workers, 1 child therapist, 3 teachers, and 12 nurses. The majority of the staff members have been with the unit several years, and some since it opened in 1971. Most of the caseload is outpatient and, to a lesser extent, day-patient, the inpatient unit being viewed as primarily for crisis intervention and for short-stay diagnostic and/or treatment programs. Patients from outside the greater Auckland area are not favored for admission to the unit because of difficulties in implementing follow-up treatment programs.

Reliabilities were calculated using the kappa coefficient for unequal numbers of judges per subject (10). A kappa of 0.70 is here considered to reflect an acceptable level of reliability. There was poor compliance with ratings on axes IV and V, so this part of the study was discontinued.

RESULTS AND DISCUSSION

Subjects

The demographic and other background characteristics of the 195 children are presented in table 1. Maoris (indigenous Polynesians) are underrepresented, but this difference is not significant. There are more children in the sample with unemployed fathers than in the Auckland

TABLE 1. Background Data—Total Group (N = 195)

Age			S.D. =	
	Mean = 10.2 yrs		3.25 yrs	Range, 2–17
Sex and age	5–9 yrs*		10–14 yrs*	Total*
	M F		M F	
Percent of sample	34 13		31 23	64
Percent of New Zealand population	25 24		26 25	51
Ethnic group	Maori/Maori Descent		Other	
Percent of sample	14		86	
Percent of population	17		83	
Father's occupational group	Professional	Manual	Other	
Percent of sample	14	50	36	
Percent of population	14	49	37	
Father unemployed				
Percent of sample	7*			
Percent of population	2.6			
One-parent families				
Percent of sample	26*			
Percent of population	8			

*p = 0.001

population, and this difference is significant (chi^2 = 15.7; df = 1; p<0.001), although the majority of patients, by far, come from the classes that constitute most of the population in New Zealand (according to 1976 census data). There are also significantly more males in the sample in comparison with the New Zealand population of this age (chi^2 = 10.03; df = 1; p<0.001).

Interdiagnoser Reliability

Our data are compared with those from the other studies (3–7), the main features being summarized in table 2 and the comparative reliabilities, in table 3.

Overall reliability. It can be seen that, overall, the system is of satisfactory reliability and that the value of kappa obtained (0.71) approximates that of the other studies that used this statistic, most of which are also around 0.70.

Major category reliability. Seven of the major categorizations—in rank order, substance use, eating disorders, anxiety (adult), other physical disorders, organic disorders, attention deficit disorder, and schizophrenic disorders—proved reliable (kappa >0.69), whereas two more—anxiety (child) and mental retardation—came close (kappa <0.70 >0.60). Moderately unreliable (i.e., kappa <0.60 >0.45) were conduct, psychotic (n.e.c.),* and somatoform disorders; and other, factitious, and adjustment disorders and other conditions proved highly unreliable.

Again, the results resemble those from most other studies, especially with regard to conduct, eating, schizophrenic, anxiety (adult), organic, and substance use disorders and mental retardation, but are discrepant to varying degrees for attention deficit, anxiety (child), and other physical disorders (higher reliability in this study). In other, psychotic (n.e.c.), factitious, somatoform, and adjustment disorders and additional codes, the range of variation across all studies is too wide to assess the results of the present study, as is the discrepancy in V codes, additional codes, other physical disorders, and other disorders, in which only one other study has reported reliability.

Subcategories. Subcategorization reliability can be looked at in several ways. The first is simply to question the reliability of individual subcategories. Ratings on attention deficit disorder with hyperactivity, separation anxiety, anorexia nervosa, enuresis, encopresis, obsessive-compulsive disorder, and delirium are reliable (kappa >0.69); those on overanxious disorder, adjustment disorder with depressed mood, and substance use, mixed or unspecified, are borderline (kappa <0.49 >0.70).

---

*n.e.c. = not elsewhere classified.

TABLE 2. Comparative Data across Studies

I. Age

% Cumulative Frequency

Study	<5	6	7	8	9	10	11	12	13	14	15	16	17	18	>18	DK
Werry (N=195)	7.2	18	24.5	30	43	49	59	68	80.5	93	98	99	100			
Spitzer (N=281)					Approx 50										100	
Field trials (N=126)															100	
Cantwell (N=24)	8	12	12	16	33	33	37	50	54	58 (adolescent)	76	89	100			42
Strober (N=95)								5	25	48	89		100			0

II. Sex ratio

Study	% Male	% No data
Werry (N=195)	64	0
Spitzer (N=281)	100	
Field Trials (N=126)	100	
Cantwell (N=24)	58	17
Strober (N=95)	51	0

III. Race

Study	White (not Hispanic)	Other
Spitzer	81%	19%
Werry	77%	23%

IV. Method

	Werry (N=195)	Spitzer (N=281)	Field Trials (N=126) Phase I / Phase 2	Cantwell (N=24)	Strober (N=95)
Number of observers	2-4	274	84	20	2
Patient status					
Inpatient	100%	33%			100%
Outpatient		34%		100%	
Other		33%			
No information			100%		
Information source	Initial diagnostic evaluation	Initial diagnostic evaluation	Initial diagnostic evaluation	Case history	Initial diagnostic evaluation
Interview type	Joint in case conference setting	Joint 53.4% Separate 46.6%	Joint 60% Separate 30% / Joint 66% Separate 33%	Separate 100%	Joint in structured interview setting

The list of unreliable categories (kappa >0.50) is, however, clearly much larger; and they are to be found within all major categories except "Other disorders with physical manifestations."

The second question is, To what extent does subcategorization impair or improve reliability of the major categories? The categories schizophrenic, psychotic (n.e.c.), and substance use disorders are impaired by subcategorization in that no subcategory has a reliability even close to that of the major category. In one instance, an individual subcategory (adjustment disorder with depressed mood) achieves a much greater reliability than the major-category disorder itself. In one or two instances (other physical, anxiety—child), reliabilities of subcategories are all, or nearly all, similar to those of the major category itself, which suggests good subcategorization; but in the majority of cases, one subcategory is of a reliability similar to that of the major category while all the other subcategories are far behind, which suggests that in these instances, little is gained by subcategorization.

No other study has addressed subcategories except that of Cantwell and co-workers (4,5), in which only one or two subcategories were apparently either used or reported, so that no comparisons are really possible.

Sources of disagreement. While kappa coefficients index reliability, they tell little about how unreliability is generated. A purely descriptive way of looking at this for some of the more important categories is presented in table 4. The columns indicate the diagnostic category, and the rows, the other diagnoses offered. Thus, for example, in the case of attention deficit disorder, the diagnosis was made 30 times. In 21 of these, at least 1 other rater made the same diagnosis; in 3, a dissenting diagnosis of conduct disorder; in 3, oppositional disorder; and in 3, other disorders. It can be seen that some diagnoses, such as attention deficit and conduct disorder, have rather consistent competitors, while others simply generate a variable amount of "noise" across the entire system (e.g., anxiety, oppositional, and adjustment disorders).

In our opinion, oppositional disorder, an entirely new category, resembles a mild conduct disorder in diagnostic criteria; it was found in this study to predominate in girls and to have unsatisfactory reliability and high "noise"-generating capacity. We therefore created a combined conduct/oppositional category and recalculated reliabilities. This elevated two unreliable categories (kappa = 0.53 and kappa = 0.39) to one nearly reliable (kappa = 0.67) category. Other such analyses could be useful in future studies.

Some peculiarities of this study. There was no majority agreement on 20% of the children, who therefore could not receive a diagnosis. This figure, however, compares favorably with previous DSM systems, in which

TABLE 3. Comparative Reliabilities across Categories and Studies

I Childhood Disorders (Disorders with DSM-III No.)	Werry (N=195) K	Werry %	Spitzer (N=281) I Joint (N=150) K	I Joint %	II Test-Retest (N=131) K	II Test-Retest %	DSM-III Field Trials (N=126) Phase I (N=71) K	Phase I %	Phase II (N=55) K	Phase II %	Cantwell (N=24) % Agreement (N=20) I With Expected Diagnosis	II Interrater	Strober (N=95) K	Strober %	Mean Weighted Kappa (All Studies)
Overall major category	0.71		0.78		0.66		0.68	15.5	0.52	14.6			0.74		0.70
Attention deficit	0.76	9.2					0.58		0.50		75	75	—	1	0.68
314.01 with hyperactivity	0.73	8.2													
314.00 without hyperactivity	0.05	1.0													
Conduct	0.53	30.1					0.61	26.8	0.61	38.2			0.75	22.1	0.60
312.00 Undersocialized, aggressive	0.57	8.2											0.86		0.67
312.10 Undersocialized, nonaggressive	0.18	9.2									30	30	0.60		0.32
312.23 Socialized aggressive	−0.04	3.1									70	70	0.46		
312.21 Socialized nonaggressive	0.32	6.2													
312.xx Unspecified subtype	0.40	3.1													
Anxiety—childhood & adolescence	0.67	21					0.25	8.5	0.44	16.4	15	55	0.47	6.3	0.52
309.21 Separation anxiety	0.72	14.4													
313.21 Avoidant	0.05	2.1													
313.00 Overanxious	0.65	4.6													
Other disorders	0.39	24.6					0.79	8.5	0.73	9.1			1.00[a]	2.1	0.64
313.22 Schizoid	0.37	3.6											1.00	2.1	0.59
313.81 Oppositional	0.39	20.0													
313.82 Identity	0.28	1.0													
Eating	0.91	2.1	−0.01	2.1	0.85	2.1	0.66	2.8	1.0	3.6			0.94[b]	11.5	0.69
307.10 Anorexia nervosa	1.00	1.5											0.94	11.5	0.98
Other physical	0.91	23.6							0.48	5.5					0.81
307.60 Functional enuresis	0.96	4.6													
307.70 Functional encopresis	0.91	19.0													
Mental retardation	0.62[c]	1.5	0.66	5.6	0.85	5.6	1.0	8.5	1.0	3.6	90	90	0.76		0.76
317.0 Mild	0.62	1.5									75	75			

[a]Both cases diagnosed as oppositional disorder.
[b]All cases diagnosed as anorexia nervosa.
[c]All cases diagnosed as mild mental retardation.

TABLE 3. (cont)

II Adult-type Disorders (Disorder with DSM-III No.)	Werry (N=195) K	Werry %	Spitzer (N=281) I Joint (N=150) K	I Joint %	II Test-Retest (N=131) K	II Test-Retest %	DSM-III Field Trials (N=126) Phase I (N=71) K	Phase I %	Phase II (N=55) K	Phase II %	Cantwell (N=24) % Agreement (N=20) I With Expected Diagnosis	II Interrater	Strober (N=95) K	Strober %	Mean Weighted Kappa (All Studies)
Organic mental	0.89	2.6	0.74	12.9	0.83	12.9			0.66	3.6					0.81
293.00 Delirium	1.00	1.0													
Substance use	1.00	2.6	0.90	22.0	0.74	22.0	1.00	5.6	0.54	9.1			1.0	2.1	0.89
305.9 Other, mixed, unspecified	0.62	1.6													
304.6 Other specified	0.02	1.0													
Schizophrenic	0.70	5.1	0.82	12.9	0.82	12.9	1.00	5.6	0.66	3.6	25	70	0.82	15.7	0.79
295.3x Paranoid type	0.16	2.1									45	45	1.00		0.44
295.9x Undifferentiated	0.35	3.6											0.62		0.44
Psychotic n.e.c.	0.47	3.1	0.85	7.0	0.43	7.0	0.85	5.6							0.61
295.4 Schizophreniform	0.19	2.6													
298.9 Atypical psychosis	0.05	1.0													
Anxiety—adult	0.91	4.6	0.74	10.5	0.43	10.5	1.0	2.8	1.0	1.8	40	40	0.64	2.1	0.76
300.29 Simple phobia	0.27	1.0													
300.30 Obsessive-compulsive	0.94	3.1													
300.00 Atypical	0.27	1.0													
Factitious	0.05	1.5	0.49	1.4	1.00	1.4									0.45
300.16 with psychological symptoms	0.05	1.5													
Somatoform	0.49	5.6	0.53	4.2	0.66	4.2	1.00	1.4	−0.009	1.8	55	55	1.0	2.1	0.61
300.81 Somatization	0.11	1.5													
300.11 Conversion	0.37	2.1													
307.80 Psychogenic pain	0.50	3.1													
Adjustment	0.23	8.7	0.74	11.2	0.60	11.2	0.66	31.0	0.36	32.7					0.50
309.00 with depressed mood	0.67	1.0													
309.24 with anxious mood	−0.04	2.6													
309.28 with mixed emotional features	0.06	1.5													
309.30 with disturbance of conduct	0.05	2.1													
309.40 with mixed disturbance of emotions and conduct	0.20	3.6													
V Codes	0.14	6.2					−0.02	4.2	0.54	9.1	35	35			0.17
V65.20 Malingering	−0.10	1.5													
V61.20 Parent-child problem	0.22	4.6													
Additional codes	0.28	7.2					1.0	1.4	−0.03	5.5			0.47	14.7	0.39
300.90 Unspecified disorder	0.28	3.1													0.34
V71.09 No axis I diagnosis	0.41	3.6													
799.90 Diagnosis deferred	−0.10	1.0													

Note: Diagnoses that occurred in only one subject were omitted (atypical conduct, atypical eating, transient tic, hebephrenic schizophrenic, brief reactive psychosis, residual schizophrenic, social phobia, atypical somatoform, psychosomatic reaction, adjustment disorder with withdrawal, academic problem, dementia, organic personality syndrome, and alcohol intoxication).

TABLE 4. Agreement/Disagreement among Diagnostic Categories

	Attention deficit (N=30)	Conduct (N=79)	Anxiety (Child) (N=72)	Other Childhood* (N=14)	Physical (N=72)	Anxiety (Adult) (N=17)	Factitious (N=7)	Somatoform (N=17)	Adjustment (N=14)	Other conditions (N=5)	V Codes (N=6)	Additional (N=5)	Oppositional (N=26)	Miscellaneous (N=14)
Attention deficit	21/3													
Conduct		41/6												
Anxiety (child)		2	50/2											
Other childhood		2	1	6										
Physical			1		66									
Anxiety (adult)						15								
Factitious							1/3							
Somatoform			3					12/1						
Adjustment		4	2	4	1	1	1		5/1					
Other conditions	3	4	3	1		1		3	1	1				
V codes		1	3		1	1					2/1			
Additional		2	1	2	2							2/2		
Oppositional	3	17	5	1	1				6	1			25/1	
Miscellaneous			1		1		2	1	1	3	3	1	1	14

No disagreement: Psychotic/schizophrenic (N=16)
Substance use (N=5)

Miscellaneous: Movement, organic, mental retardation, personality, dissociative, eating

*Excluding oppositional.

"No diagnosis" was frequently reported and even was often the commonest category (8). Certain categories were not needed at all, notably affective disorder, though one case of bipolar disorder was found, in a 14-year-old female, but had to be excluded because of the severity of her condition; discussion of the diagnosis during ward rounds appeared clinically necessary and thus transcended the needs of the research. None of us considers the frequency of major affective disorder other than rare in children, despite current thinking in American child psychiatry. It should be noted, however, that in this study adjustment disorder with depressed mood may be the New Zealand equivalent of depression in the United States.

Other diagnoses that did not occur, or but rarely, are noted at the bottom of table 3; but the wide range of diagnoses used is rather striking and compares favorably with previous diagnostic systems (8).

Local patterns. It is pertinent to look at whether the addition of a psychiatric diagnosis to already existing information increases our knowledge of local patterns of psychiatric care. Only children on whose diagnoses a majority of raters agreed and diagnoses with a frequency of occurrence of more than three were included in our study. In interpreting our findings it is important to bear in mind that the data are for inpatients only, and thus do not necessarily reflect the frequency of the disorders as such. This is not an epidemiological or validity study, as our sample is necessarily unrepresentative and reflects local peculiarities. An example of this is the high frequency of referrals for encopresis, which is a result of a recognized staff competence in treating this disorder.

Population factors. Because of small numbers in some categories, statistical tests were done only on those with more than nine subjects. Only when the overall statistic was significant were paired comparisons made.

Table 5 illustrates a number of features of interest. Males predominated in attention deficit, elimination (eneuresis and encopresis), conduct, and anxiety (child) disorders, and females in anxiety (adult), oppositional, and eating disorders. Diagnoses of somatoform and schizophrenic disorders and of the combined conduct-oppositional disorder were made equally frequently for both sexes. Of these diagnoses only childhood anxiety, oppositional and conduct disorders, and encopresis had sufficient numbers for analysis. The differences among these were significant when oppositional disorder was included ($chi^2 = 14$; $df = 3$; $p < 0.005$), but not significant when it was omitted ($chi^2 = 5$; $df = 2$; $p > 0.10$). Only the findings for anxiety and conduct disorder (without oppositional disorder) are at all unexpected (see Graham [11]). It is of interest that combining the conduct and oppositional disorders eliminates the male bias with regard to the former.

Disorders appearing in younger children (under 10 years) were encopresis and attention deficit disorders; anxiety (adult) and schizophrenic and somatoform disorders were observed in older children (over 11 years). Again, the results are as expected, all differences among diagnoses (encopresis, childhood anxiety, attention deficit, conduct-oppositional, and schizophrenic disorders) being significant except those between attention deficit disorder and encopresis, childhood anxiety and the combined conduct-oppositional category, and childhood anxiety and the schizophrenic disorders ($F = 18.89$; $df = 4$, 106; $p<0.001$).

There are no clear patterns in family size except that the somewhat larger size (more than two siblings) is unexpected and differs significantly from the New Zealand population (New Zealand census data, 1976; $chi^2 = 49.28$; $df = 4$; $p<0.001$ [12]). Family "intactness" (defined as both natural or adopted parents still living together) shows an excess of broken homes in the histories of children with conduct-oppositional disorder. Comparable figures are not available for the total New Zealand population. Adopted children seemed randomly distributed throughout the categories, but sample sizes were too small for any statistical analyses.

Length of stay. Differences in duration of hospitalization were a function of diagnosis, from the extreme brevity of a stay for enuresis, reflecting a particular treatment (13), through shorter stays for encopresis and attention deficit disorder, to longer ones for eating disorders (principally anorexia nervosa) and somatoform disorders (principally conversion and psychogenic pain disorders). These points are illustrated in table 5 and figures 1A and 1B.

Duration of the disorder. In table 6 and figure 2 are shown the patterns of the duration of the disorders. Unfortunately, in about one-third of the cases, this information was missing. Nevertheless, it can be seen that the disorders are separable into a few with a history of less than a year's duration and a majority that seem to be chronic (always bearing in mind that these are inpatients and thus more likely to be chronically ill).

CONCLUSIONS

This study differs from previous ones in that it grafted a test of reliability onto an ongoing clinical program without distorting usual clinical procedures in any way. The result has both the strength of naturalness and the liability of error through deficient, prejudged, or

TABLE 5. Descriptive Indices

	Age		Number of Sibs		Sex Ratio,	Family Situation,	%	%	Length of Stay (Median Range)	
	Mean	S.D.	<1	>2	% Male	% Intact	Adopted**	Maori**	Weeks	Days
Anxiety (child) N=21	*11.4	1.8	8	12	*94	*70	15	5	*3.3	1–187
Anxiety (adult) N=7	12.7	1.8	2	5	29	71	14	0	5	10–85
Encopresis N=33	*7.7	2.4	13	19	*76	*51.5	3	25	*3	1–106
Enuresis N=8	10.3	3.4	0	7	88	57	0	28.6	1	2–14
Oppositional N=15	9.8	3.1	6	8	*33	43	7	13	*4	1–199
Conduct N=23	10.5	2.7	8	14	*61	30.4	4	17.4	*3	1–114
Oppositional/conduct N=44	*10.5	3.0	16	26	52	*35.7	7	16	3.4	1–199
Somatoform N=6	12.8	2.0	3	3	50	50	33	0	5	5–125
Schizophrenic/ psychotic N=9	*13.3	2.7	5	4	56	77.7	11	44	5.2	2–80
Eating N=4	11.0	3.3	1	3	0	75	0	0	10.5	11–248
Attention deficit N=10	*6.4	1.3	6	4	80	60	0	0	3.25	5–43
	$F = 18.9$ df = 4, 106 $p < 0.001$		$X^2 = 49.28$ df = 4 $p < 0.001$		$X^2 = 14$ df = 3 $p < 0.005$	$X^2 = 0.14$ df = 2 n.s.			$X^2 = 8.83$ df = 3 $p < 0.005$	

*Used in analyses.
**Numbers too small for analysis.

FIGURE 1A. Time Spent in Hospital by Diagnosis

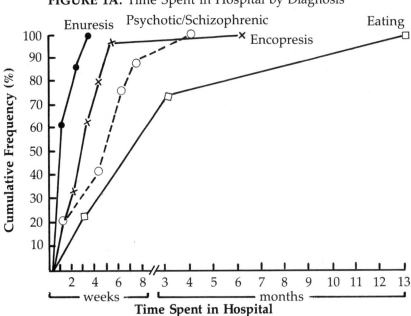

contaminated data, the latter because of unwittingly given clues and mutual shaping of diagnostic concepts by close professional association in the clinical situation. The study does, however, shed some light, we hope, on how DSM-III might work in the hands of the average clinician in the average clinic.

As in most other relevant studies, DSM-III as a whole proved reliable for major categories. But a large amount of "noise" has been added to the system by a relatively few categories, principally oppositional and adjustment disorders and "no mental disorder." The last suggests that DSM-III might do well to provide a general definition of "no mental disorder," though Strober and co-workers (7) apparently experienced no difficulty with this, and indeed used "no mental disorder" in 14% of their cases. Insofar as oppositional disorder is concerned, it seems that better reliability is produced when it is treated as a conduct disorder rather than a separate category.

Some studies have fared a little better and others a little worse, but the overall level of agreement on diagnoses is rather similar—around

FIGURE 1B. Time in Hospital by Diagnosis

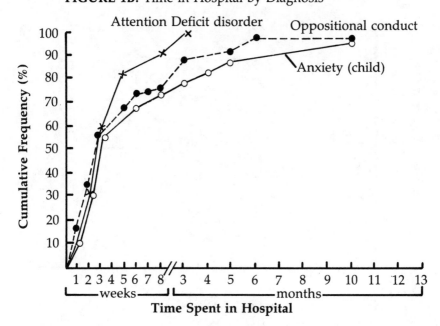

TABLE 6. Duration of Problem before Admission

	Percent of Patients				
Disorder	<3 Months	<1 Yr	5 Yrs	> 5 Yrs	N
Total	10	21	39	30	132
Psychotic/Schizophrenic	33	43	14	0	07
Conduct	20	05	43	33	21
Oppositional	7	21	43	29	14
Separation anxiety	20	47	27	07	15
Somatoform	33	50	0	17	06
Eating	0	25	0	75	04
Adult anxiety	0	43	43	14	07
Encopresis	0	13	44	44	32
Enuresis	0	0	43	57	07
Attention deficit	0	0	50	50	10
Overanxious	0	0	67	33	03

Note: Unknown (N = 8) excluded from analysis.

FIGURE 2. Duration of Disorder before Admission

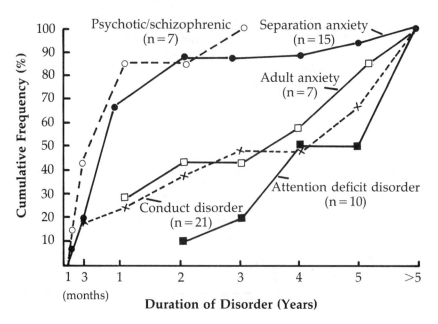

the kappa 0.70 level. There is also variation across studies in the reliability of particular categories, but these are not substantial except in one or two instances peculiar to each study. The present study also shows that, in contrast to DSM-II (8), with DSM-III clinicians are prepared to use a wide range of diagnostic categories.

Although the major categories appear robust, and could well be "tidied up" with but a little effort, our study suggests that many subcategories have serious reliability problems, as gloomily predicted by Quay (2) and Rutter and Shaffer (9). If other studies confirm our findings in this regard, in order to justify the continued existence of subcategories, a great deal of work will need to be done, in the area of the diagnostic criteria themselves and/or in the data-collection process, at least in child psychiatry. The superior results achieved by Strober and co-workers (7) for the major categories suggest that structuring the interview to cover the full range of information required by DSM-III improves reliability. However, to persuade child psychiatrists to abandon their usual practice of the informal interview in history taking and examination for a structured, comprehensive, time-consuming interview is likely to be a difficult proposition—unless critically needed validity studies can show that such standardized diagnostic procedures in child psychiatry greatly improve understanding and management.

Studies of reliability and validity of diagnosis are difficult, often intrusive, and in many ways threatening; but if child psychiatry insists on having official diagnostic systems like DSM-III and ICD-9, such systems must be vindicated, not simply adulated or vilified.

REFERENCES

1. Achenbach TM: DSM-III in light of empirical research on the classification of child psychopathology. J Am Acad Child Psychiatry 19:395–412, 1980
2. Quay HC: Classification, in Psychopathological Disorders of Childhood, 2nd ed. Edited by Quay HC, Werry JS. New York, Wiley, 1979
3. American Psychiatric Association: Diagnostic and Statistical Manual, 3rd ed. Washington, DC, American Psychiatric Association, 1980
4. Cantwell DP, Russell AT, Mattison R, et al: A comparison of DSM-II and DSM-III in the diagnosis of childhood psychiatric disorders. I. Agreement with expected diagnosis. Arch Gen Psychiatry 36:1208–1213, 1979
5. Cantwell DP, Mattison R, Russell AT, et al: A comparison of DSM-II and DSM-III in the diagnosis of childhood psychiatric disorders. IV. Difficulties in use, global comparisons and conclusions. Arch Gen Psychiatry 36:1227–1228, 1979
6. Spitzer RL, Forman JBW, Nee J: DSM-III field trials: I. Initial interrater diagnostic reliability. Am J Psychiatry 136:815–820, 1979
7. Strober M, Green J, Carlson G: The reliability of psychiatric diagnosis in hospitalized adolescents: interrater agreement using the DSM-III. Arch Gen Psychiatry 38:141–145, 1981
8. Cerreto MC, Tuma JM: Distribution of DSM-II diagnoses in a child psychiatric setting. J Abnorm Child Psychol 5:147–156, 1977
9. Rutter M, Shaffer D: DSM-III: A step forward or back in terms of the classification of child psychiatric disorders? J Am Acad Child Psychiatry 19:371–394, 1980
10. Fleiss JL, Cusick J: The reliability of dichotomous judgments: unequal numbers of judges per subject. Applied Psychological Measurement 3:537–542, 1979
11. Graham PJ: Epidemiological studies, in Psychopathological Disorders of Childhood, 2nd ed. Edited by Quay HC, Werry JS. New York, Wiley, 1979
12. Schlesinger G: The New Zealand family: present trends. J Comparative Family Studies 10:455–459, 1979
13. Foxx RM, Azrin NH: Dry pants: a rapid method of toilet training in children. Behav Res Ther 11:435–442, 1973

22

A COMPARISON OF DSM-III AND ICD-8/ICD-9 DIAGNOSES OF FUNCTIONAL PSYCHIATRIC DISORDERS IN HOSPITALIZED PATIENTS

Alv A. Dahl, M.D.

Evaluation of DSM-III includes comparing it with other systems of psychiatric classification in current use. In the Scandinavian countries, except Iceland, the eighth revision of the International Classification of Diseases (ICD-8) has been the official classification for mental disorders since 1969. Although the ninth revision (ICD-9) is almost identical with the eighth in terms of the main functional disorders (1), it has been officially approve only in Iceland.

In this paper, Norwegian ICD-8 diagnoses are compared with the DSM-III diagnoses of a sample of adult, hospitalized, mental patients with various functional disorders. This comparison gives an indication of the agreement between these two diagnostic systems in clinical practice.

MATERIAL AND METHOD

The sample was drawn from among all the patients between 18 and 40 years of age admitted to the University Psychiatric Clinic (Psykiatrisk klinikk) and the University Psychiatric Hospital (Gaustad sykehus) in Oslo during one year. The following categories were excluded: patients with organic cerebral disorders, patients who had spent more than 10% of their lives in mental institutions, and patients admitted to the

Address correspondence to: Alv A. Dahl, M.D., Lecturer in Psychiatry, Institute for Psychiatry, Gaustad Hospital, University of Oslo, Oslo, Norway emergency service as drug abusers. Twenty-two patients declined to take part in the study, which left a sample of 231 patients.

The patients were given two different diagnoses, a research diagnosis and a hospital diagnosis, that were completely independent of each other.

Research Diagnosis

All the patients had two extensive interviews with a research clinician during the second week after admission. Psychopathology was evaluated according to the Schedule for Affective Disorders and Schizophrenia (SADS) (2) and the Schedule for Interviewing Borderlines (SIB) (3). The interviewer also read the case record, since tentative diagnoses had not been made up to that time. The psychopathological data led to diagnoses according to the Research Diagnostic Criteria (RDC) (4), and these diagnoses plus the psychopathological data were used to make DSM-III axis I and axis II diagnoses (5).

Hospital Diagnosis

The hospital diagnoses were established at discharge on the basis of all the information collected about the patients. Clinical workup, but no special diagnostic instruments, was used. The doctor or psychologist in charge of the patient presented the case to the psychiatrist-in-chief, and they agreed upon an ICD-8 diagnosis.

Reliability Test

Ten percent of the interviews, all audiotaped, were picked out at random for a test of reliability of the research clinician. Seven experienced psychiatrists evaluated three cases each, following a seminar on theory and common evaluation of two cases. The research clinician's diagnoses were confirmed in 22 of the 23 cases (96%—6 cases of agreement, or 26%, could have been expected by chance).

RESULTS AND DISCUSSION

The findings with regard to axis I diagnoses are summarized in table 1, and to personality disorders (axis II), in table 2. With due consideration of the limits set by the methodology, the following conclusions seem reasonable.

The agreement on substance use disorders is high (84%) in the two systems and indicates that the DSM-III concept of substance use disorder is close to the Norwegian ICD-8 concept.

The findings concerning schizophrenia reveal that the old gap between the "broad" American and the "narrow" Scandinavian concepts of schizophrenia is considerably closed by DSM-III. It is remarkable that the concepts of bipolar and schizoaffective disorder are applied in virtually the same way to patients in both systems.

Many of the cases that would be diagnosed in DSM-III as schizophreniform disorder are covered by the Scandinavian concept of reactive psychoses, as predicted by Retterstøl and Dahl (see their paper in this collection).

Although DSM-III has omitted neurosis as a diagnostic class, the DSM-III descriptions of disorders that include the term *neurosis* in parentheses correspond closely to the Norwegian concept of neurosis (86% overlap), at least for hospitalized patients (see the Retterstøl and Dahl article).

The findings point to two classification problem areas: depression and personality disorders. The Norwegian classification of major depressive episodes is quite confusing. DSM-III has a spectrum approach to affective disorders and includes the findings of much recent research in that area. These results need to be included in a revised ICD classification of depression.

The findings also clearly reflect current inconsistencies in Norwegian attitudes toward the personality disorders. Symptom aspects, especially in terms of substance use, are used as bases for diagnoses much more than an evaluation of personality traits. The current interest in borderline disorders has given an impetus to rethinking concerning the Norwegian use of the term *personality disorder*, in which it has been nearly synonymous with the term *antisocial personality disorder* (301.7) (see the Retterstøl and Dahl paper).

CONCLUSION

There is some variation in the understanding of ICD-8 among the Scandinavian countries, so these results from Norway should not be generalized too broadly. There seems, however, to be good agreement between the current use of ICD-8 in Norway and DSM-III concerning such diagnoses as substance use, schizophrenia, and bipolar, schizoaffective, and "neurotic" disorders. The DSM-III classifications of personality disorders and major depressive episode are covered by various labels in ICD-8, just as the ICD-8 reactive psychoses are covered by various DSM-III labels. These, then, are the problem areas in comparing the classification of functional disorders in ICD-8/ICD-9 and DSM-III.

TABLE 1. DSM-III Axis I Diagnoses Compared with ICD-8 Hospital Diagnoses

DSM-III Diagnoses		ICD-8 Hospital Diagnoses		
Substance use disorder (Alcohol dependence)	24	303	Alcohol dependence	17
		301	Personalitas pathologica	5
		300.4	Depressive neurosis	1
		298.3	Acute paranoid reaction	1
Substance use disorder (Other substances)	50	304	Drug dependence	45
		298.1	Reactive excitation	3
		295	Schizophrenia	1
		301	Borderline personality	1
Schizophrenia	46	295	Schizophrenia	40
		298	Reactive psychoses	6
Schizophreniform disorder	12	295	Schizophrenia	7
		298	Reactive psychoses	5
Brief reactive psychosis	1	298.3	Acute paranoid reaction	1
Schizoaffective disorder	8	295.7	Schizoaffective psychosis	6
		298	Reactive psychoses	2
Atypical psychosis	2	298.3	Acute paranoid reaction	2
Major depressive episode	12	296.1	M-D psychosis, depressed	1
		298.0	Reactive depressive psychosis	4
		300.0	Anxiety neurosis	1
		300.4	Depressive neurosis	2
		301.1	Affective personality	1
		301	Borderline personality	1
		304	Drug dependence	1
		307	Transient situational disorder	1

DSM-III Diagnoses		**ICD-8 Hospital Diagnoses**		
Bipolar disorder	8	296	M-D psychosis, circular	8
Atypical bipolar disorder	4	295.3	Schizophrenia, paranoid	1
		298.3	Acute paranoid reaction	1
		300.4	Depressive neurosis	1
		301	Borderline personality	1
Cylcothymic disorder	4	300.4	Depressive neurosis	2
		301.1	Affective personality	1
		301	Borderline personality	1
Dysthymic disorder (Depressive neuroses)	18	300.1	Hysterical neurosis	1
		300.4	Depressive neurosis	11
		300.8	Character neurosis	3
		303	Alcohol dependence	3
Phobic disorders (Phobic neuroses)	3	300.0	Anxiety neurosis	2
		300.9	Neurosis	1
Anxiety states (anxiety neuroses) Generalized anxiety disorder	15	300.0	Anxiety neurosis	7
Panic disorder	0	300.1	Hysterical neurosis	2
		300.8	Character neurosis	2
		300.9	Neurosis	1
		301	Borderline personality	2
		304	Drug dependence	1
Somotoform disorders Somatization disorder	2	300.1	Hysterical neurosis	1
		300.2	Obses.-Compuls. neurosis	1

TABLE 2. DSM-III Axis II Diagnoses Compared with ICD-8 Hospital Diagnoses

DSM-III Diagnoses*		ICD-8 Hospital Diagnoses		
Paranoid personality		297	Paranoid psychosis	1
disorder	2	298.3	Acute paranoid episode	1
Schizoid personality		300.4	Depressive neurosis	1
disorder	5	301	Borderline personality	3
		304	Drug dependence	1
Schizotypal		295	Schizophrenia	3
personality disorder		298.3	Acute paranoid	
	39		reaction	3
		297	Paranoid psychosis	1
		300	Symptom neuroses	8
		300.8	Character neurosis	5
		301	Borderline personality	12
		303	Alcohol dependence	2
		304	Drug dependence	5
Histrionic personality		300	Symptom neuroses	4
disorder	35	300.8	Character neurosis	5
		301	Borderline personality	6
		303	Alcohol dependence	3
		304	Drug dependence	17
Narcissistic		301	Borderline personality	1
personality disorder	3	304	Drug dependence	2
Antisocial personality		301	Borderline personality	5
disorder	31	301.7	Antisocial personality	3
		303	Alcohol dependence	2
		304	Drug dependence	21
Borderline personality		295.7	Schizoaffective	
disorder	34		psychosis	1
		298.3	Acute paranoid	
			reaction	1
		300	Symptom neuroses	3
		300.8	Character neurosis	4
		301	Borderline personality	10
		303	Alcohol dependence	4

---

*Many patients have more than one personality disorder.

DSM-III Diagnoses		ICD-8 Hospital Diagnoses		
		304	Drug dependence	10
		306.5	Anorexia nervosa	1
Avoidant personality		295.7	Schizoaffective	
disorder	14		psychosis	1
		300	Symptom neuroses	6
		301	Borderline personality	4
		303	Alcohol dependence	1
		304	Drug dependence	1
		306.5	Anorexia nervosa	1
Passive-aggressive		306.5	Anorexia nervosa	1
personality disorder	1			
Dependent		300.4	Depressive neurosis	1
personality disorder	3	300.8	Character neurosis	1
		303	Alcohol dependence	1
Compulsive		300.0	Anxiety neurosis	1
personality disorder	1			

REFERENCES

1. World Health Organization: Mental Disorders: Glossary and Guide to Their Classification in Accordance with the Ninth Revision of the International Classification of Diseases. Geneva, World Health Organization, 1978
2. Endicott J, Spitzer RL: A diagnostic interview: The Schedule for Affective Disorders and Schizophrenia. Arch Gen Psychiatry 35: 837–844, 1978
3. Baron M: Schedule for Interviewing Borderlines (SIB), 2nd ed. New York, New York State Psychiatric Institute, 1979
4. Spitzer RL, Endicott J, Robins E: Research Diagnostic Criteria (RDC) for a Selected Group of Functional Disorders, 3rd ed. New York, New York State Psychiatric Institute, 1978
5. Williams JBW, Spitzer RL: Research Diagnostic Criteria and DSM-III. An annotated comparison. Arch Gen Psychiatry 39: 1283–1289, 1982

23

COMPARISON OF ICD-9 AND DSM-III DIAGNOSES OF 71 PATIENTS FIRST PRESENTING WITH SEVERE MENTAL ILLNESS

Susan Gregory, M.B., Ch. B., M.R.C. Psych., M. Med. Sc.,
and John E. Cooper, B.A, B.M., F.R.C.P., F.R.C. Psych., D.P.M.
(London)

Diagnoses according to the ninth revision of the International Classification of Diseases (ICD-9) and DSM-III were compared for 71 patients being studied in Nottingham, England. These patients form part of a follow-up study (of a total of 99 patients) being conducted in collaboration with the Mental Health Division of the World Health Organization (WHO), Geneva, Switzerland.

The Nottingham University Department of Psychiatry is a field research station in the current WHO Collaborative Study on the Determinants of Outcome of Severe Mental Disorders, and in the process of this study has collected a group of 99 patients who are now in a two-year follow-up study. They comprise all those patients who are now in a two-year follow-up study. They comprise all those patients

Address correspondence to: Susan Gregory, M.B., Ch.B., Research Fellow, University Department of Psychiatry, The University of Nottingham, Mapperley Hospital, Porchester Road, Nottingham NG3 6AA, England

The patients reported on here are part of a group studied in Nottingham during the course of the World Health Organization Collaborative Study on the Determinants of Outcome of Severe Mental Disorders, coordinated by the Division of Mental Health, World Health Organization, Geneva (Director, Dr. Norman Sartorius; Project Coordinator, Dr. Asen Jablensky). We are grateful to the World Health Organization and to the project staff in Nottingham for their support and collaboration, which provided the diagnoses upon which this report is based. (The other ten collaborating centers are in Aarhus, Denmark; Agra, India; Cali, Colombia; Chandigahr, India; Hawaii, USA; Ibadan, Nigeria; Moscow, USSR; Nagasaki, Japan: Prague, Czechoslovakia; and Rochester, N.Y., USA.)

resident in the Nottingham catchment area (population approximately 400,000) who have had contact with the psychiatric services over a two-year period because of their first serious mental illness. They have been included in the study after passing through a two-stage, symptom-based, screening procedure designed to include all those patients who have, or might have, a psychotic illness that might warrant a diagnosis of schizophrenia, even on the basis of the most liberal criteria. This group of patients includes all those with obviously schizophrenic symptoms plus a number with affective psychoses who also have delusions and hallucinations of various kinds and a small group with few or no positive psychotic symptoms, but inexplicable behavior disturbance or social deterioration.

A short time after entry into the study, all the patients were given an ICD-9 diagnosis, following a review of all the information available about them. This diagnosis was in all cases made by at least two psychiatrists working on the project, and is therefore a consensus diagnosis. The patients were given a "main diagnosis," a "subsidiary diagnosis," and an "alternative diagnosis," as was thought appropriate. At the time of writing, the first 71 of this group of patients have now been given a diagnosis according to DSM-III criteria as well, and we shall here report on some of the differences and similarities between the ICD-9 project diagnoses and the DSM-III diagnoses.

The DSM-III diagnoses were made by two psychiatrists, the present writers, initially working independently. The information available was the same as that used for the ICD-9 diagnoses, that is, the hospital clinical case notes, together with the special documents prepared by the staff working on the WHO project. These latter consisted of a clinical narrative account of the patient at entry into the study (including personal history and development, present illness and behavior, and mental state), plus the special schedules designed for the study, covering mental state (Present State Examination), history, and social and family background. These schedules are largely in the form of precoded ratings. When the two diagnosticians had made independent diagnoses, an agreed consensus diagnosis was then arrived at after discussion. This consensus diagnosis, available at the time of writing for the first 71 patients in the study, is the one discussed in this paper. (A separate report will be prepared on the reliability of DSM-III diagnoses between the two diagnosticians.)

It must be emphasized that because of the nature of the study, only a narrow range of diagnoses is being considered here. Virtually all the patients have a main diagnosis of one of the psychotic categories, and a large majority of these were of schizophrenia or schizophrenia-related categories. Also, it should be borne in mind that the diagnosticians were aware of the ICD-9 diagnoses while they were looking through the information in order to prepare the DSM-III diagnoses; there was no practical way in which the ICD-9 diagnosis could be excluded from the records since it was present in both the study documents and in the hospital case notes. Moreover, the nature of the study made it inevitable that a diagnosis of schizophrenia, or a closely related diagnosis, would be expected in most of the patients.

Despite these limitations, the comparison between the two sets of diagnoses is of interest, because it represents a fairly searching and detailed use of the DSM-III and ICD-9 categories concerned. Also, the patients are of unusual interest in that they represent a virtually complete sample of people living in a defined catchment area who were experiencing their first serious mental illness.

EXPECTATION OF DIFFERENCES BETWEEN THE TWO SETS OF DIAGNOSES

The unusually complete set of clinical and social information available about the patients under study should make the diagnoses more reliable than is often the case in ordinary clinical work, but the information was not collected with DSM-III diagnoses specifically in mind. The differences between ICD-9 and DSM-III led us to expect that some differences between the two sets of diagnoses might be found.

Since the ICD-9 categories are less precisely defined and are therefore potentially more flexible than those in DSM-III, it seemed likely that apparently specific diagnoses according to ICD-9 might be given to some patients whose DSM-III diagnoses would be one of the seemingly less specific ones. An example of what is meant by "specific" versus "less specific" would be the attribution of "paranoid schizophrenia" to a patient according to ICD-9 compared with "schizophreniform disorder" or "paranoid disorder (paranoia)" according to DSM-III. We are aware that to use "specific" in this sense is to some extent a value judgment, derived from the hierarchical set of concepts that underlie the ICD-9. However, this type of approach to psychiatric diagnosis is probably shared by many English and European psychiatrists, so we use it quite openly in our comparison.

We also expected that more patients would be given alternative and subsidiary diagnoses in addition to their main diagnoses in the ICD-9 than in the DSM-III evaluations. It seemed that additional or alternative diagnoses that were a distinct possibility might well be identifiable by means of the general description given in ICD-9, but would not meet all the detailed criteria often needed for an equivalent DSM-III diagnosis.

We were interested in gaining experience in the application of the more detailed "operational definitions" in DSM-III so as to identify problems and advantages compared with the use of ICD-9.

AGREEMENT AND DISAGREEMENT AND LOSS OF SPECIFICITY

As expected from the nature of the study, there was a very high degree of agreement between the two sets of diagnoses; indeed, only one serious disagreement was recorded (see cell 5 in table 1), in a patient with a puerperal illness that began with affective symptoms, but changed rapidly to those of typical schizophrenia. It is likely that this disagreement was due more to the difficulty of exactly matching the sets of information used for the two diagnostic procedures, which were completed at different times (in the case of a patient whose clinical state changed rapidly day by day), than to a profound diagnostic disagreement based upon exactly the same data.

The most obvious form of disagreement found was combined with some loss of specificity in the implications of the diagnostic terms used, and was most obviously manifest in 18 patients in whom the ICD-9 diagnosis was one of the four-digit schizophrenic categories (usually 295.3—paranoid schizophrenia) and the DSM-III diagnosis was schizophreniform disorder. This difference was due entirely to the six-month duration criterion in the DSM-III category of schizophrenic disorder (see cell 3 in table 1).

This and other grades of disagreement are shown in table 1; for the sake of simplicity, only the main diagnosis is presented in this table.

The expectation of loss of specificity in terms in DSM-III was fulfilled in that, for example, of the 53 patients with an ICD-9 diagnosis of schizophrenia, 33 (cells 3, 4, and 5 in table 1) had a less specific diagnosis according to DSM-III criteria. The majority of these (18) were those already described, for whom the DSM-III term *schizophreniform disorder* had to be used because the symptoms were of less than six months' duration.

USE OF MAIN, ALTERNATIVE, AND SUBSIDIARY DIAGNOSES

Table 2 shows the number of patients who received various combinations of main, subsidiary, and alternative diagnoses in the two systems. This table deals only with the use of the different types of diagnoses and takes no account of agreements or disagreements between them.

Contrary to our expectations, the different types of diagnoses were used equally in the two systems in 53 of the 71 patients. In the remaining

TABLE 1. Agreement–Disagreement and Loss of Specificity: 71 Patients with Consensus

Diagnosis According to ICD-9 and DSM-III (Main Diagnosis Only)

3-Digit Diagnosis ICD-9	Comments on ICD-9 4-Digit Diagnosis	Number of Patients	Comments on DSM-III 4-Digit Diagnosis
Schizophrenia (295)	1. Specified subtype of hebephrenic (295.1), catatonic (295.2), or paranoid (295.3)	17	Complete agreement on specified subtype
	2. Specified subtype of hebephrenic, catatonic, or paranoid	4	Different specified subtype of disorganized, catatonic, or paranoid
	3. Specified subtype of hebephrenic, catatonic, or paranoid	18	Six-month criteria of schizophrenia not fulfilled; therefore, schizophreniform disorder (295.4)
	4. Specified subtype of hebephrenic, catatonic, or paranoid	2	Specified subtype of undifferentiated (295.9)
	5. Specified subtype of hebephrenic, catatonic, or paranoid	13	Not schizophrenia. Paranoid disorder (297); atypical psychosis (298.9); major depression, single episode (296.2)—1 case
Affective psychosis (296)	6. Specified subtype	10	Complete agreement
Other categories	7. Complete agreement	3	—
	8. Minor disagreement	2	—
	9. Minor disagreement and some loss of specificity Paranoid state (297.0)	1	Atypical psychosis (298.9)
	Acute paranoid reaction (298.3)	1	Brief reactive psychosis (298.8)
	Total	71	

18 patients there were equal numbers of patients who were assigned more or fewer categories according to the two systems.

SPECIFIC POINTS

Translation of Codes for Affective Psychoses from ICD-9 to DSM-III

At first sight there appears to be a discrepancy between the ICD-9 equivalent code numbers assigned to the DSM-III categories and the

TABLE 2. Main, Alternative, and Subsidiary Diagnoses—71 Patients

	Number of Patients	Patients Given Different ICD-9 and DSM-III Diagnoses		
		Main	Subsidiary	Alternative
No differences	19	ICD-9 DSM-III		
	7	ICD-9 DSM-III	ICD-9 DSM-III	
	2	ICD-9 DSM-III	ICD-9 DSM-III	ICD-9 DSM-III
	25	ICD-9 DSM-III		ICD-9 DSM-III
ICD-9 uses more categories	2	ICD-9 DSM-III	ICD-9	
	7	ICD-9 DSM-III		ICD-9
DSM-III uses more categories	3	ICD-9 DSM-III	DSM-III	
	6	ICD-9 DSM-III		DSM-III
Total	71			

same code numbers in the World Health Organization version of ICD-9. This is most noticeable with regard to the major affective disorders. For instance, DSM-III equates code 296.2. with "major depression, single episode," but ICD-9 specifies 296.2. for manic-depressive psychosis, circular type but currently manic, an illness that "appears in both manic and depressed forms."

This problem arises because the code numbers quoted in DSM-III are not the straightforward ICD-9 code, but those of ICD-9-CM, i.e., ICD-9, Clinical Modification, specially prepared for DSM-III by the American Psychiatric Association in 1979 because of dissatisfaction with the ICD-9 itself. This important and potentially confusing point is given little prominence in the DSM-III text; it is mentioned briefly on page 5 of the Introduction, and the differences between ICD-9 and ICD-9-CM are listed in Appendix D, page 446. The quick reference, pocket-size version of DSM-III diagnostic criteria contains no mention at all of these differences, and this is the version likely to be most widely used. A more prominent warning should be displayed in both the *Manual* and the *Quick Reference*, pointing out that the code numbers are not necessarily the same as in the ICD-9 itself. Surprisingly, only 15 of a total of about 250 ICD-9 4-digit codes have been given a different meaning in ICD-9-CM (10 under 296—affective psychoses; 5 under 312—disturbance of conduct not elsewhere classified). It is not clear to the outsider why such an elaborate solution was chosen to deal with such a small number of differences of opinion.

Schizophrenic Disorders

We felt uncomfortable using the criteria of age, duration of symptoms, and social disability as essentials of the diagnosis of schizophrenia. We feel obliged to point out that the presence of these criteria are bound to cause some difficulties in the acceptance of DSM-III among a number of European psychiatrists. For instance, we had 2 men in the study only a year or so over the DSM-III age limit of 45 years who were, in all other respects, typical schizophrenic patients, and it was frustrating to have to give them a diagnosis of "atypical psychosis." In both these patients, adequate information was available, and there was no suggestion of prodromal states preceding the more obvious onset of typical symptoms.

Some other terms in the criteria for schizophrenia are particularly difficult to apply, such as "bizarre" and several of the terms in criteria A6 concerning incoherence and thought disorder. The word *bizarre* is notoriously difficult to define, yet in the DSM-III system the diagnosis of schizophrenia may rest upon the evaluator's judgment on whether a particular delusion is bizarre or not, without any further specification or guidance. Criterion F needs further specification in that the phrase "not due to" can give rise to problems. In a number of patients, organic mental disorder or mental retardation may also be present during the course of the schizophrenic illness, but psychiatrists are likely to disagree on whether in these cases the schizophrenia is due to the initial condition or simply conclude that the two conditions are coexistent.

Paranoid Disorders

In criterion E, the diagnosis may rest upon what is judged to be a "prominent" hallucination. This proved to be a difficult judgment to make in several patients.

Schizoaffective Disorder

The category "schizoaffective disorder" is not defined in any specific way. This causes problems, because patients in whom schizophrenic and affective symptoms are approximately evenly balanced are quite common, forming between 5% and 10% of cases in some large surveys. The concept of schizoaffective disorders has always been problematic, and we thought attempts should be made to be more specific in view of the frequency of this category and the well-defined nature of most other categories.

Atypical Psychosis

The category "atypical psychosis" has its uses, but it seemed to us that two very different types of patients might come to rest in this category if DSM-III were applied to larger and more heterogeneous groups of patients. One group of patients might have atypical or poorly described symptoms for which such a vague term would be appropriate, but they might be joined by a few patients who, though they had very typical symptoms of schizophrenia, because of their age could not be put in the schizophrenic disorder category.

Major Affective Disorders

The ten patients diagnosed as having major affective disorders presented no difficulties in terms of agreement between DSM-III and ICD-9 except in relation to the coding problems already noted.

Cyclothymic Disorder and Personality Disorder

The categories "cyclothymic disorder" and "personality disorder" were used very infrequently in our study, but we were left with a very strong impression that we would be unlikely to be able to make many diagnoses in these categories unless the information for the study had been collected using schedules specifically designed for use with the DSM-III system.

OTHER AXES

Our patients were also assigned codes on axis IV (psychosocial stresses) and axis V, (highest level of adaptive functioning in the past year). It is immediately evident, when one tries to use these axes, that they are still in a very elementary stage of development. Their present form is one of crude rating scales with very little specification of the categories and their code numbers. During the discussions of reliability, a comparison of differences in the codes on these axes assigned to the patients by the two raters showed that many more instructions and examples of the different code levels for both these axes will be necessary before they can be used to convey a great deal of information.

CONCLUSIONS

Although this study of the comparison between the two diagnostic systems is not yet complete, it clearly indicates that application of DSM-III's specific criteria to information not collected with the DSM-III in mind presents some disadvantages and problems. Even when an unusually large amount of information is available about patients, a significant proportion of the diagnoses tend to be rather disappointingly nonspecific compared with those made according to ICD-9.

In research projects, this problem might be minimized, or even abolished, through use of schedules keyed to the final diagnostic system from the beginning of data collection. When DSM-III criteria are applied to ordinary clinical information, however, many similar problems will arise, and clinicians accustomed to the more flexible ICD-9 system may well feel frustrated.

Moreover, we found that the length and detail of the DSM-III system needed a considerable amount of familiarization before it could be used with any ease. It was not unusual to spend 20 minutes making a DSM-III diagnosis; in some respects, the more information was available, the longer the process took. It is difficult to see how DSM-III can be used satisfactorily in a busy clinical setting. There would doubtless be a temptation, in order to save time, to use less specific categories in preference to those set out in considerable detail.

24

FUTURE DIRECTIONS
IN RESEARCH
COMPARING DIAGNOSTIC
SYSTEMS

Ian F. Brockington, M.D., F.R.C.P., and John E. Helzer, M.D.

"Diagnosis" is placing patients in the appropriate disease class within a diagnostic system. Nosology is the art or science of drawing up such systems, searching for homogeneous groups of patients. While medicine as a whole has moved steadily toward classification by causes (microorganisms, enzyme defects), psychiatry must still, *faute de mieux*, classify by clinical phenomena (symptoms, course). The abstract concepts that result are universally recognized as unsatisfactory and preliminary, but clinical classification is a necessary stage, and should be pursued with rigor, in a search for better definitions and for concepts with objective utility in the prediction of outcome or response to treatment. Clear definitions, reliable criteria, homogeneity of patients within each class, and construct validity are the marks of a sound clinical classification, and require demonstration by empirical studies.

When there are rival classificatory systems, empirical studies should give rational grounds for choosing among them. The best way of comparing diagnostic systems is the "polydiagnostic method," in which the *same* series of patients is diagnosed according to several different sets of rules. In this way, reliability, the number of patients qualifying,

Address correspondence to: Ian F. Brockington, M.D., Professor of Psychiatry, University of Birmingham, Birmingham, B15 2TH, England

This work was supported in part by United States Public Health Service Grants AA-03852 and MH-33883 and the overlap of different concepts can be plainly seen. Validity, however, is even more important, and requires independent criteria.

NATIONAL DIAGNOSTIC TRADITIONS

The emergence of objective validating tests puts us in a position to take up the challenge presented by the diversity of national diagnostic traditions. Diagnostic systems have to some extent evolved independently, encapsulated by language barriers. Within each linguistic sphere of influence, the fertile intuition of generations of able clinicians and investigators, well versed in their own literature, has created a tradition that molds the thinking of local practitioners, but is poorly understood, even ridiculed, outside these boundaries. Thus, we have a disunity that has the potential for a more complex international synthesis.

The World Health Organization has attempted to draw these ideas into a single system acceptable to all, of which the ninth revision of the International Classification of Diseases (ICD-9) is the latest model; this is the best compromise of worldwide opinion, but has not been widely accepted. The United States does not subscribe to it, and has developed its own DSM-III, which can claim to be the most detailed diagnostic system yet devised for psychiatry. Although they are less formalized, DSM-III's European rivals also have a great deal to offer. British diagnostic ideas, have, through Sir Aubrey Lewis and the Institute of Psychiatry, had an influence on the International Classification of Diseases, and have been codified in Wing's "Catego" (1) diagnostic system. Scandinavian diagnostic ideas include the concepts of reactive and cycloid psychosis, and in Sweden a multidimensional classification has been developed. The French have interesting ideas on the classification of paranoid disorders, with what are known as *bouffées délirantes*, their separation of chronic delusional states from schizophrenia, and the subdivision, by delusional mechanism, of the delusional psychoses into hallucinatory, interpretive, emotional, and imaginative subtypes. Nosology could make progress by thoroughly comparing these diagnostic systems.

One method of comparing the diagnostic systems of different countries has been undertaken by the Task Force on Assessment Instruments, which is a component of the International Program on Diagnosis and Classification of Alcoholism, Drug Abuse, and Mental Disorders. This is a joint project of the World Health Organization and the U.S. Alcohol, Drug Abuse, and Mental Health Administration (ADAMHA). One of the efforts of the task force has been to combine the British Present State Examination, by Wing and colleagues (1), with the Diagnostic Interview Schedule (DIS) devised by Robins and colleagues (2). The latter is a structured interview designed for a multicenter general population prevalence and incidence study being done in the United States. The DIS enables physician or nonphysician examiners to gather the clinical data necessary to make diagnoses according to any of three systems—DSM-III, the Feighner criteria (3), or the Research Diagnostic Criteria (RDC) (4). The combined interview instrument is called the Composite International Diagnostic Interview (CIDI), which aims to provide a single instrument that can be used by lay or clinician examiners to make diagnoses according to DSM-III or ICD as codified in Catego. This effort has served as a springboard for discussions, by the task force's multinational representatives, of how to incorporate in the various instruments diagnostic concepts unique to their own countries and components of these regional diagnoses that overlap with more widely recognized disorders and those that are unique.

Another approach involves a more extensive application of the polydiagnostic method. Attempts to communicate across national boundaries can be, and have been, made through the literature and by discussion among representatives of different countries, describing typical case histories and drawing up diagnostic criteria. But the polydiagnostic approach, in which all the diagnostic ideas are applied by experts to the same cohort of patients, is a more direct and powerful way of exploring the overlap among these ideas and, if validating criteria are also applied, of choosing among them. As Shapiro and Strömgren (5) have pointed out, the cumulative impact of research is less than it should be because clinicians in different countries do not comprehend the diagnostic system used and therefore cannot interpret new findings. An international diagnostic exercise of this kind would greatly improve cross-national understanding of each other's systems, and would probably result in an improved system that took ideas from several national traditions and was more widely acceptable than any of those in use at the present time.

EMPIRICAL STUDIES OF DSM-III

Perhaps the first attempt to compare the validity of rival definitions by the polydiagnostic method was that of Hawk, Carpenter, and Strauss (6), who compared Langfeldt's and Schneider's methods of diagnosing schizophrenia with their own 12-point system using outcome as the external criterion. Later, Brockington, Kendell, and Leff (7) compared ten definitions and found that four of them (RDC, Langfeldt's, Carpenter's, and Catego) were superior in outcome prediction. These studies were all done before DSM-III was introduced, and there has not been much time to evaluate this new system; however, several analyses have already been made, comparing DSM-III definitions of schizophrenia, depression, and mania with other systems.

In an analysis of follow-up data from the US/UK Diagnostic Project, DSM-III schizophrenia was found to be more restrictive than RDC and Catego, only 19 patients qualifying, compared with 28 and 52, respectively under the latter systems (8). Curiously, Feighner criteria selected almost exactly the same patients as DSM-III, although the psychopathological requirements for the two are substantially different, only the six months' duration of illness being shared. DSM-III schizophrenia and schizophreniform disorder, which share psychopathological criteria and differ only in duration, have totally different outcomes (table 1). All but 4 of the 28 RDC-defined schizophrenics also met the Catego criteria. Those defined by Catego who met the RDC definition had a worse outcome than those who were RDC negative (table 2). However, DSM-III-defined schizophrenics had a significantly poorer outcome than even the RDC cases (table 3).

Using the same series of 125 patients from the US/UK Diagnostic Project, followed for 6.5 years, an outcome study of depression (9) demonstrated the utility of the DSM-III distinction between nonpsychotic, mood-congruent psychotic, and mood-incongruent psychotic depression. Large numbers of significant differences were found, in spite of the small number of patients (45, 11, and 14) in the 3 groups. The mood-congruent psychotic patients differed from the nonpsychotic in the greater frequency of depressed, manic, and schizoaffective episodes during the follow-up period. The mood-incongruent psychotic group (which corresponded closely to RDC schizoaffective depression) had schizophrenic symptoms during the follow-up period, and were often given a final diagnosis of schizophrenia by British psychiatrists,

TABLE 1. Comparison of DSM-III Schizophrenia and Schizophreniform Disorder

	Schizophrenia	Schizophreniform disorder	p
Number of patients	19	7	
Outcome criterion			
Manic scale	3.4	13.0	0.04
Time in hospital	46%	12%	0.02
Social status score*	54	34	0.03
Outcome regression score*	2.53	1.46	0.02

*A high score indicates poor outcome; on both these scales the schizophreniform patients have scores better than the average for psychotic patients.

TABLE 2. Comparison of Catego Schizophrenics Who Met RDC and Those Who Did Not

	RDC+	RDC−	p
Number of patients	24	28	
Outcome criterion			
Delusions of control	8	1	0.01
Passivity scale	20.7	5.3	0.02
Delusions scale	37.2	22.1	0.03
Psychopathology discriminant score*	−0.16	+0.68	0.02
Final diagnosis of schizophrenia	21	16	0.04
Final diagnosis of affective psychosis	1	9	0.03

*A positive score indicates an excess of affective symptoms; a negative score, an excess of schizophrenic symptoms.

TABLE 3. Comparison of RDC Schizophrenics Meeting DSM-III Criteria with Those Who Do Not

	DSM-III+	DSM-III−	p
Number of patients	18	10	
Outcome criterion			
Manic scale	3.6	13.2	0.05
Defect symptoms	23.6	10.3	0.20
Time in hospital	48.1%	10.8%	0.003
Social status	53.1	33.0	0.009

though their general outcome was much better than is usually the case in DSM-III schizophrenia. When the mood-congruent and mood-incongruent groups were compared, the former had more manic symptoms; 6 of 11 were given a final diagnosis of bipolar psychosis, a diagnosis made in only 1 of 14 mood-incongruent patients.

A study of mania (10) showed that the RDC distinction between mania and schizoaffective mania was useful in predicting the pattern of symptoms during the follow-up period, schizoaffective patients (N = 19) having a marked predominance of schizophrenic symptoms, and manics (N = 20), a similar excess of affective symptoms (p = <.0005). No clear difference in general outcome emerged; the schizoaffective patients had a significantly poorer social adjustment, but spent less time in the hospital. DSM-III had no advantage over the RDC because there were no significant differences between mood-congruent and mood-incongruent psychotic mania.

These three studies were all in the area of psychosis. Work has also begun on comparative evaluation of DSM-III criteria in the areas of alcoholism (11) and drug abuse (12).

THE METHODOLOGY OF OUTCOME STUDIES

The above-described studies are only the very beginning of the evaluation of DSM-III and its comparison with other systems. There is a need to improve the methodology of longitudinal clinical studies. Much recent work has been based on either the US/UK Diagnostic Project or the International Pilot Study of Schizophrenia (6). The patients were not first admissions, and were not taken from a defined population; extensive clinical data were obtained for only the index admission, and there was no detailed assessment at the time of discharge from the hospital. Future studies should start with the first episode, so that premorbid personality and adjustment and the setting of the illness in relation to life events and difficulties can be assessed with less interference from secondary effects.

There is a need for a collaborative effort to generate more reliable, sensitive, and comprehensive outcome measures and diagnostic criteria based on the lifetime course of the illness (rather than the clinical picture of episodes). Much better data on the course of illness and symptoms of subsequent episodes are required, based on "follow through" strategies, in which each episode is documented so that the consistency of the clinical picture in successive episodes can be observed. The present strategy of studying only one "index" episode and reconstructing the course from hospital case records and a retrospective follow-up interview leaves too much uncertainty. The consistency of symptoms from one episode to another is important in assessing diagnostic concepts, but has scarcely been studied so far.

OTHER VALIDATING CRITERIA

Outcome prediction is only one of a number of validating criteria, and a complete evaluation would employ several others. One of these is *heritability*. This is based on the principle that inherited diseases breed true. Thus, we are searching for definitions of mental illness that will yield the same diagnosis when first-degree relatives suffer from similar illnesses. Turning the argument round, we can use the range of clinical features found in closely related patients (e.g., monozygotic twins) to develop more accurate definitions. The mere finding of heritability is not enough, since several mental illnesses have a pronounced familial tendency. A definition of schizophrenia that merely selected patients with high rates of familial mental illness would not necessarily thereby be validated, because an overinclusive definition that encompassed manic-depressive patients would have even higher rates. The validating principle is the *consistency* of diagnoses in family members.

Finding that illnesses do not breed true is equivalent, at one remove, to finding that episodes of illness experienced by a single patient are dissimilar. If many patients with DSM-III schizophrenia later develop typical manic episodes *or* are found to have relatives meeting DSM-III criteria for affective psychosis, there is obviously something amiss with the DSM-III categories. Occasional occurrences of this kind of dissimilarity can be tolerated, since even in an etiological classificatory system there are sporadic instances of persons with two disorders or other atypical cases. Nevertheless, the DSM-III diagnostic criteria aim at the delineation of unitary processes, and are shaken by heterogeneity in either the course of the illness or the inherited pattern of the disorder.

The clearest answer to the question of whether diseases breed true is to be found in studying the phenomena and course of an illness in pairs of homozygous twins. Since it takes years to build up twin series, the best strategy would be to take existing series, e.g., the Maudsley series or the National Academy of Sciences panel (13), and use them for a blind polydiagnostic study.

Treatment response is another possible validating strategy. Here we are searching for definitions that select patients with an identical treatment response, different from that of patients in other categories. If this could be done, it would be of great service to clinicians. Electroconvulsive therapy response could thus be used as a validating criterion for definitions of melancholia, and lithium for mania. The response of schizophrenia to neuroleptics is more problematic, since a broad spectrum of psychotic states responds to these drugs, and chronic schizophrenics respond incompletely, although they may require neuroleptic prophylaxis to remain in partial remission. As with follow-up and genetic studies, the tests can be applied only in a formal setting, in this case a double-blind, randomized, controlled, treatment trial. There is a case for taking data from completed trials, such as the nine hospitals collaborative study of phenothiazines (14), and applying a polydiagnostic approach.

We all hope and expect that these crude objective criteria (outcome, heritability, and treatment response) will soon be superseded by tests that reflect or measure directly the biological faults responsible for the psychoses (*biological markers*). The most promising biological leads to date are enlargement of the ventricles and other signs of organic brain damage in chronic schizophrenia, the dexamethasone suppression test in depressive psychosis, and, possibly, increase in rapid eye movement (REM) sleep in the affective disorders. Again, the strategy is to apply the polydiagnostic method to large sets of patients concerning whom there are good data on these variables.

CLINICAL DATA REQUIRED FOR INTERNATIONAL STUDIES

Careful thought needs to be given to the data required for an international polydiagnostic comparison of classification systems. Such data are not at present available, because of limitations in past clinical techniques. Recent studies (e.g., the US/UK Diagnostic Project and the International Pilot Study of Schizophrenia) have relied on ratings made by experts using a glossary of psychopathology. This is not appropriate for an international comparison because concepts of psychopathology differ from one country to another, and the approach to diagnosis may be radically different. An American or British psychiatrist will want a full inventory of symptoms, together with an account of the patient's social functioning and the duration of the illness. A Frenchman will want to know a good deal about the content of delusional ideas and how they evolved. A Danish psychiatrist will emphasize the setting of the illness, and its relation to personality and events. A Swedish psychiatrist would want details of the variations in symptoms from day to day during an episode. No extant diagnostic interview provides all the data required, and new standards of data collection are required for the task.

Psychiatrists have, in recent times, somewhat overvalued the symptom-based, cross-sectional, structured interview as a source of clinical information. The development of these interviews is one of the achievements of the last 20 years, and they are still the best source of diagnostic data. They are not, however, adequate in themselves for obtaining a complete picture of an episode of mental illness (15). A body of information sufficient to allow nosologists from several countries to practice their art would include structured mental state and history interviews carried out with patients and their closest relatives, but they would also require a day-to-day account of the episode, reconstructed from repeated briefer interviews and nursing notes.

The greatest departure from current practice would be the replacement of numerical ratings by narrative data. It would not be justifiable to entrust raters from one country, however senior, with the task of identifying the phenomena of an illness. The diagnosticians themselves will want to do this, and will require an account of the symptoms in the patient's own words, and of the patient's behavior in the words of observers, with minimal use of professional jargon. Thus, to meet the needs of all, the data would have to be preserved in the form of a detailed, descriptive narrative. Incidentally, a narrative record has another advantage over numerical ratings—its versatility. Any rating system can be used with it, provided the language is understood. Conversion to ratings is, of course, necessary in order that the data can be analyzed statistically, but it should be carried out only at the final stage of reviewing all the accumulated data, and only by a team of the most experienced research workers.

A proposal for the kind of study suggested here is currently under consideration, with World Health Organization support. It would involve the collection of about 200 cases of first admissions for psychoses, based on a case register. The data would be collected by structured interviews, nursing observations, and videotaped interviews, and would be condensed into 5,000-word narrative summaries. The summaries would be diagnosed by pairs of experts in Britain, the USA, France, Denmark, and the USSR, with a sixth pair using Leonhardian concepts (including cycloid psychosis) (16). The prognostic validity of the disease concepts diagnosed would be assessed by a follow through study in which all subsequent admissions would be studied in a similar way.

Although much has been achieved, during the last 20 years, in improving psychiatric diagnosis, particularly by structured interviews and operational definitions, we should not rest on our laurels. We have barely started to evaluate the concepts we have. Profound divisions and misunderstandings exist among diagnosticians in different countries, and compared with the rest of medicine, our classificatory system is rudimentary.

REFERENCES

1. Wing JK, Cooper JE, Sartorius N: Measurement and Classification of Psychiatric Symptoms. London, Cambridge University Press, 1974
2. Robins LN, Helzer JE, Croughan J, et al: National Institute of Mental Health Diagnostic Interview Schedule: Its history, characteristics, and validity. Arch Gen Psychiatry 38: 381–389, 1981
3. Feighner JP, Robins E, Guze SB, et al: Diagnostic criteria for use in psychiatric research. Arch Gen Psychiatry 26:57–63, 1972
4. Spitzer RL, Endicott J, Robins E: Research Diagnostic Criteria: rationale and reliability. Arch Gen Psychiatry 35: 773–782, 1978
5. Shapiro RW, Strömgren E: The relevance of epidemiological method techniques and findings for biological psychiatry, in Handbook of Biological Psychiatry Part I. Edited by Van Praag HM. New York, Marcel Dekker, 1979, pp 135–161
6. Hawk AB, Carpenter WT, Strauss JS: Diagnostic criteria and five-year out-

come in schizophrenia: A report from the International Pilot Study of Schizophrenia. Arch Gen Psychiatry 32: 343–347, 1975

7. Brockington IF, Kendell RE, Leff JP: Definitions of schizophrenia: concordance and prediction of outcome. Psychol Med 8: 387–398, 1978

8. Helzer JE, Brockington IF, Kendell RE: Predictive validity of DSM-III and Feighner definitions of schizophrenia: A comparison with Research Diagnostic Criteria and CATEGO. Arch Gen Psychiatry 38: 791–797, 1981

9. Brockington IF, Helzer JE, Hillier VF, et al: Definitions of depression: concordance and prediction of outcome. Am J Psychiatry 139: 1022–1027, 1982

10. Brockington IF, Hillier VF, Francis AF, Helzer JE, et al: Definitions of mania: concordance and prediction of outcome. Am J Psychiatry (in press)

11. Mulford HA, Fitzgerald JL: On the validity of the Research Diagnostic Criteria, the Feighner criteria and the DSM-III for diagnosing alcoholics. J Nerv Ment Dis 169: 654–658, 1981

12. Rounsaville BJ, Rosenberger P, Wilber C, et al: A comparison of the SADS/RDC and the DSM-III. Diagnosing drug abusers. J Nerv Ment Dis 168: 90–97, 1980

13. Cohen SM, Allen MG, Pollin W, et al: Relationship of schizoaffective psychosis to manic depressive psychosis and schizophrenia. Findings in 15,909 veteran pairs. Arch Gen Psychiatry 26:539–546, 1972

14. Goldberg SC, Klerman GL, Cole JO: Changes in schizophrenic psychopathology and ward behavior as a function of phenothiazine treatment. Br J Psychiatry 111: 120–133, 1965

15. Brockington IF, Meltzer HY: Documenting an episode of psychotic illness: The need for multiple information sources, multiple raters and narrative. Schizophr Bull 8:485–492, 1982

16. Leonhard K: Die Aufteilung der Endogenen Psychosen. Berlin, Akademie Verlag, 1957

SECTION V

Conclusion

25

INTERNATIONAL PERSPECTIVES: SUMMARY AND COMMENTARY

Robert L. Spitzer, M.D., and Janet B. W. Williams, D.S.W.

The contributors to this book have raised a variety of important issues. Space (as well as, we imagine, the patience of our readers) does not allow us to comment on all of them, or to mention all of the contributors who commented on the issues that we have chosen to discuss. We shall attempt to summarize the views of the contributors as accurately as possible, and in cases in which we disagree with a criticism of DSM-III, we shall offer (as nondefensively as possible) an explanation for the approach taken by the group that developed DSM-III. Finally, in the many instances in which we agree with the identification of a particular problem, we shall offer our own thoughts about possible solutions or the research that might provide the data necessary for a solution.

It will take only a few words for us to express our agreement with a contributor; inevitably, we shall use far more words to explain our reasons for disagreeing. This seeming imbalance should not be seen as a lack of appreciation on our part of the extremely positive reaction to the major features of DSM-III expressed in the pages of this book by so many contributors. The reader should, of course, recognize that in all our comments we are speaking only for ourselves. We appreciate the opportunity to add our comments to those of our colleagues.

Address correspondence to: Robert L. Spitzer, M.D., Chief of Psychiatric Research, Biometrics Research Department, New York State Psychiatric Institute, 722 West 168th Street, New York, New York 10032, U.S.A.

DESCRIPTIVE APPROACH

A central feature of DSM-III is its descriptive approach. By this is meant, as noted in the introduction to DSM-III (page 7), an approach that is "atheoretical with regard to etiology or pathophysiological process except for those disorders for which this is well established and therefore included in the definition of the disorder." This approach was taken so that clinicians of varying theoretical orientations with regard to the etiology of mental disorders would be able to use the classification without compromising their own viewpoints. The widespread acceptance of DSM-III in the United States by clinicians of such disparate theoretical perspectives as psychoanalysis (1) and behavior therapy (2) indicates that this strategy, with some notable exceptions (3), has been successful.

By and large, the contributors have agreed that DSM-III's descriptive approach, or what Pichot, Guelfi, and Kroll have termed an "agnostic" approach, is one of its most valuable features. Engels, Ghadirian, and Dongier, however, noted a colleague's apparent lack of enthusiasm for this approach in his comment that "DSM-III is like a bikini—it shows you everything but the essentials." Pichot, Guelfi, and Kroll express ambivalence about DSM-III's many breaks with traditional nosologic concepts: "One may, following one's own orientations, either salute the courage that has necessitated total rejection of a tradition that has lasted more than a century, or well regret this iconoclastic zeal, which risks the loss of much of importance that has been gained."

In his chapter, Kendell joins others (4) in noting that despite DSM-III's claim to be atheoretical with regard to etiology, even some of the axis I nonorganic disorders are "contaminated" with etiological assumptions. He cites, as examples, adjustment disorder, brief reactive psychosis, and conversion disorder.

It is certainly true that the definitions of these disorders (and a few others) do contain etiologic assumptions. We should argue, however, that it is precisely these few nonorganic axis I disorders for which it is "well established" that a psychological factor is necessary (although perhaps not sufficient) for the development of the disorder. The developers of DSM-III, of course, reached their own consensus about which categories had "well-established" etiologies; our Scandinavian colleagues, Strömgren, and Retterstøl and Dahl, argue that there is convincing evidence for the etiologic role of psychological factors in a major grouping of psychotic disorders that they call reactive psychoses. They express disappointment that DSM-III has only a single category, brief reactive psychosis, for disorders that develop following psychosocial stress.

A comparison of the DSM-III concept of brief reactive psychosis and the Scandinavian concept of the reactive psychoses is useful. Brief reactive psychosis can be diagnosed only if the psychosocial stressor is so severe that it would "evoke significant symptoms of distress in almost anyone." In contrast, for reactive psychoses, according to Retterstøl and Dahl, the psychosocial stressor need not be objectively severe, so long as it is judged that "the psychosis would not have occurred in its absence" when evaluated against the background of the premorbid personality and the life situation of the person. Furthermore, the DSM-III category of brief reactive psychosis assumes a duration of less than two weeks, whereas the Scandinavian concept of a reactive psychosis is that although usually brief, it can last for months or longer.

We believe that no one doubts the role of psychological factors in the development of brief, florid psychoses associated with objectively severe psychosocial stress (the DSM-III category). However, the rarity with which psychiatrists outside Scandinavia use the diagnosis of reactive psychosis indicates that the etiological role of psychological factors in these conditions is controversial.

Ideally, we should know the etiology of all mental disorders: that would then be the basis for their classification. Unfortunately, we are a long way from that point, and the task for nosologists is to decide for which conditions there is sufficient evidence to include in the definition of the disorder the presumed etiology. We believe that the developers of DSM-III were conservative in their decisions about which categories to define etiologically. We also believe that they were wise in rejecting suggestions to be wholly descriptive in all their diagnoses of the nonorganic mental disorders by not adhering to this restrictive principle in dealing with such well-recognized categories as conversion disorder and adjustment disorder, categories that by definition contain etiologic assumptions.

THE MULTIAXIAL SYSTEM

All the contributors recognize the value of DSM-III's multiaxial system of evaluation. Strömgren notes that Skodol and Spitzer are incorrect in claiming that DSM-III is the first official classification system of mental disorders to include a multiaxial system (5): the 1952 Danish classification of mental disorders was biaxial, with separate axes for symptoms and etiology. This biaxial system was not abandoned until 1965, when ICD-8 was adopted.

Both Pichot, Guelfi, and Kroll and Kendell question the basis for the distinction between the mental disorders coded on axis I and those on axis II. Kendell notes that the DSM-III explanation for this distinction, that the axis II disorders tend to be overlooked when attention is paid to the usually more florid axis I conditions, is conceptually weak. He argues, and perhaps convincingly, that axis II should be redefined to include "all lifelong but stable handicaps," thus adding mental retardation, and perhaps pervasive developmental disorders, to personality disorders and specific developmental disorders—now the only disorders noted on axis II.

Many contributors comment on problems in the use of axes III, IV, and V and point to the need for their further development and operationalization. Kendell is perhaps the most critical of axes IV and V, stating that "if they were seriously intended to provide useful information either about individual patients or about patient populations, they are a failure. . . . It is difficult to believe that either will survive into DSM-IV without radical alteration."

Roth notes ambiguities in the use of axis III, questioning the limits of what should be recorded, e.g., how recently a serious illness must have occurred in order to be recorded on axis III. At the present time, it seems to us, it is hard to know the best temporal limits to recommend. We believe, however, that the clinical utility of axis III would be enhanced by including a convention that directed the clinician to note, perhaps in parentheses after the appropriate axis III physical condition, whether that condition had etiologic significance for the axis I or II mental disorder. For example,

Axis I: Dementia

Axis III: Metastatic carcinoma (etiologic).

Two major problems with axis IV are noted. Kendell points out, we believe correctly, that the DSM-III axis IV scale assumes that the most important distinction among stressful events is their degree of severity when, in fact, a great deal of research has indicated that chronic stresses, even when mild, contribute more to the development of mental disturbance than acute stresses (6). In the inevitable revision of axis IV, we should anticipate that there will be a way to note the chronicity of the stressors.

Roth criticizes the axis IV reference to how stressful the hypothetical "average" person would find the stressor and instead suggests that the "contextual measure of threat" Brown employed in his research studies would be more useful. We suspect that Roth has overlooked the statement in DSM-III that the axis IV rating should be based on "the clinician's assessment of the stress an 'average' person in similar circumstances and with similar sociocultural values would experience from the particular psychosocial stressor(s)." By this statement, which is frequently overlooked, DSM-III does attempt to take into account the context, that is, the life circumstances, in which the stress occurred. There are doubtless more refined ways of evaluating stress by examining contextual issues. The problem is whether these refinements, which are clearly called for in research studies, would result in a rating procedure for axis IV that would be too complicated for routine clinical use.

Both Kendell and Roth question the utility of axis V as a rating of the highest level of adaptive functioning during the past year. They note that this rating does not take into account the duration of the present episode. For example, a patient with a two-year depression is likely to receive a low rating yet may have a full recovery, with return to a high level of functioning. The inclusion of axis V was based on the assumption that despite its simplicity, it would have important prognostic value. We are aware of only one study* of the value of axis V. That study did show that axis V ratings were correlated with a clinical decision to hospitalize, but that ratings of the *current* level of functioning were even more highly correlated.

We acknowledge the serious limitations of axes IV and, to some extent, V, though we think Kendell may be unduly harsh in his overall assessment of their value. We suspect, however, that the generally favorable response of clinicians to axes IV and V is due more to a general conviction that systematically including psychosocial stress and level of adaptive functioning in a case formulation is clinically useful than to the actual way these axes are constructed. We agree with the contributors that further research is necessary to determine the most practical way to operationalize these concepts and that major revisions in axes IV and V can be expected in the future. We also agree with Roth's suggestion that a program of research needs to be undertaken to study the relevance of axes II, III, IV, and V to the various axis I clinical syndromes.

DIAGNOSTIC CRITERIA

The contributors seem generally to agree that a major advance in DSM-III is the inclusion of specified diagnostic criteria. According to Kendell,

> The great achievement of the developers of DSM-III was not just that they appreciated the advantages of operational definitions, but that they mustered the energy and the determination to produce suitable definitions for nearly all the 200 diagnostic categories in the glossary and to obtain the American Psychiatric Association's approval of them. . . . this was a formidable task and an impressive accomplishment.

Also music to our ears is Strömgren's remark that "The 'diagnostic

---

*JE Mezzich, KJ Evanczuk, RJ Mathias, et al: Admission decisions and multiaxial diagnosis. Presented at the Annual Meeting of the American Psychiatric Association, Toronto, Ont, Canada, May 15-21, 1982.

criteria', which are the backbone of DSM-III, are formulated—conceptually and typographically—with admirable clarity."

Several contributors, however, while acknowledging the value of the diagnostic criteria, express concern that they make DSM-III too complicated for routine purposes. On the other hand, with the exception of Gregory and Cooper's study comparing ICD-9 and DSM-III diagnoses, in none of the empirical studies reported in this book do the authors, after using DSM-III, anticipate that its complexity will pose a problem in its routine use in their country.

Retterstøl and Dahl and Pichot, Guelfi, and Kroll express dissatisfaction with the seemingly arbitrary number of symptoms required for many diagnoses. In addition, the latter note that a common criticism of French psychiatrists is that patients with different combinations of symptoms within a particular set of criteria will be given the same diagnosis, which will result in heterogeneous groups of patients.

It is quite true that there is no empirical basis for the number of symptoms required for the vast majority of DSM-III categories that utilize such an index. For example, the requirement that there should be four, not three or five, associated symptoms of depression for a diagnosis of a major depressive episode has no empirical basis. This requirement was set by clinicians who based their decision on extensive experience with depressed patients (7). Moreover, numerous studies have found these criteria useful for a variety of clinical research purposes. Until it has been demonstrated by further investigations that a different number of symptoms yields a more valid definition of this category, it seems reasonable to rely, as did DSM-III in this case and many others, on the most expert clinical judgment available. Regarding the issue of heterogeneity, we believe that for many diagnostic categories (including the example of a major depressive episode), patients with the same diagnosis (or even subtype) may in fact present somewhat different clinical pictures, and that it is therefore appropriate for the diagnostic criteria to allow for some symptom heterogeneity.

Roth, Retterstøl and Dahl, and others question the basis for assigning equal weight to all symptoms within a symptom index. It is quite true that clinical wisdom would suggest that of the eight symptoms included in the B criteria for major depressive episode, for example, some, such as insomnia, are quite diagnostically nonspecific, whereas others, such as psychomotor retardation, are far more diagnostically specific. Weights could have been assigned to individual items on the basis of clinical impressions of their relative diagnostic salience (there being no available empirical data), but this would have greatly increased the complexity of the diagnostic criteria and perhaps thus limited their clinical acceptability. We should agree, however, with Roth's suggestion that multivariate statistical analyses should be applied to data based on

DSM-III in order to determine the relative contributions of the individual items to a diagnosis. Such analyses might well lead to the elimination of items that contribute little to a diagnosis or, as Roth proposes, to the assignment of differential weights to the symptoms.

THE DSM-III CLASSIFICATION

All the contributors comment on various aspects of the DSM-III classification. We shall limit our remarks to several major nosologic issues that were touched on by a number of the contributors.

The Omission of Neurosis as a Diagnostic Class

A consequence of the descriptive approach to classification adopted in DSM-III was the omission of neurosis as a diagnostic class. The traditional subtypes of neurosis are distributed in diagnostic classes according to shared phenomenologic features. The omission of neurosis from DSM-III was extremely controversial in the United States and sparked a scientific and political controversy that was resolved only following a complicated process of compromise and negotiation.*

In four of the chapters the contributors praise DSM-III's omission of neurosis: ". . . words such as *neurosis* and *hysteria* had become so encrusted with multiple layers of meanings and trailed so many false assumptions in their wake that we are better off without them" (Kendell); ". . . Few terms are used in so many different ways, or with so many unclear and vague definitions, as *neurosis*" (Strömgren); DSM-III avoids "the confusion usually created by the different etiological connotations of this term" (Berner, Katschnig, and Lenz); ". . . the firmly entrenched 'theory' of neuroses has been discarded and replaced by more pragmatic and useful classification of these disorders" (Wig). In only two chapters do contributors object to the omission of neurosis, arguing that abandoning the psychoanalytic etiologic assumptions need not have prevented the use of the diagnostic class of neurosis, defined descriptively (Retterstøl and Dahl and López-Ibor and López-Ibor).

It is significant that no contributor argues for the retention of neurosis in the classification of mental disorders as an etiological concept. The only remaining disagreement, therefore, is about whether or not it is possible and useful to attempt to define neurosis descriptively and, in addition, to use it to define a diagnostic class. DSM-III does contain a descriptive definition of "neurotic disorder," but the DSM-III disorders that meet this definition are scattered throughout the classification. To

---

*R Bayer, RL Spitzer: Neurosis, psychodynamics, and DSM-III: a history of the controversy. Unpublished manuscript.

have grouped them together under a single diagnostic rubric, "Neurotic Disorders," would have required, as noted in the Introduction to DSM-III, separating some affective disorders from the other affective disorders, some psychosexual disorders from the other psychosexual disorders, and some dissociative disorders from other members of that class. The possible advantages of this approach seemed to be far outweighed by the disadvantage of fragmenting several diagnostic classes that shared essential symptomatic features.

Organic Mental Disorders

Several contributors note the problem of DSM-III's forcing the clinician to make a dichotomous judgment about whether an illness represents an organic or a nonorganic mental disorder. Roth and Cassano and Maggini note the difficulty of deciding when an organic factor has contributed to the development of an affective syndrome. Wig points out that in Third World countries it is common for the clinician to be faced with a patient with psychotic features who also has a fever or suffers from malnutrition; in such cases all that can be said is that an etiologic role of organic factors in the mental disturbance is strongly suggested.

We believe that a possible solution to these problems is to include in the classification a category for the clinician to use when he or she is unsure, but strongly suspects, the etiologic role of organic factors. This suggestion acknowledges the important fact that clinical reality is not faithfully expressed in classification systems based on the nosologic ideal of mutually exclusive diagnostic categories.

Affective Disorders

Hanada and Takahashi and Strömgren find the DSM-III category of major depressive episode too inclusive, although they do not indicate how they think it should be restricted. DSM-III recognizes that the category of major depressive episode is diagnostically heterogeneous. For that reason this category is further subdivided into the following subtypes: without melancholia, with melancholia, with psychotic features, and in remission. Admittedly, this subdivision is not entirely satisfactory, for many reasons, one being that the basic issue of whether depression should be conceptualized as a continuum with varying degrees of severity or as qualitatively different subtypes has not yet been resolved. Furthermore, recent genetic data do not provide any guidelines concerning the limits of the concept of major depressive episode or how it should be subdivided (8).* Future research, perhaps aided by the availability of biological markers, may shed light on this continuing controversy.

Retterstøl and Dahl note that in the Scandinavian tradition, affective disorders are regarded as psychoses, whereas DSM-III classifies as affective disorders relatively mild conditions, including disorders that traditionally are regarded as personality disorders (e.g., cyclothymic disorder) or neuroses (e.g., dysthymic disorder). Grouping all the disorders with prominent mood disturbance together as affective disorders was based on the heuristic assumption that this would facilitate research and effective treatment. In fact, recent research does indicate that cyclothymic disorder is best conceptualized as a mild form of bipolar disorder (9) rather than as a personality disorder. The issue of dysthymic disorder and its relationship to personality disorder requires further study, although it is known that dysthymic disorder is very frequently associated with major depression (10).

Schizophrenia

In the chapters from Scandinavia and France, the contributors noted that the DSM-III restricted concept of schizophrenia and its distinction from schizophreniform disorder bring American psychiatry closer to their own national traditions in defining the nonorganic psychoses. Wig also expresses approval of the DSM-III distinction between schizophrenia (a disorder with a minimum degree of chronicity) and acute psychoses, which are very common in Third World countries. On the other hand, both Kendell and Roth take serious exception to the inclusion of a six-month duration of illness in the DSM-III criteria for schizophrenia. According to Roth, "unresolved problems in diagnosis should be made explicit rather than dealt with by means of arbitrary dividing lines. . . . [The six-month duration criterion] assumes in advance what is in need of proof." And Kendell states that one of the "cardinal purposes of making a diagnosis is to determine treatment . . . and this can hardly be done effectively if the diagnosis has to be delayed for several months and until the outcome is largely determined."

Roth here suggests that the arbitrary six-month dividing line is "in need of proof" and therefore should not become part of the definition of schizophrenia. It was the judgment of the developers of DSM-III

---

*RMA Hirschfeld: The lack of familial evidence for a "biological" depression: data from the clinical studies of the National Institute of Mental Health's Clinical Research Branch collaborative program on the psychobiology of depression. Presented at the Annual meeting of the American College of Neuropsychopharmacology, San Juan, Puerto Rico, 1981.

that there was, even then, convincing evidence that the six-month duration of illness separated patients with a generally poor prognosis and with a familial loading for schizophrenia from those who had a generally good prognosis and no familial predisposition to schizophrenia (11–13). Since the publication of DSM-III, additional evidence has accumulated that further supports the validity of the six-month criterion (14–16). Therefore, this criterion cannot be considered strictly arbitrary, and in fact seems useful.

Kendell raises an issue of concern to others as well (17), namely, whether the six-month duration criterion is merely a tautology that expresses the obvious: chronicity predicts chronicity. Kendell himself, however, is a coauthor of a significant recent study that indicates that although six months of illness is an important component of the DSM-III definition of schizophrenia, it is hardly evidence of established chronicity since many patients who meet this criterion have relatively good long-term outcomes (15). Furthermore, the authors of the study argue that the DSM-III six-month duration criterion is more an indication of insidious onset than of established chronicity. Finally, they demonstrate that it is the combination of the required psychotic symptoms *and* the six-month duration criterion that predicts a generally poor outcome for the patient with schizophrenia; neither the psychotic symptoms nor the six-month duration alone presages a poor outcome. (Two other studies have found that the DSM-III definition of schizophrenia, compared with other definitions, has good predictive validity [14,16].) Regarding Kendell's point about delaying treatment, patients who fail to meet the six-month duration criterion requirement are not left without a diagnosis; they are most likely diagnosed as having schizophreniform disorder and, at least for the acute phase, would probably receive the same treatment: neuroleptics.

The DSM-III definition of schizophrenia requires that the onset of the illness, including prodromal features, occur before the age of 45. This was done to distinguish from schizophrenia illnesses that have similar presenting symptoms, but usually have a more benign course and less familial loading for schizophrenia. Such conditions have been referred to as paraphrenia or late onset schizophrenia. Both Kendell and Roth argue that this criterion, like the six-month duration one, is arbitrary and serves no useful purpose. As Kendell remarks, "what ought to be an empirical observation is thereby converted to an axiom, . . . [and] unless there is convincing evidence that such cases are fundamentally different," age should not be used as a criterion.

Clearly, if there are laboratory procedures that could validate a clinical diagnosis of schizophrenia (as the electrocardiogram and other laboratory tests do for myocardial infarction), there would be no need for age at onset to be used as a criterion. Unfortunately, we are a long way from that point. In the absence of such laboratory procedures, we are forced to define disorders, such as schizophrenia, solely by clinical features (symptoms, course, age at onset, etc.), hoping that our clinical definition maximizes the likelihood that we shall make the "correct" diagnosis. In the case of schizophrenia, the developers of DSM-III believed that defining schizophrenia by a symptom picture alone, as was done in DSM-I and -II, resulted in an extremely heterogeneous concept of the illness in terms of such validating features as long-term outcome and family history. They thought that a more homogeneous category would be defined if a maximum age at onset were incorporated in the diagnostic criteria. We are not aware of any studies done since the publication of DSM-III that test this assumption. We look forward to studies that will examine whether or not late-onset schizophrenia-like illnesses are "fundamentally different"—to use Kendell's phrase—as the developers of DSM-III assumed.

We should point out that most clinicians, even those who disagree with the DSM-III age requirement, do not refer to patients whose schizophrenia-like illness began after the age of 45 as having "schizophrenia." Instead, such patients are said to have "late-onset schizophrenia" or "paraphrenia." In other words, there is widespread agreement that a schizophrenia-like disorder beginning in late life should probably not be diagnosed the same as one beginning earlier in life. We do think it unfortunate, however, that the DSM-III system, as noted by Gregory and Cooper, throws this group of late-onset schizophrenia-like illnesses into the category of atypical psychosis, along with other, very different, clinical pictures. Perhaps in the revision of DSM-III, the ICD-9 category of "paraphrenia" can be added to the DSM-III classification for this group of patients.

Paranoid Disorders

The contributors are in agreement with an American critique (18) that the developers of DSM-III have mistakenly limited the concept of paranoid disorders to illnesses involving persecutory delusions or delusional jealousy. Traditionally, dating back to Kraepelin, all delusions of self-reference, such as hypochondriacal and grandiose delusions, are included in the concept of paranoia.

We offer no defense of the DSM-III approach: in this instance we believe the developers of DSM-III (including ourselves) goofed. Consideration can be given to correcting this situation in the revision of DSM-III.

Categories Not Included in the DSM-III Classification

As expected, many of the contributors describe clinical syndromes frequently seen in their countries that are not included in the DSM-III classification as separate categories. Examples of such syndromes include: *timopatia ansiosa* (López-Ibor and López-Ibor); *taijin-kyofu* (Honda); puerperal psychosis (Kendell, Honda); chronic hallucinatory psychosis (Cosyns, Ansseau, and Bobon); reactive psychosis (Strömgren; Retterstøl and Dahl; van Groos); hysterical psychosis, disintegration psychosis, and hospitalization syndrome (van Groos); *dhat* syndrome, amok, *latah, koro,* brain-fag syndrome, and possession syndromes (Wig).

A formidable but important task is to study these syndromes (perhaps by examining prototypical cases) and, first of all, to determine how such cases would be diagnosed in DSM-III. (The authors attempted to do this in the case of *taijin-kyofu* during a visit to Japan; it seemed that most cases would be classified according to DSM-III as atypical psychosis—but this is not entirely satisfactory.) It would then be necessary to review the literature on these syndromes, or actually conduct longitudinal studies, and decide whether a particular syndrome was a valid diagnostic category that should be included in some way in the revised DSM-III or in DSM-IV, perhaps in an appendix or as an example of a category included in the official classification.

DSM-III AND THIRD WORLD COUNTRIES

Wig points out several problems in the use of DSM-III in the developing countries of the Third World. First of all, Third World priorities make it necessary to use non-mental-health professionals for delivery of mental health care. Therefore, they need "a classification that is simple. . . . On the other hand [they] cannot isolate themselves from the rapid advances in psychiatric knowledge in the industrialized world. A balance has to be struck between these two partly contradictory needs." According to Wig, DSM-III contains "Complicated definitions and long lists of criteria . . . [that] are very difficult to remember and apply in the average busy outpatient psychiatric clinic of a developing country, with all its constraints of time, privacy, and frequent language problems."

The need for a simplified classification of mental disorders for use by nonprofessionals in developing countries has been recognized by the World Health Organization, and a model of such a classification has been developed (19).

EMPIRICAL STUDIES AND FUTURE DIRECTIONS FOR RESEARCH

The studies of the reliability of DSM-III that have been conducted in Australia, Japan, and New Zealand indicate that clinicians outside the United States have been able to attain the same degree of reliability using DSM-III as did U.S. clinicians during the DSM-III field trials (20). This demonstrates that the DSM-III classification is useful for research and clinical work in other countries despite differences in language and culture.

Dahl's study comparing the application ICD-8/ICD-9 and DSM-III to a group of hospitalized patients in Norway yielded good agreement between diagnoses for schizophrenia and for substance use, biopolar, schizoaffective, and "neurotic" disorders. There are major differences in the two systems' approaches to classifying personality disorders and major depression (DSM-III) and reactive psychoses (ICD-8).

Gregory and Cooper's study indicates that the application of DSM-III to information originally collected to make ICD-9 diagnoses is difficult since the specified criteria of DSM-III often require considerably more information. In contrast to the conclusions of the authors of the other empirical studies included in this book, Gregory and Cooper state, "we found that the length and detail of the DSM-III system needed a considerable amount of familiarization before it could be used with any ease. . . . It is difficult to see how DSM-III can be used satisfactorily in a busy clinical setting."

Brockington and Helzer discuss the value of a polydiagnostic approach in research (also noted by Berner, Katschnig, and Lenz in their chapter) in which the comparative validity of different diagnostic systems is assessed. They demonstrate that such studies offer a powerful technique for providing an empirical basis for revisions in the classification of mental disorders. Brockington and Helzer also consider the value of standardizing the procedures for obtaining the clinical data necessary to apply diagnostic criteria. Such standardized procedures have been developed specifically for collecting the information necessary to make DSM-III diagnoses. The National Institute of Mental Health Diagnostic Interview Schedule (NIMH-DIS) was developed by Robins and her associates at Washington University, in St. Louis, to enable lay interviewers to collect from subjects, in community epidemiologic surveys, the clinical data necessary for a computer program to make DSM-III diagnoses (21). Robins and her group have been joined by John Wing in England in developing an interview instrument that combines the NIMH-DIS and the Present State Examination (22) and can be used by lay interviewers.

We have started work on a new instrument for use by clinicians, called the Structured Clinical Interview for DSM-III (SCID) (23). Whereas the NIMH-DIS and its international sibling are highly structured so that they can be used by lay interviewers, the SCID is modeled on the clinical interview, and allows for greater flexibility and clinical judgment (24).

CONCLUSIONS

The developers of DSM-III tried, whenever possible, to rely on the results of empirical studies for making decisions about the classification. In this regard they were in a far more advantageous position than were the developers of DSM-I, in the 1950s, and DSM-II, in the 1960s.

Since the appearance of DSM-III there has been an explosion of diagnostic studies bearing on the DSM-III classification, as the bibliography in Appendix 1 to this book demonstrates. Some of these studies support the validity of aspects of the DSM-III classification; as expected, some do not.

What is important, however, is recognition that progress in psychiatric nosology can now be based, more than ever before, on empirical data. It will take many years to develop an adequate data base to resolve the many controversies that are highlighted in the chapters of this book. Our hope is that this book, in helping to clarify these controversies, will serve as a stimulus to the collaborative research necessary for the development of an internationally acceptable and useful classification of mental disorders.

REFERENCES

1. Frances A, Cooper AM: Descriptive and dynamic psychiatry: a perspective on DSM-III. Am J Psychiatry 138:1198–1202, 1981
2. Kazdin AE: Psychiatric diagnosis, dimensions of dysfunction, and child behavior therapy. Behav Ther 14:73–99, 1983
3. Eysenck HJ, Wakefield JA Jr, Friedman AF: Diagnosis and clinical assessment: the DSM-III. Ann Rev Psychol 34:167–193, 1983
4. Cooper AM, Michels R: DSM-III: an American view [Book Forum]. Am J Psychiatry 138:128–129, 1981
5. Skodol AE, Spitzer RL: DSM-III: rationale, basic concepts and some differences from ICD-9. Acta Psychiatr Scand 66:271–181, 1982
6. Rutter M, Shaffer D: DSM-III. A step forward or back in terms of the classification of child psychiatric disorders? J Am Acad Child Psychiatry 19:371–394, 1980
7. Feighner JP, Robins E, Guze B, et al: Diagnostic criteria for use in psychiatric research. Am J Psychiatry 26:57–63, 1972
8. Weissman MM, Gershon ES, Kidd KK, et al: Psychiatric disorders in the relatives of probands with affective disorders: the Yale-NIMH collaborative family study. Arch Gen Psychiatry (in press)
9. Akiskal HS, Djenderedjian AH, Rosenthal RH, et al: Cyclothymic disorder: validating criteria for inclusion in the bipolar affective group. Am J Psychiatry 134:1227–1233, 1977
10. Keller MB, Shapiro RW: "Double depression": superimposition of acute depressive episodes on chronic depressive disorders. Am J Psychiatry 139:438–442, 1982

11. Astrup C, Noreik K: Functional Psychoses: Diagnostic and Prognostic Models. Springfield, Ill, Thomas, 1966
12. Sartorius N, Jablensky A, Shapiro R: Cross cultural differences in the short term prognois of schizophrenic psychoses. Schizophr Bull 4:102–113, 1978
13. Tsuang MT, Dempsey GM, Rauscher F: A study of "atypical schizophrenia." Arch Gen Psychiatry 33:1157–1160, 1976
14. Helzer JE, Brockington IF, Kendell RE: Predictive validity of DSM-III and Feighner definitions of schizophrenia. A comparison with Research Diagnostic Criteria and CATEGO. Arch Gen Psychiatry 38:791–797, 1981
15. Helzer JE, Kendell RE, Brockington IF: The contribution of the six month criterion to the predictive validity of the DSM-III definition of schizophrenia. Arch Gen Psychiatry (in press)
16. Stephens JH, Astrup C, Carpenter WT Jr, et al: A comparison of nine systems to diagnose schizophrenia. Psychiatry Res 6:127–143, 1982
17. Fenton WS, Mosher LR, Matthews SM: Diagnosis of schizophrenia: a critical review of current diagnostic systems. Schizophr Bull 7:452–476, 1981
18. Kendler KS: Are there delusions specific for paranoid disorders versus schizophrenia? Schizophr Bull 6:1–3, 1980
19. Williams JBW, Spitzer RL: A proposed classification of mental disorders for inclusion in a multiaxial classification of health problems, in Psychosocial Factors Affecting Health. Edited by Lipkin M Jr, Gulbinat W, Kupka K. New York, Praeger Scientific, 1982
20. Williams JBW, Spitzer RL: DSM-III fields trials: interrater reliability, in Diagnostic and Statistical Manual of Mental Disorders, 3rd ed. Washington DC, American Psychiatric Association, 1980, pp 209–218
21. Robins LN, Helzer JE, Croughan J, et al: National Institute of Mental Health Diagnostic Interview Schedule. Its history, characteristics, and validity. Arch Gen Psychiatry 38:381–389, 1981
22. Wing JK, Cooper JE, Sartorius N: The Measurement and Classification of Psychiatric Symptoms: An Instruction Manual for the PSE and CATEGO Program. London, Cambridge University Press, 1974
23. Spitzer RL, Williams JBW: Structured Clinical Interview for DSM-III (SCID). New York, Biometrics Research Department, New York State Psychiatric Institute, 1983
24. Spitzer RL: Psychiatric diagnosis: are clinicians still necessary? Compr Psychiatry (in press)

APPENDIX 1

An Indexed Bibliography of DSM-III

Prepared by
Andrew E. Skodol, M.D., and Robert L. Spitzer, M.D.

This appendix contains a bibliography of 357 DSM-III-related articles indexed according to 16 diagnostic categories and 13 general topics relevant to the diagnosis and classification of mental disorders. The articles chosen are of several types: 1) explanations of the DSM-III classification or of the approach taken by DSM-III to particular categories; 2) critiques of the DSM-III system or approach to a category; 3) empirical or case studies that bear on the reliability or validity of a DSM-III diagnostic class or category; 4) discussions of issues in training; 5) comparisons of DSM-III with other diagnostic systems; and 6) descriptions of the use of DSM-III in a particular setting or as applied to a specific patient group. The majority of the articles have appeared in the literature since the publication of DSM-III in 1980, but several are included from before 1980 because of their importance in influencing the approach taken by the American Psychiatric Association's Task Force on Nomenclature and Statistics and its advisory committees that were responsible for DSM-III. The articles in the bibliography augment the lists of references and additional readings that follow the individual chapters in this book.

PREPARATION

In the preparation of this bibliography we used the computer search capabilities of the library of the New York State Psychiatric Institute. We conducted a retrospective Medline search covering the period January, 1978, through March, 1981, for 40 selected, English-language journals most likely to contain articles about DSM-III. We included all DSM-III diagnostic terms plus more general terms such as "classification," "validity," "reliability," "prognosis," etc. In March, 1981, we also conducted retrospective computer searches focused specifically on DSM-III, utilizing the National Clearing House of Mental Health Information (from 1969 on), the Social Science Citation Index (from 1977 on), and Psychological Abstracts (from 1975 on). Since that time, we have received monthly updates of the Medline search.

In addition, we have supplemented the computer searches with manual searches of ten of the most popular psychiatric journals: *American Journal of Psychiatry* (January, 1980, through February, 1983); *Archives of General Psychiatry* (January, 1980, through February, 1983); *British Journal of Psychiatry* (January, 1981, through February, 1983); *Psychological Medicine* (November, 1980, through November, 1982); *Journal of Nervous and Mental Disease* (January, 1980, through January, 1983); *Comprehensive Psychiatry* (January, 1981, through December, 1982); *Hospital & Community Psychiatry* (January, 1981, through February, 1983); *Schizophrenia Bulletin* (March, 1980, through September, 1982); *Journal of the American Academy of Child Psychiatry* (January, 1982, through January, 1983); and *Psychiatry Research* (April, 1981, through January, 1983).

This bibliography thus contains articles published before March, 1983, plus several articles of which we are aware that are in press.

INDEX TERMS

The index terms that follow are intended to facilitate the location of articles by investigators, teachers, students, or clinicians with particular areas of interest. The first list of terms includes most of the DSM-III major diagnostic classes. Instead of using the DSM-III class of "Disorders Usually First Evident in Infancy, Childhood, or Adolescence" as a term, we chose simply "Children and Adolescents," since many articles discuss the applicability of diagnostic categories, such as major depression, from other sections of the classification to a child or adolescent population. This is in accordance with the DSM-III convention of not limiting diagnoses given to children and adolescents below the age of 18 to those in the "Disorders Usually First Evident in Infancy, Childhood, or Adolescence" category. Articles referring to the DSM-III category "Psychological Factors Affecting Physical Illness" (316.00) are classified simply as "Physical Disorders" (see below).

The second list includes other terms relevant to the literature on psychiatric nosology. The brief descriptions of these terms summarize the principles used in assigning the articles. Many of the articles are indexed by more than one term, both diagnostic and nondiagnostic, depending on the content of the article.

LIST OF DIAGNOSTIC INDEX TERMS

ADJUSTMENT DISORDER
AFFECTIVE DISORDERS
ANXIETY DISORDERS
CHILDREN AND ADOLESCENTS
DISORDERS OF IMPULSE CONTROL NOT ELSEWHERE CLASSIFIED
DISSOCIATIVE DISORDERS
ORGANIC MENTAL DISORDERS
PARANOID DISORDERS
PERSONALITY DISORDERS
PSYCHOSEXUAL DISORDERS
PSYCHOTIC DISORDERS NOT ELSEWHERE CLASSIFIED
SCHIZOPHRENIC DISORDERS
SOMATOFORM DISORDERS
SUBSTANCE USE DISORDERS
V CODES

LIST AND DEFINITION OF NONDIAGNOSTIC INDEX TERMS

BIOLOGICAL TESTS	Biological variables related to subtyping, validation, or use as a diagnostic test.
COMPUTER APPLICATIONS	Computer programs for making diagnoses, e.g., CATEGO, NIMH Diagnostic Interview Schedule (DIS); computers for interviewing or training; computerized record-keeping systems.
DIAGNOSTIC PROCESS	Clinical variables that affect diagnosis, e.g., professional training, experience; clinical tests, e.g., amytal interview, mental status examination. (Excludes physical examination.)
EDUCATION	Teaching and training.
EPIDEMIOLOGY	Distribution of diagnostic categories by settings, age; procedures for community case identification.
MATHEMATICAL MODELS	Factor analytic studies, discriminant function.
MULTIAXIAL	Includes other proposed axes, e.g., psychodynamic, severity, prognosis.

NON-DSM-III DIAGNOSES	Cross-referenced, if possible, under a corresponding DSM-III class, e.g., hysterical psychosis, monosymptomatic hypochondriasis (cross-referenced under psychotic disorders not elsewhere classified).
NOSOLOGY	Comparison or evaluation of systems of classification, e.g., ICD-9 and DSM-III, book reviews of DSM-III; purposes and misuse of classification; principles of validity; general use of diagnostic criteria; frames of reference, e.g., psychodynamic; definition of mental disorder.
PHYSICAL DISORDERS	Psychological symptoms in physical disorder; physical disorder as a cause of mental disorder; physical examination; includes 316.
PSYCHOMETRICS	Use of psychological tests, rating scales, and other screening procedures in clinical settings for making diagnoses.
RELIABILITY	General problems of diagnostic reliability or reliability of specified categories. (Excludes reliability of structured interview schedules, rating scales, or psychometric procedures.)
STRUCTURED CLINICAL INTERVIEWS	For diagnosis, e.g., NIMH DIS, Structured Clinical Interview for DSM-III (SCID).

INDEX OF REFERENCES

The numbers listed in the following index refer to the number of the article appearing in the alphabetically arranged bibliography that follows.

DSM-III BIBLIOGRAPHY

1. Abraham SF, Beumont PJV: How patients describe bulimia or binge eating. Psychol Med 12:625–634, 1982

2. Abrams R, Taylor, MA: Importance of schizophrenic symptoms in the diagnosis of mania. Am J Psychiatry 138: 658–661, 1981

3. Achenbach TM: DSM-III in light of empirical research on the classification of child psychopathology. J Am Acad Child Psychiatry 19: 395–412, 1980

4. Akhtar S, Thomson JA Jr: Overview: narcissistic personality disorder. Am J Psychiatry 139: 12–20, 1982

5. Akiskal HS: Dysthymic disorder: psychopathology of proposed chronic depressive subtypes. Am J Psychiatry 140: 11–20, 1983

6. Akiskal HS, Hirschfeld RMA, Yerevanian BI: The relationship of personality to affective disorders: a selective methodologic review. Arch Gen Psychiatry (in press)

7. Alarcon RD: A Latin American perspective on DSM-III. Am J Psychiatry 140: 102–105, 1983

8. Allen JR: DSM-III: leaving the darkness unobscured. J Okla State Med Assoc 73: 343–353, 1980

9. Amies PL, Gelder MG, Shaw PM: Social phobia: a comparative clinical study. Br J Psychiatry 142: 174–179, 1983

10. Andreasen NC, Grove WM: The classification of depression: traditional versus mathematical approaches. Am J Psychiatry 139: 45–52, 1982

11. Andreasen NC, Hoenk PR: The predictive value of adjustment disorders: a follow-up study. Am J Psychiatry 139: 584–590, 1982

12. Andreasen NC, Olsen S: Negative versus positive schizophrenia: definition and validation. Arch Gen Psychiatry 39: 789–794, 1982

13. Andreasen NC, Spitzer RL: Classification of psychiatric disorders, in Handbook of Biological Psychiatry, Part I: Disciplines Relevant to Biological Psychiatry. Edited by van Praag HM, Lader MH, Rafaelsen, OJ, Sachar, EJ. New York, Marcel Dekker Inc, pp 377–395, 1979

14. Andreasen NC, Wasek P: Adjustment disorders in adolescents and adults. Arch Gen Psychiatry 37: 1166–1170, 1980

15. Andrulonis PA, Glueck BC, Stroebel CF, Vogel NG: Borderline personality subcategories. J Nerv Ment Dis 170: 670–679, 1982

16. Angst J, Grigo H, Lanz H: Classification of depression. Acta Psychiatr Scand 63, Suppl 290, 23–28, 1981

17. Astrada CA, Licamele WL, Walsh TL, Kessler ES: Recurrent abdominal pain in children and associated DSM-III diagnosis. Am J Psychiatry 138: 687–688, 1981

18. Atkinson RM, Henderson RG, Sparr LF, Deale S: Assessment of Viet Nam veterans for posttraumatic stress disorder in Veterans Administration disability claims. Am J Psychiatry 139: 1118–1121, 1982

19. Barnes RF, Raskind MA: DSM-III criteria and the clinical diagnosis of dementia: a nursing home study. J Gerontol 36: 20–27, 1981

20. Baron M, Asnis L, Gruen R: The Schedule for Schizotypal Personalities (SSP): a diagnostic interview for schizotypal features. Psychiatry Res 4: 213–228, 1981

21. Battle AO: Diagnostic and Statistical Manual of Mental Disorders, 3rd ed.: Case Book [book review]. J Develop Behav Pediatrics 2: 175–176, 1981

22. Bayer R, Spitzer RL: Edited correspondence on the status of homosexuality in DSM-III. J Hist Behav Sci 18:32–52, 1982

23. Beeber AR, Pies RW: The nonmelancholic depressive syndromes. An alternate approach to classification. J Nerv Ment Dis 171:3–9, 1983

24. Bell CC: DSM-III Case Book: a learning companion to the Diagnostic and Statistical Manual of Mental Disorders, 3rd ed. [book review]. JAMA 246: 2078, 1981

25. Berner P, Katschnig H, Lenz G: Poly-diagnostic approach: a method to clarify incongruences among the classification of the functional psychoses. Psychiatr J Univ Ottawa 7: 244–248, 1982

26. Bishop ER, Torch EM: Dividing "hysteria": a preliminary investigation of conversion disorder and psychalgia. J Nerv Ment Dis 167: 348–356, 1979

27. Blazer D: The diagnosis of depression in the elderly. J Am Geriatr Soc 28: 52–58, 1980

28. Bobon DP: [Description and comparison of two revised classifications of mental disorders: the ICD-9 and the DSM-III (author's transl)]. Acta Psychiatr Belg 80: 846–863, 1980

29. Boeringa JA, Castellani S: Reliability and validity of emotional blunting as a criterion for diagnosis of schizophrenia. Am J Psychiatry 139: 1131–1135, 1982

30. Boyd JH, Weissman MM: Epidemiology of affective disorders: a reexamination and future directions. Arch Gen Psychiatry 38: 1039–1046, 1981

31. Braden W, Bannasch PR, Fink EB: Diagnosing mania: the use of family informants. J Clin Psychiatry 41: 226–228, 1980

32. Brockington IF, Helzer JE, Hillier VF, Frances AF: Definitions of depression: concordance and prediction of outcome. Am J Psychiatry 139: 1022–1027, 1982

33. Bursten B: Narcissistic personalities in DSM-III. Compr Psychiatry 23: 409–420, 1982

34. Campbell R, Schaffer CB: Diagnosing schizophrenia with DSM-III [letter]. Am J Psychiatry 138: 1260–1261, 1981

35. Campbell RJ: The language of psychiatry. Hosp Community Psychiatry 32: 849–852, 1981

36. Cantor N, Smith EE, French R de S, Mezzich J: Psychiatric diagnosis as prototype categorization. J Abnorm Psychology 89: 181–192, 1980

37. Cantor S, Evans J, Pearce J, Pezzot-Pearce T: Childhood schizophrenia: present but not accounted for. Am J Psychiatry 139: 758–762, 1982

38. Cantwell DP: The diagnostic process and diagnostic classification in child psychiatry—DSM-III. J Am Acad Child Psychiatry 19: 345–355, 1980

39. Cantwell DP, Mattison R, Russell AT, Will L: A comparison of DSM-II and DSM-III in the diagnosis of childhood psychiatric disorders. IV. Difficulties in use, global comparison, and conclusions. Arch Gen Psychiatry 36: 1227–1228, 1979

40. Cantwell DP, Russell AT, Mattison R, Will L: A comparison of DSM-II and DSM-III in the diagnosis of childhood psychiatric disorders. I. Agreement with expected diagnosis. Arch Gen Psychiatry 36: 1208–1213, 1979

41. Carlson GA, Cantwell DP: Diagnosis of childhood depression: a comparison of the Weinberg and DSM-III criteria. J Am Acad Child Psychiatry 21: 247–250, 1982

42. Caroff S, Winokur A, Rieger W, Schweizer E, Amsterdam J: Response to dexamethasone in psychotic depression. Psychiatry Res 8: 59–64, 1983

43. Charney DS, Nelson JC, Quinlan DM: Personality traits and disorder in depression. Am J Psychiatry 138: 1601–1604, 1981

44. Chessick RD: In reply to Jones SD and Weiner MF [letter]. Arch Gen Psychiatry 40: 108, 1983

45. Cicchetti DV, Prusoff BA: Reliability of depression and associated clinical symptoms. Arch Gen Psychiatry (in press)

46. Claghorn JL, Mathew RJ: How appropriate is a "medical model" in psychiatric practice? J Clin Psychiatry 41 (12 Pt 2): 3–5, 1980

47. Clayton PJ: Schizoaffective disorders. J Nerv Ment Dis 170: 646–650, 1982

48. Conn LM: DSM-III Case Book [book review]. J Nerv Ment Dis 170: 769, 1982

49. Cooper AM, Michels R: DSM-III: An American view [Book Forum]. Am J Psychiatry 138: 128–129, 1981

50. Coryell W, Gaffney G, Burkhardt PE: DSM-III melancholia and the primary–secondary distinction: a comparison of concurrent validity by means of the dexamethasone suppression test. Am J Psychiatry 139: 120–122, 1982

51. Coryell W, Noyes R, Clancy J: Excess mortality in panic disorder: a comparison with primary unipolar depression. Am J Psychiatry 139: 701–703, 1982

52. Coryell W, Tsuang MT: DSM-III schizophreniform disorder. Comparisons with schizophrenia and affective disorder. Arch Gen Psychiatry 39: 66–69, 1982

53. Coryell W, Tsuang MT, McDaniel J: Psychotic features in major depression. Is mood congruence important? J Affective Disord 4: 227–236, 1982

54. Cox WH Jr: An indication for use of imipramine in attention deficit disorder. Am J Psychiatry 139: 1059–1060, 1982

55. Craig TJ, Goodman AB, Haugland G: Impact of DSM-III on clinical practice. Am J Psychiatry 139: 922–925, 1982

56. Crary WG: DSM-III Training Guide and DSM-III Case Book [book reviews]. J Clin Psychiatry 43: 301, 1982

57. Curtis GC, Cameron OG, Nesse RM: The dexamethasone suppression test in panic disorder and agoraphobia. Am J Psychiatry 139: 1043–1046, 1982

58. Cytryn L, McKnew DH Jr, Bunney WE Jr: Diagnosis of depression in children: a reassessment. Am J Psychiatry 137: 22–25, 1980

59. Davidson JRT, Miller RD, Turnbull CD, Sullivan JL: Atypical depression. Arch Gen Psychiatry 39: 527–534, 1982

60. DeMeyer MK, Hingtgen JN, Jackson RK: Infantile autism reviewed: a decade of research. Schizophr Bull 7: 388–451, 1981

61. Dessonville C, Gallagher D, Thompson LW, Finnell K, Lewinsohn PM: Relation of age and health status on depressive symptoms in normal and depressed older adults. Essence 5: 99-117, 1982

62. Dreger RM: First-, second-, and third-order factors from the children's behavioral classification project instrument and an attempt at rapprochement. J Abnorm Psychol 90: 242–260, 1981

63. Dunn CG: The diagnosis and classification of anxiety states. Psychiatr Annals 11: 11–16, 1981

64. Earls F: Application of DSM-III in an epidemiological study of preschool children. Am J Psychiatry 139: 242–243, 1982

65. Edelsohn G: Guillain-Barré misdiagnosed as conversion disorder. Hosp Community Psychiatry 33: 766–767, 1982

66. Endicott J: Diagnostic Interview Schedule: reliability and validity [letter]. Arch Gen Psychiatry 38: 1300, 1981

67. Endicott J, Nee J, Fleiss J, Cohen J, Williams JBW, Simon R: Diagnostic criteria for schizophrenia: reliabilities and agreement between systems. Arch Gen Psychiatry 39: 884–889, 1982

68. Evans JW, Elliott H: Screening criteria for the diagnosis of schizophrenia in deaf patients. Arch Gen Psychiatry 38: 787–790, 1981

69. Eysenck HJ, Wakefield JA Jr, Friedman AF: Diagnosis and clinical assessment: the DSM-III. Ann Rev Psychol 34: 167–193, 1983

70. Feder R: Factitious disorder vs malingering [letter]. Psychosomatics 22: 469, 1981

71. Feighner JP: Nosology of primary affective disorders and application to clinical research. Acta Psychiatr Scand 63, Suppl 290, pp 29–41, 1981

72. Fenton WS, Mosher LR, Matthews SM: Diagnosis of schizophrenia: a critical review of current diagnostic systems. Schizophr Bull 7: 452-476, 1981

73. de Figueiredo JM, Baiardi JJ, Long DM: Briquet syndrome in a man with chronic intractable pain. Johns Hopkins Med J 147: 102–106, 1980

74. Finn SE: Base rates, utilities, and DSM-III: shortcomings of fixed-rule systems of psychodiagnosis. J Abnorm Psychol 91: 294–302, 1982

75. Fogelson DL, Cohen BM, Pope HG: A study of DSM-III schizophreniform disorder. Am J Psychiatry 139: 1281–1285, 1982

76. Foltz D: Judgment withheld on DSM-III, new child classification pushed. APA Monitor 11: 1, 33, 1980

77. Fox HA: The DSM-III concept of schizophrenia. Br J Psychiatry 138: 60–63, 1981

78. Frances A: The DSM-III personality disorders section: a commentary. Am J Psychiatry 137: 1050–1054, 1980

79. Frances A.: Categorical and dimensional systems of personality diagnosis: a comparison. Compr Psychiatry 23: 516–527, 1982

80. Frances A: DSM-III Training Guide. Edited by Webb L, et al [book review]. Hosp Community Psychiatry 33: 312, 1982

81. Frances A, Andreasen N: DSM-III case studies. Woman displays manic symptoms after separation from lover. Hosp Community Psychiatry 32: 533–534, 1981

82. Frances A, Cooper AM: The DSM-III controversy: a psychoanalytic perspective. Bull Assoc Psychoanal Med 19: 37–43, 1980

83. Frances A, Cooper AM: Descriptive and dynamic psychiatry: a perspective on DSM-III. Am J Psychiatry 138: 1198–1202, 1981

84. Frances A, Frosch W: DSM-III case studies. Knife-throwing incident brings sergeant to army psychiatrist. Hosp Community Psychiatry 32: 830–831, 1981

85. Frances A, Kaplan HS: DSM-III case studies. Patient on hypertensive drug has increasing erectile problems. Hosp Community Psychiatry 33: 431–432, 1982

86. Frances A, Klein DF: DSM-III case studies. Anxious, precise, demanding man seeks help soon after marriage. Hosp Community Psychiatry 33: 89–90, 1982

87. Frances A, Preven D, Manley M: DSM-III case studies. Dialysis patient shows confusion, mood swings, bizarre behavior. Hosp Community Psychiatry 33: 613–614, 1982

88. Frances A, Shapiro T: DSM-III case studies. Child with new parent is amenable at home, has problems at school. Hosp Community Psychiatry 32: 243–244, 1981

89. Frances A, Strauss JS: DSM-III case studies. Lawyer with delusions of persecution, depression. Hosp Community Psychiatry 32: 385–386, 1981

90. Frances A, Tupin JP: DSM-III case studies. Patient's mood swings send him to prison, then to hospital. Hosp Community Psychiatry 32: 683–684, 1981

91. Friedman D, Jaffe A: Anxiety disorders. J Fam Pract 16: 145–152, 1983

92. Friedman RD, Clarkin JF, Corn R, Aronoff MS, Hurt SW, Murphy MC: DSM-III and affective pathology in hospitalized adolescents. J Nerv Ment Dis 170: 511–521, 1982

93. Frye JS, Stockton RA: Discriminant analysis of posttraumatic stress disorder among a group of Viet Nam veterans. Am J Psychiatry 139: 52–56, 1982

94. Gallagher D, Breckenridge JN, Thompson LW, Dessonville C, Amaral P: Similarities and differences between normal grief and depression in older adults. Essence 5: 127–140, 1982

95. Ganguli M, Saul MC: Diagnostic Interview Schedule [letter]. Arch Gen Psychiatry 39: 1442–1443, 1982

96. Garmezy N: DSM-III: Never mind the psychologists—is it good for the children? Clin Psychologist 32: 4–6, 1978

97. Garvey MJ, Spoden F: Suicide attempts in antisocial personality disorder. Compr Psychiatry 21: 146–149, 1980

98. Giovacchini PL: The axes of DSM-III [letter]. Am J Psychiatry 138: 119–120, 1981

99. Goethe JW: DSM-III: implications for nonpsychiatric physicians. J La State Med Soc 133: 101–104, 1981

100. Graber B, Kline-Graber G: Research criteria for male erectile failure. J Sex Marital Ther 7: 37–48, 1981

101. Grunhaus L, Gloger S, Weisstub E: Panic attacks. A review of treatments and pathogenesis. J Nerv Ment Dis 169: 608–613, 1981

102. Gunderson JG, Siever LJ, Spaulding E: The search for a schizotype. Crossing the border again. Arch Gen Psychiatry 40: 15–22, 1983

103. Haier RJ: The diagnosis of schizophrenia: a review of recent developments. Schizophr Bull 6: 417–428, 1980

104. Halmi KA, Falk JR, Schwartz E: Binge-eating and vomiting: a survey of a college population. Psychol Med 11: 697–706, 1981

105. Halmi KA, Long M, Stunkard AJ, Mason E: Psychiatric diagnosis of morbidly obese gastric bypass patients. Am J Psychiatry 137: 470–472, 1980

106. Harris SL: DSM-III—its implications for children. Child Behav Ther 1: 37–46, 1979

107. Harrow M, Silverstein M: In reply to Taylor M: the road to nosologic nirvana [letter]. Arch Gen Psychiatry 38: 1298–1299, 1981

108. Helmchen H: Multiaxial classification in psychiatry. Compr Psychiatry (in press)

109. Helzer JE, Brockington IF, Kendell RE: Predictive validity of DSM-III and Feighner definitions of schizophrenia. A comparison with Research Diagnostic Criteria and CATEGO. Arch Gen Psychiatry 38: 791–797, 1981

110. Helzer JE, Kendell RE, Brockington IF: The contribution of the six month criterion to the predictive validity of the DSM-III definition of schizophrenia. Arch Gen Psychiatry (in press)

111. Helzer JE, Robins LN: In reply to Endicott J: Diagnostic Interview Schedule: reliability and validity [letter]. Arch Gen Psychiatry 38: 1300–1301, 1981

112. Hendin H, Pollinger A, Singer P, Ulmar RB: Meanings of combat and the development of posttraumatic stress disorder. Am Psychiatry 138: 1490–1493, 1981

113. Hesselbrock V, Stabenau J, Hesselbrock M, Mirkin P. Meyer R: A comparison of two interview schedules: the Schedule for Affective Disorders and Schizophrenia - Lifetime, and the National Institute for Mental Health Diagnostic Interview Schedule. Arch Gen. Psychiatry 39: 674–677, 1982

114. Hirschowitz J, Casper R, Garver DL, Chang S: Lithium response in good prognosis schizophrenia. Am J Psychiatry 137: 916–920, 1980

115. Hodges K, McKnew D, Cytryn L, Stern L, Kline J: The Child Assessment Schedule (CAS) diagnostic interview: a report on reliability and validity. J Am Acad Child Psychiatry 21: 468–473, 1982

116. Hoenig J: Nosology and statistical classification. Can J Psychiatry 26: 240–243, 1981

117. Hollender MH: Pathological intoxication—is there such an entity? J Clin Psychiatry 40: 424–426, 1979

118. Horowitz LM, Post DL, French R de S, Wallis KD, Siegelman EY: The prototype as a construct in abnormal psychology: 2. Clarifying disagreement in psychiatric judgments. J Abnorm Psychol 90: 575–585, 1981

119. Horowitz MJ, Wilner N, Kaltreider N, Alvarez W: Signs and symptoms of posttraumatic stress disorder. Arch Gen Psychiatry 37: 85–92, 1980

120. Hsu LKG: Is there a disturbance in body image in anorexia nervosa? J Nerv Ment Dis 170: 305–307, 1982

121. Hudson JI, Pope HG Jr, Jonas JM, Yurgelun-Todd D: Family history study of anorexia nervosa and bulimia. Br J Psychiatry 142: 133–138, 1983

122. Hyler SE, Spitzer RL: Hysteria split asunder. Am J Psychiatry 135: 1500–1504, 1978

123. Hyler SE, Sussman N: Chronic factitious disorder with physical symptoms (the Munchausen syndrome). Psychiatr Clin North Am 4: 365–377, 1981

124. Hyler SE, Williams JBW, Spitzer RL: Reliability in the DSM-III field trials: interview versus case summary. Arch Gen Psychiatry 39: 1275–1278, 1982

125. Irwin M: Diagnosis of anorexia nervosa in children and the validity of DSM-III. Am J Psychiatry 138: 1382–1383, 1981

126. James RL, May PR: Diagnosing schizophrenia: Professor Kraepelin and the Research Diagnostic Criteria. Am J Psychiatry 138: 501–504, 1981

127. Janulis PT: Tribute to a word: neurosis [letter; also reply from Spitzer RL, Skodol AE, Gibbon M]. Arch Gen Psychiatry 39: 623–624, 1982

128. Jarvik LF: Dementia in old age. Reflections on nomenclature. Psychiatr Clin North Am 5: 105–106, 1982

129. Jones SD: Borderline personality [letter]. Arch Gen Psychiatry 40: 107, 1983

130. Karasu TB, Skodol AE: VIth axis for DSM-III: psychodynamic evaluation. Am J Psychiatry 137: 607–610, 1980

131. Kasahara Y: [DSM-III (Diagnostic and Statistical Manual of Mental Disorders, 3rd ed.), a new diagnostic criteria in the United States]. Seishin Shinkeigaku Zasshi 83:607–611, 1981

132. Kashani JH, Cantwell DP, Shekim WO, Reid JC: Major depressive disorder in children admitted to an inpatient community mental health center. Am J Psychiatry 139:671–672, 1982

133. Kashani JH, Manning GW, McKnew DH, Cytryn L, Simonds JF, Wooderson PC: Depression among incarcerated delinquents. Psychiatry Res 3:185–191, 1980

134. Kashani JH, Venzke R, Millar EA: Depression in children admitted to hospital for orthopaedic procedures. Br J Psychiatry 138:21–25, 1981

135. Katona CLE: Puerperal mental illness: comparisions with non-puerperal controls. Br J Psychiatry 141:447–452, 1982

136. Keisling R: Underdiagnosis of manic-depressive illness in a hospital unit. Am J Psychiatry 138:672–673, 1981

137. Keller MB, Shapiro RW: "Double depression": superimposition of acute depressive episodes on chronic depressive disorders. Am J Psychiatry 139:438–442, 1982

138. Kemp KV: DSM-III Case Book [book review]. J Nerv Ment Dis 170:769–770, 1982

139. Kendell RE: DSM-III: A British perspective [Book Forum]. Am J Psychiatry 137:1630–1631, 1980

140. Kendell RE: The choice of diagnostic criteria for biological research. Arch Gen Psychiatry 39:1334–1339, 1982

141. Kendler KS: Are there delusions specific for paranoid disorders versus schizophrenia? Schizophr Bull 6:1–3, 1980

142. Kendler KS, Gruenberg AM: Genetic relationship between paranoid personality disorder and the "schizophrenic spectrum" disorders. Am J Psychiatry 139: 1185–1186, 1982

143. Kendler KS, Gruenberg AM, Strauss JS: An independent analysis of the Copenhagen sample of the Danish adoption study of schizophrenia. I. The relationship between anxiety disorder and schizophrenia. Arch Gen Psychiatry 38: 973–977, 1981

144. Kendler KS, Gruenberg AM, Strauss JS: An independent analysis of the Copenhagen sample of the Danish adoption study of schizophrenia. II. The relationship between schizotypal personality disorder and schizophrenia. Arch Gen Psychiatry 38: 982–984, 1981

145. Kendler KS, Gruenberg AM, Strauss JS: An independent analysis of the Copenhagen sample of the Danish adoption study of schizophrenia. III. The relationship between paranoid psychosis (delusional disorder) and the schizophrenic spectrum disorders. Arch Gen Psychiatry 38: 985–987, 1981

146. Kendler KS, Gruenberg AM, Strauss JS: An independent analysis of the Copenhagen sample of the Danish adoption study of schizophrenia. IV. The relationship between major depressive disorder and schizophrenia. Arch Gen Psychiatry 39: 639–642, 1982

147. Kendler KS, Gruenberg AM, Strauss JS: An independent analysis of the Copenhagen sample of the Danish adoption study of schizophrenia. V. the relationship between childhood social withdrawal and adult schizophrenia. Arch Gen Psychiatry 39: 1257–1261, 1982

148. Kendler KS, Hays P: Schizophrenia subdivided by the family history of affective disorder: a comparison of symptomatology and course of illness. Arch Gen Psychiatry (in press)

149. Klein DF, Liebowitz MR: Hysteroid dysphoria [letter]. Am J Psychiatry 139: 1520, 1982

150. Koenigsberg HW, Kernberg OF, Schomer J: Diagnosing borderline conditions in an outpatient setting. Arch Gen Psychiatry 40: 49–53, 1983

151. Kosten TR, Rounsaville BJ, Kleber HD: DSM-III personality disorders in opiate addicts. Compr Psychiatry 23: 572–581, 1982

152. Kraupl-Taylor F: A logical analysis of disease concepts. Compr Psychiatry (in press)

153. Kroll J, Carey K, Sines L, Roth M: Are there borderlines in Britain? A cross-validation of US findings. Arch Gen Psychiatry 39: 60–63, 1982

154. Kroll J, Sines L, Martin K, Lari S, Pyle R, Zander J: Borderline personality disorder: construct validity of the concept. Arch Gen Psychiatry 38: 1021–1026, 1981

155. Kruger G, Haubitz I: Classification of organic brain syndromes by cluster analysis. Arch Psychiatr Nervenkr 228: 299–315, 1980

156. Kuehnle J, Spitzer RL: DSM-III classification of substance use disorders, in Substance Abuse: Clinical Problems and Perspectives. Edited by Lowinson JH. Baltimore, Williams & Wilkins, 1981, pp 19–23

157. Langfeldt G: Definition of "schizophreniform psychoses" [letter]. Am J Psychiatry 139: 703, 1982

158. Leckman JF, Merikangas KR, Pauls DL, Prusoff BA, Weissman MM: Anxiety disorders associated with episodes of depression: family study data contradict DSM-III convention. Am J Psychiatry (in press)

159. Leckman JF, Weissman MM, Merikangas KR, Pauls DL, Prusoff BA: Panic disorder increases risk of depression, alcoholism, panic and phobic disorders in families of depressed probands. Arch Gen Psychiatry (in press)

160. Lehmann HE: Affective disorders in the aged. Psychiatr Clin North Am 5:27–44, 1982

161. Lerner HD, Sugarman A, Gaughran J: Borderline and schizophrenic patients. A comparative study of defensive structure. J Nerv Ment Dis 169: 705–711, 1981

162. Lieberman C: Schizoaffective illness defies the dichotomy . . . and keeps DSM-III pondering. Schizophr Bull 5: 436–440, 1979

163. Linn L, Spitzer RL: DSM-III. Implications for liaison psychiatry and psychosomatic medicine. JAMA 247: 3207–3209, 1982

164. Lion JR (ed): Personality Disorders: Diagnosis and Management, 2nd ed. Baltimore, Williams & Wilkins, 1981

165. Lipkin JO, Blank AS, Parson ER, Smith J: Vietnam veterans and posttraumatic stress disorder. Hosp Community Psychiatry 33: 908–912, 1982

166. Lipkowitz MH, Idupuganti S: Diagnosing schizophrenia: criteria sets and reality. Hosp Community Psychiatry 32: 344–345, 1981

167. Lipkowitz MH, Idupuganti S: Diagnosing schizophrenia in 1980: a survey of U.S. psychiatrists. Am J Psychiatry 140: 52–55, 1983

168. Lipowski ZJ: A new look at organic brain syndromes. Am J Psychiatry 137: 674–678, 1980

169. Lipowski ZJ: Delirium updated. Compr Psychiatry 21: 190–196, 1980

170. Lipp MR, Looney JG, Spitzer RL: Classifying psychophysiologic disorders: a new idea. Psychosom Med 39: 285–287, 1977

171. Lipton AA, Weinstein AS: Implementing DSM-III in New York State mental health facilities. Hosp Community Psychiatry 32: 616–620, 1981

172. Liston EH: Delirium in the aged. Psychiatr Clin North Am 5: 49–66, 1982

173. Longabaugh R, Fowler DR, Stout R, et al: Validation for a problem focused nomenclature. Arch Gen Psychiatry (in press)

174. Looney JG, Lipp MR, Spitzer RL: A new method of classification for psychophysiologic disorders. Am J Psychiatry 135: 304–308, 1978

175. Looney JG, Spitzer RL, Lipp MR: Classifying psychosomatic disorders in DSM-III [editorial]. Psychosomatics 22: 6–8, 1981

176. Loranger AW, Oldham JM, Tulis EH: Familial transmission of DSM-III borderline personality disorder. Arch Gen Psychiatry 39: 795–799, 1982

177. Lowenkopf EL: Anorexia nervosa: some nosological considerations. Compr Psychiatry 23: 233–240, 1982

178. Lyskowski JC, Tsuang MT: Precautions in treating DSM-III borderline personality disorder. Am J Psychiatry 137: 110–111, 1980

179. Macaskill ND, Macaskill A: Use of the term "borderline patient" by Scottish psychiatrists: a preliminary survey. Br J Psychiatry 139: 397–399, 1981

180. McDonald A, Kline SA, Billings RF: The limits of Munchausen's syndrome. Can Psychiatr Assoc J 24: 323–328, 1979

181. McEnvoy JP: Organic brain syndromes in DSM-III [letter]. Am J Psychiatry 138: 124–125, 1981

182. McGlashan TH: DSM-III schizophrenia and individual psychotherapy. J Nerv Ment Dis 170: 752–757, 1982

183. MacKenzie TB, Popkin MK, Callies AL: DSM-III in consultation-liaison psychiatry: contributions and quandaries. Hosp Community Psychiatry (in press)

184. McLemore CW, Benjamin LS: What ever happened to interpersonal diagnosis? A psychosocial alternative to DSM-III. Am Psychol 34: 17–34, 1979

185. McReynolds WT: Diagnostic and Statistical Manual of Mental Disorders and the future of clinical psychology. Catalogue of Selected Documents in Psychology. 8(69) MS 1734

186. McReynolds WT: DSM-III and the future of applied social science. Prof Psychol 10: 123–132, 1979

187. McReynolds WT: Psychologists' reaction to DSM-III [letter]. Am J Psychiatry 137: 1468–1469, 1980

188. Maletta GJ, Pirozzolo FJ, Thompson G, Mortimer JA: Organic mental disorders in a geriatric outpatient population. Am J Psychiatry 139: 521–523, 1982

189. Mattes J: DSM-III criteria for major depressive episode [letter]. Arch Gen Psychiatry 38: 1068–1069, 1981

190. Mattison R, Cantwell DP, Russell AT, Will L: A comparison of DSM-II and DSM-III in the diagnosis of childhood psychiatric disorders. II. Interrater agreement. Arch Gen Psychiatry 36: 1217–1222, 1979

191. Maurer RG, Stewart MA: Attention deficit without hyperactivity in a child psychiatry clinic. J Clin Psychiatry 41: 232–233, 1980

192. Maxmen JS: DSM-III and psychiatric education: the future is now. Compr Psychiatry 20: 449–453, 1979

193. Mellsop G, Varghese F, Joshua S, Hicks A: The reliability of axis II of DSM-III. Am J Psychiatry 139: 1360–1361, 1982

194. Meltzer HY, Perline R, Lewine R: Biological studies of DSM-III psychotic disorders. I. Platelet measure and apomorphine-induced growth hormone response. J Nerv Ment Dis 170: 758–765, 1982

195. Mezzich JE: Patterns and issues in multiaxial psychiatric diagnosis. Psychol Med 9: 125–137, 1979

196. Mezzich JE, Coffman GA, Goodpastor SM: A format for DSM-III diagnostic formulation: experience with 1,111 consecutive patients. Am J Psychiatry 139: 591–596, 1982

197. Milich R: DSM-III versus DSM-II: how much more reliable? [letter]. Arch Gen Psychiatry 37: 1426–1427, 1980

198. Miller LC: Dimensions of adolescent psychopathology. J Abnorm Child Psychol 8: 161–173, 1980

199. Millon T: Disorders of Personality: DSM-III: Axis II. New York, Wiley, 1981

200. Mitchell JE, Pyle RL, Eckert ED: Frequency and duration of binge-eating episodes in patients with bulimia. Am J Psychiatry 138: 835–836, 1981

201. Monroe RR: DSM-III style diagnosis of the episodic disorders. J Nerv Ment Dis 170: 665–669, 1982

202. Morey LC: Differences between psychologists and psychiatrists in the use of DSM-III. Am J Psychiatry 137: 1123–1124, 1980

203. Morey LC, Blashfield RK: A symptom analysis of the DSM-III definition of schizophrenia. Schizophr Bull 7:258–268, 1981

204. Morphy MA: DSM-III and the future orientation of American psychiatry. Psychol Med 12: 241–242, 1982

205. Morrison JR: Who needs change? Moving from research to clinical studies. J Clin Psychiatry 41(12 Pt 2): 16–20, 1980

206. Mulford HA, Fitzgerald JL: On the validity of the Research Diagnostic Criteria, the Feighner criteria, and the DSM-III for diagnosing alcoholics. J Nerv Ment Dis 169: 654–658, 1981

207. Munro A: Paranoia revisited. Br J Psychiatry 141: 344–349, 1982

208. Murphy GE: Dexamethasone suppression test and diagnosis of melancholia [letter]. Arch Gen Psychiatry 38: 1067–1068, 1981

209. Murphy JM: Continuities in community-based psychiatric epidemiology. Arch Gen Psychiatry 37: 1215–1223, 1980

210. Murray RM: A reappraisal of American psychiatry. Lancet i: 255–258, 1979

211. Nadelson CC: DSM-III Case Book [book review]. Hosp Community Psychiatry 32: 873, 1981

212. Nasrallah HA, Jacoby CG, McCalley-Whitters M, Kuperman S: Cerebral ventricular enlargement in subtypes of chronic schizophrenia. Arch Gen Psychiatry 39: 774–777, 1982

213. Nathan PE: DSM-III and schizophrenia: diagnostic delight or nosological nightmare? J Clin Psychol 35: 477–479, 1979

214. Nelson JC, Charney DS, Quinan DM: Evaluation of the DSM-III criteria for melancholia. Arch Gen Psychiatry 38: 555–559, 1981

215. North C, Cadoret R: Diagnostic discrepancy in personal accounts of patients with "schizophrenia." Arch Gen Psychiatry 38: 133–137, 1981

216. Nurnberger, J Jr, Roose SP, Dunner DL, Fieve RR: Unipolar mania: a distinct clinical entity? Am J Psychiatry 136: 1420–1423, 1979

217. O'Grady KE: Sex, physical attractiveness, and perceived risk for mental illness. J Pers Soc Psychol 43: 1064–1071, 1982

218. Okimoto JT, Barnes RF, Veith RC, Raskind MA, Inui TS, Carter WB: Screening for depression in geriatric medical patients. Am J Psychiatry 139: 799–802, 1982

219. Pauls DL, Cohen DJ, Heimbuch R, Detlor J, Kidd KK: Familial pattern and transmission of Gilles de la Tourette syndrome and multiple tics. Arch Gen Psychiatry 38: 1091–1093, 1981

220. P'erez Urd'aniz A, Prieto Aguirre JF: [Review of the literature and considerations on the latest classification of mental diseases. The DSM-III of the American Psychiatric Association]. Actas Luso Esp Neurol Psiquiatr 10: 191–204, 1982

221. Pfohl B: Effects of clinical experience on rating DSM-III symptoms of schizophrenia. Compr Psychiatry 21: 233–235, 1980

222. Pfohl B, Stangl D, Zimmerman M: Increasing axis II reliability [letter]. Am J Psychiatry 140: 270–271, 1983

223. Pfohl B, Vasquez N, Nasrallah H: The mathematical case against unipolar mania. J Psychiatr Res 16: 259–265, 1981

224. Pfohl B, Vasquez N, Nasrallah H: Unipolar vs. bipolar mania: a review of 247 patients. Br J Psychiatry 141: 453–458, 1982

225. Pichot P: [The nosology of depressions (author's transl)]. Sem Hop Paris 57: 739–743, 1981

226. Pichot P: The diagnosis and classification of mental disorders in French-speaking countries: background, current views and comparison with other nomenclatures. Psychol Med 12: 475–492, 1982

227. Pichot P, Pull C: Is there an involutional melancholia? Compr Psychiatry 22: 2–10, 1981

228. Pitman RK, Moffett PS: Somatization disorder (Briquet's syndrome) in a male veteran. J Nerv Ment Dis 169: 462–466, 1981

229. Pinsker H, Spitzer RL: Classification of mental disorders, DSM-III, in International Encyclopedia of Psychiatry, Psychology, Psychoanalysis, and Neurology, vol III. Edited by Wolman BB. New York, Human Sciences Press Periodicals, 1977, pp 160–164

230. Pope HG Jr, Jonas JM, Cohen BM, Lipinski JF: Failure to find evidence of schizophrenia in first-degree relatives of schizophrenic probands. Am J Psychiatry 139: 826–828, 1982

231. Pope HG Jr, Jonas JM, Hudson JI, Cohen BM, Gunderson JG: The validity of DSM-III borderline personality disorder. A phenomenologic, family history, treatment response, and long-term follow-up study. Arch Gen Psychiatry 40: 23–30, 1983

232. Pope HG Jr, Jonas JM, Jones B: Factitious psychosis: phenomenology, family history, and long-term outcome of nine patients. Am J Psychiatry 139: 1480–1483, 1982

233. Pope HG Jr, Lipinski JF, Cohen BM, Axelrod DT: "Schizoaffective disorder": an invalid diagnosis? A comparison of schizoaffective disorder, schizophrenia, and affective disorder. Am J Psychiatry 137: 921–927, 1980

234. van Praag HM: A translantic view of the diagnosis of depressions according to the DSM-III: I. Controversies and misunderstandings in depression diagnosis. Compr Psychiatry 23: 315–329, 1982

235. van Praag HM: A transatlantic view of the diagnosis of depressions according to the DSM-III: II. Did the DSM-III solve the problem of depression diagnosis? Compr Psychiatry 23: 330–338, 1982

236. Puig-Antich J: The use of RDC criteria for major depressive disorder in children and adolescents. J Am Acad Child Psychiatry 21: 291–293, 1982

237. Raskin M, Peeke HV, Dickman W, Pinsker H: Panic and generalized anxiety disorders. Developmental antecedents and precipitants. Arch Gen Psychiatry 39: 687–689, 1982

238. Raskin RN, Hall CS: A narcissistic personality inventory. Psychol Rep 45: 590, 1979

239. Rieder RO: Borderline schizophrenia: evidence of its validity. Schizophr Bull 5: 39–46, 1979

240. Ries RK: DSM-III differential diagnosis of Munchausen's syndrome. J Nerv Ment Dis 168: 629–632, 1980

241. Ries RK, Bokan JA, Katon WJ, Kleinman A: The medical care abuser: differential diagnosis and management. J Fam Pract 13: 257–265, 1981

242. Robins LN, Helzer JE: In reply to Ganguli M, Saul MC and Von Korff M, Anthony JC, Kramer M [letters]. Arch Gen Psychiatry 39: 1443–1445, 1982

243. Robins LN, Helzer JE, Croughan J, Ratcliff KS: National Institute of Mental Health Diagnostic Interview Schedule. Its history, characteristics, and validity. Arch Gen Psychiatry 38: 381–389, 1981

244. Robins LN, Helzer JE, Ratcliff KS, Seyfried W: Validity of the Diagnostic Interview Schedule, Version II: DSM-III diagnoses. Psychol Med 12: 855–870, 1982

245. Rosenthal TL, Akiskal HS, Scott-Strauss A, Rosenthal RH, David M: Familial and developmental factors in characterological depressions. J Affective Disord 3: 183–192, 1981

246. Rounsaville BJ, Rosenberger P, Wilber C, Weissman MM, Kleber HD: A comparison of the SADS/RDC and the DSM-III. Diagnosing drug abusers. J Nerv Ment Dis 168: 90–97, 1980

247. Rounsaville BJ, Weissman MM, Wilber CH, Kleber HD: Pathways to opiate addiction: an evaluation of differing antecedents. Br J Psychiatry 141: 437–446, 1982

248. Rudden M, Gilmore M, Frances A: Erotomania: a separate entity. Am J Psychiatry 137: 1262–1263, 1980

249. Russell AP, Tanguay PE: Mental illness and mental retardation: cause or coincidence? Am J Ment Defic 83: 570–574, 1981

250. Russell AT, Cantwell DP, Mattison R, Will L: A comparison of DSM-II and DSM-III in the diagnosis of childhood psychiatric disorders. III. Multiaxial features. Arch Gen Psychiatry 36: 1223–1226, 1979

251. Russell AT, Mattison R, Cantwell DP: DSM-III in the clinical practice of child psychiatry. J Clin Psychiatry 44: 86–90, 1983

252. Rutter M, Shaffer D: DSM-III. A step forward or back in terms of the classification of child psychiatric disorders? J Am Acad Child Psychiatry 19: 371–394, 1980

253. Schacht T, Nathan PE: But is it good for the psychologists? Appraisal and status of DSM-III. Am Psychologist 32: 1017–1025, 1977

254. Sacks MH: Millon T: Disorders of Personality: DSM-III: Axis II. New York, Wiley, 1981 [book review]; and Personality Disorders: Diagnosis and Management, 2nd ed. Edited by Lion J R. Baltimore, Williams & Wilkins, 1981. Hosp Community Psychiatry 33: 943–944, 1982

255. Schatzberg AF, Rothschild AJ, Stahl JB, Bond TC, Rosenbaum AM, Lofgren SB, MacLaughlin RA, Sullivan MA, Cole JO: The dexamethasone suppression test: identification of subtypes of depression. Am J Psychiatry 140: 88–91, 1983

256. Schiffer RB: Psychiatric aspects of clinical neurology. Am J Psychiatry 140: 205–207, 1983

257. Schover LR, Friedman JM, Weiler SJ, Heiman JP, LoPiccolo J: Multiaxial problem-oriented system for sexual dysfunctions: an alternative to DSM-III. Arch Gen Psychiatry 39:614–619, 1982

258. Shader RI, Greenblatt DJ: Antidepressants: the second harvest and DSM-III. J Clin Psychopharmacol 1: 51–52, 1981

259. Silverstein ML, Warren RA, Harrow M, Grinker RR Sr, Pawelski T: Changes in diagnosis from DSM-II to the Research Diagnostic Criteria and DSM-III. Am J Psychiatry 139: 366–368, 1982

260. Simonds JF, Kashani J: Drug abuse and criminal behavior in delinquent boys committed to a training school. Am J Psychiatry 136: 1444–1448, 1979

261. Singerman B: DSM-III: historical antecedents and present significance. J Clin Psychiatry 42: 409–410, 1981

262. Singerman B, Stoltzman RK, Robins LN, Helzer JE, Croughan JL: Diagnostic concordance between DSM-III, Feighner, and RDC. J Clin Psychiatry 42: 422–426, 1981

263. Skinner HA: Toward the integration of classification theory and method. J Abnorm Psychol 90: 68–87, 1981

264. Skodol AE: The case of Sylvia Frumkin: misdiagnosis or misfortune? In DSM-III Case Studies. Edited by Frances A. Hosp Community Psychiatry 33: 807–808, 1982

265. Skodol AE, Spitzer RL: DSM-III differential diagnosis in the elderly. Psychopharmacol Bull 17: 94–96, 1981

266. Skodol AE, Spitzer RL: DSM-III: rationale, basic concepts and some differences from ICD-9. Acta Psychiatr Scand 66: 271–281, 1982

267. Skodol AE, Spitzer RL: The development of reliable diagnostic criteria in psychiatry. Annu Rev Med 33: 317–326, 1982

268. Skodol AE, Spitzer RL: Depression in the elderly: clinical criteria, in Depression and Aging: Causes, Care, and Consequences. Edited by Breslau LD, Haug MR. New York, Springer, 1983

269. Skodol AE, Spitzer RL, Williams JBW: Teaching and learning DSM-III. Am J Psychiatry 138: 1581–1586, 1981

270. Small GW, Jarvik LF: Depression in the aged. A commentary. Psychiatr Clin North Am 5: 45–48, 1982

271. Snyder S, Pitts WM Jr, Goodpaster WA, Sajadi C, Gustin Q: MMPI profile of DSM-III borderline personality disorder. Am J Psychiatry 139: 1046–1048, 1982

272. Snyder S, Pitts WM Jr, Gustin Q: Absence of borderline personality disorder in later years [letter]. Am J Psychiatry 140: 271–272, 1983

273. Snyder S, Pitts WM Jr, Gustin Q: CT scans of patients with borderline personality disorder [letter]. Am J Psychiatry 140: 272, 1983

274. Snyder S, Sajadi C, Pitts WM Jr, Goodpaster WA: Identifying the depressive border of the borderline personality disorder. Am J Psychiatry 139: 814–817, 1982

275. Socarides CW: The sexual deviations and the diagnostic manual. Am J Psychother 32: 414–426, 1978

276. Soloff PH, Millward JW: Psychiatric disorders in the families of borderline patients. Arch Gen Psychiatry 40: 37–44, 1983

277. Sonnenberg SM: In reply to Walker JI [letter]. Hosp Community Psychiatry 33: 666, 1982

278. Sovner R, Hurley AD: Do the mentally retarded suffer from affective illness? Arch Gen Psychiatry 40: 61–67, 1983

279. Spar JE: Dementia in the aged. Psychiatr Clin North Am 5: 67–86, 1982

280. Spitzer RL: An in-depth look at DSM-III. An interview with Robert Spitzer [interview by John Talbott]. Hosp Community Psychiatry 31: 25–32, 1980

281. Spitzer RL: In reply to Taylor MA and Harrow M, Silverstein M [letter]. The road to nosological nirvana. Arch Gen Psychiatry 38: 1299–1300, 1981

282. Spitzer RL: Nonmedical myths and the DSM-III. APA Monitor 12: 3, 1981

283. Spitzer RL: The diagnostic status of homosexuality in DSM-III: a reformulation of the issues. Am J Psychiatry 138: 210–215, 1981

284. Spitzer RL: Psychiatric diagnosis: are clinicians still necessary? Compr Psychiatry (in press)

285. Spitzer RL, Andreasen NC, Endicott J: Schizophrenia and other psychotic disorders in DSM-III. Schizophr Bull 4: 489–509, 1978

286. Spitzer RL, Andreasen N, Endicott J, Woodruff RA Jr: Proposed classification of schizophrenia in DSM-III, in Nature of Schizophrenia. Edited by Wynne L. New York, Wiley, 1978, pp 670–685

287. Spitzer RL, Cantwell DP: The DSM-III classification of the psychiatric disorders of infancy, childhood and adolescence. J Am Acad Child Psychiatry 19: 356–370, 1980

288. Spitzer RL, Endicott J: DSM-III: read before reacting. Psychiatric Opinion 16: 26–33, 1979

289. Spitzer RL, Endicott J: The DSM-III classification of depression and affective disorders, in Progress in the Functional Psychoses. Edited by Cancro R, Shapiro LE, Kesselman M. New York, S.P. Medical and Scientific Books, 1979, pp 119–127

290. Spitzer RL, Endicott J: The justification for separating schizotypal and borderline personality disorders. Schizophr Bull 5: 95–104, 1979

291. Spitzer RL, Endicott J, Gibbon M: Crossing the border into borderline personality and borderline schizophrenia. The development of criteria. Arch Gen Psychiatry 36: 17–24, 1979

292. Spitzer RL, Endicott J, Robins E: Clinical criteria for psychiatric diagnosis and DSM-III. Am J Psychiatry 132: 1187–1192, 1975

293. Spitzer RL, Forman JBW: DSM-III field trials: II. Initial experience with the multiaxial system. Am J Psychiatry 136: 818–820, 1979

294. Spitzer RL, Forman JBW, Nee J: DSM-III field trials: I. Initial interrater diagnostic reliability. Am J Psychiatry 136: 815–817, 1979

295. Spitzer RL, Gibbon M, Skodol AE, Williams JBW, Hyler SE: The heavenly vision of a poor woman: a down-to-earth discussion of the DSM-III approach. J Operational Psychiatry 11: 169–172, 1980

296. Spitzer RL, Sheehy M: DSM-III: a classification system in development. Psychiatr Annals 6: 102–109, 1976

297. Spitzer RL, Sheehy M, Endicott J: DSM-III: guiding principles, in Psychiatric Diagnosis. Edited by Rakoff VM, Stancer HC, Kedward HB. New York, Brunner/Mazel, 1977, pp 1–24

298. Spitzer RL, Skodol AE, Gibbon M, Williams JBW: DSM-III Case Book. Washington DC, American Psychiatric Association, 1981

299. Spitzer RL, Skodol AE, Gibbon M, Williams JBW: The experts' opinion, a comment on Frances A [editor] DSM-III case studies: 38-year-old mother with psychotic symptoms and affective disorder. Hosp Comm Psychiatry 32: 243–244, 1981

300. Spitzer RL, Skodol AE, Gibbon M, Williams JBW: Psychopathology: A Case Book. New York, McGraw-Hill, 1983

301. Spitzer RL, Skodol AE, Williams JBW, Gibbon M, Kass, F: Supervising intake diagnosis: a psychiatric "Rashomon." Arch Gen Psychiatry 39: 1299–1305, 1982

302. Spitzer RL, Williams JBW: Dehumanizing descriptors? [letter]. Am J Psychiatry 136: 1481, 1979

303. Spitzer RL, Williams JBW: Classification of mental disorders and DSM-III, in Comprehensive Textbook of Psychiatry, 3rd ed. Edited by Kaplan H, Freedman A, Sadock B. Baltimore, Williams & Wilkins, 1980, vol I, pp 1035–1072

304. Spitzer RL, Williams JBW: In reply to Mattes J [letter]. Arch Gen Psychiatry 38: 1068–1069, 1981

305. Spitzer RL, Williams JBW: Hysteroid dysphoria: an unsuccessful attempt to demonstrate its syndromal validity. Am J Psychiatry 139: 1286–1291, 1982

306.   Spitzer RL, Williams JBW, In reply to Klein DF, Liebowitz ML [letter]. Hysteroid dysphoria. Am J Psychiatry 139: 1521, 1982

307.   Spitzer RL, Williams JBW: Psychodynamic perspective on DSM-III [letter]. Am J Psychiatry 139: 702, 1982

308.   Spitzer RL, Williams JBW, Skodol AE: DSM-III: the major achievements and an overview. Am J Psychiatry 137: 151–164, 1980

309.   Spitzer RL, Williams JBW, Wynne LC: A revised decision tree for the DSM-III differential diagnosis of psychotic features. Hosp Community Psychiatry (in press)

310.   Spring B: Stress and schizophrenia: some definitional issues. Schizophr Bull 7: 24–33, 1981

311.   Stangler RS, Printz AM: DSM-III: psychiatric diagnosis in a university population. Am J Psychiatry 137: 937–940, 1980

312.   Stephens JH, Astrup C, Carpenter WT Jr, Shaffer JW, Goldberg J: A comparison of nine systems to diagnose schizophrenia. Psychiatry Res 6: 127–143, 1982

313.   Stephens JH, Shaffer JW, Carpenter WT: Reactive psychoses. J Nerv Ment Dis 170: 657–663, 1982

314.   Stewart RS, Lovitt R, Stewart RM: Are hysterical seizures more than hysteria? A Research Diagnostic Criteria, DSM-III, and psychometric analysis. Am J Psychiatry 139: 926–929, 1982

315.   Stoltzman RK, Helzer JE, Robins LN, Croughan JL, Singerman B: How does DSM-III differ from the systems on which it was built? J Clin Psychiatry 42: 411–421, 1981

316.   Straker M: Adjustment disorders and personality disorders in the aged. Psychiatr Clin North Am 5: 121–129, 1982

317.   Strauss JS: Developing a comprehensive treatement for schizophrenia. J Natl Assoc Priv Psychiatric Hosp 10: 75–79, 1979

318.   Stroeber M, Green J, Carlson G: Reliability of psychiatric diagnosis in hospitalized adolescents: interrater agreement using DSM-III. Arch Gen Psychiatry 38: 141–145, 1981

319.   Summers F, Hersh S: Psychiatric chronicity and diagnosis. Schizophr Bull (in press)

320.   Swartz CM, Pfohl B: A learning aid for DSM-III: computerized prompting of diagnostic criteria. J Clin Psychiatry 42: 359–361, 1981

321. Tamminga CA, Carpenter WT Jr: The DSM-III diagnosis of schizophrenic-like illness and the clinical pharmacology of psychosis. J Nerv Ment Dis 170: 744–751, 1982

322. Targum SD, Sullivan AC, Byrnes SM: Compensatory pituitary-thyroid mechanisms in major depressive disorder. Psychiatry Res 6: 85–96, 1982

323. Targum SD, Sullivan AC, Byrnes SM: Neuroendocrine interrelationships in major depressive disorder. Am J Psychiatry 139: 282–286, 1982

324. Thompson JW, Green D, Savitt HL: A preliminary report on a crosswalk from DSM-III to ICD-9-CM. Am J Psychiatry 140: 176–180, 1983

325. Treece C: DSM-III as a research tool. Am J Psychiatry 139: 577–583, 1982

326. Treece C, Nicholson B: DSM-III personality type and dose levels in methadone maintenance patients. J Nerv Ment Dis 168: 621–628, 1980

327. Tu JB: Epilepsy, psychiatry, and DSM-III. Biol Psychiatry 15: 515–516, 1980

328. Varner RV, Gaitz CM: Schizophrenic and paranoid disorders in the aged. Psychiatr Clin North Am 5: 107–118, 1982

329. Von Korff M, Anthony JC, Kramer M: Diagnostic Interview Schedule [letter]. Arch Gen Psychiatry 39: 1443, 1982

330. Walker JI: A disputed diagnosis of posttraumatic stress disorder [letter]. Hosp Community Psychiatry 33: 665–666, 1982

331. Waller DA, Rush AJ: Differentiating primary affective disease, organic affective syndromes, and situational depression on a pediatric service. J Am Acad Child Psychiatry 22: 52–58, 1983

332. Wallot H: [The new psychiatric classification. Scheme of I and II axials in the DSM-III classification soon to be approved by the American Psychiatric Association (APA)]. Union Med Can 108: 661–671, 1979

333. Walton H: Personality Disorders: Diagnosis and Management, 2nd ed. Edited by Lion JR. Baltimore, Williams & Wilkins, 1981 [book review]. Br J Psychiatry 141: 105–106, 1982

334. Webb LJ, DiClemente CC, Johnstone EE, Sanders JL, Perley RA (eds): DSM-III Training Guide. New York, Brunner/Mazel, 1981

335. Webb LJ, Gold RS, Johnstone EE, DiClemente CC: Accuracy of DSM-III diagnoses following a training program. Am J Psychiatry 138: 376–378, 1981

336. Weinberger DR, DeLisi LE, Perman GP, Targum S, Wyatt RJ: Computed tomography in schizophreniform disorder and other acute psychiatric disorders. Arch Gen Psychiatry 39: 778–783, 1982

337. Weiner MF: Borderline personality [letter]. Arch Gen Psychiatry 40: 107–108, 1983

338. Weissman MM: The myth of involutional melancholia. JAMA 242: 742–744, 1979

339. Weissman MM: In reply to Mattes J [letter]. Arch Gen Psychiatry 38: 1068–1069, 1981

340. Weissman MM, Myers JK, Leckman JF, Harding PS, Pauls DL, Prusoff BA: Anxiety disorders: epidemiology and familial patterns. Presented at Research Conference on Anxiety Disorders, Panic Attacks and Phobias. Key Biscayne, Florida, December 9–11, 1982

341. Werner A: DSM-III Case Book: A Learning Companion to the Diagnostic and Statistical Manual of Mental Disorders, 3rd ed [book review]. Am J Psychiatry 140: 120, 1983

342. Wilkinson G: Treatment Planning in Psychiatry. Edited by Lewis JM, Usdin G. Washington, DC, American Psychiatric Association, 1982 [book review]. Br J Psychiatry 142: 210–211, 1983

343. Williams JBW: DSM-III: a comprehensive approach to diagnosis. Social Work 26: 101–106, 1981

344. Williams JBW, Spitzer RL: The reliability of the diagnostic criteria of DSM-III, in What Is A Case? The Problem of Definition in Psychiatric Community Surveys. Edited by Wing J, Bebbington P, Robins L. London, Grant-McIntyre Ltd, 1981, pp 107–114

345. Williams JBW, Spitzer RL: DSM-III Forum. Focusing on DSM-III's multiaxial system. Hosp Community Psychiatry 33: 891–892, 1982

346. Williams JBW, Spitzer RL: Idiopathic pain disorder: a critique of pain-prone disorder and a proposal for a revision of the DSM-III category psychogenic pain disorder. J Nerv Ment Disease 170: 415–419, 1982

347. Williams JBW, Spitzer RL: Research Diagnostic Criteria and DSM-III: an annotated comparison. Arch Gen Psychiatry 39: 1283–1289, 1982

348. Williams, JBW, Spitzer RL: DSM-III Forum. Clarifying principal diagnosis, dealing with duplicate codes. Hosp Community Psychiatry 34: 13–14, 1983

349. Williams, JBW, Spitzer RL: DSM-III Forum. Focusing on the diagnosis of organic mental disorders. Hosp Community Psychiatry 34: 290–210, 1983

350. Williams JBW, Wilson HS: A psychiatric nursing perspective on DSM-III. J Psychosoc Nurs Ment Health Serv 20: 14–20, 1982

351. Winters KC, Weintraub S, Neale JM: Validity of MMPI codetypes in identifying DSM-III schizophrenics, unipolars, and bipolars. J Consult Clin Psychol 49: 486–487, 1981

352. Wolberg LR: DSM-III and the taxonomic stew [editorial]. J Am Acad Psychoanal 7: 143–145, 1979

353. Wood D, Wender PH, Reimherr FW: The prevalence of attention deficit disorder, residual type, or minimal brain dysfunction, in a population of male alcoholic patients. Am J Psychiatry 140: 95–98, 1983

354. Woods DJ: Carving nature at its joints? Observations on a revised psychiatric nomenclature. J Clin Psychol 35: 912–920, 1979

355. World Wide Medical Press: DSM-III one year later: are we seeing eye to eye? Frontiers of Psychiatry 11: 1, 6, 11, 1981

356. Zubin J: But it is good for science? Clin Psychologist 31: 5–7, 1977

357. Zucker KJ: Childhood gender disturbance: diagnostic issues. J Am Acad Child Psychiatry 21: 274–280, 1982

Appendix 2

DSM-III Classification: Axes I and II Categories and Codes

All official DSM-III codes and terms are included in ICD-9-CM. However, in order to differentiate those DSM-III categories that use the same ICD-9-CM codes, unofficial non-ICD-9-CM codes are provided in parentheses for use when greater specificity is necessary.

The long dashes indicate the need for a fifth-digit subtype or other qualifying term.

DISORDERS USUALLY FIRST EVIDENT IN INFANCY, CHILDHOOD, OR ADOLESCENCE

Mental retardation

(Code in fifth digit: 1 = with other behavioral symptoms [requiring attention or treatment and that are not part of another disorder], 0 = without other behavioral symptoms.)

317.0(x) Mild mental retardation, _____
318.0(x) Moderate mental retardation, _____
318.1(x) Severe mental retardation, _____
318.2(x) Profound mental retardation, _____
319.0(x) Unspecified mental retardation, _____

Attention deficit disorder

314.01 with hyperactivity
314.00 without hyperactivity
314.80 residual type

Conduct disorder

312.00 undersocialized, aggressive
312.10 undersocialized, nonaggressive
312.23 socialized, aggressive
312.21 socialized, nonaggressive
312.90 atypical

Anxiety disorders of childhood or adolescence

309.21 Separation anxiety disorder
313.21 Avoidant disorder of childhood or adolescence
313.00 Overanxious disorder

Other disorders of infancy, childhood, or adolescence

313.89	Reactive attachment disorder of infancy
313.22	Schizoid disorder of childhood or adolescence
313.23	Elective mutism
313.81	Oppositional disorder
313.82	Identity disorder

Eating disorders

307.10	Anorexia nervosa
307.51	Bulimia
307.52	Pica
307.53	Rumination disorder of infancy
307.50	Atypical eating disorder

Stereotyped movement disorders

307.21	Transient tic disorder
307.22	Chronic motor tic disorder
307.23	Tourette's disorder
307.20	Atypical tic disorder
307.30	Atypical stereotyped movement disorder

Other disorders with physical manifestations

307.00	Stuttering
307.60	Functional enuresis
307.70	Functional encopresis
307.46	Sleepwalking disorder
307.46	Sleep terror disorder (307.49)

Pervasive developmental disorders

Code in fifth digit: 0 = full syndrome present, 1 = residual state.

299.0x	Infantile autism, _____
299.9x	Childhood onset pervasive development disorder, _____
299.8x	Atypical, _____

Specific developmental disorders
Note: These are coded on axis II.

315.00	Developmental reading disorder
315.10	Developmental arithmetic disorder
315.31	Developmental language disorder
315.39	Developmental articulation disorder
315.50	Mixed specific developmental disorder
315.90	Atypical specific developmental disorder

ORGANIC MENTAL DISORDERS

Section 1. Organic mental disorders whose etiology or pathophysiological process is listed below (taken from the mental disorders section of ICD-9-CM).

Dementias arising in the senium and presenium

Primary degenerative dementia, senile onset,
290.30	with delirium
290.20	with delusions
290.21	with depression
290.00	uncomplicated

Code in fifth digit: 1 = with delirium, 2 = with delusions, 3 = with depression, 0 = uncomplicated.

290.1x	Primary degenerative dementia, presenile onset, _____
290.4x	Multi-infarct dementia, _____

Substance-induced

Alcohol
303.00	intoxication
291.40	idiosyncratic intoxication
291.80	withdrawal
291.00	withdrawal delirium
291.30	hallucinosis
291.10	amnestic disorder

Code severity of dementia in fifth digit: 1 = mild, 2 = moderate, 3 = severe, 0 = unspecified.

291.2x	Dementia associated with alcoholism _____

Barbiturate or similarly acting sedative or hypnotic
305.40	intoxication (327.00)
292.00	withdrawal (327.01)
292.00	withdrawal delirium (327.02)
292.83	amnestic disorder (327.04)

Opioid
305.50	intoxication (327.10)
292.00	withdrawal (327.11)

Cocaine
305.60	intoxication (327.20)

Amphetamine or similarly acting sympathomimetic
305.70	intoxication (327.30)
292.81	delirium (327.32)
292.11	delusional disorder (327.35)
292.00	withdrawal (327.31)

Phencyclidine (PCP) or similarly acting arylcyclohexylamine
305.90	intoxication (327.40)
292.81	delirium (327.42)
292.90	mixed organic mental disorder (327.49)

Hallucinogen
305.30	hallucinosis (327.56)
292.11	delusional disorder (327.55)
292.84	affective disorder (327.57)

Cannabis
305.20	intoxication (327.60)
292.11	delusional disorder (327.65)

Tobacco
292.00	withdrawal (327.71)

Caffeine
305.90	intoxication (327.80)

Other or unspecified substance
305.90	intoxication (327.90)
292.00	withdrawal (327.91)
292.81	delirium (327.92)
292.82	dementia (327.93)
292.83	amnestic disorder (327.94)
292.11	delusional disorder (327.95)
292.12	hallucinosis (327.96)
292.84	affective disorder (327.97)
292.89	personality disorder (327.98)
292.90	atypical or mixed organic mental disorder (327.99)

Section 2. Organic brain syndromes whose etiology or pathophysiological process is either noted as an additional diagnosis from outside the mental disorders section of ICD-9-CM or is unknown.

293.00	Delirium
294.10	Dementia
294.00	Amnestic syndrome
293.81	Organic delusional syndrome
293.82	Organic hallucinosis
293.83	Organic affective syndrome
310.10	Organic personality syndrome
294.80	Atypical or mixed organic brain syndrome

SUBSTANCE USE DISORDERS

Code in fifth digit: 1 = continuous, 2 = episodic, 3 = in remission, 0 = unspecified.

305.0x	Alcohol abuse, _____
303.9x	Alcohol dependence (Alcoholism), _____
305.4x	Barbiturate or similarly acting sedative or hypnotic abuse,
304.1x	Barbiturate or similarly acting sedative or hypnotic dependence, _____
305.5x	Opioid abuse, _____
304.0x	Opioid dependence, _____
305.6x	Cocaine abuse, _____
305.7x	Amphetamine or similarly acting sympathomimetic abuse,
304.4x	Amphetamine or similarly acting sympathomimetic dependence, _____
305.9x	Phencyclidine (PCP) or similarly acting arylcyclohexylamine abuse, _____ (328.4x)
305.3	Hallucinogen abuse, _____
305.2x	Cannabis abuse, _____
304.3x	Cannabis dependence, _____
305.1x	Tobacco dependence, _____
305.9x	Other, mixed, or unspecified substance abuse, _____
304.6x	Other specified substance dependence, _____
304.9x	Unspecified substance dependence, _____
304.7x	Dependence on combination of opioid and other non-alcoholic substance, _____
304.8x	Dependence on combination of substances, excluding opioids and alcohol, _____

SCHIZOPHRENIC DISORDERS

Code in fifth digit: 1 = subchronic, 2 = chronic, 3 = subchronic with acute exacerbation, 4 = chronic with acute exacerbation, 5 = in remission, 0 = unspecified.

Schizophrenia,
295.1x   disorganized, _____
295.2x   catatonic, _____
295.3x   paranoid, _____
295.9x   undifferentiated, _____
295.6x   residual, _____

PARANOID DISORDERS

297.10   Paranoia
297.30   Shared paranoid disorder
298.30   Acute paranoid disorder
297.90   Atypical paranoid disorder

PSYCHOTIC DISORDERS NOT ELSEWHERE CLASSIFIED

295.40   Schizophreniform disorder
298.80   Brief reactive psychosis
295.70   Schizoaffective disorder
298.90   Atypical psychosis

NEUROTIC DISORDERS: These are included in Affective, Anxiety, Somatoform, Dissociative, and Psychosexual Disorders. In order to facilitate the identification of the categories that in DSM-II were grouped together in the class of Neuroses, the DSM-II terms are included separately in parentheses after the corresponding categories. These DSM-II terms are included in ICD-9-CM and therefore are acceptable as alternatives to the recommended DSM-III terms that precede them.

AFFECTIVE DISORDERS
Major affective disorders

Code major depressive episode in fifth digit: 6 = in remission, 4 = with psychotic features (the unofficial non-ICD-9-CM fifth digit 7 may be used instead to indicate that the psychotic features are mood-incongruent), 3 = with melancholia, 2 = without melancholia, 0 = unspecified.

Code manic or mixed episode in fifth digit: 6 = in remission, 4 = with psychotic features (the unofficial non-ICD-9-CM fifth digit 7 may be used instead to indicate that the psychotic features are mood-incongruent), 2 = without psychotic features, 0 = unspecified.

	Bipolar disorder,
296.6x	mixed, _____
296.4x	manic, _____
296.5x	depressed, _____

	Major depression,
296.2x	single episode, _____
296.3x	recurrent, _____

Other specific affective disorders

301.13	Cyclothymic disorder
300.40	Dysthymic disorder (or Depressive neurosis)

Atypical affective disorders

296.70	Atypical bipolar disorder
296.82	Atypical depression

ANXIETY DISORDERS

	Phobic disorders (or Phobic neuroses)
300.21	Agoraphobia with panic attacks
300.22	Agoraphobia without panic attacks
300.23	Social phobia
300.29	Simple phobia

	Anxiety states (or Anxiety neuroses)
300.01	Panic disorder
300.02	Generalized anxiety disorder
300.30	Obsessive-compulsive disorder (or Obsessive-compulsive neurosis)

	Post-traumatic stress disorder
308.30	acute
309.81	chronic or delayed
300.00	Atypical anxiety disorder

SOMATOFORM DISORDERS

300.81	Somatization disorder
300.11	Conversion disorder (or Hysterical neurosis, conversion type)
307.80	Psychogenic pain disorder
300.70	Hypochondriasis (or Hypochondriacal neurosis)
300.70	Atypical somatoform disorder (300.71)

DISSOCIATIVE DISORDERS (OR HYSTERICAL NEUROSES, DISSOCIATIVE TYPE)
300.12   Psychogenic amnesia
300.13   Psychogenic fugue
300.14   Multiple personality
300.60   Depersonalization disorder (or Depersonalization neurosis)
300.15   Atypical dissociative disorder

PSYCHOSEXUAL DISORDERS

Gender identity disorders

Indicate sexual history in the fifth digit of Transsexualism code: 1 = asexual, 2 = homosexual, 3 = heterosexual, 0 = unspecified.

302.5x   Transsexualism, _____
302.60   Gender identity disorder of childhood
302.85   Atypical gender identity disorder

Paraphilias

302.81   Fetishism
302.30   Transvestism
302.10   Zoophilia
302.20   Pedophilia
302.40   Exhibitionism
302.82   Voyeurism
302.83   Sexual masochism
302.84   Sexual sadism
302.90   Atypical paraphilia

Psychosexual dysfunctions

302.71   Inhibited sexual desire
302.72   Inhibited sexual excitement
302.73   Inhibited female orgasm
302.74   Inhibited male orgasm
302.75   Premature ejaculation
302.76   Functional dyspareunia
306.51   Functional vaginismus
302.70   Atypical psychosexual dysfunction

Other psychosexual disorders

302.00   Ego-dystonic homosexuality
302.89   Psychosexual disorder not elsewhere classified

FACTITIOUS DISORDERS
300.16   Factitious disorder with psychological symptoms
301.51   Chronic factitious disorder with physical symptoms
300.19   Atypical factitious disorder with physical symptoms

DISORDERS OF IMPULSE CONTROL NOT ELSEWHERE CLASSIFIED
312.31   Pathological gambling
312.32   Kleptomania
312.33   Pyromania
312.34   Intermittent explosive disorder
312.35   Isolated explosive disorder
312.39   Atypical impulse control disorder

ADJUSTMENT DISORDER
309.00   with depressed mood
309.24   with anxious mood
309.28   with mixed emotional features
309.30   with disturbance of conduct
309.40   with mixed disturbance of emotions and conduct
309.23   with work (or academic) inhibition
309.83   with withdrawal
309.90   with atypical features

PSYCHOLOGICAL FACTORS AFFECTING PHYSICAL CONDITION
Specify physical condition on axis III.
316.00   Psychological factors affecting physical condition

PERSONALITY DISORDERS
Note: These are coded on axis II.
301.00   Paranoid
301.20   Schizoid
301.22   Schizotypal
301.50   Histrionic
301.81   Narcissistic
301.70   Antisocial
301.83   Borderline
301.82   Avoidant
301.60   Dependent
301.40   Compulsive
301.84   Passive-Aggressive
301.89   Atypical, mixed, or other personality disorder

V CODES FOR CONDITIONS NOT ATTRIBUTABLE TO A MENTAL DISORDER THAT ARE A FOCUS OF ATTENTION OR TREATMENT

V65.20	Malingering
V62.89	Borderline intellectual functioning (V62.88)
V71.01	Adult antisocial behavior
V71.02	Childhood or adolescent antisocial behavior
V62.30	Academic problem
V62.20	Occupational problem
V62.82	Uncomplicated bereavement
V15.81	Noncompliance with medical treatment
V62.89	Phase of life problem or other life circumstance problem
V61.10	Marital problem
V61.20	Parent–child problem
V61.80	Other specified family circumstances
V62.81	Other interpersonal problem

ADDITIONAL CODES

300.90	Unspecified mental disorder (nonpsychotic)
V71.09	No diagnosis or condition on axis I
799.90	Diagnosis or condition deferred on axis I
V71.09	No diagnosis on axis II
799.90	Diagnosis deferred on axis II

MULTIAXIAL EVALUATION

A multiaxial evaluation requires that every case be assessed on each of several "axes," each of which refers to a different class of information. In order for the system to have maximal clinical usefulness, there must be a limited number of axes; there are five in the DSM-III multiaxial classification. The first three axes constitute the official diagnostic assessment.

Each individual is evaluated on each of these axes:

Axis I	Clinical Syndromes
	Conditions Not Attributable to a Mental Disorder That Are a Focus of Attention or Treatment (V Codes)
	Additional Codes
Axis II	Personality Disorders
	Specific Developmental Disorders
Axis III	Physical Disorders and Conditions

Axes IV and V are available for use in special clinical and research settings and provide information supplementing the official DSM-III diagnoses (axes I, II, and III) that may be useful for planning treatment and predicting outcome:

Axis IV   Severity of Psychosocial Stressors

Axis V   Highest Level of Adaptive Functioning Past Year

Use of the DSM-III multiaxial classification ensures that attention is given to certain types of disorders, aspects of the environment, and areas of functioning that might be overlooked if the focus were on assessing a single presenting problem.

Appendix 3

ICD-9 Classification
of Mental Disorders

ICD-9 Classification of Mental Disorders (without inclusion and exclusion terms) from **Manual of the International Statistical Classification of Diseases, Injuries, and Causes of Death,** Volume 1, World Health Organization, Geneva, 1977

Italics indicate ICD-9 codes and their categories not included in DSM-III that are acceptable to most record-keeping systems.

ORGANIC PSYCHOTIC CONDITIONS

Senile and pre-senile organic psychotic conditions

290.0	Senile dementia, simple type
290.1	Pre-senile dementia
290.2	Senile dementia, depressed or paranoid type
290.3	Senile dementia with acute confusional state
290.4	Arteriosclerotic dementia
290.8	Other
290.9	Unspecified

Alcoholic psychoses

291.0	Delirium tremens
291.1	Korsakov's psychosis, alcoholic
291.2	Other alcoholic dementia
291.3	Other alcoholic hallucinosis
291.4	Pathological drunkenness
291.5	Alcoholic jealousy
291.8	Other
291.9	Unspecified

Drug psychoses

292.0	Drug withdrawal syndrome
292.1	Paranoid and/or hallucinatory states induced by drugs
292.2	*Pathological drug intoxication*
292.8	Other
292.9	Unspecified

Transient organic psychotic conditions

293.0	Acute confusional state
293.1	*Subacute confusional state*
293.8	Other
293.9	Unspecified

Other organic psychotic conditions (chronic)

294.0	Korsakov's psychosis (non-alcoholic)
294.1	Dementia in conditions classified elsewhere
294.8	Other
294.9	Unspecified

OTHER PSYCHOSES

Schizophrenic psychoses

295.0	*Simple type*
295.1	Hebephrenic type
295.2	Catatonic type
295.3	Paranoid type
295.4	Acute schizophrenic episode
295.5	*Latent schizophrenia*
295.6	Residual schizophrenia
295.7	Schizo-affective type
295.8	Other
295.9	Unspecified

Affective psychoses

296.0	*Manic-depressive psychosis, manic type*
296.1	*Manic-depressive psychosis, depressed type*
296.2	Manic-depressive psychosis, circular type but currently manic
296.3	Manic-depressive psychosis, circular type but currently depressed
296.4	Manic-depressive psychosis, circular type, mixed
296.5	Manic-depressive psychosis, circular type, current condition not specified
296.6	Manic-depressive psychosis, other and unspecified
296.8	Other
296.9	Unspecified

Paranoid states

297.0	*Paranoid state, simple*
297.1	Paranoia

297.2	*Paraphrenia*
297.3	Induced psychosis
297.8	Other
297.9	Unspecified

Other non-organic psychoses

298.0	*Depressive type*
298.1	*Excitative type*
298.2	*Reactive confusion*
298.3	Acute paranoid reaction
298.4	*Psychogenic paranoid psychosis*
298.8	Other and unspecified reactive psychosis
298.9	Unspecified psychosis

Psychoses with origin specific to childhood

299.0	Infantile autism
299.1	*Disintegrative psychosis*
299.8	Other
299.9	Unspecified

NEUROTIC DISORDERS, PERSONALITY DISORDERS, AND OTHER NONPSYCHOTIC MENTAL DISORDERS

Neurotic disorders

300.0	Anxiety states
300.1	Hysteria
300.2	Phobic state
300.3	Obsessive-compulsive disorder
300.4	Neurotic depression
300.5	*Neurasthenia*
300.6	Depersonalization syndrome
300.7	Hypochondriasis
300.8	Other
300.9	Unspecified

Personality disorders

301.0	Paranoid
301.1	Affective
301.2	Schizoid
301.3	*Explosive*
301.4	Anankastic
301.5	Hysterical
301.6	Asthenic
301.7	With predominantly sociopathic or asocial manifestations

301.8   Other
301.9   Unspecified

Sexual deviations and disorders

302.0   Homosexuality
302.1   Bestiality
302.2   Paedophilia
302.3   Transvestism
302.4   Exhibitionism
302.5   Trans-sexualism
302.6   Disorders of psychosexual identity
302.7   Frigidity and impotence
302.8   Other
302.9   Unspecified

303.   Alcohol dependence

Drug dependence

304.0   Morphine type
304.1   Barbiturate type
304.2   *Cocaine*
301.3   Cannabis
303.4   Amphetamine type and other psycho-stimulants
304.5   *Hallucinogens*
304.6   Other
304.7   Combinations of morphine type drug with any other
304.8   Combinations excluding morphine type drug
304.9   Unspecified

Non-dependent abuse of drugs

305.0   Alcohol
305.1   Tobacco
305.2   Cannabis
305.3   Hallucinogens
305.4   Barbiturates and tranquilizers
305.5   Morphine type
305.6   Cocaine type
305.7   Amphetamine type
305.8   *Antidepressants*
305.9   Other, mixed, or unspecified

Physical conditions arising from mental factors

306.0   *Musculoskeletal*
306.1   *Respiratory*

306.2	*Cardiovascular*
306.3	*Skin*
306.4	*Gastro-intestinal*
306.5	*Genito-urinary*
306.6	*Endocrine*
306.7	*Organs of special sense*
306.8	*Other*
306.9	*Unspecified*

Special symptoms or syndromes not elsewhere classified

307.0	Stammering and stuttering
307.1	Anorexia nervosa
307.2	Tics
307.3	Stereotyped repetitive movements
307.4	Specific disorders of sleep
307.5	Other disorders of eating
307.6	Enuresis
307.7	Encopresis
307.8	Psychalgia
307.9	Other and unspecified

Acute reaction to stress

308.0	Predominant disturbance of emotions
308.1	Predominant disturbance of consciousness
308.2	Predominant psychomotor disturbance
308.3	Other
308.4	Mixed
308.9	Unspecified

Adjustment reaction

309.0	Brief depressive reaction
309.1	*Prolonged depressive reaction*
309.2	With predominant disturbance of other emotions
309.3	With predominant disturbance of conduct
309.4	With mixed disturbance of emotions and conduct
309.8	Other
309.9	Unspecified

Specific non-psychotic mental disorders following organic brain damage

310.0	*Frontal lobe syndrome*
310.1	Cognitive or personality change of other type
310.2	*Post-concussional syndrome*
310.8	Other

310.9   Unspecified
311.   *Depressive disorder, not elsewhere classified*

Disturbance of conduct not elsewhere classified

312.0   Unsocialized disturbance of conduct
312.1   Socialized disturbance of conduct
312.2   Compulsive conduct disorder
312.3   *Mixed disturbance of conduct and emotions*
312.8   Other
312.9   Unspecified

Disturbance of emotions specific to childhood and adolescence

313.0   With anxiety and fearfulness
313.1   *With misery and unhappiness*
313.2   With sensitivity, shyness, and social withdrawal
313.3   *Relationship problems*
313.8   Other or mixed
313.9   Unspecified

Hyperkinetic syndrome of childhood

314.0   Simple disturbance of activity and attention
314.1   *Hyperkinesis with developmental delay*
314.2   *Hyperkinetic conduct disorder*
314.8   Other
314.9   Unspecified

Specific delays in development

315.0   Specific reading retardation
315.1   Specific arithmetical retardation
315.2   Other specific learning difficulties
315.3   Developmental speech or language disorder
315.4   *Specific motor retardation*
315.5   Mixed development disorder
315.8   Other
315.9   Unspecified

316.   **Psychic factors associated with diseases classified elsewhere**

317.   **Mild mental retardation**

Other specified mental retardation

318.0   Moderate mental retardation
318.1   Severe mental retardation
318.2   Profound mental retardation

319.   **Unspecified mental retardation**

INDEX

405